Other Immigrants

Other Immigrants

The Global Origins of the American People

David M. Reimers

NEW YORK UNIVERSITY PRESS

New York and London

NEW YORK UNIVERSITY PRESS
New York and London
www.nyupress.org

Library of Congress Cataloging-in-Publication Data
Reimers, David M.
Other immigrants :
the global origins of the American people / David M. Reimers.
p. cm.
Includes bibliographical references and index.
ISBN 0–8147–7534–9 (alk. paper) —
ISBN 0–8147–7535–7 (pbk. : alk. paper)
1. Ethnology—United States—History.   2. Minorities—
United States—History.   3. Immigrants—United States—History.
4. United States—Ethnic relations.   5. United States—Emigration
and immigration—History.   I. Title.
E184.A1R4435   2004
305.8'00973—dc22   2004016632

New York University Press books are printed on acid-free paper,
and their binding materials are chosen for strength and durability.

Manufactured in the United States of America

c 10 9 8 7 6 5 4 3 2 1
p 10 9 8 7 6 5 4 3 2 1

To Emanuel and Nathaniel

Contents

Preface

A good deal of my prior research and writing has focused on immigrants other than Europeans, migrants some scholars label "people of color." These immigrants include Latinos, Asians, and blacks. I pulled together some of my thoughts on these millions of persons for an essay published by the American Historical Association's Teaching Diversity series, under the title "Immigration of People of Color to the United States." That essay was short, requiring much condensing, and I believe that the topic required a larger study. The result is this book, which gives a fuller picture of these newcomers to the United States.

Some of my thoughts have been presented to other historians. The title of the book owes much to a course on the global origins of Americans, about which I learned when I was invited by Professor George Kirsch and Dean Mary Ann O'Connell of Manhattan College to give the Robert Christian Lecture there in 1999. I benefited from preparing the lecture and also from a meeting with the members of the history department to discuss the book. Special thanks go to Professor Linda Place and the organizers of the conference "The Legacy of the Korean War" held at the President Harry S. Truman Library in the fall of 2001. I gave a paper there on the impact of the Korean War and immigration of Koreans to the United States. Thanks also go to Bill Stueck for inviting me to speak on new Asian immigration to the South at the University of Georgia in June 2002.

Many libraries have been helpful, especially that of New York University and the New York Public Library. The New York University staff has promptly responded to my request for materials. Marian Smith of the Immigration Service was helpful in providing materials from her agency. While I do not agree with the conclusions of many papers published by the Center for Immigration Studies in Washington, D.C., Mark Krikorian's generous e-mails have been of great assistance, especially in providing newspaper coverage of immigration to the United States.

Several friends have read the manuscript. Nancy Foner read a first draft and was of enormous help. She not only read with care and made many suggestions but also returned material quickly. Len Dinnerstein, per usual, made many suggestions on the first five chapters. Richard Alba and Marilyn Halter provided criticism on several chapters. Richard Hull read the material on black immigrants. Elliott Barkan was especially helpful in dealing with Asians and Middle Easterners. K. Scott Wong commented on the chapters on Asian immigrants, and Steve Scheinberg read an early draft of the entire manuscript and provided criticism. Kat Morgan and Rebecca Reimers proved to be excellent copy editors and proofreaders. Kat also prepared the index. Thanks, too, to Fred Binder and Roger Daniels.

Introduction

Thirty-five years ago this book, which is a history of the first generation of blacks, Asians, and Hispanics coming to America, could not have been written. The essential scholarship was uneven, and in many cases historians and other scholars had no knowledge of particular immigrant and ethnic groups. The history of African Americans was studied largely by looking at slavery. Before Kenneth Stampp's *The Peculiar Institution,* the most important book on the subject was Ulrich Phillips's *American Negro Slavery*, published in 1918, which painted a benign picture of slavery.[1] Since the publication of Stampp's book, a stream of new scholarship has vastly changed our view of slavery. Eugene Genovese, *Roll, Jordan, Roll: The World the Slaves Made* (1974), Herbert Gutman, *The Black Family in Slavery and Freedom, 1750–1925* (1976), and John Blassingame, *The Slave Community: Plantation Life in the Antebellum South* (1979), are only a few of the books that stand out. Ira Berlin's *Many Thousands Gone: The First Two Centuries of Slavery in North America* (1998) summarizes much of the scholarship, as does his *Generations of Captivity: A History of African American Slaves* (2003).[2] While historians have examined the slave trade, most works on slavery deal not with the first generation but with subsequent ones. Walter Johnson's fine *Soul by Soul: Life inside the Antebellum Slave Market* (1999) explores the interstate and intrastate slave trade, not the international one.[3]

At the same time, scholars have probed the history of free blacks not only in the South but throughout the entire nation. In the last three decades a flood of studies has examined the history of African Americans extensively, looking at urbanization, civil rights protests, family life, women, individual leaders, and racial segregation and disfranchisement. One of the most recent works, for example, is Steven Hahn, *A Nation under Our Feet: Black Political Struggles in the Rural South from Slavery to the Great Migration*, published in 2003.[4] Some of the same story was discussed by Leon Litwack in *Trouble in Mind: Black Southerners in the Age of Jim Crow* (1998).[5]

In spite of the huge outpouring of books and articles on African Americans, gaps in the literature remain. Especially missing is the history of African immigrants after the Civil War, whose children became African Americans. Marilyn Halter's *Between Race and Ethnicity: Cape Verdean American Immigrants, 1860–1965* (1993) is a pioneering book, for few historians have looked at African immigration to the United States.[6] Within the last few years, scholars (though not historians) have begun to explore the new immigration from Africa. John Arthur's *Invisible Sojourners: African Immigrant Diaspora in the United States* (2000) is one such work; others are Jon Holtzman, *Nuer Journeys, Nuer Lives: Sudanese Refugees in Minnesota* (2000); Rogaia Mustafa Abusharaf, *Wanderings: Sudanese Migrants and Exiles in North America* (2002); and Paul Stoller, *Money Has No Smell: The Africanization of New York City* (2002).[7]

By contrast, the literature on black Caribbean immigration to the United States is greater than the literature on twentieth-century African migration. The oldest, most useful study was by Ira De A. Reid, *The Negro Immigrant*, published in 1939.[8] The best newer studies are authored by Winston James (1998), Philip Kasinitz (1992), Milton Vickerman (1999), Irma Watkins-Owens (1996), and Mary Waters (1999).[9] Nancy Foner has published a number of articles on Caribbeans in New York and has edited several important books about this migration.[10] Overall, however, the few attempts to pull the literature together are brief and lacking in historical depth.[11]

When one turns to Asians and Hispanics, it is only in recent years that historians have begun to examine these groups in detail. While a general history of immigration was published by George M. Stephenson in 1926, it concentrated on immigrants from northern and western Europe.[12] During the 1930s and 1940s important scholars such as Marcus Hansen, Carl Wittke, and others studied European immigration. Wittke specialized on the Irish and Germans, and Hansen's major work, *The Atlantic Migration, 1607–1860* (1940), dealt with northern and western European migration to the United States.[13] Carl Wittke's summary of immigration, first published in 1939, neglected southern and eastern Europeans and gave "people of color" little notice. Scholarship after 1940 about immigrants (mainly Europeans) prompted Wittke to revise *We Who Built*

America and publish a new edition in 1964. Even then one reaches page 407 before encountering a discussion of post-1890 European immigration in a book totaling 539 pages, and 51 pages of the rest of the book deal with nativism. The 1964 edition included 2 pages on Mexicans and only 15 on Asians. About Asians, Wittke concluded, "The story of Oriental immigration is a brief and strange interlude in the general account of the great migrations to America."[14]

Oscar Handlin helped to draw more attention to immigration when he published his prize-winning book *The Uprooted* in 1952. However, it is difficult to find black, Hispanic, or Asian immigrants fitting Handlin's overall thesis.[15] Maldwyn Jones's *American Immigration* (1960) focused overwhelmingly on Europeans, although his revision, published in 1992, included much more material on Asians, Latinos, and Caribbeans.[16]

John Higham's classic, *Strangers in the Land: Patterns of American Nativism, 1860–1925* (first published in 1955), had no entry in the index for Mexicans, but he had more to say about anti-Chinese sentiment. Clearly he was focusing on nativism toward Europeans. Higham, of course, wrote long before important studies such as Andrew Gyory's *Closing the Gate: Race, Politics and the Chinese Exclusion Act* (1998) pointed to the importance of Chinese exclusion in the immigration restriction movement.[17]

As early as 1909, Mary Roberts Coolidge wrote of Chinese immigrants and the racism they encountered.[18] However, few historians took up the task of writing about Asians until after 1960. No historian has been as important as Roger Daniels in bringing Asians into the story of American immigration and American history generally. In 1962 he published *The Politics of Prejudice: The Anti-Japanese Movement in California and the Struggle for Japanese Exclusion,* and since then he has authored a number of other works that tell the history of Asian immigration and Asian Americans.[19]

In the past two decades a number of younger scholars have followed Daniels's lead and published important works about Japanese in America. Gary Okihiro's *Margins and Mainstreams: Asians in American History and Culture* (1994) summarizes much of the writing of the 1970s and 1980s.[20] Okihiro himself has written widely about Japanese immigrants, including those who settled in Hawaii as well as on the mainland. See also Evelyn Nakano Glenn, *Issei, Nisei, War Bride: Three Generations of Japanese American Women in Domestic Service* (1986); Yuji

Ichioka, *The Issei: The World of the First-Generation Japanese Immigrants* (1988); and Akiko S. Hosler, *Japanese Immigrant Entrepreneurs in New York City: A New Wave of Ethnic Business* (1998).[21]

Chinese immigrants have attracted even greater attention from a younger generation of historians. Examples of the new writing are Judy Yung's *Unbound Feet: A Social History of Chinese Women in San Francisco* (1995) and Erika Lee's *At America's Gates: Chinese Immigration during the Exclusion Era, 1882–1943* (2003).[22] Both New York and San Francisco have been studied extensively. New York's Chinese explorations include gender, social class, patterns of settlement, racism, and occupations.[23] A recent study of Manhattan's Chinatown dealt with religion, which is often neglected in the emerging literature about Asian immigrants (excluding Koreans).[24]

Wayne Patterson (2000) has written about the turn-of-the-twentieth-century immigration of Koreans, while important sociological and anthropological studies have looked at the post-1965 immigrants. Among the best are Ji-Yeon Yuh, *Beyond the Shadow of Camptown: Korean Military Brides in America* (2002), and Pyong Gap Min, *Changes and Conflict: Korean Immigrant Families in New York* (1998).[25]

Karen Isaksen Leonard explores the first Asian Indians in California in *Making Ethnic Choices: California's Punjabi Mexican Americans* (1992), and Madhulika S. Khandelwal's *Becoming American, Being Indian* (2002) deals with the recent Indian immigrants. Another readable study of Asian Indians is Johanna Lessinger, *From the Ganges to the Hudson: Indian Immigrants in New York City* (1995).[26]

Although large-scale migration of Southeast Asian refugees began only in 1975, sociologists and anthropologists have written about these groups. One example is Jeremy Hein, *From Vietnam, Laos, and Cambodia: A Refugee Experience in the United States* (1995); another is Cathleen Jo Faruque, *Migration of Hmong to the Midwestern United States* (2002). Part of a series edited by Nancy Foner is James M. Freeman, *Changing Identities: Vietnamese Americans, 1975–1995* (1995).[27]

Filipinos are the second-largest Asian group in the United States, behind the Chinese, but they have not been studied as extensively as the Chinese or Japanese. Older studies, such as Bruno Lasker's *Filipino Immigration to Continental United States and Hawaii* (1931), remain useful.[28] Some recent works, however, including Yen Le Espiritu, *Home Bound: Filipino American Lives across Cultures, Communities, and*

Countries (2003); Dorothy B. Fujita-Rony, *American Workers, Colonial Power: Philippine Seattle and the Transpacific West, 1919–1941* (2003); and Barbara Posadas, *Filipino Americans* (1999), point to a potential for future scholarship.[29]

Another sign of the growing interest in Asian, as well as black and Hispanic, immigration is the large number of articles and book reviews appearing in the *Journal of American Ethnic History*, the quarterly of the Immigration and Ethnic History Society. There are specialized journals for Asians, such as *Amerasia Journal*, and courses dealing with Asians (and Hispanics) have proliferated on college campuses. Moreover, several presses, including those of the University of Illinois and Temple University, have special series devoted to Asians. In addition, presses concentrating on immigrants generally, such as Greenwood, Twayne, and Allyn and Bacon, devote volumes to the new and old Asian immigration. So great has been the outpouring of scholarship on Asians, only hinted at in this discussion, that two major historians have integrated their history. Whereas Sucheng Chan's *Asian Americans: An Interpretive History* (1991) is geared toward scholars and students, Ronald Takaki's *Strangers from a Different Shore: A History of Asian Americans* (1989) is more accessible for general audiences.[30]

Within the past three decades a number of new books by historians have been added to the older literature on Hispanics or Latinos. Mexicans, the most numerous group to emigrate to the United States, have drawn the greatest attention. An older but still useful book is Carey McWilliams, *North from Mexico*, published in 1949 and reissued in 1990.[31]

Albert Camarillo wrote one of the first significant new books, *Chicanos in a Changing Society: From Mexican Pueblos to American Barrios in Santa Barbara and Southern California* (1979). Other studies have dealt with different communities. See, for example, Mario Garcia, *Desert Immigrants: The Mexicans of El Paso, 1880–1920* (1981); Arnoldo De León, *Mexican Americans in Texas: A Brief History* (1993); prizewinning George Sanchez, *Becoming Mexican American: Ethnicity, Culture, and Identity in Chicano Los Angeles, 1900–1945* (1993); Douglas Monroy, *Rebirth: Mexican Los Angles from the Great Migration to the Great Depression* (1999); and Juan Garcia, *Mexicans in the Midwest, 1900–1932* (1996).[32] Vicki Ruiz has covered Mexican American women in *From Out of the Shadows: Mexican Women in Twentieth-Century America*

(1998).[33] There are several overall studies of Mexicans in America, the most readable being Manuel Gonzales, *Mexicanos: A History of Mexicans in the United States* (1999).[34]

Because Mexican immigration has been so substantial in the last thirty years, it has also drawn the attention of demographers, sociologists, and journals. Roberto Suro's *The Strangers among Us: How Latino Immigration Is Transforming America* (1998) is a journalist's attempt to explain Latino migration. Frank Bean and Gillian Stevens, in *America's Newcomers and the Dynamics of Diversity* (2003), and Richard Alba and Victor Nee, in *Remaking the American Mainstream: Assimilation and Contemporary Immigration* (2003), have much to say about Mexican immigration.[35] The Mexican–United States border and Mexican emigration are the center of attention for Douglas S. Massey, Jorge Durand, and Norlan J. Malone, *Beyond Smoke and Mirrors: Mexican Immigration in an Era of Economic Integration* (2002).[36]

Dominicans are covered by Sherri Grasmuck and Patricia R. Pessar in their *Between Two Islands: Dominican International Migration* (1991). Cubans receive attention in Felix Robert Masud-Piloto, *With Open Arms: Cuban Migration to the United States* (1988); Masud-Piloto, *From Welcomed Exiles to Illegal Immigrants: Cuban Migration to the United States, 1959–1995* (1996); Alex Stepick, Guillermo Grenier, Max Castor, and Marvin Dunn, *This Land Is Our Land: Immigrants and Power in Miami* (2003). An attempt to compare Cubans and Mexicans is Alejandro Portes and Robert L. Bach, *Latin Journey: Cuban and Mexican Immigrants in the United States* (1985).[37]

The *Harvard Encyclopedia of American Ethnic Groups*, published in 1980, contained entries for relatively small groups such as the Wends, who were Slavic immigrants from Germany; the author of the entry on Central and South America wrote, "More than one million immigrants from Central and South America have settled in the United States since 1820, but their role in the development of American society remains uncharted."[38] An updated sourcebook (1999), edited by Elliott Robert Barkan, offered more detail about Central and South Americans, but the authors also noted that scholarly writing about these people "has been increasing at a slow pace since the mid-1980s."[39]

However, several excellent micro-studies have been done about Central Americans. Terry A. Repak, *Waiting on Washington: Central American Workers in the Nation's Capital* (1995), and Sarah Mahler, *American Dreaming: Immigrant Life on the Margins* (1995), are the best, and Maxine Margolis, *Little Brazil: An Ethnography of Brazilian Immigrants in New York* (1994), is especially good on Brazilians. The Maya of Central America and Mexico have attracted several scholars, the most recent book being Leon Fink, *The Maya of Morganton: Work and Community in the Nuevo New South* (2003).[40]

Scholarship on immigration from the Middle East has been limited mainly to sociologists and anthropologists, although several works do have a historical focus: Anny Bakalian, *Armenian Americans: From Being to Feeling Armenian* (1993); Robert Mirkak, *Torn between Two Lands: Armenians in America, 1890–World War I* (1983); and Alixa Naff, *Becoming American: The Early Arab Immigrant Experience* (1985) stand out.[41] Collections of essays about Middle Easterners have being appearing lately. One example is Mehdi Bozorgmehr and Alison Feldman, eds., *Middle Eastern Diaspora Communities in America* (1996).[42]

Immigrants from Canada, New Zealand, and Australia are certainly "beyond Europe," but they are not "people of color," so I have not discussed them here. They often closely resemble white Americans of European background, and they are from predominantly English-speaking cultures. Many South American immigrants are also closely tied to their European backgrounds, but most do come from a primarily Spanish-speaking culture, so I do include them in my consideration of those beyond Europe.

American Indians are also not Europeans and are often called people of color, but this book concentrates on the first generation of newcomers to America. Scholars do not agree on how or when these first Americans arrived. There is a general consensus that they originated in Asia and crossed over the land bridge connecting Siberia and Alaska thousands of years ago. But how long ago remains in dispute. Some scholars believe that they may have made the journey by boat, hugging the coastline. Each new discovery of possible sites of these early Americans brings forth debates about when they arrived. But whether they first journeyed 14,000 years or 30,000 years ago, we know nothing about the first generations. When Europeans and Africans began to arrive after 1492, they encountered Indian civilizations that had been here for thousands of years.

Drawing upon the new studies and my own research, I tell the story of the first generation of Asian, black, and Hispanic (or Latino) immigrants. Two themes dominate the book. First, the history of Latino, black, and Asian migration goes back a long time; thus, the period prior to World War II forms the basis for the first three chapters. Santa Fe was founded before the Pilgrims landed, and the Southwest (especially the state of New Mexico), which did not become part of the United States until 1848, has had a strong Hispanic presence for generations. The great migrations of Mexicans occurred after 1960, and today the vast majority of the nearly 10 million Mexicans living in the United States arrived in the last four decades. But there was a substantial migration before 1930. Most blacks arriving in the New World before 1860 came in chains during the seventeenth and eighteenth centuries, yet some free blacks entered during the colonial era and the early nineteenth century. The Asian presence dates to the eighteenth century. In sum, the narrative will talk about the early immigrants of people of color as well as focusing on the last half century, when their numbers have dominated immigration to the United States.

A second theme in the narrative is the great diversity of Latinos, Asians, and blacks. These names cover a great many groups. Scholars and critics remind us that terms such as "race" are social constructions and that "race" has no scientific basis. Much the same is true about other terms used in this book and elsewhere. Scholars and government and ethnic leaders often call the groups under discussion here "people of color." It should be noted that many such newcomers do not see themselves as people of color. About one-half of Hispanics or Latinos reported to the 1900 and 2000 censuses that they were white; another 40 percent labeled themselves neither black nor white and told the census that they are another race.[43] "People of color" is actually a shorthand for blacks, Asians, and Latinos or Hispanics.

The term "Hispanic" emerged from Spanish-speaking bureaucrats working for the Department of Health, Education, and Welfare in 1975. According to journalist Darryl Fears, the Ad Hoc Committee on Racial and Ethnic Differences in the department choose the term, which was used for the first time on the census in 1980.[44] Others have preferred the term "Latino," but the Pew Hispanic Center and the Henry J. Kaiser Family Foundation found in a 2002 study that 53 percent of "Hispanics" or "Latinos" do not use either term and call themselves Mexicans, Mexican Americans, Mexicanos, Dominicans, Dominican Americans, or some other nationality or ethnic group. Those making a choice of the two terms had a slight preference for "Hispanic" over "Latino." *Hispanic* magazine reported similar results from its survey.[45]

Regardless of which term is used, the fact that so many different cultures are included under the title "Hispanic" or "Latino" (or "people of color") should be a caution about making sweeping generalizations.

Cuban immigrants are not the same as Mexican migrants any more than Italian and Jewish immigrants arriving around 1900 were identical. If "Hispanic" is used, then Portuguese-speaking Brazilians are excluded. In addition, among the new Central Americans and Mexicans are Indians, who do not always speak Spanish well. Much can also be said about the term "Asian." Because diversity is a central theme in this book, I have tried to note the many differences when discussing various specific groups.

As the United States moved into the twenty-first century, blacks and Latinos together made up more than one-quarter of the American population, and Asians accounted for another 4 percent. Some observers pointed out that by the middle of the twenty-first century these three groups would account for nearly one-half of the American population and that Hispanics alone would be approximately one-quarter. It is risky to predict the long-range future. Birth rates might drop, immigration policies could shift, and social and economic conditions might change the flow of immigration. Finally, because of the great ethnic mixing in American society, what exactly the changes will bring is not known. I do not attempt to make predictions in this book. Rather, the narrative tries to bring together the experiences of the first generation of those who arrived from beyond Europe.

PART I

From beyond Europe, 1492–1940

After 1492 the French, Spanish, and English were the major explorers of America, but the Dutch West India Company was also active. Once the colonies became established, Europeans, especially those from the British Isles, were most influential. Europeans had the greatest numbers, and they had the power to control the largest group of non-European peoples, black slaves from Africa, who made up 20 percent of the American population at the time of the Revolution.

The French influence was limited to Canada and New Orleans, whereas the Spanish presence was restricted to Florida and the Southwest, which did not become part of the United States until 1848. Amid the English colonies along the Atlantic Coast, small settlements of Swedes and Dutch were established, but they were quickly absorbed by the English.

During the eighteenth century, substantial numbers of Germans and Scots-Irish settled in the colonies. The Scots-Irish, Protestant settlers from the northern part of Ireland, were especially prominent in Pennsylvania and the backcountry of the southern colonies. Germans also scattered to the frontier, but they were most prominent in Pennsylvania. Smaller numbers of French Huguenots, Dutch, Catholic Irish, Scots, and Jews from Brazil and Amsterdam also arrived. A few immigrants settled in towns and cities, but most lived in agricultural areas. Pennsylvania and New York City, with their ethnically diverse populations, became models for the American future, a pluralist society.

In the 1790s Germans, Irish, and French came to America, but their numbers were not large, and immigration was disrupted during the Napoleonic Wars. The federal government took little interest in immigration and did not even begin to count the new arrivals until 1819. But then immigration picked up again. The Irish potato famines after 1840 sent hundreds of thousands of Irish to the United States. Germans were also forced by economic conditions to head for the United States, and

Germans became the largest group of immigrants until they were surpassed in recent years by Mexicans. Five million immigrants arrived between 1840 and 1860, representing the first mass immigration to America. After the lull during the Civil War, immigration again increased from
Ireland and Germany. In the late nineteenth century, large numbers of
southern and eastern Europeans—Poles, Slovaks, Greeks, Italians, and
Russian and Polish Jews—migrated to America. They were joined by
Scandinavians: Norwegians, Swedes, and Danes. After 1900, Germans
and Irish still came but in reduced numbers. During this period of mass
immigration, French speakers from Canada also came to farm and work
in New England mill towns. Overall, some 24 million immigrants settled
in the United States from the 1880s to the 1920s. In 1910 the American
foreign-born population, overwhelmingly European, accounted for 14.7
percent of the United States population, the highest proportion in American history.

The flow from Europe did not diminish until Congress put up barriers
in the 1920s. The new system was strictly enforced during the Great Depression and World War II. Only 700,000 persons arrived from 1930 to
1945, a figure that was surpassed annually in the first decade of the twentieth century.

While Europeans dominated the immigration statistics before the
1940s, people of color—Asians, blacks, and Latinos—also joined the
movement to the United States. Most black newcomers were slaves, but
black West Indians came voluntarily, especially after 1900. In the nineteenth century Asians also decided on their own to make America their
new home. When the numbers of Asians grew, the American government
banned their entrance. Some Latinos settled in the United States in the
second half of the nineteenth century, but more substantial numbers of
Hispanics from Mexico entered from 1900 until the 1930s. The stories of
these first people of color to settle in the United States before World War
II are the subject of the first three chapters.

1

The Beginnings, 1550–1900

European men and women were not the only people exploring and settling in what is now the United States. Although Africans did not send ships to the Western Hemisphere, they worked on European vessels, sometimes in positions of authority; it was not unheard of for persons of one nationality or ethnicity to captain ships of another. Everyone knows that Christopher Columbus, an Italian, sailed under the flag of Spain when he made his famous voyage of 1492. But a black Portuguese also commanded a vessel, flying the flag of Spain, that entered New York City's harbor in 1526. Two blacks accompanied Ponce de León during his "pacification" campaigns in the Caribbean.[1] Among the first persons on European vessels to reach Texas was the Moor Estevanico, who was considered a black man. Estevanico, along with three whites, landed there in 1528 by chance when their vessel lost its way in a storm. In other cases ships' crews were made up of a variety of ethnic groups.

How was it possible for blacks to work on ships sailing to the New World? North Africans had traded with Spain and had even settled there before the Spanish and the Portuguese explored the west coast of Africa. Among the exchanges from trading were west Africans; as a result, Africans, both slave and free, were found living along the Atlantic rim.[2] By 1550, 10,000 people of African origin lived in Lisbon alone, and Seville claimed 6,000. One scholar has compared Seville to a "chessboard with equal numbers of black and white pieces."[3] Although blacks were found in other regions and nations, Spain and Portugal claimed the largest number, most of whom were slaves.[4] Ira Berlin reports that some won their freedom and found niches in the Iberian Peninsula, as interpreters, peddlers, merchants, artisans, and sailors. Thus it was that black sailors accompanied European vessels to America, including the ships of Christopher Columbus. In other cases, after coming to America in chains, they were manumitted and went to sea as free men. Berlin notes that one

Sebastian Cain from Massachusetts won his freedom, took to the sea, and settled in Virginia after visiting it several times.[5] A number of these sailors decided to stay in the New World when their ships took them there, and by the end of the seventeenth century free blacks formed communities in the Western Hemisphere.[6]

Among these communities of Africans in the New World were free blacks in the Chesapeake region of Virginia and Maryland. Some historians believe that the first vessel of blacks to arrive in 1619 with "twenty Negars" was transporting black indentured servants to Jamestown. John Russell found evidence of black indentured servants who became free when their term was over.[7] Slaves who had obtained their freedom, black indentured servants who had been freed after serving their term, and the small number of those who were free when they entered the country joined to form a free black community.[8] Timothy Breen and Stephen Innes and others have traced free blacks in the Chesapeake region. The black settlers acquired property, married, used the courts, and raised tobacco.[9]

As slavery became more important to the economic development of the colonies, it became more difficult to purchase one's freedom. Because of the tightening grip of slavery and because so few free blacks migrated to Virginia and Maryland, the free black population grew slowly until the American Revolution.

A small free black community also developed in South Carolina in the eighteenth century. As was the case in Virginia and Maryland, some of these blacks were indentured servants who obtained their freedom after a term of years; others were slaves who were manumitted; still others came in as free men and women. Marina Wikramanayke reports, "Free black immigration was also not uncommon, particularly in the coastal areas of Charleston, Beaufort and Georgetown." She notes that James Mitchell, a prominent free black in antebellum South Carolina, was "a Portuguese mulatto seaman who, finding conditions in Charleston more congenial, forsook the sea and became a landowner."[10]

The small number of free blacks in the southern colonies did not have the same rights as those of English or other immigrants. As white colonists increasingly turned to slavery to satisfy their labor needs, they feared that free blacks might become a troublesome presence. Planters and white farmers enacted a number of restrictions on free blacks, such as the right to vote or to serve in the militia, and free blacks had to pay special taxes.[11] In contrast, the vast majority of European immigrants, in-

cluding indentured servants whose terms were over, could become naturalized under the various acts passed by the English, the most important
being the Naturalization Act of 1740. Naturalization carried certain
rights and privileges, including equal access to the ballot. More than
10,000 European immigrants were naturalized in the eighteenth century,
of whom about 94 percent were Germans. In the critical days at the beginning of the American Revolutionary era, 2,600 Pennsylvania Germans
became English citizens, and they voted in the assembly elections.[12]

In New Amsterdam, while under Dutch rule, slaves were permitted to
have "half freedom." This status did not grant them equality with white
immigrants; it was given mainly to elderly slaves, and even then they had
to pay an annual tribute. Moreover, "half freedom," which allowed individuals to be virtually free, left the legal status of their children in the
hands of the parents' former owners. Slaves and free blacks did have
some rights in the judicial system, such as testifying in court, but not total
equality.[13]

Free blacks, although not equal to whites, nonetheless were better off
than those who entered as slaves and remained enslaved for life.[14] Moreover, slaves from Africa and the West Indies were brought to America
under horrendous conditions. The story of the slave trade is a familiar
one. Once bought or captured in Africa, slaves were taken to the New
World like cattle. In a classic study, authors wrote of the Middle Passage,
"Along with human cargoes, crowded, filthy, undernourished, and terrified out of the wish to live, the ships also carried an invisible cargo of mi-
crobes, bacilli, spirochetes, viruses, and intestinal worms from one continent to another; the Middle Passage was a crossroads and marketplace of
diseases."[15] Conditions were so bad that about 10 percent died en route,
a figure twice that for whites crossing the Atlantic, and those who survived still suffered deprivation and illness on the journey. In America they
were sold on ship or in slave markets. By the first third of the eighteenth
century, the native-born slave population outnumbered those who came
from Africa, but the slave trade was still an important source for labor.
Those engaged in the Atlantic slave trade were only too eager to provide
black slaves for ready purchasers.

Historians differ over how much control slaves had of their own lives
and how much of their African culture they were able to maintain in colonial America, but there is little disagreement about the brutality of the
American slave system for either imported slaves or those born in the
colonies. In many cases, especially in the early days of the colonies, slaves

sometimes worked side by side with their owners or with white indentured servants. As the plantations turned increasingly to slave labor after
1700, white indentured workers became less common. By the eighteenth
century life for the majority of incoming slaves was located on the growing plantations of the American southern colonies, cultivating rice, in-
digo, and tobacco. Working and living conditions were especially harsh
on rice plantations, where health conditions were deplorable.[16] On the tobacco plantations Ira Berlin notes, "Confined to the plantation, African
slaves faced a new harsh work regimen as planters escalated the demands
they placed on laborers in the tobacco fields."[17]

As the century wore on, slaves lost much of the independence that had
permitted them to grow their food and maintain a family life. Because
slaves were defined as property, they could be bought and sold, thus
breaking up their families. As for working conditions, Berlin concludes,
"As plantation production expanded and the planters' domination grew,
slaves in mainland North America faced higher levels of discipline,
harsher working conditions, and greater exploitation than ever before.
Without question, members of the plantation generations worked longer,
harder, and with less control over their own lives than did the members
of the mixed labor force of slaves, servants, and wage workers, who had
preceded them."[18]

Because white owners feared the growth of an independent free black
class, they grew increasingly reluctant to manumit their slaves and enacted a growing number of restrictions on slaves. Thus legislatures declared that conversion to Christianity did not entitle one to freedom. In
the case of children born of parents where one was free and the other enslaved, the law declared the child would follow the mother. Most unions
of free persons and slaves involved white men and black women slaves;
hence, these children were slaves.[19]

During the American Revolutionary era, several northern states took
steps to end slavery. Religion and the revolutionary rhetoric about equal
rights played roles in the antislavery movement. Quakers, for example,
were among the leaders persuading their members to rid themselves of
slavery. In Massachusetts the courts declared that the new state constitution of 1780 providing for equal rights of men meant that no one could
be a slave in that state. But the fact that slavery was not especially important to the economies of the northern states certainly explains why
they abolished slavery. Most laws provided for gradual manumission,
and slavery was not totally eliminated from the North until well into the

nineteenth century. In addition, once freed, former slaves were not granted equal rights. They lacked the ballot in many states, were segregated in schools as well as in some public accommodations and facilities, and faced growing hostility as the antislavery movement became more radical after 1830.[20]

Some blacks entered northern states as free persons. In 1850 16 percent of the blacks in Boston were foreign born. A few came from the West Indies, but about half of them migrated from Canada, and a few entered from Europe, South America, or Africa. One scholar suggests that those born in Africa were originally slaves who had obtained their freedom, but at least some blacks had probably entered as free immigrants.[21]

In the slave South the spirit of religion and the American Revolution also had an impact. In the 1770s and 1780s southern states and religious groups took steps to make it easier for planters and other owners to free their slaves. Many did so, and the free black population began to grow more rapidly. In Virginia, for example, the free black population grew from 2,000 in 1782 to 30,000 in 1810. In Maryland between 1755 and 1790, it increased more than 300 percent.[22] Until the 1830s there were societies in the upper South that supported colonies for blacks in Africa. Although the colonizers wanted to send only free blacks, some within the colonization movement believed that it was possible to end slavery only if blacks were freed and then sent to Africa and the West Indies.

Yet even this mild form of antislavery, if it was that, ended after 1830. The development of cotton explains why antislavery sentiments were doomed, for the American South became dependent on slave labor as it became the Cotton Kingdom. England and the growing factories of the North were able to consume nearly all the cotton produced by the slave states. In this atmosphere free blacks were considered a troublesome presence. As a result, southerners made it more difficult for planters and others to free their chattel, and they tightened the slave system further as abolitionism grew after 1830 in the North.

It was not northern abolition alone that southerners feared. In 1791 slaves in Saint Domingue (Haiti) rebelled against their status, and a bloody civil war followed, in which many slaves killed their masters. It has been estimated that 90 percent of the French in Saint Domingue eventually fled the rebellion, along with several hundred thousand of their slaves and "free people of color," who were free in Haiti but lacked equality with whites. "Free people of color" were free, light-skinned blacks who had a niche in Haiti below equality but above slavery. About 10,000 refugees came to the United States in the 1790s, and more followed in the next decade. New Orleans was a close port, and with a substantial French-speaking population, it drew many of the exiles. The wave of 3,226 "people of color" doubled the population of free blacks in the Crescent City. A number had skills that were in demand in New Orleans. They formed a battalion that fought in the War of 1812. They were also active in the Catholic Church and even established a branch of the Ursuline Sisters, and some helped to educate black children.[23]

New Orleans was not the only port of entry for the white French elite, their slaves, and "free persons of color." Shane White reports that among those refugees fleeing Haiti from 1790 to 1793 were French Royalists and free blacks who settled in New York City. They also landed in Philadelphia. In 1793 Baltimore reported that ships from Saint Domingue were unloading refugees at the docks. In Mobile and Pensacola free people of color made up nearly 30 percent of the population in 1810.[24] In 1793 a French fleet set sail for American ports from Charleston to Boston. Philadelphians raised money to assist the refugees, and some 500 slaves landed with their French owners. The slaves believed they were entitled to freedom, at least under Pennsylvania's gradual emancipation act of 1780, which had a provision stating that any slave entering the state would be free within six months. The Haitian slave holders denied that the law applied in their case, but the antislavery forces won. Nearly 500 Domingue slaves were granted freedom by 1796.[25] In Charleston the mulatto Brown Fellowship Society was established by many of these immigrants, and "it was maintained throughout the antebellum period by their descendants."[26]

One of these free immigrants, Jean Baptiste Pointe DuSable, ventured west. He established a trading post on the Chicago River and became the founder of the city of Chicago. DuSable's post did business for several hundred miles, trading furs with those eager for western goods.[27]

Many Americans welcomed the French exiles and raised money to assist them. In New York City, for example, a committee was formed to raise funds for the poorest to go to France or to the city's almshouse, and New Orleans organized relief for white immigrants.[28] Other cities and states offered aid, and the U.S. Congress appropriated $15,000 for the white immigrants' relief.[29] Some refugees had gone to Cuba, where they received a temporary welcome; but in 1809 the Spanish government, angered by the French occupation of Spain, expelled them. Many headed for the United States, bringing a second wave of French speakers to this country.[30]

As the exiles poured into American cities after 1790, Americans, especially white slave holders in the South, became increasingly alarmed. At first glance the French elite and their slaves seemed to be no threat to American slavery. But some Americans pointed out that these slaves knew of the bloody rebellion in the Caribbean and that they would spread sedition among American slaves. What should be done with those free persons of color who might carry ideas of racial equality among American slaves? Even before the Louisiana Purchase, some in the new nation grew uneasy at the arrival of free people of color and slaves from Haiti. In 1793 a white man in Richmond reported that he overheard black émigrés threaten to lead an uprising. When fires broke out a few years later in Charleston, some residents insisted that they were set by blacks who had been inspired by the Haitian rebellion. One of the largest American slave rebellions, that of Gabriel Prosser in Virginia, was foiled, but white Virginians said it, too, was inspired by the Saint Domingue revolution. The white South responded by making it more difficult for slaves to obtain freedom.[31] As white southerners changed their view of the Haitian revolution from humanitarian acceptance to increased vigilance and constraints, they passed laws to keep Haitians from landing on American shores. South Carolina banned blacks from both the West Indies and Africa from entering. In 1794 North Carolina followed suit and barred the slave trade. Others added similar restrictions, and the federal government declared that any ship bringing in blacks would be forfeited.[32] As provided by the Constitution, in 1808 Congress outlawed the slave trade. To be sure, this was a victory for the antislavery movement, but as John Baur points out, "The example of Haiti was almost universally cited by advocates of these moves."[33]

It was in Louisiana and its port of New Orleans, where the largest number of émigrés eventually settled, that fears of rebellion became most acute, especially in view of the fact that slaves and free people of color outnumbered white Haitian émigrés. It was understandable that the white French-speaking elite would want to settle in New Orleans, even after it became part of the United States in 1803. French was the second language of the territory, commonly heard in the streets. In 1810 French speakers still made up about one-fifth of the white population.[34] Moreover, Louisiana sanctioned slavery, and in the 1809 movement the

French-speaking "whites in New Orleans clamored for the entry of the refugees with their slaves."[35] Over time members of the French exile group were integrated into New Orleans society, and not a few of the later leading families had their origins in Saint Domingue.[36]

But free people of color were another matter. In 1769 they numbered only 99 and constituted just 3.2 percent of Louisiana's population. In 1805 they numbered 823 and made up 15.5 percent of the population. Then came the 1809 refugees. From May 19 to June 18 of that year, thirty-four ships docked at New Orleans from Cuba, bringing 5,574 émigrés. Free people of color numbered 1,566 in 1805 and 4,950 in 1810—an increase of 316 percent. Not all of these were free immigrants, but a substantial number—probably a majority—were.[37] In response to the growing number of blacks, the territory of Louisiana continued a Spanish prohibition on West Indian slaves and in 1806 banned the entrance of free blacks from the French Caribbean.[38] This legislation was obviously not enforced with rigor, as free blacks continued to enter. Shortly after it was passed, the mayor complained, "Many worthless free people of colour or persons calling themselves free arrive here daily without our being able to prevent it, or to drive them away after they had come."[39] The city's French residents favored taking in French exiles and their slaves, in part because many had skills, and in part because they could provide unskilled slave labor.

A particularly vexing issue for New Orleans's white residents was the potential participation of free blacks in the militia, something they had done under the Spanish. If they proved loyal to the slave system, these free black militiamen would be of great assistance in the event of a slave insurrection. Moreover, the spirit of the Revolution still lived among some Louisianans in the 1790s and 1800s, and that spirit seemed to indicate that free blacks had some rights, including participation in the militia. The first territorial legislature, meeting in 1806, authorized that the militia should contain a certain "portion of chosen men from among the freemen of colour."[40] But black men with arms were troublesome to slave holders. The issue became an important one with the outbreak of the War of 1812 and the potential for an English assault on New Orleans. When Andrew Jackson assumed command of the forces defending New Orleans in December 1814, he mustered in the city's 350 free black militiamen, including the recent black immigrants. He addressed them, "Soldiers, I invited you to share in the perils and to divide the glory of your white countrymen. . . . The President of the United States shall be informed of your conduct . . . and the voice of the Representatives of the American Nation shall applaud your valor, as your General now praises your ardor."[41] General Jackson promised each of them the same pay as white soldiers and 160 acres of land. White Louisianans did not agree, and the New Orleans city council passed laws "prohibiting free blacks from moving about the city after dark."[42] Nonetheless, Jackson mustered in two battalions of free blacks, totaling 600 in the force of 3,000. The militiamen fought well and were an important cog in the celebrated victory in the Battle of New Orleans. Their units were acknowledged as consisting of brave men taking to the field "to face the enemy a few hours after its formation." But such military valor did not bring equality.[43] Free people of color from Haiti spoke French, were often educated, and were mostly Roman Catholic. Later a few of the prosperous ones even sent their children to Paris to be educated. They found an economic niche in skilled trades working as carpenters, tailors, goldsmiths, saddle makers, and painters. The New Orleans free blacks had skills and education, and along with slaves they helped to introduce Caribbean culture to Louisiana.[44] Ultimately, however, they were still second-class citizens who had to be on guard to prove they were free and not slaves.[45]

After the American Revolution but before Congress outlawed the slave trade, South Carolina imported 90,000 slaves, who mostly ended up on plantations, suffering the same fate as those slaves born in the United States.[46] Following Congress's outlawing of the international slave trade, some ruthless shipowners still imported slaves from Africa and the West Indies. Precise figures are not available, but profits were too great to deter unscrupulous merchants. The largest source for the slave trade was internal, with thousands sold from the upper to the lower South. Blacks continued to migrate from the Caribbean, but the numbers were not large, and they faced restrictions intended to keep them out.

After the Civil War and the end of both slavery and the slave trade, Congress passed a number of laws intending to give newly freed African American citizens some rights. Before the war free blacks lacked equality even in the free states of the North. Only occasionally did this issue come to the courts. The Fourteenth Amendment changed the status, at least in law, of free blacks; it gave citizenship to all persons born in the United States and subjected to the jurisdiction of the United States. This meant that the former slaves born in the United States were now U.S. citizens.[47] But what of future black immigrants? The old state laws barring their entry were swept away, and Congress extended naturalization rights to

those who did immigrate to America. The Naturalization Act of 1790 restricted naturalization to "free white persons," which meant that Haiti's
free persons of color could not become U.S. citizens. The Naturalization
Act of 1870 added persons of African descent to whites. Now black aliens
could become U.S. citizens, but few in Congress expected many blacks to
immigrate to the United States. They were correct. In 1900 the census
recorded only a few thousand blacks born abroad, and most of them
hailed from Canada. They were the descendants of blacks who had fled
or been taken to Canada during the Revolutionary era and those slaves
who made it to Canada before the Civil War. Around the turn of the century, however, a small migration of blacks from the Bahamas to Florida
occurred, as did another larger movement from the Caribbean to New
York City. (The story of these people will be told in chapter 3.)

While newcomers from England and Africa were peopling the eastern
seaboard, the Spanish concentrated on the Southwest and Florida. Before
Hernán Cortés's spectacular conquest of Mexico, Spanish explorers led
by Ponce de León searched in Florida in 1513 for the fountain of youth.
Although they failed to find this mythic treasure, Spain sent other groups
to look for riches in Florida. Among those heading for Florida were free
blacks living in Spain. The Spanish established a base at Saint Augustine
in 1582, but it did not develop into an important colony for the founders.
The British took over Florida, sent some colonists there, and tried to develop plantations outside the city, but these were not notably successful.
Spain won Florida back in 1783 but failed to develop the territory into an
important colony.[48] When the United States finally annexed Florida in
1819 via a treaty with Spain, the 5,000 Spanish citizens there became part
of the United States.[49] In the long run it was in the present-day southwestern United States that Spain's influence became an influential force,
even though the actual number of Spanish immigrants to that region was
not large.

Not content with their 1519 conquest of Mexico by Hernán Cortés
and the conquistadors or with other victories in an emerging New Spain,
the Spanish headed north in search of gold or other riches. In 1540
Vásquez de Coronado, accompanied by a thousand men (mostly Indians), led an expedition into what is now Arizona and New Mexico. They
discovered Pueblo Indian tribes but no golden cities. Other Spanish ex-
peditions made their way into California, but this trip also failed to bring
instant riches in the form of gold. Because little wealth was found to the
north, Spanish immigrants and explorers concentrated on Mexico, the

Caribbean, and Central and South America, where gold was found.[50] For years the Spanish lost interest in the future Southwest of the United States.

When Spain did colonize the Southwest, it was in part due to a fear of English expansion. Francis Drake and others claimed land for England. To offset these claims, Spain developed a string of settlements in New Mexico, the first ones founded by a band under Juan de Onate. Their most important garrison, or presidio, was Santa Fe, founded in either 1609 or 1610 (the records are not precise). Soldiers were allowed to bring their families on occasion, but duty in the presidio was hardly ideal and could mean long, isolated years. Eventually most fears of European encroachment into the Southwest dissipated, and a large Spanish presence was not required as a buffer against other nations.

However, the Spanish did meet some opposition from Indians. They viewed the Indians as inferior, but they feared those who resisted their colonization, such as the Apaches. Spain had horses and superior military power and was able to gain control over most of the Indians. Many Indians found themselves working as forced laborers for their new conquerors. And because Spanish explorations were overwhelmingly male, Indian women were seen as sexual partners, either voluntarily or by force.[51]

In addition to searching for gold and establishing buffers against other Europeans in the New World, the Iberian conquerors aimed to convert Indians to Catholicism. Along the frontier, Franciscans, Jesuits, and Dominicans accompanied the military men; the Franciscans were the most important in numbers. They brought some Indians into the Spanish and Christian fold and used their labor for agriculture; in the missions, they used Indians held in virtual slavery. While missionaries used the forced labor of Indians, they did urge milder treatment than the military, for they believed that too harsh a policy would hinder efforts at evangelism.[52]

The end result of Spanish conquest was a disaster for the Pueblo and other Indians of the Southwest, for Spaniards brought disease and not simply conquest, just as the English had in New England and Virginia. To the Indians, Spanish rule was harsh and unwelcome. In 1680, the Pueblos successfully revolted against their rulers, who numbered fewer than 3,000, and for a few years Indians lived outside Spanish rule. The Franciscans, if not killed, were forced to flee. The uprising proved to be short-lived. Santa Fe was recaptured in 1692. By 1694 Spain had subdued the Indians, although it did make some concessions to head off future discontent.[53]

Once again in control, the Spanish extended their domain in the Southwest by establishing new garrisons in New Mexico and Arizona. Yet Arizona did not become a major settlement during the colonial era. By the middle of the eighteenth century only a few hundred Spanish missionaries, soldiers, and civilians and their families lived there.[54] The main center for Hispanics was Tucson, but its population was also small.[55] Mining had taken place in the Arivaca region in the 1730s, but the mines were abandoned shortly thereafter.[56]

In New Mexico, Spanish influence was much more pronounced. The Spanish rebuilt towns lost in 1680 and extended their rule into new areas. As before, the black robes, civilians, and soldiers dominated the colony of New Mexico. A century after the reconquest, New Mexico had about 25,000 Spanish and mestizos (persons of mixed Spanish and Indian blood) in addition to its Indian population.[57]

The Spanish were also interested in Texas. Early explorers told of great wealth there, but such talk was not uncommon, as rumors and myths of fabulous wealth inspired many adventurers to the New World. It was not until the eighteenth century that Spain expanded its domination to Texas and later, Louisiana, which became a Spanish colony in 1763. Spain founded two missions in Texas in 1690 that were abandoned within a few years. They resulted in no conversions, but they brought smallpox that devastated Native Americans.[58]

In the early years of the eighteenth century, the Spanish set up communities to act as a barrier against French expansion down the Mississippi River. In 1716 the government in Mexico City sent a few dozen soldiers and civilians into east Texas, and others followed. Fifteen years later Spain sent fifty-six immigrants from the Canary Islands to Texas.[59] While claiming the land, Spain sent few colonists to its sparsely settled Texas. By the middle of the century San Antonio claimed about half of Texas's 1,200 Spanish priests, soldiers, and civilians. During the late colonial period Spain gave a number of land grants to selected persons, and the population grew as ranching became the basis for the economy in southern Texas. Moreover, towns also grew; by 1770 the towns of the lower Rio Grande claimed about 3,000 settlers.[60]

As late as 1819 the total number of Spanish inhabitants living in Texas numbered only a few thousand. About one-half resided in the San Antonio area, with other settlements in La Bahia and Nacogdoches. Along the future border between the United States and Mexico, some 14,000 persons lived in the river settlement of Laredo. These settlers had a considerable degree of independence from the Spanish crown and generated friction between themselves and the Spanish government.[61] With Spain being awarded Louisiana in 1763, the French threat disappeared, as did the need for a military presence in Texas, although the Hispanic ranchers maintained a presence in lower Texas for generations.[62]

When Spain was granted Louisiana in 1763, the province contained only 5,000 or so Europeans, the rest of the population being African slaves or Indians. Spain sought to bolster its new territory by sending immigrants in the hope that eventually the colony would take on a Spanish character. By the 1770s, however, few potential immigrants could be found in Spain for settlement north of the Rio Grande. Among those who did come were Canary Islanders. In 1778 and 1779 Spain recruited 2,373 Canary Islanders, who became one of the largest contingents of Spanish speakers in the colonial scheme. A few others followed, but their numbers were not large.[63] The colonists were plagued by illness, adverse weather conditions, and poor planning. Moreover, Louisiana changed hands to French control and then quickly was sold to the United States as part of the Louisiana Purchase in 1803. A few of the settlers left for west Florida, which remained under Spanish rule for a few more years, but most stayed and accepted the changes in governmental control.

Canary Islanders and their descendants became a forgotten people in the history of Louisiana. Without further immigration from Spain or New Spain, they gradually lost their distinct Hispanic character, even though some prospered in Louisiana.[64] Commenting on the post–World War II Canary Islanders who still spoke Spanish, Gilbert Din noted, "Those who have clung to the use of Spanish and a traditional way of life have lived in isolated and out-of-the-way places. . . . The majority of the descendants of the Islenous in Louisiana have been assimilated."[65] Since World War II, Louisiana has received Latino immigrants from the Western Hemisphere, but these peoples do not mix much with the descendants of the eighteenth-century Canary Islanders.

California, currently the nation's most populous state, has become the center of Latino immigration. Yet in the early days of New Spain, the Spanish government paid it little heed.[66] In the second half of the eighteenth century, however, Spain decided to colonize California. In 1769, Father Serra founded the first of the California missions at San Diego. Other missions followed, at San Francisco, Santa Barbara, and Los Angeles, replacing the presidios as the chief Spanish settlements. Missions generally consisted of a church, places for the padres, and surrounding grounds (cultivated by Indians) to produce food for both the Native Americans and the missionaries.

By 1800, Spain had solidified its claim to Texas and the American Southwest. Several features of these colonies stand out. First, they were sparsely settled. As noted, Texas had only a few thousand "Hispanics," and Arizona even fewer. In Alta California, Spain had established missions and presidios in the southern half, but settlers, priests, and soldiers numbered only a few thousand. New Mexico contained the largest number of Spanish immigrants. When the United States annexed the Southwest, New Mexico had approximately 60,000 of the region's 75,000 Mexicans. This isolation meant that life was hard for both men and women, especially in view of the fact that many Indians remained hostile in spite of the reconquest that took place in the 1690s. Second, the settlements were overwhelmingly male, and Spanish soldiers and civilians took Indian wives. Describing Texas in 1780 one scholar noted:

> Demographers know that the term "Spanish" did not necessarily identify European, white-skinned Spaniards; instead it represented a society categorization. . . . European Spaniards, therefore, included but a few government or church appointees. The rest of those labeled Spaniards by the census enumerators were undoubtedly mixed-bloods who "passed" as Spaniards.[67]

To be a Hispanic or Latino today usually means one is of mixed heritage—a mestizo. To be sure, today some Mexican Americans can claim an unbroken lineage back to the days of the first Spanish settlements.[68] For example, scholars have found Jews among the first Spanish settlers along the Southwest frontier. These Jews were fleeing persecution and the Inquisition and found the frontier of New Spain more tolerant. One scholar believes that 1,500 families in the Southwest "have retained an unbroken chain of Jewish matrilineal descent."[69]

Arizona, New Mexico, California, and western Texas were only loosely connected to Mexico, the center of Spanish power. Ruling was also made difficult because of the clash of interests between civilian officials and the clergy. Finally, although the family was a key institution, women and children had prescribed roles, and an elite dominated, the societies in these regions were less hierarchical than other large population centers in New Spain.[70]

A revolution in 1821 against Spanish rule led to the independence of Mexico. At first the triumphal march into Mexico City by the revolutionaries made little difference to Tejanos (as Mexicans in Texas came to be called). They continued to raise stock and farmed or labored as craftsmen in the towns. The new threat came from the north as "Anglos" looked to Texas as fertile field for settlement. Mexico at first encouraged this immigration and gave persons such as Moses Austin a land grant to settle several hundred Catholics. The Americans brought slaves with them, which did not bother Texans because they, too, held slaves. But in 1829 Mexican authorities freed the slaves of Texas, which did not endear them to the thousands of Americans. By 1830, Americans already outnumbered Mexicans 25,000 to 4,000, and more were streaming into the new Texas during the 1830s. The American immigrants not only wanted to keep their slaves but had little use for Catholicism, the religion of the Tejanos. For that matter, many had little use for Mexicans. Clashes over slavery and religion ultimately led to the Texas Revolution and a new nation, the Texas Republic, in 1836.[71] Mexican rule had lasted only fifteen years.

Ranchers in southern Texas managed to hang on to their lands. Many of these *ricos* were descendants of the Canary Islanders or of Spanish officeholders, while the *pobladores*, usually of mixed blood, performed common labor.[72] Not many Mexicans immigrated to the United States during the Texas Republic era, and, because many Americans did come to Texas, whites outnumbered Mexicans by a margin of ten to one. Mexicans found that the dominant group in Texas did want them to settle or stay in their new nation. Mexicans became Texas citizens in 1836, but they were never regarded as equals.[73]

Elsewhere, the transformation from Spanish to Mexican rule did not produce an immediate surge in Anglo immigration. In the borderland regions, the threat of Indians, present from the beginning, appeared more important than the revolution in Mexico. California's 3,200 Spanish were divided about the revolution. Some of California's small elite favored independence, while the Franciscans favored Spain over the revolution. Once Texas was independent from Spain, and part of Mexico, a new threat arose: the arrival of the Americans who were moving west to satisfy their hunger for land.

The period from 1821 to 1848 in California is sometimes believed to have been a golden era for the Californios, when the elite ranchers dominated society. These were mostly whites, often soldiers, who under Mexican authority received 500 land grants from the Mexican government. Some grants were given to the poor Indian neophytes who had worked on the land, but in the end some 200 families of European origin dominated the region. Men ran the ranches, and women had a prescribed role in the household. Indians remained at the bottom of society, as they did in other regions of northern Mexico; many became virtual serfs. The missions had offered some protection before 1821, but the churches declined in power and influence as the large estates grew in importance. The elite grew a variety of crops and raised cattle and horses, which seemed to promise a bright future. Cattle provided hides and tallow (used for soap and candles); ships from as far away as New England came to collect hides and tallow in exchange for manufactured goods.[74] Below the elite, but higher than Indians, were persons of mixed blood who worked on the larger ranches as vaqueros in this pastoral society. In addition, some practiced crafts, and a few became soldiers. This society would later seem romantic after it was swamped by an American invasion following the Mexican War of 1848.[75]

Little development took place in Arizona during the Mexican era. Only two settlements were, in the words of Manuel Gonzales, "of any consequence in the valley, both of them presidios: Tubac, just above today's United States–Mexican border, and Tucson, a few miles farther north."[76] Arizona had been a center of much hostility between the Spanish and Indians, and this conflict did not end in 1821; Tubac itself was abandoned in 1848. "Tucson lacked gold, silver, iron, lead, tin, quicksilver, copper mines, or marble quarries," but it did have some agriculture due to the floodplain of the Santa Cruz River. However, agriculture did not bring a large number of settlers.[77] The Mexican government tried to support settlement in Arizona, and in the first years of independence it handed out many land grants, including some supplied with livestock.[78] But fierce Apache opposition hindered major ranching, and many of the land grants were abandoned after a few years.[79]

As in California, life in New Mexico changed during the Mexican era. But this arid land would not support cattle as did the land in California, and instead sheep became the mainstay of ranching. At the top of this society stood a number of prominent families who ruled New Mexico politically, socially, and economically. The largest ranches were located along the Rio Grande Valley south of Santa Fe. Expanding trade with Americans along the Santa Fe Trail helped stimulate growth. Beneath the elite were town dwellers and owners of small farms. There, too, Indians remained at the bottom of society. Although New Mexico's growth was not spectacular, it claimed more Hispanics than all other regions of the Southwest annexed by the United States in 1848.[80]

The Mexican Southwest changed radically after its annexation by the United States as a prize of the Mexican War. The Treaty of Guadalupe-Hidalgo ending that war promised that the approximately 75,000 Mexicans in the region could become American citizens and that the United States would honor their claims on the land. The Naturalization Act of 1790 had restricted naturalization to "free white persons," and, as noted, in 1870 Congress added persons of African descent. Clearly many, if not most, of the Mexicans living in the Southwest were partly Indian, and Congress did not permit American Indians to become citizens until 1924. As late as 1938 a federal court held that an immigrant who was one-quarter African and three-quarters American Indian was not eligible to become naturalized as a person of African descent.[81] In 1897 a federal court in Texas declared that if strict scientific evidence were employed Mexicans would not be considered white. However, the courts held that since Congress had permitted Mexicans in the annexed territory to become citizens through treaties, then Mexican immigrants had that right as well.[82] In the 1920s, when Congress prohibited "aliens ineligible for citizenship" from immigrating to the United States, the ban was directed at Asians; Mexicans were not prohibited from migrating.

The right of citizenship did not, however, grant equal rights to Mexicans, whether they were part of the annexed Southwest or new immigrants. Indeed, after 1848 Mexicans suffered from racial hatred that on occasion erupted into violence. Mexicans were called "greasers" and thought to be lazy, a dark-skinned people who constituted an inferior race. It did not help matters that most Mexicans were Roman Catholic, against whom prejudice also existed.

Nor did the promises in the Treaty of Guadalupe-Hidalgo protect their claims to land. The Californios encountered difficulties in proving their claims for landownership.[83] As Americans streamed into California, they rapidly outnumbered Mexicans. Land claims were sometimes vague, but even if they rested on solid legal foundations, Mexicans often did not speak English, were unfamiliar with the American legal system, and found themselves cheated. Some hired expensive attorneys and they ended up land-rich but indebted. Forced to sell tracts of land to pay these debts, the rancheros soon knew that the romantic days were history. Nor was fraud unknown. There were exceptions, and some Hispanics did hold on to their property. Moreover, the elite had little choice but to accept American rule, and some even intermarried with Americans. Of course most Mexicans did not have landed estates, and they remained landless workers, only one step higher than Californian Indians who suffered new blows as the Americans brought more violence and disease.

For Californios legal issues were not the only problem. Droughts in the 1860s, a depression in the 1870s, and finally a bust in cattle raising added to Mexican woes.[84] Some conflicts ended in violence. Historians have traced the history of Mexican bandits, especially Joaquin Muerietta, or possibly several persons with the first name of Joaquin. Americans allegedly stole Muerietta's mining claim, killed his brother, and raped his wife. In response Muerietta allegedly terrorized his foes and was sheltered by Mexicans until he was finally killed. Thus he became a virtual Robin Hood as well as a bandit in the myths that developed around him.[85]

What changed California so quickly was the discovery of gold in 1848. On January 24, 1848, James W. Marshall, an employee of John Sutter's sawmill, discovered gold. At that time the 15,000 Hispanics in the state were about equal in population to the Americans, but the news of the discovery spread quickly. It drew gold seekers, or argonauts, from the other states, Europe, south of the border, and even many Irish from Australia. For the next dozen years, the gold fields continued to attract fortune seekers. Of course, only a few made their fortunes, but many who could not strike it rich mining gold used their skills to service the miners. As a result, not only did the gold fields attract men and women, but towns, including what would become the city of San Francisco, grew rapidly.[86]

Among those arriving in California were immigrants from South America and Mexico. In the first year about 5,000 South Americans arrived; a total of 50,000 Latin Americans are said to have headed north between 1848 and 1852. Many of the Peruvians had worked in the silver mines around Potosi.[87] The news of the gold mines came to Chile on August 19, 1848, when a ship anchored in the port of Valparaiso; the stories triggered a mass movement to California. By the end of 1849, ninety-two ships registered in Chilean ports were reported to be rotting in San Francisco Bay because they had no passengers. Their passengers had disembarked and headed for Sacramento.[88] But they were easily outnumbered by the other argonauts. The Chileans, who were the largest number from South America, had come from an agricultural region where many worked small plots of land. As the Chilean population grew in the nineteenth century and left many with little or no land, some of the men thought they might find opportunities in the gold fields.[89]

Mexicans, usually called "Sonorans," sent the largest number of Latinos to California. They hailed mostly from Sonora, the northernmost state in Mexico and a region somewhat isolated from the center of power in Mexico City. Between 1848 and 1850, 10,000 left Sonora, and others followed. Some might have had experience in mining before they left, but in any case the news of the gold fields brought hope for a better day.[90] Like other groups that worked in the gold fields, Mexican argonauts were overwhelmingly male.

Mexican miners, because they were close to California and heard the news quickly, were among the first to reach the Sacramento region. Indeed, some of the other miners learned the placer method, which consisted of panning for the precious metal in streams and rivers, from Latinos. Some Hispanic argonauts panned for gold, made money, and returned home.[91] But being first did not spare them from economic and ethnic conflict or from being driven from the diggings. American miners wanted the Latin Americans out of the mines. Some squabbles over claims also took place between the Americans and the French or among the Americans themselves; others involved Mexicans and non-Mexicans who were concentrated in the southern mines, where the mixture of peoples was greater than in the north. Once the Indians were pushed aside, Latinos "became the first targets, to be followed later by the Chinese."[92] In 1849–50, conflict between the Chileans and Americans and foreign-born Europeans erupted in the "Chilean War," in which several miners lost their lives. If violence were not enough to rid the gold fields of competitors, Americans resorted to the power of the state. In 1850, California passed a foreign miners' tax, but opposition from the foreign miners got it lowered.[93] It was repealed altogether a few years later, but by 1852 Latinos had largely left the mines. The legislature also passed other laws to harass immigrants from Latin America.[94]

Ethnic conflict was not the only trial faced by the Latin Americans. After the first years, placer mining yielded poor results, and the growing number of argonauts intensified the competition to find profits. As it became more difficult to dig gold, large-scale commercial enterprises began to replace individual claims. As a result, many miners returned home. Still others, Mexicans among them, sought different ways to make a living. They opened shops to sell necessary goods to the miners, provided food and lodging, and opened saloons and gambling establishments.[95]

Many of these businesses were either run or staffed by women, who had been arriving in larger numbers after the first two years of the gold rush. The southern mines reported only 800 women in a population of approximately 30,000 in 1850 (3 percent) and only 9,000 women of a total of 50,000 (19 percent) ten years later. Some who had come to join their husbands performed the accepted gender role of keeping house and attempted to bring middle-class standards to the region. A few worked beside their husbands looking for gold. Others opened businesses that conformed to traditional gender roles, running boardinghouses, laundries, restaurants, bake shops, dance halls, gambling houses, and brothels.[96] The French women were reported to be ubiquitous at gambling tables, but Chilean and Mexican women also worked in these public places. As Susan Johnson has noted, these women worked "dancing with men, dealing them cards, servicing their bodies—these were not easy ways to make a living, and each grew more difficult as the 1850s progressed."[97]

With gold no longer so easy to mine, with commercial operations replacing placer methods, and with growing hostility by Americans toward Latinos, many Mexican argonauts decided to leave the mines but stay in California, settling in San Francisco and other cities such as Santa Barbara. In these cities Mexican immigrants encountered opposition just as they had in the mines.[98] Still others labored in agriculture, which was now required to feed California's growing population.

Some Mexicans found employment in the New Almaden mercury mine located near San Jose. Along with Chileans they "became the first Latino industrial laborers in the United States."[99] Working for wages, they found unhealthy conditions, but this did not stop them from responding to the British owners of the mine. Mexicans were being driven from the gold fields; thus employees had a ready supply of laborers.[100]

With the completion of the transcontinental railroad in 1869, it was much easier to reach the West Coast.[101] As the railroads brought thousands more settlers from the East, Mexicans became a small minority. For example, even though Mexicans continued to come north, Los Angeles changed rapidly, and by the 1880s Anglos outnumbered Mexicans.[102] Some Mexicans in Los Angeles managed to enter new occupations and hold skilled employment, but many found themselves laboring in unskilled jobs or as citrus workers.[103] They formed their own organizations, published newspapers, and, in the words of one historian, developed "an emerging ethnic consciousness."[104] In Santa Barbara, Mexicans maintained their majority until the end of the century.[105] The 1900 census found only 8,000 foreign-born Mexicans in California, less than 10 percent of the Mexican immigrant population in the United States. The great surge of Mexicans to California was a twentieth-century movement.[106]

Half of the Chileans left the mines by 1853 to return home. The largest group staying in California went to San Francisco, with the 1852 census reporting 1,100 of them in that city. Their settlement, called "Chile Town," was situated at the base of Telegraph Hill, near the waterfront. Others lived in ships anchored in Yerba Buena Cove. According to one historian, South American women who were recruited as prostitutes were among the residents of Chile Town, which was often a scene of violence. Nearby in "Sydney Town," Australian thugs known as the "Sydney Ducks" congregated on the waterfront and resorted to a rough-and-tumble life.[107] The area was the center of vice and hardly a place for peaceful living. White San Franciscans resented the presence of Chileans and assaulted a number of them, which prompted some to return to Valparaiso. Of those who remained, some opened small businesses and eventually found greater acceptance and even intermarried and assimilated.[108]

California mines were not the only digs to attract Mexican immigrants. Arizona, which had few Americans and Mexicans at the time of annexation, did not seem appealing at first to prospective immigrants. In addition to war with Indians, much of the land in the area was desert. Ranching and silver mining in the south offered some opportunity, but these did not become major enterprises until 1880, when the Apaches were pacified and the railroad reached Tucson. After that, mining began to grow. Copper mining had existed in Morenci, Arizona, on a small scale before the late nineteenth century, but new mines required large amounts of capital. This created a disadvantage for the state's Hispanics, who ended up doing manual labor.[109] The mines also needed commerce to furnish the workers with food and manufactured goods. As a result, Tucson became a key center and attracted Mexican immigrants. In 1860, 37 percent of Tucson's Mexicans had been born in Mexico, but the figure reached 70 percent twenty years later.[110] A few Tucson Mexicans achieved middle-class status; one, Estevan Ochoa, was elected mayor, the only Hispanic to hold that position while Arizona was a territory. Most Mexicans in the city held more menial positions at the end of the nineteenth century when immigration from Mexico slowed.[111]

Relations between Hispanics and non-Latinos were at their worst in Texas. As Arnoldo De León writes, "In numerous ways, life in the last decades of the nineteenth century resembled that of the period before 1880 for Texas Mexicans. Racial attitudes persisted in virulent forms. Injury, death, or insult of a white by a Tejano, for example, invited certain wrath upon the entire Tejano community."[112] Although Mexican immigrants continued to settle in Texas, they were substantially outnumbered by Americans of European origin pouring in from the north. The Texas Mexican population numbered 71,000 in 1880 and 164,974 in 1900, more than half of whom were born in the United States. More Mexican immigrants lived in Texas than in any other state at the turn of the century. In the central part of the state, Mexicans found their position deteriorating as a result of the migrant influx, and they survived by becoming day laborers or farmworkers. In the west, they worked as vaqueros, shepherds, or farm hands. In the south they remained in a majority.[113] Their position was due to the fact that southern Texas, which housed about half of the state's Mexicans, attracted few "Anglos," as all European-origin Americans were called, while continuing to be a center of immigration from Mexico. Some Tejano rancheros remained moderately successful until the 1890s, although they, much like California's Mexicans, lost land grants.

But the large number of newcomers was not the only problem Mexicans faced. Like mining, cattle raising required capital for fencing and large ranches to offset falling prices. As agriculture modernized, Mexicans increasingly became farmworkers of one kind or another. Others became merchants, artisans, or storekeepers.[114]

The situation in New Mexico was quite different than in the other states and territories of the Southwest. Before the conquest, New Mexico contained 60,000 Mexicans, by far the largest number of Hispanics in the region. Mexicans constituted a majority in New Mexico, a status they maintained until the Civil War because few persons migrated into the territory. After the war some Anglos, including ex-soldiers, settled in New Mexico. More arrived after the railroad was completed, but they generally went to the mining regions and not necessarily the areas of Hispanic concentration.

New Mexico did not see the rapid development of mining that was notable in California and Arizona. Yet trade developed as the region grew, and some of the elite managed to prosper during these years by increasing their lands and herds of sheep. Prosperity was not uniform for all classes; many were unable to win fights over land claims.[115] Many Americans and well-off Hispanos, as New Mexico's Mexicans were called, intermarried, and such alliances helped maintain Hispano influence and position.[116] Thus the territory lacked the intense ethnic conflicts that were so pronounced in Texas and California. At the same time, white cattlemen pushed their claims against the Hispano sheep men, and this conflict erupted into violence.[117]

The surviving elite was able to maintain its culture for many years. Hispanos dominated isolated rural communities, which stretched into Colorado, for decades. Because of a shortage of priests, the Penitents Brotherhood and other lay orders supplemented the Roman Catholic Church, especially in the northern rural villages. After 1880, white Americans began to settle in northern New Mexico and Colorado, and Hispanos increasingly lost their dominant cultural position. Immigrants from Mexico also settled in New Mexico after the Civil War, but only a few went to the rural areas of the north. Moreover, commercial development in the north brought the land claims of Hispanos and others into conflict, and as in similar disputes elsewhere, Anglos usually won.[118] Even as sheep grazing expanded, few Hispanos had the capital to introduce better herds, and they found themselves increasingly employed as laborers for the larger commercial operations.[119] They sometimes left their homes and villages for a period and went to the mines or worked on the ranges.

Hispano culture was based on the family, the village, and the Roman Catholic Church. Men and women had clearly defined roles, but some women moved into the larger economy. Manuel Gonzales reports, for example, that Gertrude Berkeley, known as La Tules, "ran a gambling casino in Santa Fe and made a fortune, which she increased by investing in the Missouri trade."[120]

While South Americans and Mexicans migrated to the Southwest, on the East and Gulf Coasts, Cubans were the dominant Spanish-speaking group, although their numbers were small. Cuban immigrants settled in Philadelphia, New York, and New Orleans as early as the 1820s. The first immigrants were "white professionals, merchants, landowners, and students."[121] Larger numbers arrived after 1865, and from the beginning the immigrants were engaged in politics, focusing on their homeland; they wanted an independent Cuba.[122] Some also concentrated on the abolition of slavery in Cuba, and others wanted the island to be annexed to the United States.[123]

As discontent turned to revolutionary activity in Cuba, the Spanish government forced many Cuban leaders into exile; one center was New

York City and the other Florida, with only a few settling in Europe. The New York exiles tended to be middle-class professionals and business-men, and working-class exiles settled in Florida. José Martí and Tomás Estrada Palma, operating from New York's junta, organized political clubs in the United States. Martí, the main leader of the exile community, visited Tampa to arouse sympathy for the revolutionary cause and to raise money. The junta supported filibustering operations in Cuba and by the 1890s called for independence from Spain. With the defeat of Spain in the Spanish-American War, their goals were realized, although the United States quickly replaced Spain as the foreign power dominating Cuban affairs. And not all Cubans elected to return to the newly inde-pendent island.[124]

Economic issues also played a role in prompting Cuban immigration to the United States. Those locating in Florida needed employment. Dur-ing the American Civil War, Congress raised tariffs on goods, including tobacco, coming from Cuba; as a result, many Cuban tobacco manufac-turers were forced into bankruptcy. Since the 1830s, Key West, at the tip of Florida, had a small tobacco industry, and Cuban immigrants to the United States who were tobacco workers settled there and in Tampa. There they were able to support independence for Cuba as well as orga-nize for better wages and working conditions from their American em-ployers.[125] Key West claimed 3,000 Cuban workers in its tobacco facto-ries in 1885.[126]

These people rallied to support Martí's Cuban Revolutionary Party, which he created in 1892. Although they cheered Cuban independence, once the island had won its freedom from Spain, Cuba's restored tobacco industry meant competition. Moreover, new technology in the American industry threatened to change the old way of doing things, resulting in re-duced wages. Cigar workers engaged in strikes to halt the changes, but these were not especially successful, nor could the cigar workers halt the opening of new plants outside of Tampa.[127]

The Dominican migration to the United States also dates to the nine-teenth century, but the numbers were not large until the 1950s. Two scholars have noted that like the Cubans, Dominican political revolu-tionaries found the United States to be a haven as early as the 1830s. At least one Dominican, Captain José Gabriel Luperon, came to America to fight on the Union side during the Civil War.[128] A few others followed in the late nineteenth and early twentieth centuries to pursue diverse careers, especially in New York City.[129]

Among the first Asians to explore the American Pacific coast and, later, emigrate to the United Sates, were Filipinos. In 1587 a Spanish galleon landed in California. Eight Filipinos accompanied the Spanish crew, and others followed. After the Spanish exploration and annexation of the Philippines, the conquerors needed manpower and recruited Filipino men to serve as sailors aboard their ships.[130] The sailors worked the trade between the Philippines and Mexico. Between 1565 and 1815, hundreds of Filipinos jumped ship in Mexico, where their knowledge of Spanish gave them an advantage in settling. Some gradually made their way to the fishing grounds of Louisiana. Numbering only a few hundred, they formed a fishing enclave, called Manila Village, which was eventually destroyed by a hurricane.[131]

Harper's Weekly reported in 1883 that 400 Filipinos resided in another village and also made a living by fishing. Eventually some Filipinos moved to New Orleans, where they founded the first Filipino American benevolent society, known as La Union Filipina. Another authority estimated that Filipinos in Louisiana numbered 2,600 by 1906, but the census figures do not list that many.[132]

The historian Hubert Bancroft reported that Chinese skilled workers were employed in lower California as early as 1571 and that one Chinese inhabitant was recorded in Los Angeles when it was founded in 1781. Chinese seamen also appeared in American ports as early as 1785, when three sailors were left stranded in Baltimore by the captain of their ship. For a year they remained there in the care of a merchant engaged in the trade with China.[133] On the West Coast an English sea captain of the British East India Company brought a crew of shipbuilders, including some Chinese workers, to construct ships using lumber from the forests of the northwest American coast. Other Chinese followed, and a fur-trading post was established on Vancouver Island. The fate of the Chinese who stayed there is not known.[134] A few others were merchants, selling silks, tea, and art objects on the West Coast. In 1796 a Dutch agent for the Dutch East India Company settled near Philadelphia with his five Chinese servants.[135]

In addition to servants, traders, and shipbuilders, students arrived in the early nineteenth century. A year before the discovery of gold in California, the Reverend S. R. Brown, a missionary, returned from China with three Chinese boys, who went to study at Manson Academy in Massachusetts. One later graduated from Yale.[136] One Chinese man was reported to be living in Hawaii in 1794, and in 1828 between 30 and 40

Chinese were among the 400 foreigners there. In the 1830s and 1840s, Chinese merchants went to Hawaii to establish businesses. They specialized in sugar but opened other businesses as well.[137] Chinese also came early as students or visitors, but they did not develop permanent settlements. Some of these pioneers remained in the United States, however, and a few became U.S. citizens before 1882. A Chinese cabin boy named Hong Neok who settled in Pennsylvania became a U.S. citizen in 1862. He later returned to China, became a priest, and helped found Saint John University in Shanghai.[138] The main immigration of Chinese, however, began after 1849 when they heard of "gold mountain" and sailed for the United States determined to make a fortune.

A handful of stranded Japanese sailors, rescued by American ships, arrived in the United States during the 1850s.[139] The first, Joseph Heco, came in 1851. After eight years of study, work, and religious conversion to Catholicism, he returned to Japan. While in the United States, he became somewhat of a celebrity and was taken to the White House to meet President James Buchanan. Heco even became an American citizen.[140] A few other sailors whose vessels were blown off course were found by American ships. Like Heco, some of the men studied in the United States and learned English. These early "Pacific pioneers," as one scholar called them, were viewed with suspicion in a Japan that wished to remain largely closed to the West.

The Japanese government, however, remained curious about the West and sent 250 young scholars to study in America, especially to learn about its technology. Some remained in the United States during the Civil War and Reconstruction era. A few other students came on their own or were sponsored by wealthy families. Those sent by the Japanese government attended colleges in New England; upon returning to Japan, they assumed high-level posts. Students coming privately also wanted to learn English and acquire skills that would be useful when the returned home. Landing in San Francisco in the 1880s, they accounted for a majority of Japanese in the United States. They intended to return home, but some remained as laborers.[141] Many of the student-laborers found lodging in Christian institutions such as the YMCA. Life was not particularly easy for these pioneers, but they learned English and picked up American ways.[142] They were mostly young men, but a few unaccompanied Japanese women arrived in the late nineteenth century.

Japanese curiosity about America extended to utopian societies, which were common in the United States during the nineteenth century. Brocton

Colony, located in Amenia, New York, received several Japanese in the 1860s, but they found educational opportunities to be lacking and consequently left.[143]

Japan also established trade relations with Hawaii in 1871, which brought several Japanese ships to the islands.[144] A few Japanese were recruited to work in Hawaii, and some chose not to return to Japan when their contracts ended. These early contacts did not immediately lead to substantial Japanese immigration; the pioneers did bring news of America and Hawaii back to Japan, however, probably influencing others to begin migration after 1868 when the Japanese government eased restrictions on emigration.

Geographically the Middle East is the western part of Asia, and it is certainly not Europe. Only a handful of immigrants from this region came to the United States before the late nineteenth and early twentieth centuries. A "Martin the Armenian" allegedly came to Virginia in the early seventeenth century. A few other Armenians followed, but their numbers were not large. A few Armenian businessmen, students, and clergymen migrated to the United States beginning in the 1830s. Their numbers are not known, because before 1899 they were listed as being from Turkey. Those arriving with a religious purpose had already been converted by American Protestant missionaries, and they wanted to study in America so that they could eventually return home and spread American Protestantism in their native land. A few also arrived to study medicine. The merchants, of course, were interested in trade rather than religion, and a number opened oriental rug firms in the United States during the 1870s.[145] Others who emigrated wanted to work in America and return with enough money to invest at home.

Like the first Japanese and Filipinos, these early pioneers were the forerunners of the larger movements after 1880.[146] The primary influx of Chinese had occurred earlier, during the gold rush days of the 1850s and the railroad-building era of the late nineteenth century. When the Japanese were arriving during the 1880s, Congress passed the Chinese Exclusion Act to limit large-scale Chinese immigration. These groups will be discussed in the next chapter.

2

Asians in Hawaii
and the United States

While Chinese workers in Hawaii and merchants and students on the mainland related their experiences back home, it was the discovery of gold in California that prompted thousands to leave for America. In 1849 only 345 Chinese "forty-niners" arrived; 450 more joined them the next year, and then came a rapid increase: 20,026 landed in 1852. By 1870 there were more than 60,000 Chinese immigrants in America, three-quarters of them in California.[1] Betty Lee Sung tells the story of Fatt Hing, a fish peddler in China who regularly journeyed to the coast to buy his fish. In Kwanghai he heard of the outside world, and he saw white men on the vessels in the harbor. According to Sung's account, "One morning there was a great deal of commotion and excitement on the wharves. Elbowing his way to the center of the crowd, Fatt Hing caught snatches of the cause of the shouting. By putting together a word here and a word there, he surmised that there were mountains of gold for the picking somewhere beyond the oceans."[2]

Most of those who headed for California were young men from Canton. More than 60 percent were from Toisan alone. Their living conditions were grim, and like many European male immigrants, they hoped to dig enough gold to return home rich. Many were married, but they set out alone; few wives came with the Chinese immigrants. Once in the Californian fields they used the placer method (panning for gold in rivers and streams). Most worked as individuals, but a few formed or joined companies. They arrived after the flush first few years of the gold rush; the days of quick riches were "long past, and mining was simply hard work with small returns for most miners." Taking over the exhausted mines of others, they extracted what gold they could.[3] A few reported huge finds, including two who found a 240-pound gold nugget worth $30,000.[4] But for most, their labors were not conducive to great or even modest fortunes in "gold mountain." As companies moved into the mines, some Chinese became wage laborers rather than individual miners. Others opened restaurants or took in laundry. If the profits were meager and wages low, within a few years some miners returned to China. Yet conditions back home were worse, and as a result other immigrants kept coming.[5]

Other miners quickly noticed that the Chinese looked different from Europeans or the Mexicans, Chileans, and Peruvians, but they were generally welcomed at first. Chinese immigrants were invited to participate in the 1850 celebration of California's admission as a new state, where Justice Nathaniel Bennett said, "Born and reared under different Governments and speaking different tongues, we nevertheless meet here today as brothers. . . . Hence forth we have one country, one hope, one destiny."[6] But as their numbers grew and as the diggings yielded decreasing amounts of gold, welcome quickly turned to opposition. As early as April 1850, the state legislature imposed a tax on all foreign miners. To be sure, this levy included Latinos, French, and other European immigrants, but as those groups gave up on finding gold, the Chinese increasingly became the focal point of the tax, the purpose of which was to drive them from the mines. On occasion tax collectors went to Chinese mining camps and seized the miners' possessions to be sold at auction.[7] Eventually the tax was reduced and repealed, but by then the gold fields attracted very few persons eager to find a fortune.

When the gold fields and streams in California finally became overworked, Chinese miners looked elsewhere for wealth. Some began to work for companies digging other minerals such as quartz. Others worked in the coalfields in Rock Springs, Wyoming. Once the Indians were pushed out of the way, as they were in the California fields, mining companies and miners in Rock Springs moved in. The Chinese were employed in mines owned by the Union Pacific Railroad, where they refused to join a strike. On November 25, 1875, 150 Chinese reported for work, but they had to be escorted by U.S. troops because of the hostility from white miners.[8] Such hostility did not bode well for the future.

Rock Springs was a rough community, practically all male, and mostly young and unmarried. Working conditions were harsh and the pay not high. Under such conditions whites simply saw the Chinese as intruders who were taking sides with the company to break strikes and keep wages low. Clashes and friction between the Chinese and whites escalated into a full-scale riot in 1885, in which the Chinese were driven out of town and twenty-eight immigrant workers were killed. Order was restored only when U.S. Army troops arrived. When China protested the treatment of its nationals, the U.S. government did pay an indemnity but refused to take responsibility for the violence.[9] Additional incidents of violence occurred in other western mining camps and cities.

Some Chinese in the gold fields supported themselves by feeding the miners rather than panning or digging for gold. Those who began to till the soil had come to the United States to mine, not farm. Many had been farmers in China and certainly were familiar with agriculture. They quickly learned that there was a market for their produce, and not just in the mines.[10] Some of the food they ate in the fields, such as rice, was imported from China, but they could grow vegetables and they even raised hogs. Whether importing or growing, they found a large market for their efforts in the mining fields of California.[11] They grew crops and produce on the mining plots they claimed or leased from others, with some individuals working at both mining and growing. By the 1870s most of the land they farmed was leased. They soon leased land not to mine but to grow food for the hungry miners, both Chinese and non-Chinese. According to Sucheng Chan's detailed study, in 1860 the most important urban center for Chinese farmers was the city of Sacramento, which recorded 110 Chinese vegetable cultivators.[12]

Truck farming required little knowledge of English, which few immigrants, Chinese included, had. Chan notes that in some areas immigrants other than the Chinese dominated the markets. Italians, for example, were prominent as truck farmers, but English or Scottish immigrants, who spoke English, were not.[13] Farming provided an income, but it was tough work. In some cases swampland had to be drained, and truck farming required constant attention. As agricultural sectors grew in importance and size, some Chinese became tenant farmers, reclaiming land and planting orchards and crops.

Chinese also worked as cooks to serve the agricultural workers; others became merchants, those who got the crops and produce to market. The merchants became the elite of Chinese society, especially after Chinese exclusion, because they dealt with whites. Most farmers, whether they owned their own land, leased it, or worked as tenants, lived in an isolated bachelor society. In spite of the fact that their produce was needed in the cities, Chinese farmers found themselves facing a hostility similar to that encountered by Chinese miners. Over time the agricultural workers left the fields and moved into the cities. By 1920 there were few Chinese farmers left in California. The Asians who took their place hailed from Japan.[14]

Chinese immigrants found employment in areas other than mines or in the mining regions or as farmers. Perhaps the most famous of the Chinese immigrants were those who helped build the transcontinental railroads. Beginning in 1865, the Central Pacific Railroad hired 50 Chinese workers.[15] Within two years, Charles Crocker, president of the Central Pacific, had employed 12,000 Chinese immigrants to built his railroad east. According to Crocker, "They are very trusty, they are very intelligent, and they live up to their contracts."[16] Going through the mountains of the West was a daunting task. It took 300 men a month to "clear and grub a bare three miles." Then came winter. Faced with blasting mountains and contending with huge snowdrifts, a "good many men" died in the first winter, as one railroad official put it. Many lost their lives, and their bodies could not be recovered until spring. Speed was of the essence for the railroad promoters because the subsidies they received for building were tied to a limited time frame.[17] One observer recalled that the Chinese were a "great army laying siege to Nature in her strongest citadel. The rugged mountains looked like stupendous ant-hills. They swarmed with Celestials, shoveling, wheeling, carting, drilling and blasting rocks and earth."[18] The completion of the transcontinental railroad occurred at Promontory Point, Utah, in 1869. In spite of their labor, the Chinese workers were not invited to participate in the ceremonies marking the successful uniting of the nation by rail.[19] After the railroad's completion, some of the workers returned to China, but others scattered to various American cities. Jack Chen notes that it was ironic that Chinese immigrants had helped build the transcontinental railroad, for after its completion it made it easier for other workers to flood California; when a labor surplus and depression developed in the 1870s, Chinese immigrants were blamed for the deteriorating economic conditions and falling wages.[20]

Except for the few who remained in mining and those who farmed, Chinese immigrants headed for the cities to take up new occupations. Yet it was not the completion of the Central Pacific Railroad or the growing difficulty of making a living by placer mining that determined the movement to cities and the limiting of economic opportunity for Chinese immigrants. While at first the Chinese were welcomed as hard workers, a growing number of other Americans, native born and white immigrants alike, began to call for the end of immigration from China.

As the number of Chinese immigrants grew, they faced a rising tide of racist ideology. In 1869, Charles Francis Adams Jr. said the Chinese were only "semi-civilized" people who could not assimilate. Adams was by no means alone in his thoughts in the 1860s. Such attitudes were common throughout the United States, even among those who had never worked with or seen many Chinese immigrants.[21] Of course, blacks and Latinos encountered similar racism, but they were not barred from coming to the United States as Asians eventually were. Many Americans believed that the Chinese immigrants were coming as contract laborers, which was partially true, a practice that amounted to slavery in their minds. During the Civil War, Congress had passed a law permitting contract labor as a method for attracting immigrants, but in the aftermath of the war, this practice came to be viewed as undesirable, and the law was eventually repealed.[22] Labor leaders were particularly outspoken in their opposition to "coolie" labor.[23] When a southern convention called for the replacement of blacks by Chinese immigrants, and when a North Adams, Massachusetts, factory imported Chinese to break a strike, labor leaders were alarmed. The *Springfield (MA) Republican* newspaper declared, "The Chinese question . . . is being forced upon us with rapidity that no one could have anticipated."[24] In the end few Chinese came east, and even fewer eventually settled in the South.

Rumblings in Congress led to debates about restricting or ending Chinese immigration as early as the 1860s, but the legislators took no action at that time. In 1870, however, the Chinese question was debated as Congress passed a new naturalization act. When Charles Sumner moved to eliminate the word "white" from the 1870 naturalization act, the senators refused to do so. In the aftermath of the Civil War, some support for equal civil rights and racial justice existed, so a minority of senators agreed with Sumner, but in the end all that the majority in Congress would do was to add "persons of African descent" to those eligible for naturalization. Clearly Asians were not of African descent, but were they white? It was the intent of the legislators to deny the Chinese and other Asian immigrants the right to become U.S. citizens. Some of those discussing the issue insisted that Chinese immigrants worked for unfair low wages; others insisted the Chinese were an inferior race.[25] The courts later agreed that the Chinese were not permitted to naturalize, but the Supreme Court did not finally decide the issue for other Asians until the 1920s.[26] Of course those persons of Chinese ancestry born in the United States were citizens due to the Fourteenth Amendment, but because so few Chinese women had arrived, it was not expected that many such children would be born here.

Five years later the legislators limited the immigration of Chinese women when they passed the Page Act of 1875. Although there were no federal limits on Chinese women, and state laws were not effective in limiting Chinese immigration, few women accompanied their miners in the search for gold mountain. Some did immigrate with their merchant husbands, but the number of merchants were not large, and many came alone before bringing their families. The group that caused the most anxiety among Americans were prostitutes. The censuses of 1870 and 1880 recorded a few thousand prostitutes, and although nearly two-thirds of Chinese women were reported as prostitutes, scholars are not certain how accurate the official counts were. Their numbers also declined between 1870 and 1880.[27] Other immigrant women also became prostitutes, but the concentration of such Chinese women in San Francisco coupled with an increase in racism made for their exclusion. Local governments attempted with mixed success to ban Chinese prostitutes.[28] The Page Act banned immigrant prostitutes but affected Chinese women generally. Immigration officials used the act to scrutinize all Chinese women whom they regarded as morally decadent. As George Peffer notes, "Clearly, government officials who enforced anti-Chinese legislation both before and after exclusion demonstrated a consistent unwillingness, or inability, to recognize women who were not prostitutes among all but wealthy applicants for immigration."[29] Officials enjoyed growing support in the press and among Americans concerned about Chinese immigration. A San Francisco newspaper praised the Page Act, saying it promised to limit "lewd and immoral women." The *San Francisco Bulletin* noted an official report that proclaimed, "The habits and manners of the Chinese immigrating to this country are of the lowest order of that people. . . . Most males . . . are brought here under contract for servile labor." The report concluded that the women "are of the lowest and vilest class, and are brought here for the purposes of prostitution and corrupting the morals of the people and bringing disgrace upon enlightened civilization."[30] As a result, it was very difficult for Chinese men to bring their wives to America, leaving most Chinese men to live in a bachelor society.

While those whites wanting to curtail Chinese immigration focused on prostitutes, it should be acknowledged that the bachelor society was not universal. Scholars have found that Chinese women were working with their families in the fishing industry as early as the 1850s. Sucheng Chan also recorded the existence of Chinese women in agriculture in the late nineteenth century, and others reported families in western towns and communities. In spite of the laws banning interracial marriages, such unions did take place.[31]

Not content with driving Chinese men from the mines and making it more difficult for women to enter, white Californians passed laws to harass those immigrants who lived in San Francisco. These included limiting legal rights, harassing laundry owners, and blocking the small number of Chinese children from attending public schools. The courts declared some of these acts unconstitutional, but even if all were held to be valid and would have severely restricted the lives of Chinese men, they would do nothing to halt the immigration itself. Hostility toward Chinese was not limited to the West Coast; in New York, too, Chinese immigrants faced a growing enmity.[32] The Chinese fought these laws but were unable to contain the rising tide of racism.[33] The movement for immigration restriction eventually resulted in congressional action. When politicians took up the cry of Chinese exclusion in the 1870s, it was only a matter of time before treaties with China would be renegotiated to permit exclusion. In 1882, Congress appealed to both racist and labor arguments when it passed the Chinese Exclusion Act, which barred most Chinese immigrants for a ten-year period. Other measures followed, and exclusion lasted until it was repealed in 1943.[34]

Despite the law, ways for Chinese to immigrate to America still existed. Diplomats, teachers, and travelers were permitted, as were merchants. The laws did not specify women and children, and left decisions about their migration to enforcement officials. Some merchants and their wives had only very small businesses, but these sufficed to gain entry. Officials did make it difficult for wives of merchants to enter at first, but it gradually became easier for women to join their husbands.[35] Laborers were banned, as were their wives. Moreover, Chinese who had been born here were U.S. citizens and could travel back and forth between here and China.[36] Many were held at Angel Island in San Francisco Bay while officials determined their fate.

Erika Lee has found that Chinese immigrants other than merchants were nonetheless able to get around the harsh laws. A few women entered as wives of merchants but were really prostitutes. Because the San Francisco earthquake and fire of 1906 destroyed immigration records, it created a "big chance for a lot of Chinese."[37] Chinese immigrants in the United States could claim that they were born in America and hence were U.S. citizens, with the right to travel back and forth to China. While in

China they announced the birth of a son (they were overwhelmingly male), who because he was the child of an American citizen was a citizen and hence had the right to come to America. In many cases, these sons were not the sons of Chinese claiming citizenship. Rather, the "slot" was sold to another man who became a U.S. citizen, a "paper son," eligible to immigrate to the United States.

To be a paper son meant a life outside much of the mainstream, for there was always a fear of detection and deportation. After World War II, the government permitted paper sons to come forward and "confess" their illegal entry and regularize their status. Thousands did so. There were exceptions, including Tung Pok Chin. He came as a paper son and lived in Boston and New York City. Because of his liberal politics, he was fearful that he might deported. Despite harassment by the Federal Bureau of Investigation, he managed to remain in the United States and rear a family. The fear of deportation remained strong, but he did not confess. He noted that becoming a legal citizen would enable one to sponsor relatives in China for emigration. But he had no one he would sponsor, and he had no desire to return to China.[38]

In other cases, a few immigration officials took bribes; in still other incidents, Chinese entered illegally from Mexico or Canada. It is not known how many crossed the border illegally or came illegally as paper sons, but thousands of Chinese did enter the United States each year after the first exclusion act of 1882.[39] Of those arriving at Angel Island, in spite of careful screening and some long stays on the island, more than 80 percent were eventually able to convince immigration authorities that they had the right to be in America.[40] Erika Lee estimates that from the time Angel Island was established as an immigrant station in 1910 until the repeal of the Chinese exclusion act, 175,000 Chinese came through its doors.[41] The Chinese population would grow by thousands, but many Chinese remained for a few years and then returned home.

A number were women, and the ratio of women to men increased.[42] About half of all Chinese women in the United States lived in San Francisco, and by 1940 there were 20 women for every 100 men nationally. As a result, a small second generation appeared in the nation's Chinatowns.[43] A few whites even supported the increase in the number of Chinese women, for they made for a stable family life. The women often worked in family enterprises such as laundries, restaurants, and grocery stores. As the journalist and reformer Jacob Riis put it, "I would have the door opened wider—for his wife; make it a condition of his coming or staying that he bring his wife with him. Then, at least, he might not be what he now is and remains, a homeless stranger among us."[44]

Hostility did not end with exclusion. As noted, the Rock Springs, Wyoming, incident occurred after 1882, and there were riots against Chinese immigrants in other places in the American West, even though their numbers began to decline as many returned to China.[45] Overall, the Chinese population in the United States decreased in the first few decades of the twentieth century.

After exclusion most Chinese lived in the nation's urban Chinatowns, with San Francisco's being the largest. In 1940 more than 90 percent of Chinese immigrants and their children lived in cities, which were often overcrowded slums, but few Chinese were able to live elsewhere. Chinese were also limited in their ways of making a living. For a time some fished in San Francisco, but like those in the mines, they were eventually forced out of this occupation. Some found jobs in manufacturing, but they were often driven out of these occupations, too. They entered the cigar-making industry of San Francisco in the 1850s, and at one time most of the city's cigar makers were Chinese; Chinese even owned a number of the factories that produced cigars. The white cigar makers' union finally succeeded in driving out the Chinese workers and factories in the 1880s.[46] The garment trade, the boot and shoe industry, and the woolen industry also attracted Chinese workers, but here, too, they experienced opposition, and if they branched out to construction or the skilled trades, they encountered the opposition of white unionists.[47] The most important businesses were laundries and restaurants. The first San Francisco laundry was reportedly opened by one Wahn Lee, who hung a sign advertising "Wash'ng and Iron'ng."[48] The ubiquitous laundries required little capital but long hours of labor, often by one man, although many were family enterprises. These immigrants had not operated laundries at home, but it was one of the few occupations open to them in America. Many of the businesses were scattered through the cities, with the laundrymen living in the shops, mostly in white neighborhoods. But they had little contact with whites except as their customers. As a result, they felt lonely, isolated from the mainstream of American society.[49]

During the Great Depression of the 1930s, New York City authorities passed a law requiring an annual license fee and the posting of a bond in order to operate a hand laundry. Chinatown's leaders were ineffective in fighting these regulations, and as a result the city's laundrymen organized the Chinese Hand Laundry Association (CHLA). Organizers were also opposed to some of the Chinatown merchant leaders' policies toward China.[50] Such a struggle was not entirely unusual. Chinese immigrants, like other immigrants, were vitally concerned about events at home. Thus they paid particular attention to the revolution of Sun Yat-sen, the split within the Nationalist movement that pitted the communists against Chiang Kai-shek, and the Japanese invasion of China during the 1930s. They raised money to aid China in the struggle and did what little they could to alert the American public to the plight of China.[51]

As part of the tourist industry, restaurants also claimed the working days of many immigrants. Merchants and newspapers portrayed Chinatown as an exotic place with an "Oriental Atmosphere." Restaurants served the tourists, as did the many shops selling "art objects and relics." Later on tourists were told of "opium dens" and "tong wars." The *New York City Guide* told its readers that a visit to Chinatown "should include dinner at one of the numerous restaurants declared by the Board of Health to be among the cleanest in the city."[52]

While they were isolated from mainstream American society, Chinatowns were by no means without structure. The Six Companies, composed of the leading merchants, ran the Chinatowns. As noted, the CHLA of New York City opposed the companies' support of Chiang Kai-shek and his Kuomintang (the Chinese Nationalist Party).[53] Missionaries established churches and other religious organizations, such as YMCAs. Few Chinese immigrants converted to Christianity, but the missions sometimes provided a home for runaway prostitutes.[54]

Women in China usually obtained entrance because they were the spouses of merchants. A few were married to U.S. citizens, but Congress changed the rules in 1924. The law was modified again in 1930 to make it possible for some women to join their citizen husbands. About thirty Chinese women also entered each year as students.[55] Like the men, Chinese women were often detained at Angel Island and subjected to considerable questioning about their right to enter the United States.

Once in the United States, the women were responsible for care of their homes (often crowded apartments) and raising the children. Yet some women went to work for wages, which were badly needed to maintain a decent standard of living. These were usually menial jobs because the women had poor English-language skills and were not well educated. Often this meant working in Chinatown, frequently in garment factories or in family businesses.[56]

For middle-class women, community activities beckoned, especially the opportunities presented by the Chinese YWCA in San Francisco. The YWCA also provided help for working-class women in need, offering English classes and advice about immigration issues, employment, and child care. The YWCA wanted to Americanize the immigrants and at the same time was supportive of raising the status of Chinese women.[57]

Many Chinese men managed to support their families back in China, keep up with events there by letter, and return home for periodic visits. Historian Madeline Yuan-yin Hsu has told the story of people who maintained such contacts for decades. In some cases, as noted, the men managed to bring their wives and children to America, a process requiring years of planning. Their sons could arrive as paper sons, but wives sometimes slipped through Angel Island. A few men on gold mountain even managed to return home with enough savings to retire.[58]

For those Chinese who had gone to Hawaii to work in the cane fields, life was somewhat different. From 1852 to 1899, more than 50,000 Chinese went to Hawaii.[59] Like those who went to the continental United States, they were overwhelmingly men, and they intended to work only for short periods. Many returned home, but after Chinese exclusion in 1882 some went to the United States. On the plantations they were replaced by Japanese workers after 1880. Chinese migrants usually worked in the rice fields, although they began as cane workers. Planters liked these migrants because they were recruited to work at low wages.[60] As the islands' population grew, the Chinese agriculturalists branched out, growing and harvesting other crops.[61] In time some of the migrant workers moved to urban areas, where they generally began at the bottom, working as domestics, running laundries, and cutting hair. Some managed to break into skilled occupations.[62] Whatever the particular occupation, the trend was toward increased urbanization, leaving to others agricultural work.

Some southern whites wanted to utilize Chinese laborers to replace blacks, but the number of Chinese recruited for such purposes after the Civil War was not large, and few ended up working on plantations in the South. Even before the Civil War, a small number of Chinese worked as cooks, stewards, or small merchants in the southern states. A few married whites and became permanent settlers.[63] The first attempts by planters to bring Chinese workers to their plantations yielded practically no results. Still, some planters were convinced that newly freed blacks would not work and that it was necessary to find another labor source. In 1867 the first Chinese began to arrive in Louisiana.[64] Several hundred others migrated to Mississippi and Arkansas and began by picking cotton, but these newcomers hardly constituted a mass movement. Complications involving labor contracts made such movement difficult, and the Chinese themselves believed that they could make better wages in California. Once the workers were on the plantations, the labor contracts proved difficult to enforce, and some of the field hands moved to cities, where they found greater opportunities. In New Orleans, Chinese families utilized their contacts with California to establish small businesses. As elsewhere, they opened the ubiquitous hand laundries, restaurants, and small grocery stores.[65]

Marriages of Chinese men to southern whites or blacks produced children who were classified as Chinese in the census of 1880. But in other cases the children were classified as white, and some "passed" into white society. Others were classified as blacks and identified with blacks. Because the numbers of such children were not great, they did not cause much concern among white southerners.[66] But there were limits. Mississippi's Chinese children were sent to black schools, unless they numbered only one or two; in those cases they attended the white schools. When local officials would not permit his daughter to attend the white school, a Chinese merchant in Rosedale, Mississippi, took his case all the way to the U.S. Supreme Court in the 1920s. The Mississippi Supreme Court had already declared that because Chinese children were not "white," they must attend a "colored" school. The U.S. Supreme Court agreed, and not until the 1950s did Mississippi permit many Chinese students to attend the white schools.[67]

Like some other immigrants, the first Japanese arrivals were students or stranded sailors who were picked up and brought to America. Others followed who either were sent by the Meiji government or came on their own, often sponsored by wealthy families. These scholars were, of course, not immigrants intending to settle permanently in the United States. Those sent by the government attended colleges in New England, and upon returning to Japan they assumed high government posts. Some others had backing neither from the government nor from wealthy families; they had to work their way through American schools. Their goals were similar to those of other students: to acquire English and skills that would be useful when they returned home. Landing in San Francisco, they accounted for a majority of Japanese in the United States for a few years after 1880. They intended to return home, but some remained as laborers.[68]

Many of these student-laborers found lodging in Christian institutions such as the YMCA. Life was not particularly easy for these pioneers, but they learned English and picked up American ways.[69] They were mainly men, but a few Japanese women also arrived in the late nineteenth century. The students were attracted to the United States by popular guides about life in America. Like countless other immigrants, they came seeking a better life, and because many returned home, they spread news about the United States in Japan. One such account, *Kitare, Nihonjin,* proclaimed, "Come merchants! America is a veritable human paradise, the number one mine in the world. Gold, silver, and gems are scattered on her streets. If you can figure out a way of picking them up, you'll become rich instantly to the tune of ten million."[70]

A favorable vision of life across the Pacific prompted many to leave their homeland, but conditions in Japan were also important. Repressive legislation created discontent among some educated young men, and the Japanese government, which had opposed large numbers of its citizens going abroad, shifted its policy to permit the recruitment of Japanese laborers to work in America or Hawaii. This shift occurred just when the United States was banning Chinese laborers. As a result, plantation owners in Hawaii searched for new workers in Japan who would work long hours for low pay. Beginning in the 1880s, several hundred thousand Japanese came to either Hawaii or the mainland. They hoped to make money quickly and then return home.[71]

Japanese laborers came to Hawaii and the United States under contracts, a government-supported system that flourished until 1907. The contractors placed them in agricultural, mining, timber, and railroad jobs. On the mainland, railroads desired their labor, as did mining interests. But it was in Hawaii that the first major migration from Japan occurred.[72]

The sugar plantations eagerly sought out new laborers when the Chinese either were banned or stopped coming. The Japanese lived in barracks on the plantations and quickly became the largest source of foreign labor. Life was not easy for these workers, who rose early and worked in the fields until late in the evening. Moreover, they were not accustomed to working in labor gangs. Ronald Takaki quoted one laborer who said about Japan, "It's okay to take the day off, since it was our own work. We were free to do what we wanted. We didn't have that freedom on the plantation. We had to work ten hours a day."[73] A few left before the end of their contracts, but most waited until the term ended.[74] Some of the contract laborers remained in Hawaii but moved to cities and towns and opened small businesses. On several occasions Japanese workers banded together with other Asians on the plantations to protest their conditions and pay and to organize unions, although these efforts were only partially successful.[75] A 1909 strike saw 7,000 thousand Japanese plantation workers engaged, and another in 1920 brought together several thousand Japanese and Filipino workers.[76]

Planters pitted one ethnic group against others during the strikes, and segregation was common among the various ethnic groups in the plantation camps, a situation that made labor solidarity difficult to achieve. Gradually some owners improved conditions and in the case of families built cottages to house them. Indeed, the owners came to believe that men in families rather than single men made better workers.[77]

In 1900 an American law made labor contracts illegal from Hawaii to the United States, and in 1907 President Theodore Roosevelt banned Japanese laborers from coming to either the United States or Hawaii. Before that time companies in the United States tried to entice them to leave Hawaii or Japan and work on mainland railroads, mines, and lumber mills, offering higher wages as the lure. Thousands responded until Japanese immigrant labor was restricted in 1907.[78] California claimed the largest number, but Japanese immigrant communities also appeared in Oregon and Washington, and even in New York City.

Those recruited for the mines and railroads gradually moved to West Coast cities or became agricultural workers. Eventually a number purchased or leased land, working it for their own profit. Japanese railroad and agricultural laborers arrived in the Hood River Valley of Oregon in 1896. The Hood River Valley proved to be a major center of fruit production, especially apples and pears, and a number of Japanese either owned or leased land there.[79] Japanese farmers were also found in Washington, where they operated nurseries and produced vegetables, dairy products, and poultry.[80] Japanese farmers were located throughout other western and southwestern states, though their numbers were small, except in California.[81] In California there were only 37 Japanese farms in 1900, accounting for 4,764 acres; by 1910, the Issei (first generation) operated 350 farms covering 17,250 acres. Many of the California Japanese began as tenants or laborers before acquiring their own land; in 1910, under several arrangements, they leased land amounting to more than 180,000 acres. A 1913 California law barred Japanese immigrants from owning land; hence some farmers put their land in the names of their children, who, as native-born Americans, were eligible to own land.[82] In 1925 about one-half of the employed Japanese were engaged in farming of one kind or another.[83] Just as Hawaiian farm laborers went on strike, so did those on the mainland. The strikes proved unsuccessful, in part because American unions did not wish to join with Asians in labor solidarity.

Urban Japanese supported themselves by opening hotels, lodging houses, and many small businesses. Initially they catered to fellow Japanese, but they later branched out and dealt with the larger community. A 1909 immigration commission reported that Japanese owned more than 3,000 enterprises; one-third of these establishments were located in San Francisco and Los Angeles.[84] Not a few were related to agriculture, selling farm products produced by Japanese farmers. Many of the other businesses, such as lodging houses, also relied on Japanese immigrants for their incomes. Common establishments included barber shops, pool rooms, restaurants, laundries, and supply stores.

These businesses did not require much capital. The immigrants either worked and saved for several years to raise the necessary funds, or they borrowed from a Japanese rotating credit association. Moreover, the labor costs were cheap because these were usually family enterprises that did not pay wages to their members. The businesses also required long hours for family members, or they were paternalistic, employing other nonfamily Japanese members at low wages.[85]

Although Hawaii and the West Coast accounted for the large majority of Japanese immigrants, a small community also developed in New York City. Some had already worked in the West before coming to New York, but others had come across the Pacific and through the Panama Canal. They included students, merchants, businessmen, and even a few professionals. In part, they were drawn to New York City because, in Japan, reports from America noted the racism of the West Coast. As historian Mitziko Sawada has noted, "Without question, Japanese on the East Coast did not encounter the virulent and continuous acts of hostility directed at Japanese in California, Oregon, and Washington."[86] Many of the first immigrants worked in the Brooklyn Navy Yard, while others ran boardinghouses or restaurants. While relatively less racism was apparent in New York, it nonetheless existed, and Japanese immigrants sometimes found the only jobs open to them were in domestic service, a traditional entry place for immigrants.[87] A few opened stores, such as tailoring enterprises.[88]

Whether in Hawaii, on the West Coast, or in New York City, the initial Japanese immigrants were overwhelmingly young men. This was especially true of the contract workers in Hawaii. A few single women on their own did manage boardinghouses, which were needed because so many of the first migrants were single men.[89] As was the case with Chinese immigrants, among the first Japanese women to emigrate were prostitutes. Taken to the port of Nagasaki, they were then shipped to America by Japanese men.[90]

Women accompanying their husbands were expected to live in a traditional culture in which men dominated. In addition to their housekeeping chores, immigrant women worked for pay. In the sugar fields of Hawaii they often worked along with their kin, and in ethnic enterprises they worked side by side with other family members. Because they did the housework as well, their days were long. One attested, "We worked from morning till night, blackened by the sun. My husband was a Meiji man; he didn't even glance at the housework or child care. No matter how busy I was, he would never change a diaper."[91]

On the mainland their chores were similar. They were expected to help with the farmwork and be involved with running the small enterprises in urban areas. For those trying to acquire their own land, the working day never seemed to end, and early conditions were primitive.[92] Domestic work had a low status in Japan, but it offered employment for Japanese women immigrants; one-quarter of Issei women working outside the home were in domestic employment.[93]

Unlike the other Asian groups arriving in the late nineteenth and early twentieth centuries, the Japanese immigrant community received many women and developed a family culture. The numbers grew gradually after 1900, until the so-called gentlemen's agreement of 1907 restricted Japanese laborers from immigrating to the United States. Many Japanese men did return to Japan, but others wanted to stay in America, at least until they retired; hence they sought to bring brides to America to form a family unit. Women continued to arrive after 1907 as the wives of immigrant husbands, and many of these were "picture brides" who married Japanese immigrants by proxy, for few of the men could afford the trip back to Japan to find a spouse. Immigrant men sent their photo along with information about their position in America to Japan, where their relatives and those of the prospective wife negotiated a marriage. Consequently, thousands of young women had never seen their husbands until they disembarked in Hawaii or the United States. Their first ordeal was passing through immigrant inspectors, but more disappointing to others were their husbands. They did not always resemble the pictures, and not a few women found that their new husbands were much older than the pictures suggested. Only then did they discover that the pictures sent to Japan were touched up.[94]

In spite of their disappointments, picture brides had no funds to return home and could not divorce their new husbands. The women not only lacked funds but also were expected to help their husbands generate income. Most ended up in rural communities, where they helped till the soil. If they settled in cities such as San Francisco, Seattle, or Los Angeles, they were expected to help in family enterprises.[95]

Americans who were opposed to Japanese immigrants became alarmed upon the arrival of picture brides. Senator James D. Phelan took up the issue in 1919, insisting that this practice was an "uncivilized" Asian custom that had no place in America. "To make matters worse, these women produced children" who, as American-born citizens, could purchase land. Responding to the pressure against picture brides, Japan decided to halt the practice, and then American laws made the practice even more difficult. As a result, while most Japanese immigrants in America were developing families, about 20 percent remained unmarried.[96]

Even though Japanese migrants accounted for only a small fraction of the immigrant population, and though they worked hard and were developing a socially conservative family life, they nonetheless faced growing racism and a movement to end their migration to the United States. In 1900 the American Federation of Labor called for a ban on "Mongolian" laborers, and the California Democratic Party supported such a ban. A meeting of a variety of organizations formed the Japanese Exclusion League in 1905, and newspapers such as the *San Francisco Chronicle* warned of an invasion from Japan.[97]

In 1906 the San Francisco Board of Education told principals to send all Asian children to the "Oriental School." Suddenly President Theodore Roosevelt was faced with a diplomatic confrontation with Japan. The president was aware of Japan's growing power and status among nations of the world, and he did not wish to offend the Japanese government. At the same time, Roosevelt knew that West Coast opposition to Japanese immigration was strong, and the president himself believed that whites were superior to Asians.[98] He was able to negotiate a gentleman's agreement with Japan, in which the Japanese government would halt the immigration of Japanese laborers to the United States in return for efforts to end the school crisis. The school board was satisfied because only ninety-three Asian children were involved, and its main desire was an end to Japanese immigration to California.[99]

In 1924 Congress passed an immigration act that put the gentlemen's agreement into the statute books. The law simply said that "aliens ineligible for citizenship" were to be barred from coming to America. The key clause meant that all Asian immigrants would be barred. As noted, according to the 1870 naturalization act, only immigrants who were white or of African descent were eligible to become citizens. Some Japanese had been naturalized before 1922, but in that year the Supreme Court (in *Ozawa v. United States*) held that Japanese immigrants were neither white nor of African descent. Now they were officially barred from naturalization, which meant that after 1924 they could no longer enter as legal immigrants.

A slight exception was made for those Japanese men who had served in the military during World War I. Some had naturalized, but in 1925 the U.S. Supreme Court ruled that Japanese war veterans were ineligible for naturalization. In 1935 Congress passed the Nye-Lea Act, which permitted 500 Asian veterans of World War I to be become American citizens. In spite of this exception, only students, diplomats, and other such visitors were permitted to come to the United States.[100]

The same clause barring their migration was used by western states to prevent Japanese immigrants from owning land. In 1913 California prohibited persons who were ineligible for naturalization from owning land in the state. Several other states followed suit. But, as noted, immigrants' citizen children could own land, and Japanese immigrants put the land in their children's names. In other cases, sympathetic whites leased land for them, but the law did have an impact.[101]

Exclusion and restrictions on landownership were only two of the hardships generated by the anti-Japanese racism. In cities the Japanese had difficulty finding housing, raising capital, and doing business. Like so many other immigrants, the Japanese immigrant community built its own institutions to act as a buffer against American hostility and to reinforce its own heritage. Japanese associations protested against their treatment, and Japanese-language schools aimed at passing the language on to immigrants' children. Newspapers were published and Buddhist temples were built for worship.[102] Worse yet, the Issei watched discrimination directed at their children.

The Nisei, or second generation, like many immigrant children, grew up wanting to be part of American culture. They excelled in school, played American sports, and listened to and danced to popular music. Some resisted attending the language schools because they saw no use for them in American society. They organized their own group, the Japanese American Citizens' League (JACL), which stressed their feelings about being Americans. After all, they were citizens and could vote. The JACL grew rapidly during the 1930s, expanding from eight to fifty chapters with a total of 5,600 members. At times members of the league did not even acknowledge racial discrimination and prejudice, and their 1940 creed, written by journalist Mike Masoka, was superpatriotic. It noted that some Americans might be prejudiced, but "such persons are not representative of the American people. . . . I am firm in my belief that American sportsmanship and attitude of fair play will judge citizenship and patriotism on the basis of action and achievement, and not on the basis of physical characteristics."[103]

Yet the second generation could not ignore racism, even if they downplayed it in public. The Nisei did well in school, and many went on to attend colleges and universities, but they could not find employment suited to their educational level. They labored on family farms or worked in small Japanese businesses in cities.[104] The ultimate test of their "Americanism" came during World War II when a group of Japanese Americans from Hawaii and the United States proved to be one of the most highly decorated units fighting in Europe.[105]

Within a few months of Japan's attack at Pearl Harbor, on December 7, 1941, the U.S. government rounded up West Coast Japanese immigrants and their children and placed them in virtual concentration camps, a move supported and advocated by many of the region's newspapers and politicians. They became, in historian Roger Daniels's words, "prisoners without trial."[106] Most of those removed from their homes and sent to the camps were second generation and therefore American citizens. Worse yet, no incident of sabotage was attributed to them. In Hawaii, the federal government declared martial law, and 1,444 Japanese were interned there as well. Unlike the California press, newspapers in Hawaii asserted that Japanese Americans were loyal, and rabble-rousing politicians were largely mute. Those few interned out of a population of 150,000 Japanese were mostly persons connected to Japanese organizations, such as language schools. Cooler heads prevailed in Hawaii, but it should be kept in mind that the Japanese accounted for nearly one-third of Hawaii's total population; incarcerating them would have seriously disrupted the economy and society of the islands.[107]

Before the end of the war the government began to release Japanese Americans. Some returned to their homes on the West Coast, but most of their possessions had been confiscated, and they received only a tiny proportion of their worth in compensation. Moreover, many were fearful of their reception; incidents of violence and hostility were reported. Gradually, however, the climate began to change, and they found more acceptance in American society, but not until the 1980s did several American presidents apologize and Congress vote funds for at least a partial restitution. A major factor was the war record of the Japanese American soldiers in Europe.

When most immigration from Japan was barred by executive agreements and finally legislation, the restrictions applied to Korea as well because Korea was a colony of Japan after 1907. In the 1880s a few Korean students came though Hawaii on their way to the United States; a few merchants arrived in Hawaii in the late 1890s. These Koreans were the vanguard of a small wave of immigrants who settled first in Hawaii and then the United States. They numbered about 8,000 between 1903 and 1920.[108] About 70 percent of Korean immigrants were literate; most were young males from a variety of occupations. Unlike most Japanese and Chinese immigrants, they came not from rural areas but from cities. They had one thing in common: limited economic opportunities and even poverty at home, and so were eager to seek their fortunes abroad. Ronald Takaki quotes one immigrant as saying, "The country had been passing thorough a period of famine years. . . . My occupation as tax collector barely kept me from starvation's door as I traveled from village to village." Politics was also a factor as many Koreans believed their future was bleak under Japanese rule.[109]

While economics certainly account for Koreans' desire to migrate to Hawaii, another factor was Christianity. Nearly half of the newcomers had been converted to Christianity, and the missionaries presented them with a rosy picture of life in Hawaii and encouraged them to migrate. Hawaii, they were told, was a "haven of peace and plenty."[110] Faced with restrictions on the Chinese, Hawaiian planters, as noted, actively recruited Japanese laborers instead. However, Japanese were considered troublesome, and planters looked elsewhere for labor, which they found in Korea. The first discussions about bringing Koreans to Hawaii occurred in 1895 and 1896, but nothing resulted from these talks. The planters then contacted Horace Allen, an American minister in Korea, to enlist him in the process of recruiting immigrants. As a result of Allen's work, recruitment on a small scale began.[111] The movement never reached large proportions because the Japanese government began to limit emigration of Koreans to prevent them from competing with Japanese labor. Shortly thereafter, through the gentleman's agreement and legislation, the United States prohibited practically all Asian immigration.[112]

The Koreans' lack of farming background meant little to planters who had contracted with them to work in the fields. About 10 percent of these migrants were women, and a few were children. When immigration was restricted, Koreans, like the Japanese, brought picture brides to the islands. As a result, by the 1920s about 20 percent of Korean immigrants were women. When their immigration was ended, a few returned home; others left Hawaii for the United States and, like most other Asians of the era, settled on the West Coast, mainly in California. Their numbers were never large; the 1940 census found fewer than 2,000 Koreans in America.[113] Like the Korean community in Hawaii, mainland Korean society was chiefly a male or bachelor one. The immigrants worked as domestics, farmers, gardeners, and janitors. The farmers tended to be migratory laborers, moving from field to field harvesting different crops. A few operated small stores that catered to the ethnic community.[114]

Mary Paik Lee has left a memoir of her experiences growing up and living on the West Coast. Her family was often poor and faced considerable prejudice in finding housing and employment in California. When she arrived in California, her family was laughed at and insulted, leaving Mary "upset." That was her first experience with American prejudice on the mainland.[115] Her family went from town to town and her father from job to job in California; life was extremely harsh. Mary and others in her family also went from job to job to earn enough to sustain the family. The Paik family, like so many other Koreans, was Christian, and Presbyterian churches were an important part of their lives. Her father's health deteriorated, which made things worse for the family.[116]

Korean immigrants, although small in numbers, were nonetheless interested in ending Japanese control over their native land. They organized groups to work for this end, but these nationalistic efforts were not realized until after World War II, when Japan was defeated and Korea became independent. The second generation did not necessarily share the nationalistic views of their parents. As one young Korean put it, "So far I have read very little about my parents' native land. I have never felt a sense of pride in knowing about my parents' native land but I have pity and sympathy for them."[117] A desire to be American did not spare either the children or the parents from the racism of the West Coast.[118]

Data from 1871 through 1899 list about 500 "Indians" coming to America, and the census of 1900 reported the presence of 2,050. These people were probably merchants, professionals, or visitors, although, as Roger Daniels notes, we know almost nothing about them.[119] The immigration authorities counted about 7,000 Punjabi Indian immigrants—mostly young men—who arrived between 1905 and 1917. Like so many immigrants, they originally intended to stay temporarily and return home with substantial earnings. Asian Indians came from a rural background that emphasized landownership; they looked to America as a possible place to farm, and many eventually ended up in California's Imperial Valley. White Americans branded them as "Hindoos" or "Hindus," but 85 percent were Sikhs. Only a few were actually Hindus, even less than the 10 percent or so who were Muslims.[120]

Some of the Punjabis had served with the British overseas. Some fought in the Boxer Rebellion in 1900 in China, and others were stationed in Hong Kong. From their migrant experience they no doubt heard of a better life in the Western Hemisphere. Karen Leonard quotes one Indian as saying, "I was born in the Punjab district of India and served on the police force in Hong Kong, China, for some years. While I was in China several Hindus returned and reported on the ease with which they could make money."[121]

Like other Asian immigrants, they faced a long voyage to America. Steamships linked India to Hong Kong, but even from that connection it was nearly a three-week voyage to the United States. America was by no means their original destination; many first went to Canada, where they received a cool reception and encountered violence intended to drive them out. From there some headed south to work in Washington, finding employers who welcomed them. They worked in agriculture but also in lumber mills. Although employers were eager to hire these young men, other Americans were not so welcoming. Asian Indians were arriving after the exclusion of the Chinese and during the growing antagonism toward Japanese immigrants. As noted, the hostility toward Asians erupted sometimes into violence, and Indians were among the victims of these outbursts. It was easy enough for racists to see Indians as economic competition. Joan Jensen reports one white worker as saying, "One of these days, by God, the whites are going to chase all of them out of camp and they won't come back either. We'll drive them all down the line with a two-by-four. If the whites only knew enough to stick together and organize we wouldn't need to work with those damned Orientals." This was no idle threat. In the summer of 1907 an angry mob in Bellingham, Washington, assaulted Indians and drove them of town.[122]

Violence followed the newcomers as they went south to California in search of jobs in mining, canning factories, and agriculture. In spite of the outbursts in the first decade of the twentieth century, several thousand stayed and carved out a position for themselves in California's Imperial Valley. Some continued to work in agricultural labor camps or moved around the state finding jobs in lumbering, but many eventually became successful farmers. Hard work and careful cultivation of their white neighbors won them a place, and the violence became infrequent.

If violence became less frequent, agitation to end this flow of immigrants grew. Newspapers called for their exclusion, politicians joined the chorus for a ban, and the Asiatic Exclusion League added Indians to the list of those it wanted kept from American shores. Immigration officials in San Francisco did turn back some would-be immigrants, citing general restrictions against those likely to be carriers of disease. Economic justifications were the most likely explanation for denial of entry. Between 1908 and 1920, the federal government refused admittance to 3,453 Indians, saying the immigrants were likely to be unemployed and become a "public charge." At the same time, some politicians and labor leaders insisted that the Indian immigrants would work and take jobs from Americans.[123] When a few women arrived, restrictionists warned that their numbers would grow and insisted on a ban. Responding to the charges that Indians were "inassimilable" or "treacherous," Congress finally excluded them in a law enacted in 1917 by establishing a "barred zone" covering India and several other Asian countries from which immigrants were to be banned.[124]

The 1917 law precluded the movement of Indian women to the United States, and only a few of the immigrants had managed to bring their spouses over before this time. The choice for Indians was either to return home, if married, or to find spouses in California. Some white women married Asian Indians, but most whites opposed such unions. As a result, the immigrants turned to Mexican women working in the fields. The first Indian-Mexican marriage took place in 1916, and within a decade or so, about half of the Indians married Mexican women. Some of those who never married lived with Indian families, becoming "uncles." The children of such unions generally became Catholic rather than Sikh, and if they spoke a language other than English, it was apt to be Spanish, not Punjabi. The Punjabis did build a Sikh temple in Stockton, California, and some of the children later exhibited an interest in attending it.[125]

Finding a marriage partner was only one problem facing the Indian immigrants. In addition to exclusion, there also remained the issue of landownership for those who remained in America. As noted earlier, California and other states prohibited "aliens ineligible for citizenship" from owning land. The question then became, could Indians become U.S. citizens? The decision in *Ozawa v. United States* (1922) settled the issue for Japanese immigrants, but were Indians "whites" as indicated in the Naturalization Act of 1870? At the local level some courts had permitted Indians to naturalize, but in other cases judges barred naturalization. A case begun by Bhagat Singh Thind finally reached the Supreme Court in 1923. Thind, a college graduate, had come to the United States in 1913 and applied for American citizenship. He contended that court rulings and general logic indicated that he was "Caucasian," and therefore "white" within the meaning of the naturalization laws. In 1920 a district court agreed with him, but three years later, in *United States v. Bhagat Singh Thind,* the Supreme Court declared that he was not white and hence could not become a naturalized U.S. citizen.[126] Following this decision, U.S. officials denaturalized sixty-five Indians during the 1920s, and states blocked Indians from owning land under the statute denying ownership of land by those ineligible for citizenship.[127] Like the Japanese, some Indians put their property into the hands of their American-born children who were U.S. citizens.

For those few who did not farm, discrimination generally restricted where they could live in cities and what they could do for a living. A few opened small grocery stores, for example, and lived among other Asians. In Los Angeles, Indians also owned bars and boardinghouses or were peddlers or elevator operators; they resided near or in the city's "Little Tokyo."[128]

Some also came to study. One source counted thirty students attending the University of California at Berkeley in 1910, but they were by no means spared discrimination. Rooming houses refused to rent to them, and some public restaurants would not serve them. If they traveled in the South, they learned to wear their turbans so as not to be taken for black Americans, but on the West Coast they encountered less hostility if they did not wear turbans.[129] The most well known of the students was Dalip

S. Saund, who arrived from England in 1919 and headed to Berkeley. He received a doctorate in math but went to work in the Imperial Valley. Married to a Czech immigrant, he farmed land in his wife's name.[130] In 1946, when the United States finally permitted Indians to naturalize, Saund became a citizen, became active in politics, and ultimately became the first Asian American to be elected to Congress, serving three terms before his death.[131]

Many Indians in the United States attempted to organize against British control of India, and some students responded to the appeals of Taraknath Das and Har Dayal, the chief leaders in the crusade against Britain. Their efforts resulted in the formation of several groups and publication of several newspapers dedicated to ending British rule in India. British authorities were convinced that they represented a threat to their colonial empire. Americans cooperated with British efforts to neutralize these activities, and during World War I the United States arrested several leaders, charged them with violation of the neutrality laws, and deported several. Actually there was no threat from such small groups.[132]

Following the *Thind* decision, in addition to denaturalizing those who had obtained citizenship, California courts began denying the right of Indians to marry whites, citing a California law that barred interracial marriage. The ban, denial of citizenship, and exclusion precluded a larger Indian community. By 1940 some Indians had returned home, and as others died, the Indian American community shrank. In 1940 the census reported only 2,405 Indians, with some 60 percent living in California and working the land. Only a few were professionals, and among the racial groups reported by the census, they had the lowest level of educational achievement.[133]

When laws and executive agreements cut the flow of immigration from Asia, Hawaiian planters and some agriculturists in the American West began to look elsewhere for laborers. In the Southwest, Mexican immigrants, both legal and illegal, filled the gap. But Mexicans did not go to Hawaii, and there was still room for others to pick crops in the Pacific Coast states; Filipinos were readily available. Following the conquest of the Philippines, the Supreme Court determined that the Constitution did not follow the flag; hence, Puerto Ricans and Filipinos were not U.S. citizens by the mere fact of their birth in American colonies. However, Congress did grant citizenship to Puerto Ricans in 1917, but not to Filipinos. Thus, Puerto Ricans could freely migrate to the United States. A few thousand did so after 1917 until the Great Depression of the 1930s curtailed migration because of the severe shortage of jobs in the continental United States.

Because legislators did not grant Filipinos citizenship, their status fell between citizenship and alien. They were declared to be nationals, so that they were not "aliens ineligible for citizenship." Their status as nationals gave them free migration to the United States until Congress decided differently in 1934. As noted in the previous chapter, some Filipino sailors left their ships in the eighteenth century and settled near New Orleans; others who deserted their ships lived in Washington.

A few others came later to study in American colleges. Before 1900 the Filipino presence in the United States was minuscule, and in 1910 the census found only 406 Filipinos living on the mainland.[134] Beginning in 1903, government-sponsored students from wealthy families, called *pensionados*, came to study in a number of colleges and universities across the United States. Most were young men, but a few women were sent to America as well. As secondary education in the Philippines expanded, higher education no longer was the sole prerogative of a few elite families. In 1923 a New York–based Filipino newspaper, the *Filipino Student Bulletin*, estimated that 2,000 Filipinos were studying in the United States, and it has been estimated that 14,000 such persons studied in the United States from 1910 until 1938.[135] The purpose of the program was to train Filipinos to be leaders in their native land, and many became successful at home. They included Jose Abad Santos, a future chief justice, and Ernesto Quirino, the uncle and guardian of a future president of the Philippines. While some returned to the Philippines with professional credentials, others went to work in the Philippine civil service when the United States turned many positions over to Filipinos after 1910. By 1920, more than 95 percent of civil service positions in the Philippines were held by Filipinos.[136]

Unlike the *pensionados*, another group of students—those who were poor and self-supporting—began to enter the United States in 1910. They usually studied at many of the same colleges and universities but had a much more difficult time because they lacked funds and hence needed to work. Whereas most Filipino immigrants went to Hawaii and the West Coast, the students were more scattered. Not all returned to the Philippines when their studies were completed, thus becoming "unintentional immigrants." A restriction of opportunities in the Philippines, especially during the 1930s, accounts for some of their reluctance to return home. Others married American women who did not want to migrate. As educated persons, these individuals had better qualifications for work than did most Americans and Filipinos on the West Coast. The 1940 census found that the median number of years of schooling for Chicago's male Filipinos, or Pinoys, as they called themselves, was 12.2, nearly double that on the West Coast. Some of the midwesterners worked in skilled crafts or, because of their educations and knowledge of English, as professionals. Yet in Chicago, too, these migrants faced prejudice in the job market and in finding decent housing. Most became service workers in hotels, restaurants, and clubs. Filipinos also found jobs in several U.S. post offices, some taking these jobs at night while they continued their educations. By 1941, reported two scholars, "Chicago Filipinos had become an immigrant community, largely in spite of their own intentions."[137] Another important Filipino student community developed in Seattle, Washington. A few were attracted to the University of Washington to advance their educations, and quite a few returned home after completing their studies.[138]

The student communities were relatively small, for the bulk of Filipinos headed to Hawaii or the West Coast for employment in canneries, agriculture, or low-wage jobs. Filipinos learned of the prospects for working in Hawaii from those who pioneered this migration. Moreover, they, unlike other Asians, were somewhat Americanized. Historian Ronald Takaki quotes one as saying, "From the time of kindergarten on our island, we stood in our short pants and saluted the Stars and Stripes which waved over our schoolyards."[139] While the Americanization of Filipino culture was connected to American colonization, this type of homage to the United States was to be repeated after World War II when American power and culture were visible in most parts of the world.

Knowledge was one part of the emigration story; desire was another. Poverty in the Philippines lay behind the migration to Hawaii and later the mainland. The migration to Hawaii was composed almost entirely of young men with little education and few prospects for remunerative work at home. Filipino culture generally looked down on single women leaving. A few of the migrants were married, but only a handful brought along their wives. They did not intend to settle permanently abroad. Like so many immigrants, they carried a somewhat romantic notion of life in Hawaii and the United States, and after a few years they hoped to be able to bring their riches acquired overseas back to the Philippines.[140] When labor recruiters arrived seeking young men for plantation work, many Filipinos eagerly signed contracts, mostly for three years. Between 1900 and 1930, about 100,000 went to Hawaii. When labor contracting became illegal, many still managed to emigrate.

Planters were eager to replace Asians who had come previously with these new sugarcane workers. But there was another reason for the planters' enthusiasm: labor conflict. When Japanese workers had organized and carried out strikes for better working conditions, planters sought new workers to replace the "militants," or at the very least they hoped to play one ethnic group off against the other. Japanese workers were aware of the entry of new unskilled workers and attempted to build unions and strikes across ethnic lines, but they had little success. Planters encouraged some married Filipinos to bring their wives and families in the hope that family life would encourage more docile and conservative workers.[141]

Like other contract workers, Filipinos found that their life in the cane fields was not what they had expected. Plantation life was closely supervised by the employers, who controlled not only wages but also prices at the company stores. Wages were low. Houses were usually small and lacked modern indoor toilets; most also lacked running water. If hardly ideal, this housing was an improvement over that at home, but still, these conditions prompted some to return home without the riches they had hoped for. But because economic conditions offered little opportunity in the Philippines, many stayed and endured a life of manual labor in Hawaii's cane fields.[142]

When their contracts expired, after 1930 some drifted into Honolulu. A few found better economic opportunities in the city, but most labored at unskilled or semiskilled jobs in canneries or in the growing tourist industry. Immigrant urban families had great difficulty finding year-round employment at adequate wages. Many remained unemployed, and some ended up on welfare.[143]

There was an alternative to returning home: migration to the mainland United States. Most did so during the 1920s, coming either directly from the Philippines or from Hawaii. Filipinos found employment in the fisheries of Alaska, where they were the third-largest ethnic group employed in the 1920s. The fisheries provided only seasonal employment, and working conditions were exceptionally poor. Most Filipinos, some 60 percent, labored in agriculture, chiefly in California, where they replaced Japanese, Chinese, Koreans, and Indians. The center of Filipino life was Stockton, California. In California they harvested cotton, oranges, tomatoes, lettuce, and other crops.[144] Growers were eager to employ Filipinos but were not enthusiastic when these workers formed or joined labor unions. When the Great Depression hit, agricultural workers had difficulty in organizing.[145]

Cities also beckoned these immigrants, who found jobs primarily as domestics, in hotels and private homes, or as gardeners. They were apt to be elevator operators or janitors in hotels.[146] Their knowledge of English helped them obtain such jobs, but these were largely low-paying positions. Moreover, in towns and cities Filipinos encountered discrimination in housing and public facilities.[147]

In one area Filipinos were unique among Asian immigrants: as seamen, whether in the merchant marine or the U.S. Navy. In 1901, while the Philippine-American War was still under way, Filipinos served as scouts under American military officers. In 1904 the navy began to recruit them, beginning with about 300 that year. During World War I, 25,000 Filipinos volunteered to enlist in the navy, and thousands more worked in the navy yards of Manila. After the war several thousand continued to work in the yards, and several thousand more stayed in the navy where, barred from other positions, they were mess attendants. The U.S. Navy actually trained Filipinos in the Philippines for these positions. Filipino servicemen obtained naturalization because of a World War I era law that permitted alien military men to become American citizens. Their status remained in doubt, however, and not until 1935 did Congress authorize naturalization to World War I veterans, even those who were considered ineligible for naturalization. Ninety Filipinos became American citizens under this law.[148] The limited enrollment of Filipinos in low-level military positions after 1900 was the forerunner of larger participation of Filipinos during World War II.

All Filipinos faced discrimination and limited occupational mobility. White-collar work was hard to come by, and most of the available domestic and agricultural tasks consisted of migratory and menial labor. Even those who upgraded their skills through additional schooling and acquisition of fluent English found their paths blocked. Growers liked this supply of cheap labor, except when the workers joined trade unions and strikes for better working conditions and wages. The workers formed a Filipino Labor Union in Stockton, but growers pitted Filipinos against other ethnic groups.

For Filipinos living in the United States, life was harsh and lonely. Because many harvested crops up and down the Pacific Coast, they did not form a distinct community along the order of a Chinatown with many businesses catering to fellow immigrants. Social life was found in the dance halls, pool halls, and Asian restaurants that these migratory workers frequented. Some Filipinos did marry white or Mexican women, but because of laws banning Asian-white intermarriage, they ventured outside California to legalize their marriages. In Chicago, for example, Barbara Posadas found that of the 532 Filipino men who were married only 54 were married to Filipino women and 478 to others.[149]

White Americans objected to Filipino wage earners, believing they were brought in to break strikes and force down wages.[150] Opposition resulted in violence on several occasions as American workers attempted to drive Filipinos from their jobs. The onset of the Great Depression aggravated fears of economic competition.[151]

Yet it was not economics alone that explained white opposition to these newcomers. When members of this overwhelmingly male community attempted to date white women or dance with them in dance halls, they touched upon the most sensitive of racial issues: sex. One reader told the *San Francisco Chronicle*, "Racial aliens may undercut us, take away our jobs, surpass us in business competition, or commit crimes against our laws, and we would be only a little harder on them than we would be on aliens from Europe of our own race. But let them start to associate with our women and we see red."[152] Some Americans considered Filipinos to be sexually aggressive toward white women; others called them "goo-goos" and "monkeys."[153]

In 1930 at Watsonville, California, "economic rivalry and sexual jealousy," as Ronald Takaki put it, erupted into an anti-Filipino riot. Four hundred white men attacked a Filipino dance hall and beat the immigrants. One Filipino was shot to death. Judge D. W. Rohrback blamed the Filipinos for the violence: "Damn the Filipino! He won't keep his place."[154]

The growing tension and violence led to a change in immigration policy toward Filipinos. With groups like the Native Sons of the Golden West urging Congress to take action, it was only a matter of time before this last Asian immigration group faced restriction. It was "absolutely illogical to have an immigration policy to exclude Japanese and Chinese and permit Filipinos en masse to come into the country. . . . If they continue to settle in certain areas they will come in conflict with white labor," declared the author of the Tydings-McDuffie Act (1934).[155] The act provided for Philippine independence after ten years, at which time immigration to America would cease.

Until then, only fifty immigrants were to be permitted annually. Hawaiian planters could still import laborers if necessary, but Filipinos were not allowed to migrate from Hawaii to the United States. In addition, Congress provided funds for those who wished to return home. Many had returned during the first years of the Great Depression, and a few more used these federal funds to leave.

With passage of the Tydings-McDuffie Act, Asian exclusion was complete for laborers. In the future only diplomats, students, a few merchants, and visitors were to be permitted to enter America.[156] The experiences of Filipinos, Chinese, Japanese, Indians, and Koreans differed in many details. Of the Asian groups, the Japanese were the most successful in building a family-style existence in the United States. Chinese, Koreans, Japanese, and Filipinos encountered American culture in Hawaii as well as along the Pacific Coast. In contrast, few Indians settled in Hawaii. The Japanese and Chinese were more numerous by far than the Koreans and Indians. The Filipinos came later than the other groups. But all Asians had much in common. Other Americans believed them to be inferior and radically different than European-origin Americans. In the end, white Americans thought that Asians could not be assimilated. The abuse and violence heaped upon Asians eventually led to their exclusion as immigrants. At the time of World War II, when mainland Japanese and their children were interned, few would have predicted that a new day would dawn in the last half of the twentieth century. Yet postwar American society did an about-face and opened the door to new (and larger) waves of Asian immigration to the United States.

3

North to America, 1900–1940

The census of 1870 counted approximately 10,000 foreign-born blacks. Nearly a third were from Canada, no doubt the descendants of those taken there after the American Revolution and those whose slave ancestors had fled to Canada before the Civil War. After that date, black migration to America resumed, although, of course, none of these immigrants entered as slaves. Black immigrants, like both Europeans and Asians, came from a variety of places with diverse languages and cultures. The numbers were not large, and the foreign-born black population was only 54,737 in 1900. It grew more rapidly from 1900 to the 1930s, but the total number immigrating to the United States from the end of the Civil War to 1930 was roughly 200,000. These black immigrants added a new dimension to the nation's African American population.[1]

It will be recalled that the Naturalization Act of 1790 limited citizenship to "free white persons," and the act of 1870 expanded to include persons of African descent. Congress added the phrase but did not think that it would lead to large-scale African immigration. As one federal judge put it in 1880, "No one seriously believed that 'the negroes of Africa' (would emigrate)."[2] When the legislators banned Asians by barring those ineligible for citizenship, they did not include black immigrants. In 1914 and 1915, however, several southern congressmen moved to bar "all members of the African or black race." Senator John Sharp Williams insisted that foreign-born blacks were even less desirable than Asians. He concluded that the United States could not maintain free institutions "except by a homogeneous race."[3] His proposal, though passing the Senate, failed in the House. During the 1920s, however, Congress restricted African immigration by giving Africa quotas (of 100) for only a few areas. British and French mandates each had quotas of 100, as did the Union of South Africa, Liberia, Ethiopia, and several other mandates. Only ethnic groups whose forebears had come to the United States voluntarily were granted a quota, a device that excluded practically all black Africans, and the small quotas for some African mandates could also be used by whites.[4]

Not many black immigrants came directly from Africa between 1870 and the 1920s, so the law's impact was not immediately apparent.[5] Moreover, the Johnson-Reed Act of 1924 did not give quotas to nations and colonies of the Western Hemisphere. Thus blacks from the Caribbean could still migrate to the United States and become citizens. Many did so, before and after the national origins system went into effect, but during the Great Depression, when economic opportunities were scarce, the number of persons from the Caribbean fell, as it did from all areas of the world.[6]

The first known immigrant from today's Sudan was Sati Majid, who arrived in 1904. He came to America to spread the teachings of Islam to those Americans "whose hearts are favorably disposed to receiving it."[7] He aimed his preaching especially at African Americans but converted only a few and eventually returned to Sudan.[8] Majid was not a forerunner of a larger wave of migration, for during the next decades few Sudanese followed. During World War II some Sudanese working on merchant ships that stopped in U.S. ports were recruited into the U.S. Navy. One migrant noted about his experience in 1942, "I worked on a Greek steamer that was affiliated with what was called the British War Ministry. After my arrival [in the United States] we were given the option to join the American navy, because the Americans were recruiting people and there was an urgent need for people to work for them."[9]

From 1855 to 1930 about 35,000 persons came from the Cape Verde Islands, located several hundred miles off the coast of Africa. Settled by the Portuguese and African slaves, the islands were home to people who were a mixture of both groups. Even before the Civil War, American whaling vessels recruited Cape Verdeans as sailors. The first arrivals appeared in New Bedford, Massachusetts, in 1860. Migration grew slowly, averaging only 204 annually during the 1890s. When steamships replaced boats with sails, this recruitment stopped. But the contacts that had been made between the islands and Massachusetts set the stage for a larger migration after 1900, which was not curbed until the 1920s.[10] Of the thousands of Africans immigrating voluntarily to the United States from 1890 to the 1920s, the Cape Verdeans are the only people to attract scholarly attention and were the largest group hailing from Africa.[11]

Like so many other immigrants, Cape Verdeans often traveled to work in the United States (or worked in whaling) and then returned home. Many stayed, however, settling in and around New Bedford, Massachusetts, and Providence, Rhode Island. Marilyn Halter's careful study indicates that these 35,000 Islanders were mostly men, but a number of women arrived, too, as well as some young children.[12]

Economic factors account for the migration to the United States, for Cape Verdeans, like so many other immigrants, were seeking better wages abroad. Some of the men found employment in the maritime trade. The Massachusetts cranberry bogs attracted the largest number of agricultural workers, but Cape Verdeans also picked other crops.[13] The workers included women and children as well as men. To be sure, mill towns were close by, but black Cape Verdean men and women faced discrimination in the mills.

Most Cape Verdeans settled in and around New Bedford, Massachusetts, not near the cranberry bogs. Women ran boardinghouses and worked as domestics, and men labored in occupations related to the maritime trades. A few men also found employment in fishing and, when factories opened up, as unskilled laborers in industry. Very few became professionals; a 1924 survey turned up only three lawyers, two physicians, and two dentists among Cape Verdeans in New Bedford.[14]

In the United States, Cape Verdeans were considered black. Some tried to identify themselves as Portuguese Americans, but light-skinned Portuguese from the Azores and Madeira "disassociated themselves from them" and would not allow black immigrants into their organizations.[15] In addition, the widespread racism of native Americans limited Cape Verdean social life. Even the local churches did not welcome them. In Saint John the Baptist Church of New Bedford, for example, whose members were mostly white Portuguese, Cape Verdeans were not allowed on the governing board, and even those who simply attended services "received an icy reception."[16] As a result, Cape Verdeans created their own churches and institutions. In part these organizations were an attempt to keep their own culture alive, but nonwhite immigrants had even less choice than whites in trying to become part of American society. The new national origins system of the 1920s limited Cape Verdean migration to the United States. They could come under the quota for Portugal, but Portugal was granted only 440 slots, hardly enough for major immigration. Moreover, during World War I the government in Lisbon placed obstacles in front of Cape Verdeans who wished to emigrate, and these barriers remained after the end of the war.[17]

Although after the Civil War a few black immigrants came directly from Africa, including the Cape Verde Islands, and Canada, the bulk of blacks hailed from the Caribbean nations and colonies. From 1900 to 1940 at least 143,397 arrived and only 33,518 departed. These black immigrants entered from British colonies of the West Indies, which they could do under the British quota. Jamaica and Barbados were the leading colonies sending immigrants to America, with most of those immigrants coming before the 1930s.[18]

Some West Indians went to nearby places before coming to America. They found work in Central America, Costa Rica, Honduras, Guatemala, Nicaragua, and Cuba. When the French attempted to build a canal and railroads across the Panama isthmus, they offered employment, and Caribbean men responded. Central America continued to attract laborers when the United States began to build the Panama Canal. From 1903 to 1913 the Canal Zone attracted thousands of Caribbean migrants; Jamaica alone sent at least 45,000 migrants to work in Panama.[19] Although these migrants encountered horrendous working conditions and racism, they received higher wages than at home. Indeed, most Jamaican and Barbadian blacks lived at the bottom of their social order under appalling conditions. Winston James notes that as late as 1919, for example, 18,000 black small landowners in Barbados held only 17,000 acres of land, while 90,000 acres were under the control of the small white elite, who "bitterly resisted the growth of a black peasantry in Barbados."[20] No wonder the blacks headed for the Canal Zone or other places in Central America. At first the overwhelming number of immigrants were men, but women joined the exodus to Panama, where they found employment as servants and in laundries.[21] When the canal was finished, some remained there; others returned home, but some headed for the United States. Irma Watkins-Owens claims that the exact number who made this trip is unknown, but a substantial group financed their journey to America with "Panama money."[22] Indeed, it was the migration of West Indians from the Canal Zone to the United States that prompted southern white congressmen to urge the barring of all black immigrants. Senator John Sharp Williams singled out these newcomers when he proposed to bar blacks. "We are," he said, "beginning to receive now some very undesirable immigration of the African race from the West Indies. A great many

Jamaican negroes have been employed upon the Panama Canal." After being accustomed to American wages, he noted, they are now settling in Gulf ports, such as those in Florida and Louisiana.[23]

When the banana trade expanded in Central America and Jamaica, small farmers were squeezed as large-scale banana planters acquired most of the land. This served as an inducement for many to look elsewhere for a livelihood. Similar poor economic conditions prevailed in Barbados. Natural disasters, such as hurricanes, only added to the woes of West Indians.[24] The United Fruit Company's steamers were the most regular ships to head for New York City, carrying people as well as bananas. Private lines also made the trips, but black immigrants received inferior accommodations. If they could not clear immigration officials, they sometimes became stowaways and entered illegally.[25]

As the tourist trade developed between the United States and the West Indies, it offered another route to America. By 1879 American steamships were taking visitors to the Caribbean; when the ships returned, they sometimes took West Indians to Boston and especially New York City.[26] Still other black immigrants came from the American possessions in the Virgin Islands, which were acquired from Denmark in 1917. And, of course, some blacks from Puerto Rico emigrated to the United States, but Congress made them American citizens in 1917, not resident aliens.[27]

Among the first Caribbeans to arrive in the late nineteenth century were Bahamians, who went to Florida as agricultural workers or to Key West to labor in fishing, sponging, and turtling. Some Bahamians had visited Florida before the Civil War, mostly to trade with Florida's Indians. The distance to Florida was short, and economic conditions in the Bahamas were poor. Many had little chance of moving beyond a subsistence level.[28] Some ventured to other places in the Caribbean, but the United States became the center of Bahamian immigration. As white farmers developed Florida, they needed workers to pick crops, and Bahamians furnished that labor. Some of these early immigrants returned to the Bahamas, but many settled permanently in southern Florida, which had Bahamian enclaves in Lemon City, Coconut Grove, and Cutler.[29] Others drifted into Miami, and when it incorporated in 1896, foreign-born blacks accounted for 40 percent of the black population.[30] The city grew steadily after 1896, with black immigrants accounting for a sizable proportion of the population in the early twentieth century. Miami had a larger foreign-born black population than any American city except for New York.[31]

Miami's building opened new opportunities other than in agriculture for these black immigrants, who found jobs in the building trades, in local lumber yards, along the docks, and as day laborers throughout the city. Some found work as domestics or as service workers in the new hotels catering to the growing tourist trade. Most of the early workers were men, but as the hotels opened, Bahamian women found employment there, as well as in restaurants, usually as low-level service workers. All the emerging resort cities offered "better jobs and higher wages than they had known in the islands."[32] Historian Raymond Mohl reports that from 10,000 to 12,000 Bahamians left for Florida between 1900 and 1920, which officials recorded as one-fifth of the entire Bahamian population.[33] So many left for the United States that Bahamian officials became alarmed at the loss of their laborers. One Bahamian planter wrote, "In a very short time our lovely islands will soon be depopulated, gone to swell the millions of the great American continent."[34] Agricultural work did not necessarily dry up as Miami grew. Bahamians continued to work in the citrus industry, and in harvesting vegetables.[35]

The immigration legislation of the 1920s created uncertainty about future immigration, but as members of British colonies in the Western Hemisphere, Bahamians were allowed to migrate to the United States. Even after the collapse of the Florida real estate boom in the 1920s, the devastating hurricane of 1926, and the depressed years of the 1930s, immigrants still arrived, but a similar number returned home, which, as Raymond Mohl has noted, suggested a short-term labor migration and return flow. The migration continued into the 1940s, when the wartime economy created a need for labor and the War Manpower Commission actively recruited Bahamian agricultural workers.[36]

Bahamians who chose to remain in the United States created their own immigrant institutions. Central to these immigrants was the Anglican (or Episcopal) Church. In 1897, in "Colored Town," a white clergyman founded Miami's Agnes Episcopal Church for these immigrants. Several other congregations were founded whose parishioners were mostly West Indian. Bahamians also attended the churches of other denominations, but the Episcopal churches were the most important for these immigrants.[37]

While wages were high compared with those in their homeland, black immigrants encountered state-enforced racism in Florida. Throughout the South after 1890, racism limited African Americans' acceptance and participation in public institutions and denied them the ballot. Mohl reported that the Miami press denigrated the immigrants as lazy and "referred to them as 'Nassau niggers.'"[38] One newcomer said, "Having passed the immigration and customs examiners, I took a carriage for what the driver called 'Nigger Town.' It was the first time I had heard that opprobrious epithet employed, and by a colored man himself."[39] Blacks could not stay at the hotels where they worked and which they had helped build. Schools and housing were segregated, and conflicts with the local police added to the immigrants' woes.[40] Mob violence was not unknown to Miami's blacks, and the Ku Klux Klan was active in Florida during the 1920s, staging a large rally in Miami in 1921.[41]

The largest number of black immigrants settled in the Northeast, especially in New York City. They came from a variety of nations and colonies in the Caribbean and Central and South America, but the dominant groups were English speakers from the Caribbean. Once immigrants had settled, they helped friends or family members to come. They arrived from places in which they were the majority, even if poor, and entered New York City, where the white majority practiced intense racism. In New York City only 1.9 percent of the city's population was black in 1900; it grew to 12.7 percent in 1930. The African American population continued to grow during the Great Depression, but mostly due to migration by southern blacks, not Caribbean migrants. Blacks were politically powerless in such an atmosphere and confronted limited economic opportunity and Jim Crow schools, hotels, and many public facilities in spite of state civil rights laws.

As was the case with most immigrant groups before 1930, a majority of Caribbean blacks were men. But whether men or women, they were usually young and unmarried. Winston James notes that of those Caribbean immigrants who arrived in the nineteenth century, quite a few were "skilled craftsmen, students, teachers, preachers, lawyers and doctors."[42] One black leader observed of these first immigrants, "It was taken for granted that every West Indian immigrant was a paragon of intelligence and a man of birth and breeding."[43] After 1900 the newcomers did conform to their reputations to some extent. Winston James reports that in 1923 nearly all immigrants were considerably more literate than were native-born black Americans and even many whites. He continues, "Allied to the high rate of literacy were two other characteristics that contemporaries often mentioned. One was an extraordinary love of books, education and the written word. The other was a similar attachment to the spoken word, in conversation as well as in the form of public oratory."[44] Moreover, these immigrants had more business and professional experience than did black Americans.[45]

Once in New York, however, most immigrants entered service occupations. For men this meant being laborers, elevator operators, and porters; women worked as domestics. A railroad porter's job was considered middle-class in the black community, as was a job in the post office. Overall, blacks were underrepresented on the public payroll and were generally blocked from most white-collar employment whether in public or private jobs. A few immigrants did utilize their education and entrepreneurial experience to open businesses, yet these enterprises were usually small with little capital, working in a segregated market. Those immigrants who were professionals, such as dentists, physicians, and lawyers, found themselves confined to the black community.[46] Many West Indians continued their quest for higher education: "Noteworthy, too is the fact that many of those who remained built upon their education and skills with which they came to America. They attended night school. They acquired more qualifications. Caribbean teachers, not infrequently, became American doctors and lawyers, but the number doing so was very small."[47]

But, confronted by racism, even the professionals faced discrimination in finding housing in white neighborhoods. West Indian immigrants settled in older, predominantly black areas. In 1900 about 5,000 Caribbean immigrants lived in New York City's scattered black neighborhoods, but as Harlem increasingly became a ghetto (followed by Bedford-Stuyvesant in Brooklyn), it developed as the center of Caribbean life. Black churches located elsewhere moved to Harlem, and various black organizations established themselves there, too. White Harlemites, who resisted the movement of African Americans onto their turf, abandoned Harlem in increasing numbers after 1920. Initially Harlem's housing, composed of many fine brownstones, was attractive, but apartments quickly became overcrowded, run-down, and segregated. There was little choice for blacks: "Few areas were open to blacks; after 1920 the black population of New York was largely concentrated in central Harlem and the Bedford-Stuyvesant section of Brooklyn."[48]

Many of the English-speaking immigrants had been Anglicans at home; in New York City a few attempted to attend white Episcopal churches, but there, as elsewhere, they were unwelcome. At Brooklyn's Holy Trinity Episcopal Church they were at first required to sit in a separate section. Black Episcopalian churches such as Saint Augustine and

Christ Church Cathedral in Brooklyn attracted immigrants. Christ Church Cathedral was headed by a Barbadian, the Reverend Reginald Grant Barrow. Some churches ran social programs that appealed to the newcomers. In Harlem newly formed churches of Methodist and Episcopal denominations reached out to the newcomers, as well as to native-born African Americans. Traditionally black denominations, such as the African Methodist Episcopal Church, attracted some immigrants. Women made up a majority of those attending, but the churches were headed by men. Religion was an important source of welcome to immigrants, though secular and radical West Indians had little to do with religion.[49]

West Indians also developed their own institutions. Caribbean peoples came from a variety of cultures, often speaking different languages; as a result, they wanted to manage their own mutual benefit societies and organizations. Among those who spoke English, there was the Bermuda Benevolent Association, founded as early as 1897; the Sons and Daughters of Barbados; the Trinidad Benevolent Association; the Grenada Mutual Association; and the Montserrat Progressive Society. Membership was based on one's nation of birth. West Indian immigrant associations functioned much like the traditional ones: to help newcomers both financially and socially. Some collected funds for education or provided money for families and individuals faced with sickness and death. They also held social functions such as boat rides and picnics. In addition, the benevolent associations became a source of funds for business activity and housing.[50]

Most West Indians were English speakers, but in New York City there were French speakers from Martinique, Guadeloupe, and Saint Martin. A few French speakers came from Senegal and Somalia in Africa. Together they formed a Franco-Colonial Club.[51] Migrants from Haiti, who spoke French or Haiti-creole, tended to be scattered and did not form many of their own particular associations. According to Ira de Reid, the 500 Haitians who migrated to New York City in the 1920s were a well-educated group and were mostly engaged in the trades or professions. The women often worked for pay but usually were not domestic servants.[52]

Although men dominated politics and ethnic organizations, Irma Watkins-Owens believes that "Caribbean women may have had more opportunities for leadership than at home."[53] In 1915, she reports, women from the Danish West Indies (now the Virgin Islands) formed their own group, and for English speakers there was the American West Indian Ladies Aid Society. Elizabeth Hendrickson, president of the Ladies Aid Society, became a well-known street corner speaker.[54]

Caribbean immigrants also joined associations that were composed predominantly of native-born blacks. The best-known Caribbean leader was Marcus Garvey, who created the Universal Negro Improvement Association (UNIA). Garvey was born in Jamaica and came to New York in 1916. He had formed the UNIA two years earlier but went to America to raise money for the group and to meet with Booker T. Washington, who died before Garvey arrived. Once in the United States, Garvey decided to make New York City the center of his activities. He began publication of *Negro World* in 1918. The Jamaican at first gathered wide support from blacks in Harlem and elsewhere with his program of black nationalism, freedom for Africa, and economic development within the African American community.

Garvey's UNIA, which urged separate economic and social development for blacks, reportedly had a worldwide membership of several million at its height. West Indians featured prominently in the organization.[55] Garvey's call for freedom for Africa drew the attention of black African leaders, and his urging of economic independence for African Americans appealed to many American blacks, including West Indians. Yet his criticism of assimilationist leaders and the National Association for the Advancement of Colored People (NAACP) aroused considerable opposition among many in the black community. Garvey hurt his cause by meeting with leaders of the Ku Klux Klan, which made him appear to accept white racism. At the same time, when his economic schemes failed, he ran afoul of the U.S. government, which considered him to be dangerous. Convicted of mail fraud, he was sent to prison and was deported a few years later upon his release.[56]

Conflicts with other black leaders and the federal government were not the only problems facing the UNIA. Women were brought into the organization and made contributions to its effectiveness, but the UNIA placed women in a clearly subordinate role. A revolt by women against their position was led by Amy Jacques Garvey, Garvey's secretary and second wife. Like Garvey, she was born in the West Indies, in Kingston, Jamaica. After Marcus Garvey's imprisonment, she became the UNIA's main leader.[57]

Marcus Garvey generally ignored politics; his program of black uplift was capitalist. In fact, some Caribbeans believed that the UNIA did not go far enough. According to Winston James, "The migrants' unavoidable everyday interaction with white people—often tinged with racism—disposed some of them to radical political activity." In addition, many had come from a background of labor union participation or nationalist activity. While some Caribbeans agreed with Garvey's nationalism and proposal for African nations' independence, radical West Indians rejected capitalism and saw socialism as the only way for black Americans to gain equality in the United States. According to James, a key radical leader was Hubert Harrison, a Virgin Islander. His dismissal from the post office was engineered by Booker T. Washington and his followers, and he then became a full-time organizer for the Socialist Party and the first person to invite Marcus Garvey to lecture.[58]

Another organization, more radical in approach, was the African Blood Brotherhood, founded by Caribbeans in 1919. It aimed to combine black nationalism with revolutionary socialism. Cyril Valentine Briggs, the leader, was born in Saint Kitts in 1888. Yet this organization never drew a large following and later ran into difficulty because of its socialism.[59] Perhaps more well known was the socialist journal the *Messenger*, founded by two native-born blacks, Chandler Owen and labor leader A. Philip Randolph. The *Messenger* never achieved a large following, but it was watched, along with other black radical groups, by the Federal Bureau of Investigation.[60]

Most blacks, whether native or foreign born, did not endorse socialism. At the turn of the century blacks in New York generally supported the Republican Party, which they identified as the party of emancipation from slavery. In the northern cities where they could vote, they still had little influence in Republican affairs. New foreign-born blacks made up about one-sixth of the city's black population, but one additional problem for them was that they first had to become citizens to obtain the franchise. They did so in growing numbers by the 1930s, switching allegiance to the Democratic Party, which offered economic assistance programs to their communities, but they still represented a small minority of the black electorate. However, they began to run for positions in both political parties, and won a few slots. One of the three black delegates to the New York Constitutional Convention in 1938 was from the Caribbean, and the only black delegate to the national conventions of the Democratic Party from New York in both 1932 and 1936 was a West Indian. A few received patronage, but black politicians in Harlem had little voice in the city's politics before World War II.[61]

Before the Great Depression of the 1930s, West Indians stopped coming to New York City in significant numbers, and during the grim years of the depression, life in that city was unappealing because employment was so scarce. To be sure, the general immigration restrictions dealing with disease and literacy posed barriers, but it was the bleak economic conditions in the United States coupled with the difficulty of obtaining relief that discouraged many from migrating. American officials rigidly enforced the "likely to be a public charge" provision of the law. The stories of those already in the United States provided direct evidence of the limited prospects for immigration. Indeed, more West Indians left the United States during the depression than arrived.[62]

From south of the border the largest number of immigrants were Mexicans. Some scholars estimate that more than 1 million Mexicans migrated to the United States from 1900 to 1940, mostly between 1900 and 1930, which was more than five times the number of blacks who came from the Caribbean. Because Congress did not include nations of the Western Hemisphere when it introduced national origins as the basis for cutting European immigration and virtual exclusion from Asia and Africa, Mexicans and Canadians, the two nationalities that sent the most immigrants, continued to arrive much as before. However, Mexicans, like all immigrants, were covered by the general immigration laws, which by the 1920s meant they had to pay a head tax, be literate, and not fall into any one of the categories for exclusion. Nonetheless, it was relatively easy for immigrants to cross into the United States along the southern border without first being cleared by officials. Some entered without inspection, worked for a limited period, and then returned home without being counted as immigrants. The federal government did not even make an attempt to count Mexican immigrants until 1908, and no border patrol existed before 1924. Even then, the federal government was more interested in keeping out Asians who attempted to avoid the laws excluding them and in halting liquor being smuggled in violation of the prohibition laws.[63]

The Immigration Bureau admitted that it had "no means of knowing" how Mexicans were entering the country. The census reported just over 100,000 foreign-born Mexicans in 1900 and nearly 500,000 in 1930. In 1908 the U.S. government calculated that between 60,000 and 100,000 Mexican immigrants entered the country each year.[64] Yet Lawrence Cardoso estimates that even before 1910, when the federal government began to count these immigrants, as many as half a million arrived from

1900 to 1910; some scholars estimate that the number was larger, with as many as 60,000 Mexicans arriving annually during the first decade of the twentieth century.[65] Officially the figure between 1900 and 1930 was more than 700,000. During the Great Depression, Mexican immigrants were forcibly deported, and few (roughly 22,000) arrived to take their places.[66]

During World War I the government waived immigration laws to permit Mexican farmworkers to enter for short periods.[67] Growers were able to convince the federal government that they needed farm hands to help harvest and pick their crops in order to win the war. As immigration from Europe dropped after 1914, growers found friendly ears in Washington, D.C. Railroads and mining interests also wanted Mexican workers. About 70,000 were finally admitted as temporary migrants; most returned home, but some chose to remain in the United States. With the end of hostilities the federal government terminated the temporary worker program in 1921.[68]

There were plenty of reasons for Mexicans to head north and not return. Many were poor, with little or no land and limited job prospects in their own country; only 3 percent of the peasants in Mexico owned any land at the turn of the twentieth century.[69] Conditions did not improve for them in the first decade of the twentieth century and were especially deplorable in central Mexico.[70] Then Mexico became plagued by violence. A government headed by Porfirio Díaz grew increasingly unpopular after 1900 until, in 1910, he was overthrown by a revolution initiated by Francisco I. Madero, who had a strong following among the middle class. When Madero was assassinated, violence erupted in many parts of Mexico and lasted for a decade. People were killed, harvests destroyed, villages looted, and trade interrupted. Peace was finally restored in 1920, but life for many went on unchanged. As a result, Mexicans continued to migrate to the United States in search of employment and peace.[71]

People usually do not move, no matter how deplorable their conditions, unless they have some hope of improving their lives. Knowledge and transportation were also essential for migration. The Southwest, especially New Mexico and Texas, was not exactly unknown to Mexicans. Pockets of Mexican settlement in these areas offered a familiar place for the newcomer. Although one could cross the border with ease, getting there was also easy once the railroads connected the border to the interior of Mexico. Railroad construction in the north of Mexico drew workers from the central and southern regions, and when lines from the United

States met Mexican railroads at the border, transportation became available for migration to America.[72] Railroads, in Lawrence Cardoso's words were "of paramount importance to northern migration."[73]

Railroads made transportation easy, but they also required labor. Beginning in the late nineteenth century, when the rail connections to the United State were being built, labor agencies, operating mostly from Mexico City, sent recruiters to the countryside for workers. Peasants were pulled to the north, where wages were higher than in central or southern Mexico. Once in the northern part of Mexico, poor Mexicans asked the question, Why not cross the border, where wages are even better? In the United States, some of these migrants could use the skills they had learned in Mexico to help build the Southern Pacific and Santa Fe Railroads as they completed their transcontinental connections. Even when the railroads were finished, hands were needed for maintenance. Railroad managers were delighted at the influx of these migrants who worked for low wages—a dollar a day—in the first decade of the twentieth century.[74] A federal government commission reported in 1909 that Mexicans were the largest source for railroad laborers in the Southwest. An immigration act of 1885 barred the use of labor agents outside the United States to recruit immigrants, but labor agents from America nonetheless went over the border to find workers. Some young Mexican men lived in boxcars and shacks as they worked the lines of the Southwest.[75] The number of such workers was not large, but they did spread the news about higher wages to the north.[76]

A railroad's upkeep required steady hands, but the lines also needed coal, and once again Mexicans were available. Texas was by no means the primary state for coal mining, but it did have a small coal industry in the early twentieth century. Mexican miners also dug coal in northern Mexico and, if they were temporarily idle, simply crossed the border to work in Texas. As was the case with railroads, the mines employed labor recruiters to find workers, especially those with experience. One authority reported on this process: "It was the customary procedure for representatives of each of the mines to ride the train . . . to Laredo or Eagle Pass in order to recruit experienced labor. The representatives would pay a certain amount to get the Mexicans across the border, and return . . . sometimes with 40 or 50 laborers."[77] Mexicans were not the only coal miners in Texas; Japanese, for example, had been recruited to dig in Mexico's fields, and some of them also crossed over to work the Texas mines.[78]

Like the railroad workers, most of those Mexicans working and living in the coal mining towns were young, single men. The number of women increased once their husbands were established, especially in the mines along the border. Women who accompanied their husbands were responsible for care of the household and rearing of the children. They did not work in the mines, but they often took in boarders. Owners encouraged family units because they believed that this provided for a more stable and reliable workforce.[79]

Coal mining was a dangerous operation, especially in the early decades of the twentieth century, and the Texas mines were no different from those elsewhere. Accidents were a constant problem, resulting in the death of many miners, and prolonged labor in the mines brought with it many health hazards. The wages for such labor may have been better than in Mexico, and highest in the pits precisely where working conditions were the worst, but even then they were hardly adequate for a decent standard of living. As a result, Mexicans joined with other miners to form unions. In Texas they were partially successful, but by the 1920s the mines were not competitive with those in other areas.[80] In addition, oil and gas were being substituted for coal. By the 1920s mines were being closed, and this Texas industry was rapidly shrinking, just at the time when Mexican immigration was increasing.

Mexican immigrants, along with American-born Hispanos, also found employment in the coal mines of southern Colorado.[81] Mexicans also worked in the copper pits of Arizona, reportedly accounting for more than 40 percent of the copper miners in that state in 1927.[82] Conditions were not much better in the copper mines than in the coal mines. Mexican miners usually worked in unskilled jobs, but even skilled workers were paid less than Europeans for the same jobs. Mexican miners organized and went on strike but with few results; the companies were simply too strong and were able to utilize the national guard effectively. In Bisbee, Arizona, in 1917 a vigilante mob rounded up more than 1,000 workers and shipped them in boxcars to neighboring Columbus. Officials in Columbus refused to let them disembark; instead, officials dumped them into the middle of the Arizona desert.[83]

Although railroad construction and maintenance and mining coal to drive the trains were among the first industries to employ Mexican immigrants, agriculture utilized many more. Mexican farmers and farm hands had been laboring in Texas and California before the region's major irrigation projects were completed in the early twentieth century. In the 1880s and 1890s Mexican migratory workers had crossed into

Texas to harvest cotton. Worried Texans, who did not believe that whites and blacks would provide needed farm labor, saw the solution in Mexicans. The *Galveston News* remarked in 1898, "In these parts of the state where cheap Mexican labor can be secured for chopping and picking cotton . . . this staple can unquestioningly be raised [at a profit]."[84]

The irrigation of the Southwest made possible an enormous expansion of agriculture. Moreover, Japanese workers were barred in 1907, Asian Indians were barred in 1917, and World War I and the immigration legislation of the 1920s reduced immigration from Europe. Filipinos and Mexicans filled the gap, with Mexicans being the most important labor source in California's rich Imperial Valley. Employment agencies, aware of the demand for Mexicans to harvest crops, stationed themselves in El Paso, where so many newcomers crossed, and quickly placed them in jobs not only in agriculture but also along railroads and in urban areas.[85] Many farm hands worked only part of the year and returned home during the winter, when harvesting ended. Perhaps half elected to stay in the United States, finding other temporary employment until their labor was needed again in the fields.[86]

During the post–World War I slump, many Mexicans found themselves out of work. Some returned home, but others headed for cities in search of employment. But conditions quickly improved, and the demand for agricultural and industrial labor increased once again.[87] Mexican immigration reached a peak in the mid-1920s. More than 400,000 were counted by immigration officials during that decade, but the exact number is unknown because many simply entered without inspection to work in California's fields.

Employed migrant workers found living conditions deplorable. Low pay, lack of sanitation, run-down housing, and inadequate diet all limited the lives of these workers. Mexicans found themselves segregated in low-paying positions. Before World War I some citrus orchards provided better housing, while others gave workers land but not housing. During the 1920s these attempts at improved living conditions virtually came to an end.[88]

While California employed the largest number of Mexican migrants, other states needed their labor, too. The sugar beet industry in rural Colorado, Utah, and the Midwest recruited Mexican labor. By the 1920s they had replaced the old workforce, "consisting mostly of Belgians, German-Russians, and Japanese."[89] The Michigan Sugar Company recruited its first Mexican hands in 1915 and enlisted more when recessions curtailed employment in cities. Wages were low and living conditions deplorable: "Chicken coops, tents, abandoned shacks and barns only recently vacated by animals often served as housing."[90] As a result, turnover was high in the fields. But other Mexicans took their place, and by the late 1920s the vast majority of sugar beet workers were Mexicans. Sugar beet fields often consumed an entire family, with the parents and children all working. Picking sugar beets was also a seasonal task. During the off-season the farm hands returned to Mexico or found employment in urban centers. As a result, small Mexican communities developed in the Midwest.[91]

Not all agricultural immigrants worked as migratory workers. Unlike the rest of the South, Texas had a large number of permanent resident Mexicans who were concentrated in the southern part of the state, along the Rio Grande. Historian Neil Foley has pointed to the importance of Mexicans in the cotton industry of Texas. The workers in this industry were often American-born Mexicans, but immigrants played a role, too. And in the twentieth century Mexicans replaced whites as farm tenants or sharecroppers. Many white owners preferred Mexicans because they believed Tejanos (Texas Mexicans) would accept lower wages or endure worse conditions. Mexicans "had suddenly become," Foley reports, "in the eyes of white landowners, the solution to the growing demand for a cheap and tractable labor force in the nation's leading cotton-producing state."[92] Sharecropping was one of the worst occupations in the first half of the twentieth century. There was little hope of eventually owning one's land, or even of escaping the poverty of tenant farming.

Due to the racism and power of landowners, attempts to unite black, white, and Mexican sharecroppers and tenants failed.[93] The collapse of the cotton market in the 1930s only served to emphasize the poverty of these rural folk, and New Deal programs scarcely affected them. The Southern Farm Workers Tenants Union had only brief success. Many blacks headed north, and poor whites went to California, as depicted in John Steinbeck's novel *The Grapes of Wrath.*

As important as agriculture, mining, and railroads were to the livelihood of Mexican immigrants, jobs in cities also beckoned them. Industrial employment had an advantage over agricultural and railroad work, which was largely seasonal and left workers without employment for several months of the year. Many of the Mexican immigrants in El Paso had been recruited by labor contractors, but some remained in the city itself.

Historian Mario Garcia has noted that El Paso's "semi-industrial" economy "largely determined the types of jobs Mexicans obtained."[94] Here
was a large force of generally unskilled labor, which could be hired for
low-level jobs in the city's industries. The El Paso Smelter Company employed more Mexicans than any other ethnic group, and by 1910 Mexicans constituted 90 percent of El Paso's smelter workers. As elsewhere,
"the cheapness of Mexican workers and their ability to be used in unskilled, semiskilled, and even skilled occupations made them attractive
employees for the railroad shops."[95]

In addition, the building boom in the city opened jobs for Mexican immigrants. Most were manual laborers, but some acquired skills and held
better jobs at higher pay. The city's cigar industry also turned to these immigrants.[96] A few even worked for the public sector, including five of El
Paso's nineteen policemen in 1894. Only a few of the newcomers became
white-collar workers, however, as most labored at low-paying, unskilled
jobs.[97] Their lack of English and low skills partly explain why so many
held menial jobs, but in El Paso as elsewhere Mexican immigrants also
encountered discrimination. Firms were reluctant to hire them, at least
for skilled positions, and labor unions did not want them as members.
The Texas Federation of Labor, for example, blamed the Immigration Bureau for admitting Mexican immigrants and went on to accuse labor recruiters of trying to keep down wages by seeking out immigrants to replace American-born workers. The American Federation of Labor (AFL)
even used cultural or social arguments to attack Mexican immigration.
The migrants were accused of being criminals and unable to become assimilated into American society. The union's journal insisted, "True
Americans do not want or advocate the importation of any people who
cannot be absorbed into full citizenship, who cannot eventually be raised
to our highest social standard. . . . the avariciously inclined will be rele-
gated to the nether darkness from which they drew their blackened
souls."[98]

The situation was little different in other Texas cities. The Texas commissioner of labor said that in 1928 Mexicans "performed up to 75 percent of all unskilled construction labor in the state."[99] Californian cities
also relied on Mexican labor. In 1928 one survey reported that Mexicans
made up about 10 percent of the state's factory employees; the most important industries were in stone, clay and glass products, textiles, metal,
food, and tobacco.[100] In Arizona they constituted over 60 percent of the
state's smelter hands.[101] For others, employment as domestic workers,

gardeners, and casual laborers was the norm, even though a small white-collar community grew in cities such as Los Angeles.[102]

While Mexican immigrants have usually been discussed in the context of the development of the Southwest (and in particular agriculture), a steady stream also headed for the states of the Midwest. Some, as noted, found employment harvesting sugar beets, but a larger number settled in cities, where they found employment in industries. In 1900 only 1,252 Mexicans were recorded in the midwestern states, but by 1930 they numbered 69,193. Some of these newcomers had pushed north from Colorado and other mountain states, but a growing number crossed at El Paso and other border points and headed directly to Chicago, Detroit, and other industrial cities. They simply followed the railroads north. Some even worked as section crews on the railroads before settling in the Midwest. Brought north as contract laborers, many simply left their contracted employment when they found other opportunities.[103]

Like many European immigrants, they sought jobs in the booming industries of Detroit and Chicago. Moreover, when the outbreak of World War I curtailed European immigration, Mexicans filled jobs formerly held by Europeans.[104] As a result, most northern Mexicans worked in factories, a much larger proportion than in Texas and California.[105] Some of those who were hired to work in the steel industry did so during the great steel strike of 1919. Employers eagerly sought them as replacements for the strikers, and after the strike ended many stayed on.[106] Inland Steel was one of the main employers of Mexican immigrants, who made up 12.9 percent of its workforce by 1922. Others worked for Youngstown Sheet and Tube and in factories in Gary, Indiana.[107] The lure of Detroit was the automobile industry. Chicago's diverse industrial economy also offered jobs in meatpacking, railroads, and foundries. In these factories, Mexicans were part of an ethnic hierarchy, with blacks at the bottom and whites at the top. Yet for the workers, these jobs were better than those along the railroads or in agriculture. They offered steadier employment and better pay than did the fields of California and Texas.

Steel and automobile industries were not immune from general economic conditions, nor were autoworkers always able to find employment during the 1920s. The recession following World War I led to many layoffs, which included Mexicans. The Santa Fe Railroad in Kansas City, Kansas, fired nearly half of its workforce. Detroit autoworkers were especially hard hit during the slump, with 80 percent of its hands out of work at the end of 1920.[108]

Like other immigrants, many Mexicans labored in unsafe factories and lived in run-down housing. But because of low pay and discrimination in the housing market, their housing conditions were especially appalling. Some landlords simply refused to rent to single Mexicans, who then found places in boardinghouses run by Mexican women. In Chicago 43 percent of Mexican families had boarders. Nor was it unusual to find several men working different shifts so they could share a bed.[109]

Most Mexicans in this great wave of migration were young men. It was generally not acceptable for single women to migrate. Not only did Mexicans themselves frown on single women going north, but immigration officials also believed that women might become public charges or prostitutes.[110] Around the turn of the century there were 100 Mexican men for every woman in the cities of the Midwest, and even in southwestern cities there were 115 men for every 100 women. The ratio improved after that, but as of 1930 Mexican communities were still heavily male.[111] Some men had families back home and were expected to save part of their wages to be sent home to support their kin. In other cases, wives accompanied their husbands heading to El Norte. Wives were expected to take care of the children, clean house, and cook meals. Men frequently opposed their wives entering the paid workforce. In 1930 in Los Angeles, 60 percent of Mexican families had only one wage earner, but as one scholar remarked, "This figure may not tell us much because those women who worked usually engaged in irregular part-time employment to supplement their husbands' or fathers' inadequate wages."[112] And what were Mexican women to do if their husbands were killed or injured on their dangerous jobs? Some returned home, but others stayed and sought employment. One "part-time" position was taking in boarders, which, as noted, was a common practice as long as so many young men needed places to sleep and eat. Women's wages enabled the family to live better, survive downturns in the business cycle, and even finance trips home to Mexico.[113]

Women who were part of agricultural Mexican communities could be expected to work in the field at least part of the time, in addition to their household responsibilities. Agricultural labor in the big fields of California was a family enterprise. Indeed, children worked too, and "mothers with infants were not uncommon sights." As Vicki Ruiz notes, rural women, "had few choices other than picking produce. Some became cooks in labor camps and others ran makeshift boardinghouses. In addition to picking produce, caring for her family, and serving as the local midwife, Irene Castaneda's mother took in laundry for which she earned $5 per week."[114]

Yet Mexican women also entered urban occupations outside their homes, often employed as low-wage domestics. Mario Garcia's El Paso study revealed that domestic employment claimed the largest group of immigrant women; it was a pattern that was repeated elsewhere. Women also labored in related industries such as laundries.[115] Such occupations paid low wages, leading some married women to seek higher-paying work in factories, such as those in El Paso's garment industry.[116]

Although male immigrants often objected to their wives' working for pay, they were more willing to send their daughters into the workforce. Indeed, most Mexican women employed outside their homes were the daughters of immigrants. The paychecks of the older daughters were essential to survival for these families. Single daughters, like sons, usually lived at home and contributed to the family income. Sons, who held higher-paying jobs than their sisters, were expected to give only part of their wages to support families, but daughters had to turn over all their earnings. Such a pattern was not usual among immigrant groups. Even so, "the meager wages that employers paid to women made life outside the family economically precarious."[117]

Some young women found jobs in canneries. This employment exposed them to poor working conditions and prompted a union effort. The Congress of Industrial Organizations' (CIO's) United Cannery, Agricultural, Packing, and Allied Workers of America successfully organized some workers in California's cannery industry, and it included women workers. Even wives of husbands who worked in canneries supported the strike by providing food for the picket lines, taunting the scabs, and fighting back when the police attacked.[118]

The changing status of Mexican immigrant women as a result of their employment in the paid workforce gave them a feeling of and at least a limited experience of independence. As one social worker put it, "If single, the Mexican women like to remain at work; they learn English and like their independence."[119] Even married women noted a change as their income became essential to the family. Some Mexican men protested against this changing status, and fathers often attempted to exercise more control over their wives and daughters. "The place of the woman after marriage is in the home, taking care of the children," noted one. A Spanish-language Chicago newspaper lamented the declining status of men and quoted one as saying, "'I have an American friend who can't even open his mouth to order a couple of eggs in his own home. She shoves him out to a restaurant because, according to her, she did not get married to a cook for any Tom, Dick or Harry, and that included . . . her husband.'"[120]

Vicki Ruiz also notes that the encounter of young Mexican women with popular culture, in movies, fashion, and consumerism, reinforced their sense of independence. Some of this contact was an attempt by various agencies and programs to "Americanize" immigrants—to teach them ways that were different from those of their own culture. To be sure, young immigrant and American-born women did not immediately drop their way of life and embrace the emerging American mass culture after 1920. Nonetheless, the lure of consumerism, noticeable among young women, was strong, and they resisted such practices as chaperoning, rejecting this form of adult control over their lives.[121] Such conflicts between immigrant parents and American-born children were by no means limited to Mexicans, for other groups experienced similar disagreements between the generations.

While racists assailed Mexican immigrants and wanted to bar their entry into the United States, Mexicans had their defenders among non-Mexican social critics. Educators and social workers attacked discrimination and promoted Americanization programs in the schools and settlement houses. Often paternalistic in conception, these programs did not represent a commitment to cultural pluralism. Some social critics went further in their views of American policies. Covering the situation in California's agricultural fields, journalist Carey McWilliams noted the miserable working conditions of migratory laborers and the power of the large growers. His portrait of Mexican agricultural workers, *North from Mexico: The Spanish-Speaking People of the United States* (1949), presented a sympathetic picture of farm life and influenced future scholarship.[122]

Some restrictionists hoped that Mexicans would not be seen as white and therefore would be ineligible for naturalization, and, according to the 1924 law, ineligible from immigrating to the United States. In a Texas case handed down in 1897, under strict interpretation of the law, the court ruled that the Mexican in question would "probably not be classed as white." The court, however, allowed him to naturalize, basing its decision on a series of treaties conferring the right of Spaniards and Mexicans to become American citizens.[123]

Although declared "white," Mexicans faced discrimination everywhere. Historian Manuel Gonzales reports, "Anti-Mexican sentiment was pronounced wherever Mexicans went, a bitter legacy from the nineteenth century. The greatest animosity occurred in Texas, where the memory of the Alamo combined with the exaggerated racial attitudes of Southerners to make life especially difficult for the immigrant."[124] Texas took extreme action to warrant this claim, but Mexicans in other states also faced discrimination. For example, California passed a "greaser act" in 1855, an antiloitering law that applied to persons who are commonly know as "greasers," persons of mixed Spanish and Indian blood "who go armed and are not peaceable and quiet persons."[125]

Texas had a history of violence against Mexicans, and although conditions improved after 1900, the state was still an oppressive place for Mexican immigrants and their children. The situation in El Paso certainly confirms this analysis. If schools were the key to future mobility, then the opportunities for Mexican El Paso residents were slim indeed. "From their inception El Paso public schools segregated most Mexican children, in practice if not legally," reports Mario Garcia. The Mexican barrio schools received fewer funds than the white ones and offered little education beyond the elementary level. Of course, such segregated arrangements also existed in other Southwest states.[126] In the early years, Los Angeles had not segregated its pupils and had offered bilingual education, but this changed as more Mexicans migrated to the state.[127]

Segregation prevailed in other public institutions, and Mexicans were expected to use facilities within the barrio, not outside of it. Segregation was often done by "custom" rather than by law. In some cases Mexicans, for example, attended schools with other students and were able to use public facilities. But whites clearly wanted Mexican immigrants to be segregated. Texas restaurants, movies, and swimming pools either refused to accommodate Mexicans or kept them separate from whites. Indeed, swimming pools were open to Mexican children in some communities only one day per week, just before they were drained and cleaned. As for the Houston schools for Mexicans, historian Guadalupe San Miguel Jr. concludes, "This public schooling [for Mexican American children], however, was of inferior quality, as evidenced by school segregation and administrative mistreatment."[128] In sum, throughout the southwestern states, "social spaces were also organized to reinforce social distance between Anglos and Mexicans. . . . When Mexicans entered Anglo territory, they were confined to certain times or sections."[129]

The League of United Latin American Citizens (LULAC), founded in 1929 in Texas, and other Mexican American organizations attacked segregation and the inadequate and unequal funding of Mexican schools. Generally conservative on economic issues, LULAC concentrated on attacking racism and the unequal treatment given to both Mexican immigrants and native-born Mexicanos. LULAC, according to historian Benjamin Marquez, believed that once discrimination ended, Mexicans would take their rightful places as useful and even middle-class Americans. To be sure, Mexicans could remain proud of their heritage, but they were to be incorporated into American society.[130] LULAC concentrated on countering the publicly expressed racist views so common in the 1920s and 1930s; it insisted that Mexicans were not "colored" and deserved an education in white schools. In 1930 the U.S. Bureau of the Census introduced a classification system that indicated that Mexicans were a separate race. The issue appeared again in 1936 when another federal agency said that Mexicans were not white. LULAC, which largely represented middle-class, American-born Mexicanos, objected and lobbied against these ruling. "We are not a yellow race," said LULAC. The organization insisted on Mexicans being called white, and the bureau dropped its separate racial category for Mexicans and did not use it again.[131] Obviously, being considered white would exempt Mexicans from the official segregation that was so common for blacks in the 1930s. Eventually Texas officials used a "white" designation for Mexicans, but this action did not halt segregation and discrimination.[132] LULAC initiated boycotts in several Texas cities against businesses that practiced racial distinctions. It also boycotted a newspaper for carrying ads stating "No Mexicans Allowed."[133] In addition, the organization campaigned for improvements in the Mexican schools.[134]

Working-class immigrants and native-born Mexicanos also turned to trade unions to win better working conditions and higher wages. In Texas, however, most unions were segregated, which weakened their effectiveness. Until passage of the Wagner Act in 1935, unions were generally successful only for highly skilled laborers, and the new labor law did little for farmworkers. Nonetheless, in Texas the United Cannery, Agricultural, Packing, and Allied Workers of America won a few contests for higher wages in the 1930s, and the Union of Mine, Mill, and Smelter Workers gained recognition by 1946. Women cigar workers also won a few strikes in the 1930s and gained higher wages.[135]

Elsewhere in the Southwest labor conflict became especially acute during the Great Depression. For years Mexican migratory farmworkers had attempted to unionize, but with little success. California was the center of much of the conflict during the 1930s, as Mexicans, sometimes joining with other ethnic groups, went on strike and attempted to organize unions. In the end most of these efforts failed, largely because growers were too strong and well organized. Growers marshaled law enforcement agencies against the strikers and "red-baited" the unions, accusing them of being dominated by "un-American" communists. Moreover, during the depression it was relatively easy to find workers to replace those on strike.[136] Camille Guerin-Gonzales explains how farmers in Contra Costa County defeated the strikers: "During another strike in 1934 . . . the Associated Farmers again used terror and vigilante action against Mexican workers. . . . Growers escorted strikers to the county line and threatened their lives if they returned. The county sheriff then deputized the growers, who subsequently arrested strikers who were picketing farms in the county. Unable to counter state and grower power, workers called off the strike."[137]

The immigrant community also created many other organizations to help immigrants' adjustment and survival. These *mutualistas* were similar to those of other immigrant groups, providing their members financial aid, such as sickness and burial insurance, and help in finding jobs.[138] The mutual aid organizations also reinforced traditional Mexican culture as they fostered community entertainment. Some of the groups were for men only, but some women also belonged and even formed their own mutual aid societies.[139]

Despite the efforts of unions, mutual aid societies, and civil rights groups, nothing could change the course of events during the Great Depression when more than 400,000 Mexican immigrants (and their American-born children) either were deported or voluntarily returned to Mexico. State, federal, county, and local governments did not want to aid Mexicanos during the bleak 1930s. These governmental agencies simply shipped the immigrants back to Mexico. It marked the first (and only) time in American history that an ethnic group that had legal residence in the United States was deported in large numbers. Repatriation began in Los Angeles and quickly spread to other California communities where Mexicans resided. Governmental agents raided places where Mexicans congregated and put them on trains and buses headed for Mexico. Many immigrants left voluntarily because they could find no work or relief and knew that eventually they would be deported.[140] The Mexican consulate offices even cooperated with the deportation efforts because they knew they had little choice and hoped to make the removal as pleasant as possible.[141] Folk singer Woody Guthrie captured this phenomenon in his song "Deportee."

Most of the deportations occurred in the early years of the Great Depression, but few immigrants entered during the 1930s. During the depressed years many of the migratory jobs that Mexicans had held in the 1920s were being taken by the Okies who left Texas and Oklahoma for California. The Mexican experience in the Midwest was little different. As Juan Garcia put it, "For Mexicans the depression was disastrous. As jobs became scarce, they were among the first fired and were replaced by 'Whites' and 'American citizens.'"[142] Detroit's Mexicans lost their jobs as automobile layoffs began. It was a situation similar to that of the 1920–21 recession, except that conditions did not improve after 1929; indeed, they grew worse.[143] As the depression deepened, those who had been able to draw public aid found themselves being removed from governmental assistance. They had little choice but to voluntarily join the exodus to Mexico.

The mass removal of so many Mexicans left a bitter taste in the mouths of those who were being sent south. For those who did manage to hang on during the Great Depression, life was not easy. A small middle class had emerged in both California and Texas, and a second generation with more education and English-language ability had better opportunities than their parents. This pattern would be repeated after World War II.

While Mexicans were by far the largest Spanish-speaking group to immigrate to the United States, after the mining days of California the numbers from South America dropped. But a steady flow of South Americans and especially Central Americans continued. In the early decades of the twentieth century, about 4,000 persons annually arrived from South America. A civil war in Chile in 1891 sent thousands north, and political instability and economic conditions continued to serve as catalysts for immigration. From Central America, Nicaraguans, for example, fled political persecution during the 1930s. At first the elite of Central America came, along with many educated immigrants who were teachers, labor organizers, and political dissidents. They settled mostly in New York, Houston, New Orleans, San Francisco, and Los Angeles.[144]

Economics explained why people left their homelands. The contacts with Central and South America dated to the gold rush days and were connected to developing trade routes and industries. San Francisco is a case in point. During the quest for riches, Latinos settled in the city when the gold fields no longer yielded quick riches. During the rush the Pacific mail steamer and other vessels "regularly plied a course between the East Coast and San Francisco via overland connections on the Central American isthmus, mainly in Panama and Nicaragua."[145] San Francisco became a port for the growing coffee crops of Central America, which led to migratory flows, both to and from the city. In addition, like West Indians, many Salvadorans, Nicaraguans, and other Central Americans helped build the Panama Canal; when that task was completed, they headed north to the West Coast's major port, and many found jobs along the waterfront.[146] Others worked in the growing banana trade, in canneries, and in industrial jobs.[147]

The refugees from mining days and the newcomers from south of the American border were mostly young men who intended to work in the United States for only a few years and then return home. Many did go back, but others remained. Their settlement in San Francisco's North Beach gave the area a reputation as a "tenderloin," a place of vice catering to young men. There one could find theaters, brothels, and other illicit activities. At the same time, in 1875 the Latino population founded Our Lady of Guadalupe, a Spanish Catholic church. Gradually the Latinos settled in the Mission District.[148] These contacts and growing Latino populations in San Francisco and other cities were not large compared with the Mexican population in the years before 1940, but they became centers of information about El Norte that would aid many more who came from Central and South America after World War II.

Some Latinos were black and suffered the same hostility as other black immigrants and native-born blacks. The Afro-Cubans in Tampa, Florida, are a case in point. In 1870 Afro-Cubans constituted 21 percent of the Cuban population in the United States; in 1920 the 11,531 Afro-Cubans accounted for only 13 percent of the Cuban American population.[149] In the 1890s in the tobacco industry of Ybor City, Florida, they and other Cuban immigrants combined a desire for the independence of Cuba from Spain with radical politics. In the early years of Ybor City's history, little racial prejudice existed; it was "an oasis of tolerance and decency in a desert of bigotry and hatred."[150] After 1900, however, relations between Afro-Cubans and other Cubans and whites deteriorated.[151] The coming of World War II placed new demands on the economy, in which Mexican immigrants would once again be welcomed for their labor skills. Yet prejudice was by no means ended in the 1940s, as two incidents in Los Angeles attested. This story is told in a later chapter.

PART II

The Emergence of a New Multicultural Society, 1940–Present

Since the end of World War II, and especially after 1965, a surge of new immigrants has been altering America's demography. When the United States entered World War II, the conditions changed for some Asians, Latinos, and blacks, though not necessarily for the better. Japanese Americans on the West Coast were interned by the federal government in relocation camps during the war. In contrast, the federal government allowed some Filipino servicemen to become American citizens, and Congress repealed the Chinese exclusion acts in 1943. The repeal was not a major change, for China received an annual quota of only 105, but it marked the beginning of a significant shift in American immigration policy.

On the basis of these modest alterations, at the end of the war few persons would have predicted the enormous changes to come. However, important legislation in 1965, 1986, and 1990 permitted millions of people to immigrate to the United States. Immigration was especially heavy after 1980, and in the 1990s surpassed the previous record of the first decade of the twentieth century. During the 1990s the foreign-born population grew at a rate nearly four times that of the native-born population. After a low point in 1970, when only 4.7 percent of the American population was foreign born, the nation's newcomers accounted for 11 percent of the population by 2003.

In the first two decades after the war, the majority of immigrants came from Europe, under either the national origins quotas or special legislation for displaced persons and refugees before a new policy was enacted in 1965. Because the Western Hemisphere lacked quotas or even a ceiling until 1965, many newcomers from Latin America entered, too. Under the new laws, beginning in 1965, Asians, blacks, and Latinos dominated the immigration flow. In the 1990s, with the end of the cold war, many persons from Poland and the former Soviet Union came in larger numbers, but those from beyond Europe still accounted for the great majority of immigrants. Mexico alone accounted for one-fifth of all immigrants during the 1990s.

The economic and social impact of the new wave of immigration has been most noticeable in the six states where most immigrants settled: California, Texas, New York, New Jersey, Florida, and Illinois. In 2000 demographers found that California became the largest state in which non-Hispanic whites were no longer in the majority.[1] Within these states, immigrants have tended to settle in large urban areas. Fast-growing urban areas such as Los Angeles, Houston-Galveston-Brazoria, Chicago-Gary-Kenosha, Washington-Baltimore, Atlanta, Miami, and Dallas–Fort Worth grew largely because of new immigrants.[2] New York City, where immigrants have always settled, received few newcomers from 1930 to 1950, but then immigration once again began to change the Empire City.

Just as impressive has been the spread of immigrants to towns, cities, and states where few had lived previously. Asian professionals practiced their crafts throughout the United States, and African refugees settled in cities such as San Diego, Minneapolis, and Atlanta. As for Latinos, the *Christian Science Monitor* noted in 2001, "In almost every growing U.S. county for which the new census numbers are available, the rise in Hispanics has outstripped overall population growth—from the Aleutians to Nantucket Island, Mass., from Green Bay, Wis., to the rural Mississippi Delta."[3] Clearly, the United States was changing as the twenty-first century dawned. These immigration changes are the topic of the chapters that follow.

4

El Norte
Mexicans, 1940–Present

Of the latest newcomers from Asia, the Caribbean, and Central and South America, Latinos constitute about half. And, among the countries sending Spanish-speaking immigrants to the United States, none have been so important as Mexico. Mexicans account for approximately 60 percent of the nation's Hispanics, and amount to about 40 percent of all immigrants arriving in California since the 1970s.[1] In 1999, sociologist Robert Smith remarked, "It's increasingly getting harder to get away from Mexico, even while living in the United States. . . . Short- and long-term Mexican migration represents the greatest economic, political and cultural impact of any other immigrant group in the United States." Given the backlog of Mexicans waiting to migrate to the United States, they will continue to influence American life for some time to come.[2] (See Table 1.)

Rather than waiting for visas or immigration permits, many choose to illegally cross the Rio Grande in order to work and live in the United States. Mexicans make up the largest nationality group (a majority) of the illegal immigrant population in the United States. In 1996, the Immigration and Naturalization Service (INS) estimated that there were 5 million undocumented persons living in the United States, of whom Mexicans numbered 2.7 million (55 percent).[3] The 2000 census revealed that these figures were out of date. Using the new data, demographers suggested that the undocumented population reached 8.7 million in 2000, with Mexicans constituting the majority.[4] Frank Bean and other scholars have suggested somewhat different numbers.[5] Most authorities believe that Mexico accounts for approximately half the total.[6] So great has been this migration that Mexico has now passed Germany as the nation sending the largest number of persons to America since the country's founding. The 2000 census counted 8.8 million persons born in Mexico and living in the United States; in 2002 the Center for Immigration Studies placed

TABLE I
*Immigration from Mexico
and Three Other Leading Emigrant Nations (1998–2001)*

Country of Birth	1998 No.	%	1999 No.	%	2000 No.	%	2001 No.	%
Mexico	206,426	19.4	173,919	20.5	147,573	22.8	131,575	20.1
India	70,290	6.6	42,046	4.9	30,237	4.7	36,482	5.6
China, People's Republic	56,426	5.3	45,652	5.4	32,204	5.0	36,884	5.6
Philippines	53,154	5.0	42,474	5.0	32,026	4.8	34,466	5.3

SOURCE: Immigration and Naturalization Service, Annual Report, 2001.

the figure at 9,659,000.[7] Official immigration totals from 1820 to 2000 indicated that persons from Mexico numbered 6,138,964. The census included some of the undocumented population but still represents an undercount. Jeffrey Passel of the Urban Institute has stated that half of the Mexicans counted were actually undocumented.[8] Moreover, these figures of more than 9 million Mexicans living in the United States do not take into consideration many of those who arrived at the turn of the twentieth century or those who have died or returned home.[9]

After the deportations of the 1930s, the Mexican government and many Mexicans were not eager for more migration to America. But World War II marked the beginning of a trend that continued for the rest of the century; indeed, the numbers increased each decade. When the United States went to war against Japan, Germany, and Italy in 1941, it eventually mobilized 15 million men and women in the armed forces. Several million Americans migrated to the cities, especially those of the West Coast, to labor in the nation's rapidly growing war industries. The lean days of the Great Depression had finally come to an end. During this war Mexicans and Mexican Americans were among the millions heading to centers of the war economy. "The best jobs were in the cities. Consequently, during the war years there was a massive influx of the Mexican population into urban centers," wrote historian Manuel G. Gonzales.[10] These centers brought Mexican Americans into contact with other ethnic groups and heightened their awareness of their second-class position in the United States. Moreover, young Mexican Americans flocked to the military or were drafted.[11] Many of them told their extended families in Mexico that opportunities again existed in the United States.

Not all negative experiences ended for Mexicans. Two particularly violent episodes occurred in Los Angeles during the war. A gang of Mexican youths were falsely accused of murdering a young white youth. Los Angeles officials put seventeen young Mexican American men on trial for the murder, which was labeled the "Sleepy Lagoon incident" because the body was found at the Sleepy Lagoon swimming hole. The trial quickly became a mockery of justice. The young men were not allowed to shave or bathe for a week; several were convicted with little evidence and under appalling courtroom procedures. The district court of appeals finally overturned the conviction after the defendants had spent two years in prison. In 1943, just after the defendants went to trial, the Zoot Suit Riots broke out in Los Angeles. Sailors attacked Mexican American youths who were wearing popular suits with baggy pants and large hats, and soon the assaults degenerated into the sailors beating any Mexican American youths they could find, regardless of their clothes. The Los Angeles police made little or no effort to halt the violence. Finally the navy restricted the sailors to their posts, thus ending a sorry and bigoted episode targeting Mexican Americans.[12] While these were the two worst episodes involving bigotry against Mexicans, they were by no means the only ones.[13]

Yet the United States needed labor. Because so many Americans, immigrants and native born, flocked to wartime industrial jobs or were drafted into the military, large-scale farms were now short of labor. The farmer-owners convinced Washington to make an agreement between the United States and the Mexican government to bring temporary workers from Mexico to pick crops. These were mostly young men, called "braceros." The total number of braceros was not large, and the Mexican government refused to allow them to work in Texas because of the extremely bad treatment of persons of Mexican heritage in the Lone Star State. Later the ban on Texas was repealed, and braceros worked in Texas and as far north as Oregon. The bracero agreement was extended after the war in one form another until Congress finally ended it in 1964, but while it was in existence about 5 million braceros labored for a time in American agriculture.[14]

They were supposed to receive the "prevailing wage" and enjoy the same federal protections as American farmworkers. In fact, farmworkers were unprotected by federal programs, and the "prevailing wage" turned out to mean wages as low as possible. Their living arrangements were primitive, including inadequate housing and unsanitary facilities. Most labored in agriculture, but a few were employed as railroad workers.[15]

Despite terrible living conditions, there was no shortage of potential braceros during the program's existence. Social and economic conditions were so appalling in Mexico that even with the low wages paid these temporary farm hands, they were able to send money home and return with additional funds to help their families and communities. Indeed, once their contracts ended, many braceros signed on again to return to American farms. If the demand exceeded the number being recruited, many were quite willing to cross the border without proper papers and find employment, often working side by side with braceros. Growers were eager to employ these undocumented immigrants because they worked for low wages and lacked legal protection. Federal officials worried about the growth of illegal labor after World War II and in 1954 carried out "Operation Wetback," an INS effort to deport illegal aliens found on American farms. To ease growers' fears that they would be unable to find enough harvest hands, the federal government doubled the number of braceros until it was more than 400,000 annually in the peak years of the late 1950s.[16]

Overall the number of illegal aliens attempting to get into the United States then dropped, but when the bracero program ended in 1965 and Congress placed a ceiling on Western Hemisphere immigration the same year, undocumented immigration once again grew. Included in the flow were women and families. The INS simply could not seal the U.S.-Mexico border, and for a variety of reasons border wardens did not raid many agricultural fields to remove illegal workers. Undocumented farmworkers found employment throughout the Southwest, and especially California, but also as far north as Washington, where apple growers were eager to employ them during harvest season.

It is important to keep in mind that farm hands could follow the crops in California and elsewhere and thus prolong their stay beyond a few months. Moreover, many migrants remained longer in the rural towns of California. New varieties of crops and methods of cultivation were extending the agricultural season. Philip Martin, a professor of agricultural economics, noted, "What's happened is that many people who used to go back and forth to Mexico have settled in California with their families." Many of these families were poor, but a growing number were reportedly buying homes and putting down roots in these rural California communities.[17] As important to agriculture as undocumented laborers were, a growing number of illegal aliens were finding employment in cities. Moreover, entire families were included in this migration, with women constituting a growing proportion of the *indocumentados*.[18]

In spite of their use of undocumented aliens, estimated to account for 42 percent of field hands by the mid-1990s, growers insisted that they were chronically short of labor during the harvest season, and they lobbied Congress over the years to import new farm laborers.[19] Under a special 1952 legislative program called H-2, some temporary farm hands were recruited after 1965, but their number never exceeded 50,000 and usually was much lower. Farmers were permitted to employ these workers if they could demonstrate that a supply of domestic labor was inadequate to pick their crops. Mostly young Jamaicans, the laborers generally worked in Florida cutting sugarcane, harvesting perishable crops, or picking apples in the Northeast.[20]

A provision in a 1986 immigration law gave an amnesty to more than 1 million farmworkers, many of whom experts believed were not really farm laborers. The INS did not have the manpower to carefully check each applicant. The law established a program for importing temporary farmworkers, but the federal government generally remained unconvinced that there was a shortage of field hands. Only a few thousand Mexicans were recruited under this program, many of whom were employed in North Carolina, not in the large fields of California.[21] After 1996 the number of H-2 workers for agriculture was increased slightly. A total of 15,000 received work permits in 1996, and nearly 42,000 did so in 1999, which hardly represented a major shift in policy. Growers insisted that hundreds of thousands were needed, if illegal aliens were to be replaced.[22]

A modest program was inaugurated in 2000 with the Mexican state of Zacatecas to bring temporary farmworkers to the United States. The U.S. government established the Zacatecas program by working with Governor Ricardo Monreal of Monterrey to bring the Mexicans to Texas. Texas businessmen convinced American officials that it was impossible to find workers in the economy of 2000 and hence the growers needed to go directly to Mexico, but the visas amounted to only 17,000 permits.[23]

Mexicans had plenty of notions about the United States. Some had previously worked as braceros. Others had worked close to the American border in maquiladoras, foreign-owned assembly plants, which boomed in the cities of northern Mexico. As Mexicans flocked to jobs in the maquiladoras they became more aware of United States cities just across the border. Although these workers were now receiving higher wages than their kin in villages and farming regions, wages to the north were much higher. Why not, many asked, simply cross the border and find a better life?[24]

Crossing the border is hazardous to say the least. Increased INS enforcement and tighter restrictions during the 1990s only made conditions worse. Stricter controls in areas of heavy crossing "pushed the traffic far from urban areas toward some of the most remote and dangerous zones, due to their topography and climate."[25] More than a thousand Mexicans died trying to cross the border between 1993 and 1997 alone.[26] As enforcement increased in southern California and some parts of Texas, the price to hire a "coyote"—someone who promised to smuggle persons across—went up. An INS official told reporters in 1998 that coyotes charged about $200 in 1996. The going rate two years later was between $800 and $1,000. This fee covered being smuggled across in large trucks supposedly bringing goods, not people, into the United States.[27] For those crossing on foot the cost also increased.[28] Restrictions tightened even more after the World Trade Center was destroyed by terrorists in September 2001. Moreover, to avoid the beefed-up border patrols, migrants crossed in deserts, with exceptionally high temperatures, where travel on foot was dangerous. With temperatures above 100 degrees, a plentiful supply of water was necessary, as was the ability to withstand such heat. In addition, it was not unknown for the migrants to be victimized by robbers along the border and for women to be raped by those stealing what few dollars they had.[29] According to INS officials, for the year ending in October 2000, a total of 369 immigrants died attempting to cross into the United States. One hundred of these deaths occurred along the Arizona border, up from only 19 the year before.[30]

A sensational episode occurred in the spring of 2001. Coyotes led a group from Mexico into the desert, promising to get them across into the United States. However, the smugglers robbed and abandoned them to the heat of Arizona. Of the original party, immigration officials found thirteen dead bodies, and a fourteenth person died on the way to the hospital.[31] Conditions were even worse during the hot summer months. In the summer of 2002, eleven Mexicans climbed into a tightly sealed railroad car, in either Texas or Mexico. Once the door was shut, their gamble turned into a disaster. Months later the sealed car reached Iowa.

When the door was finally opened, the eleven were found dead.[32] But it was by no means the only such disaster. In May, 2003, seventeen aliens were found dead in another truck in Texas.[33]

As important as Mexicans were for American farms after World War II, the overwhelming majority of Mexican immigrants lived in towns, cities, and suburbs throughout the United States. The border towns and cities of Texas and California where prior immigrants had settled received large numbers of newcomers. But Mexicans did not stop to work in places such as Brownsville, Texas, or San Diego, California. Rather, they headed from the border areas to cities such as Houston, Texas, and the Los Angeles area, where the largest single concentration of Mexican immigrants was found. Texas continues to attract many immigrants, but California has surpassed Texas in numbers and is easily the state with the largest concentration of Mexican immigrants and Mexican Americans at present.[34]

In Texas older Mexican communities have grown rapidly with the influx of immigrants. In Houston, Mexicans constituted 7 percent of the population in 1960; ten years later the figure was 12 percent of the city's population—150,000 people. The numbers have increased further since 1970, and there are several barrios in the so-called Space City.[35] As for Dallas, according to one native of Guanajuato, Mexico, "To me, it's almost like being back in my village. I live here with my family, and there are eight families we know very well. They are either from the same village as us, or we've known them a long time. . . . This feels like home."[36]

While large numbers of Mexican immigrants settled in Texas and California, others migrated to other cities and states in the Southwest. Older communities in Arizona, New Mexico, and Colorado all received new immigrants. The migration stream also headed to the Midwest, where Mexicans had settled between 1900 and 1930. Some were farmworkers following the crops and providing field hands in the sugar beet fields in California and Texas, but Minneapolis, Detroit, and Kansas City also received Mexican newcomers.[37] Chicago had several Mexican concentrations, as well as settlements in suburbs and small cities nearby. In 1970 Mexicans made up more than two-thirds of Chicago's Latino population, which amounted to 20 percent of the city's total. Two hundred thousand additional Mexicans settled in the Windy City during the 1980s, and more continued to arrive in the last decade of the twentieth century. By 2000 the Mexican-origin population numbered 1 million in the Chicago area.[38]

While new migration swelled older Mexican communities, just as impressive was the rapid growth of barrios in areas where practically no Mexicans had lived before 1980. Maria Hinojosa settled in New York City in 1979. She later recalled, "There were no Mexicans in New York in 1979—none I could find anyway. It took me a month of deep-cover detective work to find out where I could buy tortillas." She found them in an old Spanish store, but "even then all I could find were three-packs of frozen white tortillas. They were disgusting, and I was depressed."[39] New York City's Latino population consisted largely of Puerto Ricans and Dominicans in 1980, but after that date a rapid influx of Mexican immigrants bolstered the Empire City's Mexican population, which officially reached 186,000 in 2000, although some experts estimated it to be larger. Responding to criticism of sociologist John Logan, in 2003 the Bureau of the Census increased its earlier figures on the number of Latinos in New York City.[40] Of the nation's major cities, New York City ranked sixth in Mexican-origin population in 1998.[41] If New York City's Mexican population soared from practically zero in 1980, so did that of many smaller communities and states. In Georgia, Alabama, Tennessee, and the Carolinas, Mexican immigrants numbered over 1 million in 1999.[42] Mindful of the growth of Mexicans in Georgia, Governor Roy Barnes donned a sombrero after addressing a Cinco de Mayo festival.[43] Vermont, one of the nation's "whitest" states, also attracted a few Mexicans. The Latino population of Vermont grew 40 percent in the 1990s and surpassed 5,000 by 1997. The newcomers were numerous enough to begin holding a Latino festival in Burlington by 1993.[44] In Maine, another New England state with historically few Hispanics, Latinos dominated the labor force at Turner's DeCoster Egg Farm, the largest such farm in the United States. In faraway Alaska, Mexicans found jobs on fishing boats.[45]

Many migrants to states such as Georgia were drawn to work in the poultry industry.[46] Developments pioneered by Frank Perdue revolutionized the raising and marketing of chickens. Public concern over health and disapproval of meat eating gave an additional boost to the chicken boom. As the industry spread and began to exhaust the cheap native-born labor force, employers looked elsewhere for workers. In the spreading poultry (as well as meatpacking) industry they turned to immigrants from Mexico and Central America.[47] Many of the plants were located in smaller cities and towns such as Dodge City and Storm Lake, Iowa; Milan, Missouri; and Siler City, North Carolina. Noel, Missouri, a small town in the Ozarks, had only 1,300 residents before Latinos arrived after

1990 to work in Hudson Foods's poultry plant. By 1997 Noel had nearly 1,000 employees in the plant.[48]

The *U.S. News and World Report* presented the industry as a new version of Upton Sinclair's novel *The Jungle*, which told of horrible conditions in Chicago's meatpacking industry. Ninety years after Sinclair published his groundbreaking exposé of the nation's meatpacking industry, "illegal immigrants are flocking into the United States to take the dangerous, low-paying jobs most Americans won't."[49] There Mexicans found jobs that paid six to seven dollars per hour. The work was repetitive, and workplaces were dirty and sometimes unhealthy.[50] Conditions and wages were little different in other plants along the "chicken trail." A reporter covering a slaughterhouse in North Carolina wrote, "The place reeks of sweat, . . . steam and blood. . . . Everything is used, and the kill men, repeating slaughterhouse lore, say that even the squeal is sold. . . . People on the cut lines work with a mindless fury. There is tremendous pressure to keep the conveyor belts moving. . . . There is no clock, no window, no fragment of the world outside."[51] Because of these conditions, worker turnover was high. Yet other Mexican immigrants could easily be found to replace those who quit. Well-developed immigrant networks from Mexico to towns and cities all over the United States have made it easy for "employers to find laborers."[52] A few Mexicans found jobs dealing with animals other than hogs and chickens, for example, caring for horses during the racing season at Saratoga Springs, New York.[53]

Migration from Mexico had begun earlier with the recruitment of farmworkers, often under the bracero program, when, according to Professor David Hayes-Baptiste of the University of California at Los Angeles, the immigration network brought whole villages of young men to the United States. After the end of the bracero program, Mexicans kept coming because they knew how to get to the United States, either legally or illegally. As Hayes-Baptiste put it, "Those routes were hard-wired, burned in during the years of the bracero program. Today, before people leave the village for the first time, they know where they are going to go, where they are going to stay, often where they are going to work."[54] Never mind that some of the immigrants were undocumented. In Brownsville, Texas, a center of recruitment, one Mexican American citizen remarked, "The gringos arrive here from all over: Texas, Mississippi, North Carolina, Illinois and Florida. They find illegal workers who are willing to work."[55]

The story of one village in Mexico, Villa Juarez, revealed how the recruitment network functioned. In this town of about 5,000 residents, half of the population had been to the United States. One villager remarked, "People in every house have relatives in the United States." Many headed for Atlanta, Georgia, where they received information and goods from a grocery store owned by a fellow citizen from Villa Juarez. Money sent home was crucial for Villa Juarez's survival. And for those who wished to join their neighbors, the network was in place to assist them. A restaurant owner in Atlanta, also from Villa Juarez, was able to employ some of his friends and relatives when they came north. Douglas Massey, a leading authority on immigration from Mexico, said about the first immigrant to settle, "They go where he is. That's where he can provide housing and an entrée into the community."[56]

In addition to family and village networks, formal recruiting by employers aided in settlement and jobs. Conchita Gonzales, for example, obtained workers through the H-2B program, which, though small, was a legal mechanism to recruit farm hands. In another case the Foley Enterprises firm processed visas for thirty-five to forty different companies in need of help. The head of Foley Enterprises believed the word was spreading: "This year I went to a (landscaping) trade convention in Dallas, and we were just bombarded."[57] El Espresso (a Coach USA Company) is another company placing immigrants in jobs. Within a period of a few months it recruited 15,000 workers from Laredo to North Carolina to work in the tobacco fields.[58] When the InStaff Personnel employment agency discovered it could not find workers, it went to the border to recruit laborers for food processing companies and posted fliers at the Texas Workforce Commission's office in the Rio Grande Valley.[59]

Whether networks were formal or informal, the result was the same for the employers. Remarked Wayne Cornelius of the University of California at San Diego, "It's low-maintenance. [The immigrants'] friends will orient them at work, tell them how to dress, even what buses to take. The owner doesn't have to do anything."[60] With such networks, especially in the flush times of the late 1990s, workers were able to find employment easily.

Remittances are also a major part of the story of Mexican migration, and many families in Mexico could not have survived without the funds they received from America. Estimates of the amount sent to Mexico annually vary, but most experts believe that it was at least $6 billion and possibly as much as $10 billion, with total remittances to Latin America being $14.2 billion from the United States in 2002.[61] The Mexican government knows that money is badly needed in economically depressed communities. President Vicente Fox of Mexico is aware that the transfers amount to Mexico's third-largest source of income, behind only oil and manufacturing. His concern has been to make sure the funds go to Mexico without large fees or commissions to transfer the funds. He also wants the money to be used for development and not simply to buy consumer goods.[62]

In the late 1990s one problem for undocumented immigrants wanting to send money home was the lack of bank accounts. Middlemen, such as check cashing shops, took a healthy share of the funds as commission to send money to Mexico. The Mexican consulate in Los Angeles began in 2001 to issue consular identification cards to its nationals whether or not they were in the United States with proper documents. In 2001 Mexico issued 664,000 consular cards worldwide, but in 2002 the government issued more than 1.4 million in the United States alone.[63] Only 58 percent of Mexicans in the United States had bank accounts in 2001, but in November 2002 Wells Fargo, a San Francisco bank with branches in twenty-three states, agreed to accept the consular cards to permit persons to open accounts. Other banks quickly followed, making it possible for Mexicans to send money home cheaply.[64]

How frequently the illegals return home is not precisely known, but scholars believe that the pattern of back-and-forth migration has been extensive for many years since World War II. Indeed, many migrants had no intentions of settling permanently in the United States.[65] Evidence suggests that the length of stay in the United States is increasing. A 1997 study carried out by Mexico and the United States reported that migrant workers from Mexico, both illegal and legal, settle longer than previously in America. "The rate of back-and-forth movement seems to be slowing," the study concluded. Moreover, the impact of 1996 laws tightening immigration and making it more difficult for undocumented aliens to go home and return may have encouraged many to simply remain in the United States and sink roots here. This was not the intent of the framers of the 1996 law, but it probably was one of its unintended consequences.[66]

In recent years border officials have caught a growing number of Mexican women attempting to cross illegally. The women amounted to 15 percent of the total in 1992, up from just 8 percent in 1987. Some, to be sure, migrated to join their husbands, but a survey of 718 women crossing from Tijuana to America revealed that only 10 percent declared they were trying to join their families; most sought employment.[67]

For several decades after 1945 the majority of Mexicans obtaining a green card were men, but the proportion of women steadily increased over time, amounting to more than half of the flow during the 1990s. In 2001, for example, the INS reported that 81,174 Mexican men and 125,222 women entered legally. The number of young children was also increasing, duplicating the dominant pattern of postwar immigration generally.[68]

Whether men or women, Mexican immigrants have tended to be less educated than most other immigrant groups in the United States, to lack technical skills, and to know little English. Unlike Indians or Filipinos, in the 1990s only a handful of Mexicans entered with green cards as professional or executive workers.[69] As a result, Mexican immigrants typically took jobs that paid poorly. For women this meant work in the service industries or as domestics. Hotels, motels, and offices depended on foreign labor in many communities for cleaning rooms and doing laundry. Many Latino men also worked as janitors in large office buildings. This type of employment required few skills and limited English. Such jobs paid little—the minimum wage or less in some cases—though the wages were sometimes better than those in the garment industry in California, where many Mexican immigrants worked. A reporter for the *Los Angeles Times* told the story of one woman, Hilda Aguilar, who immigrated to the United States in 1992. Aguilar found employment in the garment shops of Los Angeles, where she started at the bottom of the ladder. After seven years she still had not improved her position, nor did most of the other estimated 61,000 Los Angeles sewing machine operators. As a result of competition from abroad, the wages of many women garment workers decreased in the 1990s. Many were lucky to earn California's minimum hourly wage of $5.75. The women were trapped by their lack of skills and knowledge of English. Remarked Aguilar, whose husband worked in the same shops, "We have no options. We can't go back [to Mexico]. Our children were born here. Our lives are here." A scholar agreed, "God knows what those workers will do. The women might go into domestic work."[70] Indeed, many Mexican women, especially in Texas and California, have become domestics, mainly because few other opportunities are available.

If Mexican women dominated paid housework, men dominated day labor. Standing on street corners in California communities, they waited for someone in need of labor to bargain for wages and then hire them to care for their yards or work in nurseries. Better jobs existed in construction, where they might find employment lasting weeks or even months. The appearance of Mexican immigrant street corner labor markets dated to the 1980s. In San Francisco day laborers first appeared when Mexicans gathered at Tiffany and Duncan Streets.[71] Unemployment in the early 1990s made finding work difficult, but with the booming California economy after 1995 (until 2000), employers eagerly sought these day laborers. The growth of street corner labor markets prompted several cities to regularize the industry. Los Angeles city officials set up job centers to replace scattered street corners for recruitment of day laborers. Of course, such workers were not unionized and sold their labor for relatively low wages. Some employers preferred the old system, under which they could hire men for $5 per hour instead of $7 per hour or more, as required by the job centers.[72] Although the practice of hiring day laborers began in California, it spread to other American cities and towns. Men who found day work in construction discovered their wages were higher than for those working in the "chicken trail." Jose Zjamudio was earning $18 per hour in 2000 working as a bricklayer in Detroit. In Manassas, Virginia, the site of famous Civil War battles, Miguel Rodriquez painted houses and commercial buildings for up to $250 a day in 1999.[73] In Farmingville, Long Island, a few workers make $100 per day. As one immigrant commented, "It's strange, but man, the money is here. I never dreamed about $100."[74]

A study carried out by the New School University in New York City found that 95 percent of the day laborers in the New York area were men, many of whom had families back in Mexico or Central America. They generally earned more than the minimum wage and on average were able to send $3,600 annually to their home communities. Some of the workers said that at times their employers had not paid them. As an undocumented worker from Mexico said, cheap labor was needed, and many Mexicans "are willing to provide the muscle."[75] However, when six or eight day laborers lived in a single-family home, they sometimes raised the hackles of the neighbors. During the summer months in Farmingville, one ranch house contained thirty men. One resident of Brewster, New York, said, "There's a cultural difference between Americans and Latinos. We don't stand on the street looking for work. The average person will wake up at 8 o'clock and go to work. They wake up and go stand on the street corner and look for work. I call it visual pollution."[76] Some towns have tried to halt street corner hiring, but their efforts usually failed. In 2000 in Farmingville, Long Island, shouting matches erupted between those on the street corners and some older town residents; the situation became violent when two white men assaulted Hispanic immigrants.[77] In some cases towns have passed laws limiting the number persons who could legally occupy one house.[78] It seemed as if such immigrants were wanted as low-wage and casual laborers but not as neighbors.[79] One INS official explained, "There's a fundamental ambivalence in our nation over what to do about illegal immigrants who are living in our communities and who have become contributing members."[80]

Even worse than the conditions of day laborers, housecleaners, or garment shop workers were those of deaf immigrants who had been smuggled into the United States to sell pencils or trinkets on New York City's subways and streets. The smugglers controlling this group, which included children as well as adult men and women, kept them in virtual bondage and paid them little money. Their story came to light in 1997 and led to the prosecution of the persons holding them. The immigrants themselves were allowed to stay in the United States.[81] A few months later the federal government announced that it had broken up another gang that had recruited and smuggled Mexicans to work in a T-shirt factory in Georgia. Most were young men who had paid coyotes $1,000 to cross the border and were then given work under sweatshop conditions.[82] The recruiters, legal or not, were often Mexican immigrants or Mexican American themselves. Moreover, with the expansion of barrios, employment opened for these middlemen, who served the newcomers by offering services. They ran stores that sold familiar items and where the language spoken was Spanish. Still others offered services to help immigrants get a job or a driver's license or deal with American institutions and bureaucracies. Noted one, "Most of the people I have met are humble people who just want to be productive members of the community. We cannot imagine the conditions they have come from, so it's tough to know so many people are hard on them just because they speak a different language and have a different cultural background."[83]

Journalistic accounts of the struggle of Mexican immigrants trying to make a living are backed by statistics. A study of Mexican Americans in Los Angeles revealed that these newcomers began at the bottom of the economy. A majority had not graduated from high school. Mexican-origin men were just as likely to be working as other men, but employment alone did not put them into the middle class. In 1990 Mexican immigrant men in Los Angeles averaged $18,000 a year, compared with $46,000 for white non-Hispanics. Mexican immigrant women's earnings also lagged behind those of white women in Los Angeles.[84] The gap has not changed much over time. For the most part Mexicans have not been able to improve their language skills and education levels to catch up with other workers in Los Angeles.[85] Spanish is typically spoken in the homes of Mexican immigrants; 97.5 percent spoke Spanish at home in 1980, and the figure stayed about the same (96 percent in 1990), with only 50 percent indicating that they spoke English well or very well. Lack of English and lack of education are major handicaps in the job market.[86]

At the national level, the Census Bureau reported in 2000 that only 51 percent of the Mexican-origin population had completed high school, compared with 88.4 percent of non-Hispanic whites. Second- and third-generation Mexican Americans had higher educational achievements than the first generation, earned more money, mastered English, and often lived outside the barrio.[87] In Los Angeles, whereas the Mexican immigrant generation earned an average of only $18,000 annually in 1990, native-born Mexican Americans earned $30,500.[88] Some of the immigrant generation succeeded in reaching the middle class as owners of businesses and or as white-collar workers.[89] Indicators such as home ownership, income, English language acquisition, naturalization, and intermarriage among Latinos pointed to a growing middle class, following the path of past generations of other immigrants.[90] Another study by William Clark of California during the 1990s also found a growing Latino middle class.[91]

While some Mexican immigrants and their children and grandchildren have experienced increased social mobility (albeit slowly) and visibility across the United States, there is one area where young men have been exceptionally noticeable: baseball, which has been accompanied by large salaries during the 1990s. By 2000 Latinos accounted for nearly 25 percent of major league baseball players, a figure that had nearly doubled in one decade. These included Mexicans, but Hispanic players have come from all over the Caribbean and Central and South America in addition to Mexico.[92] Latino ball players in the United States date from the turn of the century, though their numbers were not large until the last two decades. Historian Samuel O. Regalado wrote that before 1941 they "trickled into the major leagues with no great fanfare. Although all of them were considered white [blacks were banned until 1947, including Latino blacks], some were deemed a novelty and others became targets of journalistic humor."[93] During the past sixty years baseball was emerging as a popular sport throughout Latin America. As owners and managers became aware of the enormous talent virtually on America's doorstep, they began to recruit in Latin America, including in Fidel Castro's communist Cuba. They sent scouts south and helped players to obtain visas.

The desegregation of baseball, begun in 1947 when Jackie Robinson played for the Brooklyn Dodgers, aided black Latinos. Hispanics encountered discrimination, including low salaries, but gradually the fans, owners, and other players accepted them, especially if they were skilled players. If the players could not speak English, teams provided interpreters. Fernando Valenzuela, a standout pitcher during the 1980s, knew little English; he had been spotted in Mexico by a scout for the Los Angeles Dodgers. The team made provisions for him to communicate in Spanish. Not only were such players desired for their contributions to the games-won column, but the growing number of Latino players also increased attendance. The New York Yankees' general manger Bob Watson remarked in 1996, "We have made no concerted effort [to recruit Latin American players], even though we have players on our team. But common sense tells you that Fernando Valenzuela did wonders for the population in San Diego." And with the growth of the Spanish-speaking population in the United States, attendance could only go up.[94]

The vast majority of Mexicans and Latinos are Roman Catholic. By the end of the twentieth century, Latinos accounted for 30 percent of the membership of Catholic parishes in the United States, and they were the most rapidly growing group within the church. Not only were their numbers increasing but according to some studies Hispanics were more likely than others to attend mass.[95] In some dioceses, Mexican parishes were merged with older churches experiencing declining membership. In New York City, for example, Saint Bernard Church, which had seats for 700, had only a few dozen persons attending mass. Nearby, Our Lady of Guadalupe, a church of Latinos, was "bursting at the seams." Hence in 2003 the Catholic Church merged the two.[96]

This surge in membership occurred at a time when the Catholic Church in America was facing a shortage of priests and nuns as many of those who might previously have gone into the church were selecting other options and careers. For example, in November 2000, the vocation director of the Roman Catholic Diocese of Brooklyn said that the diocese could not find enough new priests; Bishop Thomas V. Daily added that the shortage had become a "crisis," as ordinations in his diocese were down 92 percent from twenty years earlier.[97] The shortage of Latino clergy is especially troublesome for the church. It is often remarked that unlike Irish Catholic immigrants, Mexicans and other Latinos did not bring their priests with them. Thus the Catholic Church had to scramble for Spanish speakers or had to send their priests (of whom the Irish were the largest group) back to school to learn Spanish. In 1990, 9 percent of priests and 6 percent of nuns were studying Spanish, but the combined figure was only 4 percent ten years later.[98] In 2000 a study commissioned by the National Conference of Catholic Bishops pointed out that nationwide the church had one Latino priest per 10,000 Latino parishioners compared with one priest per 1,200 overall all.[99] In 2000 the church had only an estimated 2,000 Hispanic priests nationwide.[100]

It was not the shortage of Spanish-speaking priests alone that caused concern among Catholic leaders. Many Latinos brought with them religious attitudes that differed from the prevailing American modes. One study indicated that Latinos wanted more Bible study and felt that they were not welcomed within Catholic churches and parishes. Some Catholic leaders worried that if the Catholic Church did not respond to Latin American immigrants' evangelism, the newcomers might be attracted to Protestantism. Remarked one Catholic leader, "I see storefront (evangelical Protestant) churches opening in increasing numbers both in San Antonio and other cities across the United States."[101] Latinos had already encountered evangelical Protestants in their homelands, and many responded favorably to the emotional pull of those churches in the United States. As the Reverend Brian Jordan noted in his study of the Pentecostal movement, the Pentecostal community "becomes a place of refuge, of cultural affirmation."[102] A survey carried out by the Graduate Center of the City University of New York in 2002 indicated that 13.1 million Hispanics were Catholics and 2.9 were Protestant. These figures were sure to alarm Catholic leaders. Moreover, the study revealed that 30 percent of Latinos had no religion.[103]

Religion was not the only institution of importance to Mexicans. The self-help organizations that had developed before World War II suddenly found themselves facing a new and growing immigrant population. Mexican farmworkers joined César Chavez's United Farm Workers (UFW) in the 1960s and 1970s. Because the UFW emphasized families, women played a prominent role in its activities; Chavez's most trusted lieutenant, for example, was Dolores Huerta. Achieving some success with help from other unions, church and political leaders, and consumers, the UFW's 1960s boycott of grapes and strikes led to a growing membership. However, faced with a tough stance by growers and a plentiful supply of migrant workers, many of whom were undocumented and willing to pick and harvest crops for low wages, the UFW lost membership after 1980 and ceased to be a driving force in Californian agriculture. Moreover, growers increasingly turned to mechanization to replace workers. When Chavez died in 1993, the movement was moribund, and two years later it was estimated that only 26,000 of the nation's 1.5 million farmworkers were members of a trade union.[104]

Mexicans and other Latinos also attempted to form or join unions in other economic sectors. The UFW itself began to organize in California's cities. Whether it will have more success there than in rural areas remains to be seen.[105] Mexicans have joined some old-line unions, such as the United Auto Workers, but trade unionism has been in decline since its peak in the late 1950s. By 2000 only about 12 percent of American workers were members of unions. Language and immigration status were problems for union organizers. Undocumented aliens have hesitated to join a union for fear that their boss will turn them over to the INS to be deported. This is not an idle threat; it has happened before. In recent years some union leaders changed their hostility toward undocumented immigrants, who they often feared would drive down wages, and began organizing activities in the 1990s. The International Ladies' Garment Workers' Union made such overtures among garment workers but with few results. The American Federation of Labor and the Congress of Industrial Organizations (AFL-CIO) concluded in the late 1990s that all illegal aliens should be granted a new amnesty and that even those without documents should be organized. Selected to spearhead this drive was a Mexican American woman, Linda Chavez-Thompson. "Immigrant workers," she declared, "work very hard for their money. They hold the worst kinds of jobs." But organizing them has been a difficult task.[106] In May 2000, California's Janitors for Justice movement won a three-year contract providing for a 24 percent increase in wages.[107] Even more difficult to organize are men in the street corner markets and women domestics. In Los Angeles the Domestic Workers Association, begun in 1992, achieved some success in supporting the claims of domestic workers for higher pay and better conditions, but this was also an uphill battle.[108]

Mexican immigrants and their children have not been unwilling to protest their living conditions. In the late 1960s young Mexican American men criticized the war in Vietnam and the discrimination they experienced in jobs, housing, and education. From these protests related to the civil rights movement of the 1960s, the Chicano movement was born. It took various forms: political, social, and intellectual. The leaders used the name "Chicano" to indicate their alliance with Mexican workers, their acceptance of Mexican American culture, and their pride in being from Mexico. They argued in favor of increasing the Chicano presence on college campuses and adding Latino studies to the curriculum. The protests spawned a movement among Mexican women who challenged some of the cultural forms of Latino life. The movement also helped the development of young Mexican American scholars who have probed the history of Mexicans in the United States.[109]

The emergence of active Mexican women in the Chicana movement was part and parcel of growing participation of these women in public life and of women's changing roles within the Mexican American community. Women's working for wages was more common in the United States than in Mexico. Wage labor, even at poorly paid jobs, did give women greater say in their households. The involvement of women in the wage economy was not limited to working per se. Indeed, women actively supported the UFW and were instrumental in strikes in the garment industry, where they found employment in large numbers. One of the strikes involving many Mexican women occurred in a 1972 walkout against Farah Manufacturing in Texas. Led by the Amalgamated Clothing Workers (ACW), women joined with men and struck at Farah plants. The strike was especially bitter and led to a national boycott, with an eventual settlement in 1974. Other women helped organize unions and community programs to improve their living conditions.[110] Historian Vicki Ruiz has noted that Mexican women were learning a great deal about unions and leadership.[111]

In addition, writers and musicians have come to the fore in recent years. The first modern novel by a Mexican American, Antonio Villareal, was *Poche*, published in 1959. Some Latinos have also appeared in films and on TV. Painters have found outlets for their work.[112] Moreover, the Latin influence on popular music grew in the 1990s, and in 2000 Hispanics created the Latin Grammy Awards.

The growing presence of Mexicans was watched with anxiety by many Americans. It was one thing when Mexicans worked in agriculture, lived in isolated rural areas, and returned home after the picking was done but quite another when they moved into large cities in huge numbers and settled in smaller towns to work in the local poultry industry, especially if they arrived with families and intended to settle permanently. Watching Latinos moving into Lexington, Kentucky, a grocer noted, "There used to be only single male Hispanics. . . . Now they are bringing their wives and children. They all go to church every Sunday. They are building their own playgrounds and forming their own baseball teams." He concluded, "They are trying to have their own lifestyle like they had in Mexico."[113] Critics believed that Mexican immigrants used public services without paying their share and that they refused to assimilate. One of the main areas of contention was education. Los Angeles, faced with a surge in public school enrollment, had only limited funds to build new classrooms and staff them with qualified teachers. The limits on property taxes, enacted under Proposition 13 in 1978, made it difficult for Los Angeles and other California urban communities to provide an adequate education to the latest newcomers.[114] In 1999 Latinos, mostly Mexicans, made up half the student population in Dallas's public schools. To instruct the city's 156,861 Latino pupils, the board of education estimated that it was short 700 bilingual teachers, in spite of special efforts to attract such teachers.[115]

Sometimes the increase of Latino students with limited English skills in areas where few Latinos existed in the 1980s was even more dramatic than it was in California or Texas, which had Latino populations dating back more than a century. Evangelina Cortez, assistant superintendent for multicultural education in Dallas, said, "The further away from the Mexico border you are, the harder it is. . . . I feel for (other states) because I know how difficult it is for us." Paterson, New Jersey—far from the Mexican border—was one such community. Of course some American-born Paterson Hispanic children knew English, but others came from homes where the parents spoke only Spanish, and these children's knowledge of English was poor at best. Of the 253 students of Mexican origin attending Paterson's schools in 1999, 187 had been born in Mexico.[116] In smaller communities along the "chicken trail" the impact of a rapidly growing school population of students with limited ability to speak English was perhaps even greater. In Siler City, North Carolina, for example, which had attracted many Mexicans to work in poultry plants, Mexican school enrollment went from only 9 percent of the total in 1994 to 39 percent just five years later. Chatham County schools were spending $731,000 for English as a second language (ESL) classes: 40 percent of it in the Siler City Elementary School, which had six ESL teachers and two assistants. Angry parents and residents clashed over the curriculum and funding. The school board wanted to devote more funds and teachers to ESL programs, but like many schools throughout the nation, Siler City found it difficult to find Spanish-language instructors.[117] While Latino parents wanted a school system more sensitive to their children's needs, white parents believed that their children were being shortchanged. As a result, some white parents took their children out of the Siler City schools and sent them to nearby Chatham County schools, which were 93 percent white. A few others placed their children in a newly formed charter school.[118]

Bilingual education became quite controversial in California. ESL was offered as one solution: teach students in regular classes, but use ESL classes to help them acquire English quickly. Other bilingual programs taught subject matter in the students' language and tried to teach the students enough English so they could be placed in the mainstream classes within two years. Such programs, it was claimed, also bolstered the children's self-esteem because they were taught about their heritage. The results of these programs were mixed, given that some students were still unable to move into regular classes after two years and that Latinos had high dropout rates. Critics insisted that bilingual education was badly flawed and should be abandoned. In California Ron Unz, a wealthy businessman, sponsored a statewide proposition to ban bilingual education, and in 1998 he succeeded in convincing voters to pass his measure. California's ending of bilingual education was followed by votes in other states.[119]

In 2000 in New York City, another city with a large Latino population, the board of education adopted the recommendations of a mayor's task force, giving more alternatives for parental choice and curtailing bilingual programs there.[120] In 1998, Miami's school board went in the opposite direction, advocating an expansion of bilingual education to make all students fluent in both English and Spanish. The plan came from the business community, which argued that all Miamians should know both languages to function properly in Florida.[121]

Language also erupted as an inflammatory issue in other states. Senator S. I. Hayakawa from California proposed that English be made the nation's official language. The main organization in the 1980s and 1990s spearheading this drive was U.S. English, headed by Hayakawa and Dr. John Tanton. About half the states passed laws or resolutions to make English their official language, but these were largely symbolic and had little impact. In addition, English-only advocates became embroiled in disputes about bilingual education and ballots in languages other than English.[122]

Like prior waves of immigrants, Mexicanos eventually turned to politics. Young Chicanos and Chicanas and the more conservative mainline politicians were keenly aware of the poverty among Mexicans and of racial discrimination they faced. One of the oldest political groups, the League of United Latin American Citizens, organized in Texas in the 1920s, consisted of second-generation, middle-class Mexican Americans, not the immigrants. The GI Forum, organized after World War II, did have members who were born in Mexico, but this organization was limited to veterans of World War II and at first concentrated on issues of interest to GIs. LULAC and the GI Forum had assimilationist goals and aimed to integrate Mexicans into American society and to eliminate discrimination. They expanded their agendas after the 1960s in response to the growing needs of the Mexican and Mexican American communities, but neither group had much influence in Washington, D.C.[123] Until the 1980s the only state in which Mexicans had political clout was New Mexico, which had sent Dennis Chavez to the senate in 1933. During the 1960s a few Mexican Americans won election to public office, including Congress. In 1960 Henry Gonzales, the son of immigrants, became the first Mexican American to be elected to Congress from Texas. He moved from local politics to the House of Representatives, eventually serving for thirty-seven years in the House. In Los Angeles, Edward Roybal took a similar route.[124] The vast majority of Mexicans in the 1950s were American born, but their numbers were not large and they were not well organized; many favored President Dwight D. Eisenhower in 1952.

The large-scale migration getting under way in the 1950s changed the political fortunes of Latinos in the United States. The formation of Viva Kennedy clubs during the 1960 election was perhaps the first step in the emergence of Mexicans in national politics. Because the Republican Party had been unresponsive to their needs, the clubs supported the Democrats. These local groups also served to bring Mexican American voters together. Even those who were not yet citizens "could support the fund-raisers, dances, and tamale sales. These people gravitated to those activities that brought Mexicans together."[125] Kennedy ran very well in Mexicano districts, and his election resulted in a few patronage appointments.[126]

By 2000 Hispanics outnumbered blacks in the U.S. population. The Bureau of the Census found in 2000 that Latinos accounted for 35.3 million persons to blacks' 34.7 million.[127] Overtaking black Americans in numbers was one thing, but equaling them as voters is another. By the 1990s, approximately 40 percent of Mexicanos were foreign born, and most had not become American citizens. They were relatively recent immigrants, but with time more would no doubt become naturalized U.S. citizens.[128] In the 1990s a growing number did so. Trying to encourage immigrants to become American citizens, the Clinton administration, under Vice President Al Gore's leadership, began a program called Citizenship USA.

No sooner had Citizenship USA been announced than Congress enacted limits on immigrant noncitizens obtaining public benefits as part of welfare reform in 1996. The legislators also tightened procedures for immigrants to enter the United States and made it easier to deport them. Immigrants drew the obvious conclusion from these actions: it was best to become U.S. citizens. Then Mexico decided to allow Mexicans living in the United States to keep their Mexican citizenship when they naturalized under American laws. As a result of these changes, Mexican immigrants rushed to become U.S. citizens. Felicitas O. Velasquez, a school janitor who had lived in the United States since 1959, said, "I just never thought I really needed it before. But I've heard a lot on the news. Everybody says that maybe now is a good time to become a citizen. If you're not, they're coming after you."[129]

The INS was overwhelmed trying to complete the application process, and its procedures prompted charges that many people had been hastily naturalized. Republicans, who had supported the 1996 laws, were especially alarmed because they believed the Clinton administration was rushing to enroll new Latino voters to support the Democratic Party. These fears became a reality as Mexican Americans and most other Latinos (Cubans are the exception) voted overwhelmingly for Democratic tickets in the 1990s elections.[130] Charges and countercharges forced INS officials to change procedures, but the numbers of people who became citizens in the late 1990s were striking. New citizens numbered only a few hundred thousand annually in the late 1980s but surged to more than 1 million after 1995, including many Mexicans, with a high of 2 million applying three years later.[131] Reformed INS procedures lessened the criticism, and in 1999 applications for naturalization fell to 800,000, while the waiting period for processing applications dropped from two years to nine months.[132] The INS commissioner, Doris Meissner, announced that from 1993 to 2000 nearly 6.9 million immigrants had applied for naturalization, more than in the previous forty years, and she noted that 2.5 million new citizens had been processed in 1999 and 2000.[133]

Beginning in 1992 Congress granted the INS additional funds for naturalization. However, the agency had to switch personnel from processing applications for immigrant visas to naturalization, and as a result, the lines for green cards grew. Per usual, the INS was denounced for the delay in processing visas. Declared one immigrant lawyer, "I'm just sick and tired of seeing the way this affects the lives of the people I represent."[134]

As more Mexicans and other Latinos became citizens with the right to vote, it opened the prospect of their increasing influence on both local and national politics. California's Mexican Americans became such a force during the 1990s, electing many members of their ethnic group to state offices, as well as sending men and women to Congress. California's Cruz Bustamante became the first Latino speaker of the state assembly in 1996; in 1998, he was elected lieutenant governor of California and was the first Latino elected to statewide office since 1878. In 1998, about 20 percent of the state assembly and senate were Mexican Americans, as were five of California's fifty-two congressional representatives.[135] In 2000 the congressional Hispanic Caucus numbered eighteen, which was under half the size of the Black Caucus, even though the number of Latinos was about the same as African Americans.

But there is every indication that Latino representation will increase at the state, federal, and local levels. Mexican Americans are a young population, and a large second generation is reaching voting age with more immigrants becoming citizens. Nationwide, Latinos generally, and not simply Mexican Americans, accounted for only 2.4 percent of the ballots cast in 1976. The figure was 4 percent in 1996 and 7 percent in 2000. Among Hispanics eligible to vote, some 71 percent did so in 2000, compared with the national voter turnout of 51 percent. Except for Cubans, Latino voters tended to favor Democrats, and Mexican Americans were solid in their support of Vice President Al Gore in the disputed 2000 presidential election. George W. Bush did reasonably well in Texas, but there, too, Mexican American voters favored Gore over Bush. Republicans could only hope in the future that the conservative social beliefs of Mexican Americans would bring them into the Republican camp, but the GOP still had an uphill battle in the early days of the twenty-first century.[136] The emergence of Mexican and Latino voters was but one sign of the growing significance of Latino Americans. Given the immigration rates of recent years, that influence would continue to spread throughout American society.

5

Central and South Americans

Although Mexican immigrants have accounted for more than 60 percent of the Latinos who arrived in the United States in the past half century, substantial numbers of Central and South Americans, who established communities in the United States before 1950, have also swelled immigration totals. According to the 2000 census, Latinos, whose numbers increased by nearly 60 percent in the 1990s, passed African Americans as the largest non-European ethnic group. The census counted 35.3 million Hispanics, slightly more than the total for blacks. The striking trend appeared to be continuing in the first years of the twenty-first century. Moreover, many experts have maintained that the Census Bureau undercounted Latinos. Sociologist John Logan, working with census and other data, concluded that Latinos were more numerous than official figures suggested. He said, for example, that New York City's Dominicans totaled 593,777—a figure 186,304 higher than the government's figures. For the city's Colombians, Logan said his results indicate that the government failed to count 36,700 of these nationals.[1] Roberto Suro, head of the Pew Hispanic Center, noted the difficulties of using census questions when counting Hispanics and agreed that many were left uncounted by census takers. Latinos hailed from a variety of cultures and nations in the Western Hemisphere and included the Cuban refugees (who will be discussed in a later chapter). But whatever the exact figures, there is no doubt about the rapid increase in Latinos since 1960 and their growing impact on American society and culture.[2] For half a century Latinos were concentrated in only a few states such as Texas and California, but now they are found in growing numbers in many regions and states.[3] (See Table 2.)

The largest number of Central American Latinos hailed from Nicaragua, El Salvador, and Guatemala, where economic necessity and limited job prospects drove many people north. These individuals were

TABLE 2

Immigration from Selected Central and South American Nations (1991–2001)

Country of Birth	1991	1992	1993	1994	1995	1996	1997	1998	1999	2000	2001
Central America	111,093	57,558	58,162	39,908	31,814	44,289	43,676	35,679	43,216	66,443	75,914
Costa Rica	2,341	1,480	1,368	1,205	1,062	1,504	1,330	1,204	886	1,324	1,744
El Salvador	47,351	26,191	26,818	17,644	11,744	17,903	17,969	14,590	14,606	22,578	31,272
Guatemala	25,527	10,521	11,870	7,389	6,213	8,763	7,785	7,759	7,308	9,970	13,567
Honduras	11,451	6,552	7,306	5,265	5,496	5,870	7,616	6,463	4,809	5,939	6,615
Nicaragua	17,842	8,949	7,086	5,255	4,408	6,903	6,331	3,521	13,389	24,029	19,896
Panama	4,204	2,845	2,679	2,378	2,247	2,560	1,981	1,646	1,646	1,843	1,881
South America	79,934	55,308	53,921	47,377	45,666	61,769	52,877	45,394	41,585	56,074	68,888
Argentina	3,889	3,877	2,824	2,318	1,762	2,456	1,964	1,511	1,393	2,331	3,328
Bolivia	3,006	1,510	1,545	1,404	1,332	1,913	1,734	1,513	1,448	1,772	1,826
Brazil	8,133	4,755	4,604	4,491	4,558	5,891	4,583	4,401	3,902	6,959	9,505
Chile	2,842	1,937	1778	1,640	1,534	1,706	1,443	1,240	1,092	1,712	1,947
Colombia	19,702	13,201	12,819	10,847	10,838	14,283	13,004	11,836	9,966	14,498	16,730
Ecuador	9,958	7,286	7,324	5,906	6,397	8,321	7,780	6,852	8,904	7,685	9,706
Peru	16,237	9,868	10,447	9,177	8,066	12,871	10,853	10,154	8,438	9,613	11,131
Venezuela	2,622	2,340	2,743	2,427	2,627	3,468	3,328	3,136	2,508	4,716	5,205

SOURCE: Immigration and Naturalization Service, Statistical Yearbook, 2001.

relatively poor, with little education, and often had agricultural skills suitable only for the crops of their own land, such as coffee and bananas. Yet another factor compelled many to leave. Beginning in the 1970s and continuing into the 1990s, their nations experienced prolonged and severe violence. The conditions varied somewhat, but civil wars prompted many of the immigrants to try to win asylum or refugee status. To be sure, some other Central and South Americans applied for asylum, too, but for Nicaraguans, Guatemalans, and Salvadorans the struggle to remain in the

United States took years and left many uncertain about their status as the twentieth century ended.

Nicaraguans began to immigrate to the United States as early as the 1930s and 1940s. These exiles were escaping political oppression by Anastasio Somoza Garcia and his family's dictatorship. Washington supported the Somoza regime and even trained some of its military in the United States. Nicaraguans settled in New York, New Orleans, San Francisco, and Los Angeles. Mostly professionals, labor leaders, intellectuals, and political dissenters, some returned to Nicaragua when the left-wing Sandinistas overthrew the Somoza family in 1979.[4] Before 1979, Somoza family members saw the handwriting on the wall and began to move their assets to the United States even before their fall from power. The dictator Anastasio Somoza Debayle died shortly after fleeing his country. Some of the elite, loyal to the Somozas—the top political officials, businessmen, bankers, and large landowners—followed the Somoza family to Florida when the Sandinista National Liberation Front took power in 1979. Altogether some 15,000 Nicaraguans moved their assets and persons to Florida in the face of their changing circumstances.[5] According to Alejandro Portes and Alex Stepick, they were among "the richest people in Florida." Following them were middle-class exiles, and the two groups created "a visible Nicaraguan presence in Miami."[6]

The administration of Jimmy Carter (1977–81) adopted a hands-off policy to events in Nicaragua, but Ronald Reagan decided to aid the Contras, a counterrevolutionary group attacking the Sandinistas. Based in neighboring Honduras and Costa Rica, the Contras operated against Nicaragua with military strikes. The subsequent U.S.-backed violence sent thousands of Nicaraguans—mostly working-class or peasant—fleeing to neighboring countries. As conditions deteriorated at home, thousands traveled to Mexico and eventually entered the United States illegally. Most drifted to Florida and especially Miami, where prior waves of Cubans had created a Spanish flavor. It was claimed the latest migrants numbered 70,000 by 1987 and were the fastest-growing Hispanic group in Florida.[7] So great was the attraction of the Miami region that the 2000 census reported that Cubans, who once made up 90 percent of the Latino population, were scarcely a majority of that group. The government counted 129,000 Central Americans in the region along with 154,000 South Americans, 38,000 Mexicans, and 36,000 Dominicans.[8] Two other Nicaraguan centers were in the New York–New Jersey area and the Los Angeles area.[9]

Gaining legal status was a problem for Nicaraguans. Prior to 1980, refugee status and asylum were granted for those opposing communism, but the Refugee Act of 1980 used a more broadly defined standard for asylum: one needed to have a well-founded fear of persecution because of national origin or membership in a particular group, religion, race. Asylum was granted on an individual basis only for those who could prove their fear was based on concrete evidence, such as demonstrating that they were the target of someone's death squad. These claims for asylum created a problem for the Reagan administration. Its policy, which was later supported by President George H. W. Bush, was to encourage immigrants to go home and join in the fight against the Sandinistas. The Republicans in Washington concentrated on aiding the Contras and winning the civil war in Nicaragua, not on assisting refugees entering the United States. President Reagan insisted that if communism gained a foothold in Central America, the United States would experience a large wave of migrants—"feet people"—seeking refuge. The position of the Immigration and Naturalization Service was little different, and the INS denied the vast majority of the requests. Of the 15,856 Nicaraguans who requested asylum between 1983 and 1986, only 14 percent won it.[10]

In 1986, however, the INS signaled a shift in policy. Perry Rivkind, the INS's Miami director, indicated that he believed undocumented Nicaraguan immigrants should be granted asylum. He noted that it was inconsistent for the U.S. government to try to overthrow a left-wing regime in Nicaragua and at the same time refuse to grant refugee status to those fleeing that regime. Moreover, Miami judge James Lawrence King halted the deportation of those in Florida, Georgia, and Alabama and gave a similar reason for his decision. A flood of undocumented Nicaraguans then asked for asylum, and the approval rate increased to 50 percent. In the face of pressure generated by this ruling and anticommunists in Congress, the Reagan administration partially switched policy and permitted Nicaraguans to remain in the United States. They could even obtain work permits, pay taxes, and not be deported. However, they were not given green cards; only a few thousand received the coveted visas. Nor were they able to receive refugee benefits. The administration did not wish to open the door for a mass exodus from Nicaragua to the United States, and it believed that granting green cards to a few would trigger a flood of requests.[11]

One additional problem with asylum was time. When Congress passed the Refugee Act of 1980, asylum requests and cases were not expected to number much more than 5,000 annually. But as large numbers of Central Americans and others began to apply for asylum, the backlog grew, reaching several hundred thousand by the 1990s; gaining asylum became a time-consuming process. It seemed as if new crises in the world prompted a movement to the United States, with new migrants requesting political asylum.

A resolution for many Nicaraguans occurred in 1986 when Congress passed the Immigration Reform and Control Act (IRCA), which gave undocumented aliens who had been in the United States before 1982 the right to become immigrants; many Nicaraguans did so. However, those arriving after the IRCA was passed were still in limbo: allowed to stay but not necessarily permitted to obtain green cards. Many hoped that they would be given refuge in the United States, and in 1988 and early 1989 thousands of refugees crossed into Texas and were taken by bus to Florida. Not all Miamians were happy with the INS and courts deciding to give asylum, for it appeared that a new wave of Latin Americans would engulf the city. In the face of increased migration and a flood of applications for asylum from Nicaragua in 1989, the INS reverted to its tough position on asylum. Agents along the Texas border effectively blocked the number arriving illegally, and as a result attempted entrants dropped considerably.[12]

Events in Nicaragua changed the situation once more when the Sandinistas called for free elections, which they lost.[13] With the Sandinistas out of power in the 1990s, it was no longer possible to claim a "well-founded fear" of escaping persecution by a left-wing government. Of course those who had green cards or who were U.S. citizens could use the regular preference system to sponsor immigrants, and many did so. The 2000 census reported that 177,684 Nicaraguans lived in the United States. Most had been admitted as immigrants between 1966 and 1996 and had used the family preferences to migrate.[14] Many more had come illegally. In 1997 congressional supporters of Nicaraguans, and indeed of all Central Americans, joined with those wanting a resolution of the situation and passed the Nicaraguan Adjustment and Central American Relief Act, which gave most Nicaraguans already in the United States the right to apply for a green card. The law placed Nicaraguans nearly on a par with Cubans.[15] For the next few years a growing number of Nicaraguans were admitted to the United States as immigrants. In 1997 Nicaragua sent 6,331 immigrants to America, followed by 13,389 in 1999, and 24,029 in 2000. The numbers dropped to 19,896 the next year. Officials believe that still more came illegally.[16]

By far the largest number of Nicaraguans settled in Miami. Portes and Stepick estimated in 1993 that as many as 100,000 Nicaraguans lived in the Miami area, and more arrived after that time. Most were working-class migrants who began to enter after the elite and middle-class exodus in the mid-1980s.[17]

The elite and middle classes faired better than the working class. A few bought and ran restaurants, ventured into banking, or sold real estate; by 1993 Nicaraguan immigrants operated 300 business in Miami.[18] Whereas the first groups were able to find employment, those arriving in the late 1980s had more difficulty in securing jobs. Some worked off the books doing manual labor or working in factories, or taking whatever jobs were available, including becoming flower vendors. Like Mexicans, many Nicaraguan men stood on street corners looking for day labor. An estimated 50 percent of the Nicaraguan men in Miami worked as labor-ers. Nicaraguan women sewed garments at home and replaced Cubans who were moving out of the garment shops. And a few followed Haitians and worked in Florida agriculture. The most successful men became con-struction workers and even became "the preferred workers in the Miami building trades."[19] But whatever they did, Nicaraguans as a group were not as welcome or successful as Cubans.

To some extent Nicaraguans worked with Cubans on political and eco-nomic issues, but clearly their needs were different. Washington was gen-erous with Cubans but not with Nicaraguans until their status was partly resolved in 1997. The new policy covered those who had arrived before that date, but those coming after were not eligible for refugee benefits.

Initially the Cuban community welcomed anticommunist Nicara-guans. Cuban doctors and other community leaders donated their service to this latest group of refugees, including giving food and providing med-ical care. As Cuban Ignacioi Martinez said, "We had our time of need, and now it's their turn."[20] Politically Cubans joined with Nicaraguans in raising funds in support of the Contras. The two groups also created the Central America Pro-Refugee Commission, which aimed to help settle refugees and support the Contras. But with the Sandinistas' fall from power that tie was gone. Moreover, just because many Nicaraguans were anticommunist and spoke Spanish did not guarantee them a favored spot in the city's economic life. For employers, the arrival of many unskilled laborers was a boon for the building industry; but some of the city's citi-zens thought that the newcomers would become a burden. Miami's black population considered assistance given to these Latinos unfair when there were so many needs in the black community. Tensions in the city resulted in several riots with strong ethnic and racial overtones.[21]

Like Nicaraguans, both Salvadorans and Guatemalans experienced a struggle winning refugee status, asylum, and green cards. In 1954 a coup backed by the Central Intelligence Agency (CIA) overthrew the Guatemalan government of Jacobo Arbenz Guzman, who had assumed power in a democratic election three years earlier. Arbenz confronted a society in which most farmers were landless and firms like the United Fruit Company had a favored position: 2 percent of the landholders owned nearly three-quarters of the country's land. The reformer Arbenz appeared too radical and too close to communism for the Eisenhower administration in Washington; hence it used the CIA to overthrow his regime and place in power one headed by Colonel Carlos Castillo Armas. Arbenz fled, but many of his supporters were arrested, and plans for land reform were scrapped.[22]

Conditions deteriorated after the Castillo coup, and a migration to the United States began. Driven largely by poverty, poor health, and a huge inequality in income and land distribution, landless Guatemalan peasants headed for the United States. They were joined by students, victims of political repression, and unemployed workers.[23] In the 1960s guerrillas emerged, determined to overthrow the government, which was supported by American funds and Special Forces personnel. As a result, Guatemala became engulfed in a violent civil war that lasted until the early 1990s. Two authorities remarked, "Central America in the 1980s was one of the most violent, politically unstable regions in the world."[24] Right-wing government forces caught and executed thousands of citizens suspected of supporting the guerrillas. Moreover, many Guatemalans who did not take sides in the conflict were caught in the violent war. As many as 200,000 were killed, and thousands more disappeared. At least 150,000 fled to Mexico for asylum, but they strained resources there.[25] Not satisfied with their prospects in Mexico or the possibility of returning home, thousands trekked through Mexico to the southern border of the United States, where they joined others seeking to enter illegally. During the 1980s Guatemalans averaged about 5,000 legal immigrants entering the United States each year, but an unknown number of undocumented Guatemalans migrated as well. Most experts believe that after 1980 undocumented immigrants outnumbered those coming as resident aliens by a considerable number.[26]

Trying to cross Mexico to enter the United States was no easy task. First there was the 2,000-mile trip from Central America through Mexico itself. Then there was the Rio Grande to cross and fences to climb along the United States–Mexico border. Because the immigrants had little knowledge about crossing, they turned to coyotes, who charged several hundred dollars, an amount that few displaced Central Americans could afford. Moreover, there were hotel bills and meals required along the journey, plus fees paid to corrupt Mexican officials. Money was usually obtained by the remittances of those who had gone before. Along the border loomed the possibility of robbery and, for women, rape by bandits. Even then the trip might end with the INS halting migrants and deporting them. Despite all this, many took the chance of going to America because, as one said, "It's the American dream. Up there, everything works itself out."[27]

Many Guatemalans intercepted by the INS were sent back, but aliens not caught until they were beyond the border applied for asylum. The INS insisted that they were coming for economic and not political reasons, and it rejected the vast majority of claims—more than 90 percent.[28] It was simply not enough to have a fear of being caught in the middle of the violence at home, according to the INS. Critics, of course, insisted that the INS's standard was much too rigid.

In the 1990s individual women from Central America began to request asylum on the grounds that they were subject to abuse by their husbands. Rodi Alvarado Pena, a Guatemalan woman, made such a claim in December 1999. Through her attorney she argued that she was threatened with violence and physically assaulted. Prior to that decision, some women had been granted asylum, such as a Haitian woman who had been gang-raped.[29] Pena was one of a number of women from countries around the world to make the case that she was a member of a group threatened with violence and therefore deserved asylum. While the INS agreed that Pena was subject to abuse and even violence, the U.S. Board of Immigration Appeals declared that she was not covered by asylum law. However, in December 2000, Janet Reno, the outgoing U.S. attorney general, voided the denial of asylum. In response to Pena's case and those of other women, the INS drafted new regulations about asylum and wife abuse, but officials did not expect a large number of such cases.[30]

Economic conditions in El Salvador were little different, and a violent civil war erupted there in the 1970s and lasted for twenty years. Commenting on the Salvadorans, anthropologist Sarah Mahler noted that the "brutality of the civil war . . . left some seventy thousand dead—one of every one hundred citizens." The violence had become a daily reality for many, especially in the rural areas.[31] Moreover, many of those fleeing the violence found that Mexico was not pleased to find another refugee population at its doorstep.[32] Members of prominent families fled first. These well-educated Salvadorans were professionals, financial executives, and owners of businesses and real estate. They did not experience the same trauma as the lower and middle classes who followed them.[33]

Some Central Americans who entered illegally before 1982 were permitted to become resident aliens under the IRCA's provisions, and once legalized, they could sponsor others. Between 1989 and 1991, Guatemalan immigrants numbered 65,000, when the IRCA amnesty migrants began to regularize their status, but many other illegals entered after the cutoff date of 1982 and thus could not become legal immigrants.[34] The violence in Central America continued well beyond that date and left those who wished to avoid the bloodshed of their homeland little choice but to stay in the United States illegally. Several churches gave refugees sanctuary during the 1980s, but the number was small, and the federal government put an end to this practice. More important was the action of church groups in taking the federal government to court. In *American Baptist Churches v. Thornburgh,* Guatemalan supporters forced the INS to admit it had improperly denied asylum requests from more than 100,000 Central Americans and agreed to hear their cases again. The subsequent settlement reached in 1991 gave asylum seekers special rules for rehearing their claims.[35] Central American applications for asylum surged under the provisions of this case, only to drop a few years later.[36]

For those not gaining legal residency but living well beyond the border, the prospect of being deported was a daily reality. However, undocumented aliens were usually not bothered by the government because the INS concentrated its efforts on deporting criminals and halting undocumented aliens at the border dividing the United States and Mexico. Moreover, Central Americans did win a stay of deportation when they were given temporary protected status (TPS) as provided in the 1990 immigration act. More than 200,000 applied for TPS, but immigrant advocates believed that about half a million Salvadorans were eligible. In 1999 the INS commissioner Doris Meissner announced that henceforth the INS would not deport the approximately 240,000 Salvadorans and Guatemalans who had fled from repressive regimes and civil war violence while their applications for asylum or immigrant status were being processed.[37] Even though TPS was extended again by President George W. Bush in 2002, these Central Americans received only temporary relief, and it covered only those who had entered before March 2001.[38]

While hailing these moves, the Hispanic Caucus in Congress and other Latino organizations, supported by liberal Democratic groups, worked to permit these aliens to become permanent resident aliens and have the same privileges awarded to Cubans and Nicaraguans and not have to seek asylum on a case-by-case basis. The opportunities granted to Cubans and Nicaraguans with passage of the Nicaraguan Adjustment and Central American Relief Act of 1997 only prompted Guatemalans and Salvadorans to push harder to legalize their status. Regulations issued by the INS in 1999 helped some but by no means ended the crisis. These new rules covered only one-third of the illegal Central Americans.[39] The results of the new regulations gave a number of Central Americans asylum, although the backlog of claims was still more than 300,000 in 2001.[40]

Another possibility for undocumented aliens was to marry an American citizen or a resident alien and thus become eligible for admission on the basis of family unification. But this was still an individual matter, and the waiting period for family members often stretched into months and years. As a result, immigrant advocates, led by the Hispanic Caucus in Congress, urged that all Salvadorans and Guatemalans be considered refugees just as Cubans were. Liberals denounced Republicans, saying that they were willing to accept those fleeing left-wing nations such as Cuba and Nicaragua, but not Haitians, Salvadorans, and Guatemalans who escaped right-wing dictatorships. The support of President Bill Clinton helped, but in the Republican-dominated Congress the Hispanic Caucus faced an uphill battle. Finally, a compromise accepted by Congress and President Clinton led to a new law. The Legal Immigrant Family Equity Act (LIFE), as passed in 2000, gave undocumented immigrants the right to apply for an immigrant visa, provided they had entered before 1982 and lived in the United States since that time and, for one reason or another, had been unable to be included in the IRCA amnesty.[41] These were individuals who had been rejected by the INS or were afraid to apply for fear of rejection. The exact number of those who missed the IRCA's deadlines was not known. In addition, LIFE permitted undocumented aliens who were married to American citizens or resident aliens to apply for immigrant status without returning to their homes. Because they had a limited time in which to apply, this particular provision created a rush to city halls for marriage licenses between undocumented and documented aliens (and U.S. citizens).[42]

LIFE also permitted family members of immigrants who were awaiting a visa to live in the United States. If they were already on American soil, they would not have to return home while their applications were being processed. The legislation also allowed undocumented aliens who had worked for a period of years in the United States (between 1994 and 1998) and who were waiting for a visa to remain in the United States.[43] Finally, the legislation allowed thousands of illegal aliens to pay a fine and remain in the United States while they awaited their applications to change their status. They would not have to return home and wait there for a period that could run into several years. Obviously working and waiting in the United States was of great benefit compared with returning home.[44] Eligible immigrants had only a few months to apply. The law was complicated to many immigrants, and observers also noted misleading advertising by attorneys who promised more than they could deliver. Although no one was certain about the exact number of persons covered by the LIFE act, estimates ran as high as several hundred thousand.[45]

Most Central Americans were not covered by the LIFE act, and for supporters of Salvadorans, Guatemalans, and Hondurans (along with some Haitians and Liberians) the legislation passed in November 2000 was not a total victory. One immigration attorney said, "People think that there's some amnesty out there. This is not a broad-sweeping reform here. It's really a kind of technical reform."[46] Critics supported an alternative Latino and Immigrant Fairness Act that would permit Central Americans who entered illegally in the 1980s and early 1990s to be able to adjust their status, but Congress and President Clinton would accept only a partial amnesty as granted by LIFE. Representative Louis V. Gutierrez (D-IL) expressed the reformers' views when he said, "I refuse to give up until we win a no-compromise victory" for the immigrants.[47]

Following the passage of LIFE, a devastating earthquake shook El Salvador in January 2001, and Washington decided to suspend deportation of Salvadorans temporarily. Friends of Salvadorans said that the government should grant TPS as well, but federal officials did not agree at first.[48] Finally, President George W. Bush granted Salvadorans TPS in May 2001. It was estimated that 150,000 Salvadorans were covered by the new TPS for a period of up to eighteen months, but 160,000 applied within a few weeks. During their TPS tenure they would be eligible to receive work permits and find legal ways to obtain green cards. El Salvador sent 22,578 immigrants to the United States in 2000 and more than 30,000 in 2001.[49] TPS was quite common, and Salvadorans joined people from nine countries who enjoyed TPS at that time.[50] Other nations that had received that status at one time or another were Angola, Burundi, Honduras, Liberia, Montserrat, Nicaragua, Sierra Leone, Somalia, and Sudan.[51] It is understandable that many people from these nations did not want to return home and face economic upheaval and violence.

At the same time, it should be noted that while being on TPS one might fulfill the provisions of the immigration laws (such as marrying an American citizen or a resident alien) and receive permanent status as an immigrant. It has become common in the last few decades for persons to receive their green cards while already in the United States; indeed, in recent decades a majority of persons becoming resident aliens are already living in the United States. In 2001, for example, of 1,064,318 immigrants, nearly two-thirds were already in America when they received their green cards.[52] Others not in the United States at the time of receiving a green card had visited at some time in the past. A new study of immigrants carried out in the late 1990s by well-known scholars found that one in five of new immigrants had at one time resided illegally in the United States.[53]

The issues of asylum and civil war changed during the 1990s as opposing forces in Nicaragua, El Salvador, and Guatemala agreed to end their conflicts and hold political elections to create stable governments. Even though the violence ended, the plight of those arriving after LIFE was still unknown. There could be little doubt that many more immigrants wanted to come to the United States, for economic conditions did not improve in the 1990s. Costa Rica had the highest per capita income and the most stable democracy of the Central American nations and, consequently, little out-migration. But life expectancy for Indians in Guatemala was only forty-eight years, and many communities in El Salvador still lacked safe drinking water. Many persons lived in poverty or only slightly above it in the post–civil war era. Migration to the United States to begin a new life working in order to wire money home was often viewed as the only way for Salvadorans and Guatemalans to survive their grinding poverty. The Pew Hispanic Center and the Inter-American Development Multilateral Investment Fund estimated that remittances to Mexico and Central America totaled $23 billion in 2001, with sharp increases reported in both 2001 and 2002. Most of the payments came from the United States.[54]

The undocumented status of so many Central American immigrants was only one of several characteristics that these Latinos shared with Mexican immigrants. Members of both groups also worked off the books or in the shadow economy and earned relatively low wages. Just as Mexicans followed the "chicken trail," so did many Central Americans. Mexicans dominated the agricultural jobs in California, but Central Americans also found employment in agriculture. As in the Mexican exodus, women constitute the majority of documented Central American immigrants in recent years. However, studies of undocumented Central Americans indicate that they were more apt to be single males, usually of working age. If they were married, their families were often left behind and lived on the money sent from the North. Women among them labored as housecleaners and were also expected to keep house and manage their families.[55]

Salvadorans journeyed as far north as New York's Long Island, where the women mainly cleaned houses and the men cared for lawns, washed dishes in restaurants, and performed unskilled construction work as day laborers.[56] As Frank P. Petrone, town supervisor of Huntington, New York, noted, "If we didn't have this population, the dishes and silverware in our diners probably wouldn't be clean."[57] Some also worked in Long Island agriculture, but the men usually found higher wages in landscaping. Other towns reported similar situations. In 1999 immigrant advocates estimated that more than 100,000 Salvadorans lived on Long Island, along with many Mexicans, Hondurans, and Guatemalans. Earning the minimum wage or perhaps slightly more proved to be a trial because of the high cost of housing in these suburbs. The chief economist for the Long Island Association put it, "They've found it almost impossible to find anything but substandard housing. So they're doubling, tripling, quadrupling. And therefore you have disasters."[58]

Sarah Mahler's study of Salvadorans on Long Island reinforced the picture painted by journalists. She found the Salvadoran community on Long Island living "on the margins." The group she studied was primarily male and undocumented. Some of the men were married, but they had left their families behind and supported them by sending money home. This was no easy task, for their wages were low. They arrived, she said, with great hopes for a better life but found the reality quite different.[59]

Central Americans were not limited to the suburbs of Long Island. Many, like Mexicans, settled in California, where their largest number was found. According to the 1990 and 2000 censuses, more than 50 percent of Salvadorans and Guatemalans lived in California.[60] There they resembled the demographic profile of those in Long Island and other suburbs. Los Angeles's Salvadorans were a predominantly immigrant population, with 80 percent being foreign born, the same distribution as Guatemalans. Central Americans' median incomes were considerably less than the Los Angeles average. A minority had completed high school, and only 3 to 4 percent were college graduates, compared with a national figure of 25 percent. One study of Los Angeles revealed that in spite of the high labor force participation (in low-paying jobs) of Central Americans in the 1990s, one-quarter lived below the poverty line.[61] At that time only 11.2 percent of native-born Americans were living below the poverty line.[62]

Next to Los Angeles, the largest settlement of Salvadorans and Guatemalans is in the Washington, D.C., area. Because so many are undocumented aliens, exact figures are unknown. Some experts believed that Salvadorans numbered 45,000 and Guatemalans 5,000 in the mid-1990s. The *Washington Post* used a higher figure in 1999, estimating that 80,000 Salvadorans lived in the city itself, with another 100,000 in the surrounding areas.[63] The Latino migration to Washington began just after World War II, when Latin American embassies proliferated and gave diplomats a taste for American life; a few of these diplomats then stayed in the United States. As the nation's capital underwent a huge expansion, it created a need for workers to help build the large number of houses and office buildings being put up in the city and the surrounding suburbs. Typically after the first migrants settled, they helped to bring in their kin. For example, from Chirilagua in El Salvador, the Zambrano family began to migrate to Washington in the late 1970s and found jobs in the growing suburbs, which needed construction workers. The first Zambrano came "to follow a friend, who had followed a brother, who had married a woman whose sister may have been working in Washington's diplomatic community." Nineteen-year-old Edith Zambrano arrived in the summer of 1983 and made burritos in a restaurant and cleaned offices at night. Her classmates from the El Salvador town of Chirilagua came one "by one, that summer and the next. . . . First were Alex and Hector, then Sandra and Cristina and Luis. Her cousins followed . . . and every Sunday she bumped into someone else from home."[64] By the late 1990s some 5,000 migrants from the village of Chirilagua alone lived in the Washington area, and by then they had established a familiar community.[65] The Zambranos' story could be repeated by others. Rosa Lopez began her family's trek to the nation's capital that eventually drew more than thirty-five other family members.[66]

The migration to Washington was often spearheaded by women, who found ready employment performing child care and house and office cleaning. Terry Repak noted about those sampled in Washington, "The most striking feature about Central American women's work profiles is that almost all of the women interviewed in Washington entered the labor market as domestic workers, no matter how high their education level."[67] Men were more apt to work in construction and restaurants, where their wages were higher.[68] Some of the women came to Washington to make money to send back home to support their families, but single women migrated, too, because housework was nearly always available. Although service jobs were hardly ideal, they were considerably better than in civil war–torn El Salvador.[69] Washington's Salvadoran women had a higher rate of participation in the paid labor force than Mexican women: 80 percent compared with only half.[70] Working for pay, whether as single mothers or as married partners, gave Salvadoran women a higher status and greater say in family matters.[71]

Other Salvadoran communities were scattered throughout Texas and Florida and even in Waldwick, New Jersey.[72] The New Jersey community, like many others, was relatively small, numbering only 100 families in 2000. Palisades Park, also in New Jersey, witnessed an influx of Guatemalans and Salvadorans beginning in the late 1980s. There, too, some stood on street corners waiting for casual labor jobs.[73]

Most of the Salvadorans found employment similar to those on Long Island and in Washington, D.C., and Los Angeles. In San Francisco, for example, married women usually worked in the paid labor market but, like their husbands, found only low-paying positions, often cleaning other people's houses. For some women California's garment industry provided employment, but these too were poorly paid jobs. One study found that 62 percent of the Salvadoran women and 80 percent of the men were in the paid workforce; both figures were above the national average for all men and women. When the economy slumped in the early 1990s in California, it was not so easy to find even these lower-paid jobs. The state's economy improved in the mid-1990s only to experience another recession in 2001.[74]

The pattern of migration and work was little different for Spanish-speaking Guatemalans, who were mostly peasants with little education or knowledge of the English language. Like Salvadorans they often escaped the violence of their homeland by fleeing to neighboring countries. Finding unsatisfactory conditions and a cool reception in Mexico, many crossed into the United States as undocumented immigrants, mostly to live in California, Texas, and Florida, and even in small communities along the "chicken trail."

Guatemalans located in particular communities because of the social networks developed by those who had arrived earlier. San Francisco's trade with Latin America had developed before World War II; thus postwar Central Americans who settled there entered an already established community.[75] In 1987 a Delaware family hired a Guatemalan field worker, Albertino Lopez; when he could not find housing, his employers purchased a home and rented it to him. In no time at all Lopez's house was filled with his relatives, who came to work for Perdue Farms, the main industry in Georgetown, Delaware. Both Guatemalan men and women found employment in the poultry plants. After 1995 the Guatemalan population increased rapidly as news of the expansion of the poultry business spread to Central America and Mexico. Within a few years Georgetown had experienced a demographic shift and more than a third of its residents were Latinos. While the change was under way, the couple who had hired Lopez bought other houses and rented them to new Guatemalan migrants. Guatemalans who managed to buy their own homes rented rooms to other Guatemalans. Soon the newcomers developed a community, supporting Catholic churches in the area and creating their own social networks and institutions. Needless to say, such a rapid influx alarmed many of the older non-Hispanic residents, who tried to halt the influx by the use of zoning codes. Others, however, moved beyond fear of the newcomers and worked for common goals in the schools and in community life.[76]

News of El Norte was carried to Central Americans by letter, telephone, and even personal visits. A study of Salvadorans in San Francisco revealed that 80 percent had received help from U.S. relatives and friends in the migratory process.[77] In 2000 the Miami airport reported that each Christmas season tens of thousands of Central Americans headed for home, taking along presents. Baggage handlers were overwhelmed by the numbers heading south, and one even reported that roosters were included among the homeland-bound treasure.[78] These trips brought valued items and news of immigrants' work and life in the United States. Information about the land to the north also came in the form of remittances. Such cash was just as important to Central American villages as it was to Mexican ones; the Central Bank of El Salvador estimated that $1.6 billion flowed annually from the United States to that country. In Intipuca, El Salvador, one reporter noted that the Western Union building was huge and active, carrying a sign that read in both English and Spanish "Welcome to Intipuca City." Similar stories could be told of other towns in Guatemala where remittances became the largest source of income.[79] In the late 1990s the Guatemalan finance minister estimated annual remittances to Guatemala to be $450 million.[80]

Honduras did not experience a violent civil war in the style of Nicaragua, El Salvador, and Guatemala, but it did share their poverty and harsh living conditions. As a result, a number of Hondurans headed north after the 1960s in search of higher wages and a better life. If they could not satisfy the requirements of immigration statutes and regulations, they joined Mexicans and other Central Americans crossing the Rio Grande and entered the United States illegally. How many did so is not known, but some officials estimate that undocumented Hondurans numbered over 100,000 in the late 1990s, only about one-third of the El Salvadoran total.[81] With smaller numbers and lacking a prolonged civil war, Hondurans found that their plight was not nearly as visible as that of the Nicaraguans, Salvadorans, and Guatemalans.

When it came to patterns of settlement and demographic profiles, Hondurans resembled other Central Americans. They settled in some of the same places and performed similar work. Houston, Chicago, the Florida farm belt, Washington, D.C., and Los Angeles were the main centers of Honduran life.

The plight of Hondurans only came to national attention when Hurricane Mitch ripped through Central America in 1998. Honduras suffered more damage than any other country, although many Nicaraguans found themselves homeless, too. International aid helped Hondurans to begin the process of rebuilding their lives, but others decided that the situation was hopeless; they reasoned that the future lay in the United States. The INS did not consider them to be refugees, even though their land had been devastated. In response to the Honduran exodus, Janet Reno, the U.S. attorney general, granted TPS to those arriving before late December 1998. Former INS commissioner Meissner remarked, "We are watching it very closely, and we want to do everything we can to avert a mass migration."[82] TPS was extended until 2001. Hondurans and the Honduran government wanted it extended again, and the administration of George W. Bush compiled. In May 2003 the U.S. Bureau of Citizenship and Immigration Services (the new name for INS under reorganization carried out in the creation of the new Department of Homeland Security) allowed those Hondurans fleeing the hurricane to remain in the United States until January 2005. An estimated 85,000 Hondurans were covered by the new TPS, along with a few thousand Nicaraguans.[83] Yet it was not American officials alone who deterred the exodus, for if those seeking refuge needed a coyote to guide them in crossing the border, they had to come up with cash for the smuggler, and several thousand dollars was a huge amount of money for a poor immigrant.

For Hondurans who saw their villages and homes destroyed by Hurricane Mitch, there was no turning back. "The hurricane left me in the street," said Joel Ramos Cruz. "The river took all our cattle. Now there is only the land. The floods wiped out everything."[84] Another put it, "I am past the years where I want adventures. I am doing this [coming north] because I have no options. In Honduras I had no way to make money. I had no house. I had no transportation. And I had no food for my family. In the United States if they pay me three dollars an hour, it will be fine by me."[85]

Central Americans, in traditional immigrant style, organized their communities. The Catholic Church was one institution in the United States that was familiar to these migrants, although some turned to evangelical Protestant churches. The struggle for winning refugee and immigrant status drew some Central Americans together, and they worked with immigrant rights groups and formed mutual aid societies. Yet because so many were undocumented, Central Americans were reluctant to engage in public life.[86]

To speak of all immigrants from Central America and Mexico as "Latinos" or "Hispanics" is misleading at best and clearly wrong in some cases. Even labels like "Mexican" can obscure important ethnic, cultural, and linguistic differences within nationality groups. In southern California, for example, Mixtec Indians from the southern Mexican state of Oaxaca have migrated to work in the agricultural fields. A survey completed in 1993 found that 40 percent of the migratory laborers in southern California were Indians, whose culture was different from that of many Mexicans and whose primary language was not Spanish. Rather, they spoke one of twelve different Indian languages. Moreover, Mexican Indians were not found simply in southern California but ranged as far as Oregon's apple orchards. They originally began to cross the border in the 1980s, and although exact figures are not known, some experts believed that in 1995 Indians numbered 50,000 of California's 800,000 agricultural workers. One grower declared, "Before, I used to just have Mexicans here. Then, slowly, it changed and now just about all of them are from Oaxaca. . . . [You] hear them talking and you realize, that's not Mexican [Spanish] they're speaking."[87] These Indians were replacing other Mexican agricultural laborers who were less willing to work at such low-paying jobs. Like previous Mexican laborers, they developed migratory and support systems to find jobs and housing for the newcomers.[88] For the first time the 1990 census provided an entry for "Latin American Indians." While the numbers were not large, an estimated 35,000 to 40,000 Latin American Indians (mostly Maya) entered during the 1990s.[89]

Indian immigrants were not solely from Mexico. From Central America and especially Guatemala, Mayan Indians were most prominent. They migrated for the same reasons as others: to escape poor living conditions and the violence of the civil wars that racked Central America during the 1970s and 1980s. If they could not obtain green cards, and few could, they joined Mexicans and other Central Americans in trying to cross the U.S.-Mexican border illegally. Journalist Roberto Suro reported that Juan L. Chanax left the Guatemalan Highlands of Totonicapan in September 1978 and ended up in Houston. There he found a job "mopping a supermarket floor. He was not alone for long. His hometown, San Cristobal, and the villages that surround it had a population of about four thousand people when he left. Within fifteen years, some two thousand of them had joined him in Texas."[90] His relatives were the first to follow, and then his friends. These Mayan immigrants performed unskilled work and gradually improved their lot.

Like most Central American and Mexican immigrants, the Maya were Roman Catholic. However, Leon Fink noted about the Maya and other Latinos of Morganton, North Carolina, that by 2000 they could attend five Spanish-speaking non-Catholic churches. The five congregations included "one Assembly of God, two Church of God (including one primarily Aguacateco, the other K'iche), one Pentecostal Independent, and one Baptist congregation."[91] They also had their own informal networks that held the community together.[92]

Another Mayan community developed in Indiantown, Florida, in an agricultural area on the edge of Lake Okeechobee. Like the Maya of Houston and other Central Americans, the Maya of Indiantown had fled violence in their home communities.[93] Using the Mayan networks, the newcomers found housing and jobs, with many working in agriculture.[94] Several thousand Maya also inhabited other towns in the Florida agricultural belt. Still others lived as far north as North Carolina.[95] In Morganton, North Carolina, Maya were drawn by the Case Farms poultry plant. In this highly competitive industry, the company tried to reduce costs, and with the possibility of hiring Central American Maya, it found the solution to its need for laborers. In 1989 the company began to hire persons from Guatemala. As in other poultry plants, the work was dangerous and provided low wages. Indeed, the working conditions were so poor that the Maya organized a union to improve their lives.[96]

James Loucky also found a Mayan community in Los Angeles, which by the 1980s had grown to several thousand. Here, too, immigrants followed routes and networks that had been established during the 1970s by a small number of Q'anjob'al, mostly from the town of San Miguel Actan.[97]

By the late 1990s women outnumbered men from Guatemala, probably the largest source for Maya. In 2001, a total of 4,787 men entered compared with 5,176 women. These, of course, are the official immigration figures.[98] Allan Burns's study of Maya in Florida turned up a majority of males (72 percent).[99] Typically Mayan men went first, sent remittances home to aid their families and communities, and provided funds to assist others in coming. The population of Indiantown increased substantially during the peak migratory labor season of October to May, when workers were needed for picking citrus fruits and vegetables. Not knowing English or even much Spanish and being undocumented left them at the mercy of employers. Even though men were the majority in Indiantown, Mayan women worked in the fields, too. But by no means were all Maya employed as agricultural workers. In the early 1990s the more successful ones found jobs in construction, landscaping, and the retail trades.[100]

A scandal of major proportions engulfed Central Americans, mostly Indians, in Immokalee, along the western coast of Florida. There immigrants had been recruited to work as agricultural laborers. Some found themselves indebted to the coyotes who had brought them across the southern border of the United States and found jobs picking crops. Some of the unfortunate immigrants were held in virtual slavery to the labor bosses. The federal government eventually prosecuted some successfully, including the foremen who had exploited them. But the worst incidents of slavery were reserved for young women, fourteen and fifteen years of age, who found themselves working in brothels. The women were required to perform "between fifteen and twenty-five sexual acts per day."[101]

In addition to field wage work, Mayan women in Indiantown and Houston were busy running households. The average household among the Maya in Florida was large, between nine and fourteen members, some of whom were boarders. Mayan men and women also discovered that raising children was difficult as the youngsters rapidly learned English and lived under the influence of America's mass culture.[102]

In San Francisco, Mayan women took the lead in migration. Some even had to leave their children behind while they became established. Such was the case with Maria Guiterrez, a Kanjobal woman from Guatemala, who never attended school and knew only a limited amount of Spanish. Her choice of occupation in San Francisco was limited to housecleaning and child care. Guiterrez told a student interviewer, "I don't like being in the United States because I have no family here, and I believe that people in [the] States don't have a sense of morals, traditions or respect for life. But I have to make it here somehow."[103]

Gaining legal status was important for Mayan immigrants, but also difficult. As noted, the IRCA provided a general amnesty for those entering before 1982 and a Special Agricultural Workers (SAW) provision for agricultural workers who had labored in farming during a four-month period in 1985 and 1986. In the case of the Maya, many had worked in agriculture and consequently applied for SAW status. From Guatemala, 225,503 persons received a general IRCA amnesty and 66,132 persons received a SAW amnesty, but how many of them were Maya is not known.[104] But for those arriving illegally after the IRCA's deadlines, it was difficult to win asylum; the INS, as noted, was reluctant to give asylum for those fleeing violence after 1986. Additional undocumented immigrants would be eligible to apply for asylum because of the 2000 law passed by Congress and signed by the president. Maya faced the same difficulties as other Central Americans. Moreover, they faced still another obstacle: simply being understood. Robert Perez applied for asylum and was given a date for a hearing in late 1998. Maya was his language; he spoke very limited Spanish and no English. "I need to be able to tell what happened to me in my own words," he said. Responding to the problem was the Maya Various Interpretation Services and Indigenous Organization Network, which provided thirty translators for the estimated 20,000 Maya in southern California.[105] Yet authorities admitted that finding Mayan translators for asylum applications and judicial procedures was difficult.[106]

A number of these Central American and Mexican Indians resented being called "Hispanic" or "Latino." In Los Angeles they established an organization called the Mexica Movement. "This whole Latin-Hispanic agenda destroys our identity as indigenous people. It's like the Spanish empire lives again," explained Olin Tezcatlipoca, head of the Mexica Movement. Mexicas rejected the label "Latino," claiming that they wanted to learn about their own past cultures. One couple living in Denver refused to allow the hospital to put "Hispanic" on their daughter's birth certificate; the parents pointed out that her name, Citlalmina, was Aztec.[107]

The largest group of Spanish speakers from the Caribbean were Cubans (who will be discussed in chapter 10), followed by Dominicans. While the Dominican Republic did not experience the violence common to Central American countries in the 1980s, it nonetheless had a long history of turmoil. Moreover, Dominicans had direct contact with American power and authority and knew about the United States. In 1916 the United States began an occupation of the Dominican Republic that lasted until 1924. As a result, some degree of "Americanization" began before the large immigration to the United States after 1962. Another brief American occupation in 1965 sided with the conservative forces in the Dominican Republic, and economic conditions did not improve after that. In the 1950s and 1960s the dictator Rafael Leonidas Trujillo (1930–61) had restricted emigration, and only "diplomats and a handful of well-to-do people of unquestioned loyalty to the government were granted visas."[108] Many who did get out during the 1950s were urban, middle-class migrants fearful of Trujillo's repressive regime. When Trujillo was assassinated in 1961 and his dictatorship fell, Dominicans began an exodus to the United States that grew at increasing rates until the late 1990s. It averaged over 25,000 annually in the 1980s and ran slightly higher in the 1990s, hitting a peak of 51,000 in 1994.[109] While some of the migrants were poor rural folk with little education, studies have revealed that many were urban middle-class dwellers.[110] The very poor did not have the resources to move. Regardless of whether they were struggling rural folk, middle-class, or urban, Dominicans had plenty of reasons to emigrate: economic conditions and political life were far from ideal in the Dominican Republic. Attempts to change the economy were only partly successful, and unemployment remained high. Even many professional and technical workers found the prospects for employment bleak, and they, too, began to leave as the gap between wages in the United States and the Dominican Republic grew.[111]

Dominicans had much in common with other newcomers from the Western Hemisphere. Until 1965 the Western Hemisphere had no numerical limits on immigration; hence it was relatively easy to enter the United States. After the new quotas were established for all nations in 1977, Dominicans found it more difficult to immigrate. The majority entered legally after that date, with members of a family or village going first, saving, and sending remittances home to help family members and neighbors survive and also to assist others in migration. But if they could not enter with documents, they came illegally. Unlike Central Americans or Mexicans entering without documents, they had no land barrier to cross. Some did manage to go to Puerto Rico and pass themselves off as Puerto Ricans who, as American citizens, could enter without restrictions. Yet this was no easy task. First they had to cross the perilous passage between the Dominican Republic and Puerto Rico, some ninety miles long. As the INS chief there summarized, they came because "these are desperate people."[112] If they avoided INS officials, they found employment in San Juan and saved money for the trip to the United States. More commonly, however, they came on tourist visas and simply overstayed their visa limits. American officials in the Dominican Republic rejected many of those applying for tourist visas, but it was impossible to determine precisely who would stay and who would return. Moreover, faked documents were plentiful and hard to detect.[113] Family networks provided undocumented and documented immigrants with ready access to jobs and housing.[114]

To talk of Dominican immigration to the United States is to talk of New York City, especially the Washington Heights area of Manhattan, where 60 percent of this rapidly growing group settled. As Roberto Suro described it, "In the 1970s and 1980s they built an enclave as vibrant as any the city had ever produced."[115] There the language of the streets was Spanish, the discourse of shopping was Spanish, and Dominican organizations were everywhere. By 1990 Dominicans were the largest foreign-born group in New York City. As noted earlier, sociologist John Logan suggests that the 2000 census count of 407,473 should have been 593,777.[116]

Some pooled their funds to enable others to open their own businesses such as bodegas, small general stores that offered services beyond selling food; they carried special items and gave customers attention often not found in supermarkets.[117] To some degree bodegas served as social centers as well as stores. Other small Dominican-run businesses catering to the community were beauty shops and businesses offering discount phone services to the Dominican Republic.[118] These ethnic enterprises were capitalized at low levels, employed few people besides the owners, and required long hours of labor. In addition, intense competition existed between the stores. One owner described the plight of bodegas: "Bodegas mean only one thing: *mucho trabajo y poco dinero* [much work and little money]."[119]

In the 1990s fewer than 10 percent of Dominicans ran their own independent businesses, and they had one of the lowest percentages of entrepreneurship of New York ethnic groups.[120] Most have entered low-paid occupations. For women, for example, this was in the garment industry, and if they were lucky, the shop was a union one, which offered better wages and health benefits. Working in the paid economy gave women greater say in their households, and many did not wish to return to the Dominican Republic, where the roles of women were more proscribed than in the United States. For men, jobs in the city's service sector, meeting the needs of the city's professionals, did not require education or a fluent knowledge of English. About 9 percent of Dominicans were employed in professional or managerial positions, a figure only one-third that for non-Hispanic whites and considerably below that for blacks and other Hispanics in the city.[121]

Studies pointed to deteriorating circumstances in the 1990s. In the early 1990s Dominican Americans' per capita income declined more than that of any other group in the city's sluggish economy.[122] Many were recent immigrants who had only limited English-language skills. Their general educational levels were much below the city's and nation's average. Only 4 percent had a college degree, and only 45 percent had graduated from high school. If they were identified as black, they also faced racial discrimination.[123]

Dominicans' low levels of education did not enable them to take full advantage of the city's booming economy of the late 1990s. Both unemployment and welfare use remained high.[124] Especially disturbing was the fact that a growing number of households were headed by women; by 1996, nearly half of all Dominican families had female heads. These households were usually managing on incomes below or just above the poverty line; Dominicans had poverty rates nearly double the city's average.[125] Dominicans in Washington Heights also lived in a dangerous neighborhood, with drug dealers operating virtually in the open. They sometimes labored in dangerous occupations, a fact brought home by the annual murder of several livery cab drivers. Rosario Vargas in San Jose De Las Matas, Dominican Republic, which had sent a number of young men to New York to drive cabs, observed, "I have two teenage sons who want to join my brother Paulo driving livery cabs, but I and a lot of other mothers have put down this rule: Go if you have to, but driving a livery cab is out of the question."[126] Even running bodegas could be risky, for there loomed the possibility of robbery; in 1992 alone forty-seven bodega owners were killed by robbers.[127] Violence against Dominicans was not restricted to the workplace. Repeated conflicts with the police erupted into violence following a police shooting of youths in 1992.[128] Residents were quick to point to overcrowding, unemployment, poverty, crime, and distrust of the police as major problems for Dominicans.[129]

The depressing statistics describing Dominican Americans' living conditions in part reflect the fact that so many newcomers had to start at the bottom when they arrived. Not surprisingly, those with a good education and English-language skills found better jobs.[130] Many Dominican boys played baseball, hoping for a trip to the big leagues and big salaries, the way that other Latinos had achieved the American dream. In the Dominican Republic and Washington Heights, young men played baseball with a passion. But only a very few, including Manny Ramirez and Sammy Sosa, made the leap.[131]

As Dominicans have become citizens in growing numbers, there loomed the possibility of political clout. Several were elected to New York City's local community and school boards. In addition, a redrawing of district boundaries and an enlarged city council resulted in the election of a Dominican to the new council. In 1996 a Dominican was elected to the New York State Assembly.[132] This could lead to better municipal services for Dominican neighborhoods and more jobs in the public sector, where Latinos generally were underrepresented.[133]

After World War II, immigration from South America also grew, but South Americans came in much fewer numbers than did Mexicans, Caribbean peoples, and Asians. Indeed, South American nations were eligible for the lottery created by the 1990 immigration act, which was granted to countries that had low immigration levels to the United States before that time.[134] From the 1950s to the 1990s, South Americans were about equal to Central Americans in immigration totals and in the census, but most experts believe that Central Americans sent considerably more undocumented immigrants to the United States. The INS estimated that in 1996 El Salvador, Guatemala, Honduras, and Nicaragua all had more undocumented immigrants in the United States than Colombia, which topped the estimates for South America.[135] Ecuador and Colombia, along with Guyana, are the leading sources for new immigrants from South America. In 2002 Colombia, with 16,333 immigrants, was in the top twenty of nations sending newcomers to the United States; Guyana and Ecuador were the next two major South American sending nations.[136] It should be kept in mind that while Guyana and Trinidad are culturally West Indian, many immigrants from these nations are ethnic Asian Indian by heritage. They are the descendants of Indian plantation workers recruited in the nineteenth century.

In general immigrants from South America are better educated and have more marketable skills than Central Americans and Mexicans. According to the 2000 census, 79 percent of South Americans had at least a high school education, compared with only 37 percent of Central Americans. South Americans were also much more apt to be college graduates than Central Americans.[137] Not surprisingly, a larger proportion of South Americans had higher rates of persons working as managers or professionals. South Americans also had higher incomes than Central Americans and Mexicans. Those who had naturalized did quite well economically.[138] Twenty-four percent of Central Americans lived in poverty in 2000, but only 11.5 percent of South Americans did, which was about the same percentage as for native-born Americans.[139]

A 1980s study by Adriana Marshall of Argentines, for example, found relatively few poor and unskilled emigrants. Indeed, Argentina remained a labor-importing country for decades after World War II. Those who did migrate were better educated and skilled than the Argentina population. On the whole, Adriana Marshall reported in 1988, Argentines in the United States were better educated than other Latin Americans.[140] Most Argentines entered as regular immigrants, but a few had come as refugees during the political repression there in the 1970s.[141] In addition, an unknown number of Argentines were Jews or third-generation Italian Argentines. European ethnics were often well educated and worked in business. Thus, although they came from the Western Hemisphere and lived in a Spanish-speaking culture, they resembled European immigrants in many ways. Most Jews who left after the 1960s headed for Israel, but some settled in the United States as well.[142]

Nonetheless, economic problems affected nearly all Argentines, especially during the early 1990s, when unemployment combined with high inflation convinced a number of Argentines to leave their homeland. A study reported in 2002 and conducted by Argentina's University of Social and Enterprises Sciences found that nearly one-quarter of Argentines expressed a desire to emigrate. These individuals were usually young (under age thirty-five), with a high school diploma or higher. The preferred destinations were Spain or Italy and, for Jews, Israel, yet a significant number indicated a desire to head north to the United States.[143]

The Argentine government did bring inflation under control briefly, but then the economy deteriorated markedly in the late 1990s. In addition, corruption scandals rocked the government. Looking back, one exile said, "Things are getting worse every day."[144] Thousands of Argentines lined up outside the embassies of Italy and Spain, the home of many of their immigrant ancestors generations ago. The United States, especially southern Florida, the home of so many Latin Americans, also received a new influx. Precise figures are unavailable because many Argentines were undocumented. A "Little Buenos Aires" in Florida hosted Argentine soccer matches and included many ethnic stores. The Argentine press claimed that 100,000 Argentine immigrants lived in Florida alone.[145]

In late 2001 and early 2002, Argentina experienced a new crisis when the country could not make its debt payments. Inflation and unemployment added to the nation's woes and prompted many to think of leaving. Fearing that many visitors would overstay their visas and become undocumented aliens, an alarmed U.S. Justice Department tightened rules for temporary visas. The number migrating on ninety-day visitors' visas dropped, but there is no doubt that many Argentines would find ways to enter the United States, especially as the financial crisis showed no indication of ending in 2002. That crisis was a more important factor than Justice Department rules.[146] During further deterioration of the economy, Argentines continued to settle in Florida. A political activist and journalist in San Francisco claimed that 6,000 additional immigrants had come to that city and the Bay Area. Still others went to New York.[147]

Pockets of South American settlement dotted other cities. Beginning in the 1960s, the Washington, D.C., area, particularly Arlington, Virginia, attracted many Bolivians, who were leaving a deteriorating economy in their homeland. The number of Bolivians arriving in the 1990s was about the same as Argentines—roughly 2,000 annually—though experts believed that the actual number was much greater than the figures reported by the INS. Some officials said as many as 60,000 to 100,000 Bolivians lived in the United States in 2000. These were not necessarily Bolivia's poorest citizens; many were educated, middle-class migrants who believed their futures were limited at home.[148]

New York City's Ecuadorans comprised a cross section of education levels, but as a group, they were not as well educated as Argentines.[149] Particularly if they lacked skills needed for success in the New York market, they scrambled for jobs. Women immigrants, for example, were more apt to work for pay in the United States than in Ecuador; they attended sewing schools and then, with the aid of friends, found employment in the garment industry.[150] A study of Ecuadoran undocumented immigration to New York City during the hard times of the 1980s included well-off migrants and poorer folks from rural areas. As elsewhere, kin ties facilitated the moves, and remittances home were vital for those left behind. The desire to leave also produced a market in forged documents.[151]

More is known about Colombians than about other Spanish-speaking immigrants from South America, in part because their immigration numbers are the highest from that continent. Colombia has sent twice as many immigrants to the United States as the next largest South American sending nation. Colombians have also attracted attention because of their connection to the drug trade and the violence that was often related to drugs. Colombian cartels had a dubious reputation as being the main source of drugs smuggled into the United States.[152]

Economic conditions did prompt many Colombians to leave, including migrants from the working class, the middle class, and even some members of the elite. Yet the economy was closely connected to the political upheavals that racked Colombian society for years. The assassination of Jorge Eliecer Guitan, a popular Liberal Party leader, in 1948 set off a decade of violence and civil war (La Violencia), which destroyed much of the country's agriculture and set in motion an exodus to the cities and the United States.[153] All classes were represented in this migration, but the majority "were people from the lower and lower-middle classes."[154] A truce was finally declared in 1957, but violent conflicts between drug lords seeking to dominate the drug trade once again led to years of violence, with large numbers of better-off Colombians as well as those from the interior cities fleeing. The drug lords were virtually at war with the government.[155] Although the economy did well in the 1970s and 1980s, it began to deteriorate in the late 1990s. The violence also increased. Many innocent people were killed in the streets of Colombia's cities, and no one was safe even in Bogotá. In 1997, 31,000 Colombians were killed.[156] As one advocate of Columbian refugees put it, "There is a greater risk of being kidnapped in Columbia than in any other country of the world."[157]

Even if not subjected to violence, several hundred thousands were displaced by the continued conflicts, and among those without homes, more than 50 percent were unemployed. Most "live in shantytowns surrounding Columbia's largest cities."[158] These unfortunate folks had only limited access to drinking water and health facilities. Moreover, a disproportionate number of those displaced were Afro-Colombians.[159]

The continued intensive violence set off a new wave of immigration to the United States in the late 1990s as left-wing guerrillas battled the army and there were conflicts over control of the drug trade. The Bush administration and Congress approved funds to aid government forces, and in the aftermath of the destruction of the World Trade Center on September, 11, 2001, the federal government increased supervision of those who intended to settle in the United States and provided additional funds for the Columbian government to fight insurgency.[160] In the late 1990s the economy was in its worst shape since the bleak days of the 1930s. In the 1990s, green cards to the United States numbered 15,000 each year on average. If Colombians could not obtain visas, they were willing to come as visitors and then simply stay on illegally (visitors' visas to the United States doubled between 1996 and 2000).[161] Lines outside foreign embassies in Bogotá grew in 1999 as the violence intensified. A number of requests for visitors' visas were rejected by American officials on the grounds that the applicants intended to settle illegally in the United States. Some Colombians hired coyotes to take them to Bimini and the Bahamas and from there by plane to Florida.[162] The INS estimated that 60,000 undocumented Colombians lived in the United States in the mid-1990s.[163] Others used higher figures. Between 1996 and 2000, some Colombian experts estimated that 1 million Colombians left the country, some 200,000 going to the United States. Colombian officials said that as many as 300,000 left in 1999 alone. Other estimates place the figure higher, but precise totals are unavailable because so many of those who left were undocumented. The immigrants tended to be middle-class people, with skills and education, who could afford to get out. But working-class Colombians were also putting together funds to send at least one person north, who would then bring others. Those who chose to stay related horror stories of escalating violence back home. One widow explained, "My husband was killed over a business deal because people can just get away with that sort of thing."[164] An immigration lawyer remarked, "The stories these people tell will make you cringe. I think Colombia is a tragedy waiting to happen."[165]

Some Colombian visitors and immigrants in the United States requested that the attorney general grant them TPS, to last until the situation at home improved. "We are asking," said one leader "for temporary protected status for the thousands of families that have fled here. We think our request is based on merit and compassion."[166] In November 2003, the Department of State announced that it would not grant TPS to Colombians, citing improved conditions in their home and the fact that a number of Colombians had been granted asylum.[167] A growing number had applied, and some had received asylum, but their numbers were not large. In 2001, a total of 5,672 Colombians received asylum, the largest figure for any one country, and the federal government did begin to process Colombian applications for persons temporarily in Ecuador.[168] Colombians faced the task of convincing the U.S. government that they were entitled to asylum on an individual basis, analogous to the Salvadorans and Guatemalans. However, the U.S. government did not appear eager to admit Colombians as regular refugees.

Colombians tended to settle where their countrymen had gone before or in communities with many other Latinos. Thus New York City had a large colony, and in New Jersey cities their presence grew. Los Angeles, where so many Latinos lived, also attracted them. The East Boston community of Colombians grew sharply. Primarily middle-class immigrants could afford to leave, and they used their business skills and education in their new home; one official in East Boston estimated that in 2002, 80 percent of the businesses there were run by Colombians.[169]

It was in southern Florida that the majority of Colombians sought a haven from the violence and economic conditions of their homeland. One university study noted that the elite did well in that part of Florida, with many having enough funds and social contacts to begin their own businesses. Others not so fortunate were the undocumented, who worked in small businesses such as restaurants. Fluency in English was also a problem for many of the newcomers, but one could survive in southern Florida by speaking Spanish alone. Upward mobility, however, was difficult for those who did not know English.[170]

Brazilian immigrants were not numerous, but there was a steady growth of Brazilian immigration after 1980. According to INS figures, from 1966 to 1979, a total of 22,310 individuals from Brazil entered the United States; from 1980 to 1991, the number increased to 33,475. Even so, the average was only slightly over 3,000 annually; in 1998 it totaled 4,401, but it increased to 9,446 in 2001.[171] Estimates of their American population varied widely. In 1990 one Brazilian newspaper put the figure at 600,000, but another said that it was only about half that. Whatever the precise figure, one scholar noted that Brazilians themselves had noticed a large increase of their numbers in the 1980s.[172] The INS reported an increase during the 1990s of those illegally trying to cross the southern border into the United States.[173] Inflation and unemployment were the underlying economic factors accounting for emigration from Brazil, with half of Brazilian immigrants relocating to the United States.[174] Brazilians coming after the 1980s headed to communities where friends and family helped them find jobs and housing. Small Brazilian communities developed in California (mainly Los Angeles and San Francisco), Miami, Atlanta, New England, and New York City. They also settled near Hispanic communities, although they were not Hispanics; Brazilian immigrants spoke Portuguese. One careful study of Brazilians noted that because they spoke Portuguese rather than Spanish, they were mostly unnoticed or invisible to Americans.[175] In Miami they were reported to be buying small businesses or starting their own.[176] In Los Angeles they opened restaurants and shops where Brazilian bands played familiar music.[177] In San Francisco they were numerous enough to hold an outdoor carnival in 1979.[178] The Atlanta Brazilian community was established more recently, but it was estimated to have 10,000 to 15,000 members by 2000.[179] Not all these newcomers entered with immigrant visas; rather, they came with nonimmigrant visas and then stayed on after the visas expired.[180]

Maxine Margolis's detailed study of New York's Brazilians, published in 1994, revealed a young, well-educated population: 31 percent of these individuals had university degrees. The newcomers identified as being white. In short, they had a higher socioeconomic status than the Brazilian population itself.[181] At first men dominated the flow, but women began to come in increasing numbers in the 1980s. Men and women were willing to "do whatever kind of work they can get that does not require documents or much command of English." They found jobs busing tables, shining shoes, cleaning houses, driving cabs, and, for women, even working in "go-go" bars. For men shining shoes and for women dancing in bars were jobs of low status, or sometimes even embarrassing. The jobs were often beneath their level of skills and education, but without documents or knowledge of English, these immigrants' choices were limited.[182] Some hoped to make money and return home with funds to purchase homes, land, or businesses. If they lacked an adequate income in this country and could not save money, plans for return were shelved for some of these immigrants. Women who entered the paid labor market (and most did) even at low-wage jobs found their status and independence higher in the United States than in Brazil and thus were less willing to think of returning home.[183]

For Brazilians, social life was built around the Catholic Church, clubs, music, family, and friends. In the West Forties of Manhattan, they began to open shops and restaurants catering to other Brazilians and tourists. The newcomers also held an annual street parade in this "Little Brazil."[184] These social events and institutions obviously were welcomed by the immigrants because they provided a taste of home.

Thus far, immigration from Mexico and Central America has outnumbered that from South America. Yet due to the economic problems faced by many nations and people of South America, immigration from that continent could easily increase. The all-important networks for migration are in place. Moreover, it has been difficult for the United States to control undocumented migration whether at the border or in the interior. Several nations, such as Colombia and Argentina, could well move into the ranks of those nations sending large numbers of people to the United States during the years to come.

6

Across the Pacific Again
East Asian Immigrants

During World War II, many Americans began to change their views about Asians. Chinese Americans especially found new economic opportunities, and their participation in the military was welcomed. As K. Scott Wong observed, "Whether or not World War II should be considered the major watershed in twentieth-century American history continues to be debated, but there is no doubt as to the significance of this period in Asian-American history. The war is perhaps as important as the passage of the 1965 Immigration Act, which finally allowed Asian immigration to the United States to proceed on a level equal to other immigrant streams."[1] China was the first Asian nation to receive a quota when Congress repealed the Chinese Exclusion Acts in 1943. The allotment was only 105, but legislation allowing war brides to immigrate eventually permitted 10,000 Chinese women to come to the United States. The original law excluded Asians, but it was amended in 1947.[2] (See Table 3.)

Chinese also arrived under the various refugees acts passed in the 1950s, and the Refugee Escapee Act of 1957 permitted "paper sons" to legalize their status; approximately 30,000 did so, although some were reluctant because they feared they might be deported.[3] In 1961 President John F. Kennedy used the parole power to admit 14,000 other refugees, this time from Hong Kong. Other Chinese refugees, numbering tens of thousands, entered from Vietnam in 1978 when the Vietnamese communists attacked the ethnic Chinese there.

When Congress replaced the national origins quotas in 1965, China (meaning Taiwan) received 20,000 places, not counting immediate family members of U.S. citizens. The new Chinese immigrants initially came from Taiwan or Hong Kong, but in 1981 the People's Republic of China (PRC) received its own quota of 20,000. Immigration was increased for all countries in 1990, and the immigration law of that year also raised the allotment for Hong Kong to 10,000.[4] The 2000 census found 1,391,000

TABLE 3
Immigration from Selected Asian Nations
(Last Residence) (1970–2001)

Country of Last Residence	1971–80	1981–90	1991–2000	1998	1999	2000	2001
Asia	1,588,178	2,738,157	2,795,672	212,799	193,061	255,860	337,566
China	124,326	346,747	419,114	41,034	29,579	41,861	50,821
Hong Kong	113,467	98,215	109,779	7,379	6,533	7,199	10,307
India	164,134	250,786	363,060	34,288	28,355	39,072	65,916
Japan	49,775	47,085	67,942	5,647	4,770	7,730	10,464
Korea	267,638	333,746	164,166	13,691	12,301	15,214	19,933
Philippines	354,987	548,764	503,945	33,176	29,590	40,587	50,870
Vietnam	172,820	280,782	286,145	16,534	19,164	25,340	34,648

SOURCE: Immigration and Naturalization Service, Statistical Yearbook, 2001.

foreign-born Chinese in the United States, a huge leap from the number reported in 1940. Approximately 2.5 million persons reported Chinese ancestry in the 2000 census, the largest Asian group.[5]

Post–World War II Chinese immigration was considerably different from the old. The nineteenth-century immigrants hailed mainly from Canton; in contrast, the new immigrants came from Hong Kong, Taiwan, and various regions of the PRC. They often spoke different dialects. Starting with the war brides legislation, women outnumbered men in the flow. On the eve of the new immigration, 80 percent of the Chinese in the United States were men. Half of the women lived in San Francisco. The war brides laws had a direct impact on the gender ratio in American Chinese communities, making it possible to unite families, as did the family unification provisions of the post-1965 immigration laws. As a result, the renewed migration was one of families and not one of single males.[6]

The new Chinese immigrants came from a variety of classes and included highly skilled and educated professionals, many of whom spoke English because they had attended school in the United States. However, these immigrants also included many working-class persons who knew no English and possessed few skills suitable for employment in the high-tech sector of the American economy. Such differences prompted some observers to note that the renewed Chinese immigration was bipolar. Foreign-born Chinese, Morrison Wong wrote, "exhibit a bipolar occupational structure of the cluster of workers in both high-paying professional and managerial occupations and low-paying service jobs."[7]

Those Chinese stranded in the United States when the communists won power in China in 1949 were mostly well-educated scholars, students, and professionals. These educated immigrants were joined by thousands from Taiwan who entered the United States to study; the Taiwanese government financed the educations of those who lacked funds. The students established networks within American colleges and universities to assist others in coming to the United States from Taiwan. Parents of students were eager for their children to be educated in the United States even if their offspring remained there, and many of the students did. Taiwanese were uncertain about the future of their country and its relation to the PRC, and migration to America was viewed as an alternative to remaining in Taiwan. As was the case with thousands of other students, young Taiwanese found employment in the United States after completing their studies. Once they had a green card, and later citizenship, they in turn could use the preferences of the 1965 immigration act to bring their spouses, minor children, and siblings to America.[8] Other students managed to stay in the United States by marrying American citizens or resident aliens. Overall, in 2001, a total of 4,126 Chinese students became permanent resident aliens.[9]

Although fewer students from Taiwan immigrated after 1990, some Taiwanese remained eager to settle in the United States even though their country's economy grew and prospered. Unsure about Taiwan's future, they moved capital abroad and continued to immigrate to the United States. Many of these immigrants were entrepreneurs who opened businesses when they arrived. Whether as families, entrepreneurs, or professionals, approximately 400,000 immigrants were counted as Taiwanese after the 1965 immigration act was passed.[10]

Like the Taiwanese, many mainland immigrants came initially to study in the United States but remained after graduation by finding employment or marrying an American citizen or resident alien. The largest single group of scholars who adjusted their status to become resident aliens were the 48,212 Chinese students already in the United States when the Chinese government violently crushed the Tiananmen Square pro-democracy revolt in June 1989. Some of these students had denounced the communist government in strong terms, leading Congress and the president to allow them to remain in the United States.[11]

Tensions between the United States and China did not lead to a reduction in the number of immigrants, nor did the number of students from China decrease after the destruction of the World Trade Center on September 11, 2001. The Institute of International Education reported that in 2001–2 a record number of foreign students—nearly 600,000—were attending American colleges and universities. Chinese students accounted for 63,211 of that total—10.5 percent.[12]

The foreign student program became a network for future immigration and not merely the Chinese. Economist George Borjas has estimated that 13 percent of all foreign students eventually become immigrants.[13] The fact that students were in the United States completing their education before they became resident aliens was part of a growing trend in the 1990s. As noted, in the past decade a large number of persons receiving immigrant status already resided in America, and in the late 1990s a majority of persons receiving green cards were living in the United States whether as students or on a temporary visitor visa. In 2001, for example, roughly two-thirds of the immigrants were already in the United States.[14]

Most of the more than 1 million Chinese immigrants arriving between 1943 and the end of the twentieth century originated in mainland China.[15] While Chinese immigration was dominated at first by persons from Taiwan, immigrants from the mainland assumed large numbers after the PRC received its own quota of 20,000. In 2001 the Immigration and Naturalization Service reported that 50,821 people entered from the PRC, as did 10,307 immigrants from Hong Kong. Immigration from Taiwan was averaging 13,000 persons annually during the 1990s.[16] Significantly, many of the Hong Kong and Taiwanese immigrants were born in the PRC and had fled or had been taken by their parents to either Hong Kong or Taiwan.

Taiwanese immigrants and later immigrants from China and Hong Kong settled throughout the United States, with the largest numbers finding homes along the East and West Coasts. The Los Angeles–Long Beach area of California received the largest number, and both San Francisco and New York City were destinations for substantial numbers of Chinese residents. New York City actually had three Chinatowns. Chinese spilled over from Los Angeles into the suburb of Monterey Park, California, and the community was quickly tagged "Little Taipei." Although Chinese communities in New York and elsewhere were often labeled "Little Taipei," or "Chinatown," Taiwanese typically lived alongside other Chinese and Asians. Some areas contained a mixture of diverse ethnic groups, not simply Chinese or Asian.[17] Of Monterey Park's foreign-born Chinese population, 38 percent were born in mainland China, 11 percent were born in Hong Kong, and 16 percent were born in Taiwan.[18]

Besides the large Chinese communities on the West and East Coasts, just as striking is the settlement of Chinese in cities and states where few had gone before 1940. In the 2000 census, Texas reported that 105,829 Chinese lived in the Lone Star State. This figure includes both immigrants and native-born Chinese, but the immigrant generation is larger than that of the native born. Florida reported 46,132 Chinese, and even Alabama and Mississippi attracted Chinese settlers, 6,900 and 3,827 respectively.[19] Chinese also located in Atlanta, Georgia. The post-1945 Atlanta Chinese community developed when many students who had attended school there remained in the region after completing their studies. Roughly 80 percent of the early settlers had "professional degrees with advanced training."[20] The dispersal of the Chinese was indicative of the general movement of Asian immigrants after 1980. The Bureau of the Census reported that although one-half of Asians were located in New York, Hawaii, and California, sizable numbers were found in all regions. About 19 percent lived in the Northeast, 11 percent in the Midwest, and 18 percent in the South.[21]

Within states and metropolitan areas, some of the more economically successful Chinese settled in predominantly white suburbs, where they found better housing and more competitive schools, something they deemed important for the education of their children. Wealthy Chinese settled in California's San Mateo, just south of San Francisco, where many homes sold for $1 million.[22]

The Taiwanese professionals settled where they found jobs that used their skills. At the top of the professional class were physicians. Others who knew English and possessed excellent educations found employment as white-collar workers, including employment with federal and local governments.[23] Still others—engineers or computer experts—settled in California's Silicon Valley, where they helped the American high-tech industry grow. Their entrance into California's technology industry began in 1979, when a small group of Chinese engineers, "while attending a banquet in San Francisco," decided to open a branch of the Chinese Institute of Engineers.[24] More than one-quarter of Chinese immigrants had college degrees, and in places such as Silicon Valley nearly one-quarter held graduate degrees.[25] The institute was initially dominated by Taiwanese, and it used its contacts in Taiwan to recruit other experts and tap knowledge. When Taiwan experienced a booming economy in the 1980s, some of the engineers returned home, in many cases drawn by active government recruitment.

Many immigrants from the PRC had professional training valued in the United States, and after experiencing initial downward mobility, they mostly found employment in higher-paying jobs.[26] The elite, like the Taiwanese, included physicians, engineers, and computer experts working in such places as Silicon Valley. By the end of the 1990s, professionals from the mainland began to outnumber Taiwanese there, but the firms they started were no less successful, until the recession beginning in 2001. In 1998 the Silicon Valley firms begun by Chinese and Asian Indians generated $17 billion in sales and created 58,000 jobs.[27]

In addition to advanced educations, some Hong Kong (as well as Taiwanese) immigrants, having sold their profitable businesses at home, also arrived with plenty of capital to invest. For example, Bernard Wong told of a Hong Kong family who had operated a restaurant and owned a condominium in Hong Kong. After selling their assets, the family members arrived in the United States with $200,000 in savings.[28] A few Hong Kong immigrants had even greater assets and could be termed wealthy, with abundant funds to invest. Indeed, such capital was partly responsible for driving up the price of housing in Chinatowns, which were among the most crowded areas in American cities.[29]

For those without professional qualifications or large amounts of capital, employment usually meant working for others or running their own small businesses such as banks, groceries, pharmacies, real estate firms, candy shops, and coffee shops. Aware of the desire of immigrants to keep in touch with families and friends in China, some Chinese-owned shops began selling phone cards. Chinese shop owners were by no means the only immigrants to sell these cards, which had become a $2 billion business by 2002. Phone cards were used by Dominicans, other Asian immigrants, and nearly all groups who wanted to keep in touch with folks at home.[30]

Entrepreneurs sometimes employed members of their families or hired fellow countrymen.[31] Small businesses, if successful, presented opportunities for social mobility, but they required long hours.[32] Many of the ethnic Chinese from Vietnam had owned small businesses in Vietnam's cities. When they arrived in the United States, they were not always welcomed either by Americans generally or by the Chinese already here. They usually were able to adjust to their new land, however, and once again become entrepreneurs in Chinatowns or in settlements of Vietnamese refugees. In 1991 in San Francisco, Chinese owned 9,028 firms, and in the five counties of the Bay Area, they ran more than 18,000 such shops. The small enterprises were mostly family run, operating by staying open for long hours while earning low profits.[33] Immigrant entrepreneurs also owned garment factories, groceries, and a large variety of family-run shops, especially restaurants, catering to tourists.[34] The immediate nuclear family was the mainstay of these firms, but other kin were employed, too.[35]

No Chinese business was as important as the restaurants, which played a vital role in the Chinese community and accounted for the largest single industry. They were especially important for the employment of male cooks, waiters, and bus boys. Women also found employment in restaurants, operating cash registers and seating customers. The growing restaurant enterprises were not limited to Chinatown, where Chinese and non-Chinese tourists ate; the popularity of Chinese food made it profitable to run restaurants in neighborhoods outside of Chinatown. In the mid-1990s the nation's Chinese restaurants reportedly numbered over 40,000 and employed several hundred thousand workers. Of no little importance was the growth of take-out Chinese eateries.[36]

For most Chinese immigrants, working-class positions in the many shops run by Chinese provided the best opportunity for employment, and many immigrants struggled to make a living scarcely above poverty. While many women labored in family businesses, most found employment working for others. The largest single concentration of these female immigrants was in the garment shops of New York, San Francisco, and other Chinatowns. When the American garment industry declined after 1960, there remained a niche for small contract firms owned by Chinese. The employers had a ready supply of women who poured into Chinatowns. With little English and a great need for income to support their families, the immigrant workers found employers eager to hire them.

They worked in factories that often were not in compliance with labor laws and that paid relatively low wages. But these women had few choices; in addition, they could on occasion bring their children to work with them.[37] Employers claimed that unions were unnecessary because as Chinese owners they had close relations with their fellow ethnic employees. But conditions and wages in New York City drove the women to join the International Ladies' Garment Workers' Union.[38] In 1982 they struck and won wage concessions and health benefits. They remained, however, working in an industry battered by foreign competition and a recession beginning in 2001.

When the World Trade Center was destroyed on September 11, 2001, it was a harsh blow for businesses in lower Manhattan's Chinatown given its proximity to "Ground Zero." A survey of 350 Chinatown businesses revealed that within a few weeks income was down by 30 to 70 percent. "From fruit stands to jewelry stores to garment factories, Chinatown's businesses need high volumes because they typically have low profit margins," noted the *New York Times*, and many customers stayed away after the September 11 attack.[39] Nor was it likely that Chinatown would recover.[40] The city contained two other areas of high Chinese population, in the boroughs of Queens and Brooklyn, and some of the Manhattan Chinatown businesses could move, but the other neighborhoods were already crowded.[41] Some of the wealthy entrepreneurs had investments not limited to Chinatown; they owned banks, hotels, and other property and were engaged in international trading, and like many of the educated professionals lived outside of the country's Chinatowns.[42]

What of those who had little money, poor English skills, limited educations, and no family connections needed for a green card? Their only way to immigrate was through illegal entry, graphically illustrated on June 6, 1993, when the cargo steamer *Golden Venture* ran aground off of Long Island, New York. Desperate passengers, illegal aliens from China, leaped from the ship into cold water in an effort to get ashore. Ten did not make it. The remainder reached land, some with help from the Coast Guard. The subsequent investigation and reports about this unfortunate vessel revealed that the passengers had paid up to $30,000 for passage from China to the United States.[43] They were taken into custody, and only after they began a hunger strike were some released on parole. Yet others were not finally released until they had been detained for nearly four years.[44] Eventually some did win asylum or the right to remain in America, but a majority were deported.[45] In spite of the deportations and the fact that the head smuggler was convicted and received a twenty-year prison sentence, other young men were willing to try to get to America under similar dangerous sailing conditions. In August 1999, another vessel was discovered in the harbor of Savannah, Georgia, with 132 undocumented Chinese immigrants aboard.[46]

These episodes highlighted that in addition to the "brain drain" from Taiwan and China, other immigrants with few prospects in China were desperate to migrate to America. In order to immigrate to the United States, they agreed to return part of their earnings in America to the smugglers. Fuzhou's main export was young men. The cost could run as high as $40,000.[47] The willingness of desperate people made it possible for organized smugglers to run profitable enterprises. Peter Kwong's study narrated how immigrants, mainly but not exclusively from Fujian Province, were willing to indenture themselves for the journey to America. The smugglers, called "snakeheads," brought thousands to the United States.[48] Judy Yung claims they numbered 100,000 from the early 1980s to 1997, but no one knows how many arrived. Once in the United States, they worked long hours at low-level jobs to pay the snakeheads and save enough to bring their relatives to America.[49] There were plenty of entry-level positions in the restaurants and garment shops of the nation's Chinatowns that were usually left untouched by the INS. Ko-Lin Chin's study of these illegal immigrants found that many earned enough to pay off their debts within a few years and even sent money home.[50]

Before the new immigration, Chinatowns were dominated by the Chinese Consolidated Benevolent Association (CCBA), known as the Chinese Six Companies. While the CCBA remained on the scene after the 1940s, new organizations appeared to deal with the many problems faced by the immigrants. Taiwanese associations also raised funds to finance cultural centers. In Texas, the Taiwanese Association of Houston spent $300,000 in 1993 to establish a community center. Similar Taiwanese groups were active elsewhere.[51] Student groups aided new scholars, and professional and business associations attempted to deal with economic issues. College alumni groups catered to the educated Chinese whether from Taiwan, mainland China, or Hong Kong.[52] And for those who could not read English or who wanted to know about events in their communities or in China, many Chinese-language newspapers appeared on newsstands.

Among the organizations established by the newcomers were special schools to help children improve their grades and prepare for the Scholastic Aptitude Test (SAT). One scholar declared that special classes after the regular school day had become the norm in New York City's China-town.[53] Immigrant parents put great pressure on their children to succeed through education, to find better jobs and a better life than they had had. As a result, many Chinese students, and Asian students generally, took honors courses and strove to gain admission to the nation's most selective schools. The children were also encouraged to major in engineering, math, computer science, and business. Asian children did gain admission to many of the most elite institutions of higher education in the nation. Such success won the attention of the national media and commentators and prompted the notion of a "model minority," an unfortunate and often inaccurate phase.[54] Educational achievement did not come without a price, as students complained of enormous pressure at home by parents to succeed: "They work hard for me, so I have to work hard for them."[55] At the other end of the spectrum remained many poor Chinese who lived in or on the edge of poverty. These included Chinese Nationalist soldiers who fled first to Taiwan when the communists seized power and then to the United States after 1960 when Taiwan did not grant them a pension. Because they knew no English, several thousand veterans lived in China-towns on meager earnings.[56]

Moreover, Chinese Americans have experienced discrimination and even violence. The most famous case was that of Vincent Chin, who in 1982 was beaten to death by two angry automobile workers who be-lieved that he was Japanese and that Asians were responsible for unem-ployment in the auto industry. Chin's attackers received only a fine and a suspended jail sentence.[57] Other hate crimes were reported after the Chin case, and Asian organizations pressed for more action against those who assaulted Asians.[58] Some of the violence came at the hands of other Chi-nese. Not the least worry of many immigrants has been the presence of Chinese youth gangs in the nation's Chinatowns. The "Born to Kill" gang, composed of ethnic Chinese from Vietnam, was alleged by author-ities to be the "biggest problem" in New York City's Chinatown, but other gangs were feared as well.[59]

Cultural institutions and activities served the Chinese community, but after the 1980s some Chinese immigrants and Chinese Americans gained access to the larger public. Maxine Hong Kingston and Amy Tan became best-selling authors, and Connie Chung a nationally known television an-nouncer, while Yo-Yo Ma became an internationally known cellist. Chi-nese cooking has become an integral part of American cuisine. In education, Chang-lin Tien became chancellor of the University of California.[60] Because so many of the newcomers lacked citizenship, it was difficult to elect Chinese Americans, even at the local level. The highest office reached by a Chinese American was by Gary Locke, whose grandfather was a Chinese immigrant; he became governor of the state of Washington.[61] Governor Locke was picked by the Democratic Party to answer President George W. Bush's State of the Union address in 2003.[62] In Monterey Park, California, Chinese residents mobilized to offset what they perceived as nativism and bigotry directed at their community. A state anti-immigrant "Official English" initiative passed in 1986 divided the community and eventually led to a diverse city council, with Judy Chu as mayor, replacing the old mayor who was identified with anti-immigrant politics.[63]

The second East Asian nation to receive a quota was the Philippines.[64] When Congress passed the Tydings-McDuffie Act in 1934, it appeared that immigration from the Philippines was at an end, because this act limited Filipino immigration to 50 persons a year for ten years; upon achievement of independence, no further immigration was to be permitted. In addition, the federal government offered to pay the passage for those wanting to return to the Philippines. Only 2,200 Filipinos used the Repatriation Act of 1935 to return home, leaving behind "old-timers" who would become an aging, predominantly male community numbering about 100,000, clustered mostly in Hawaii and California. Yet the events of World War II and the subsequent modification of postwar immigration laws changed restrictionism to a liberal immigration policy. Within a few years the Philippines became one of the major sending nations, second only to Mexico after 1970 (excluding refugees in some years), enabling the Filipino American population to become the second-largest Asian group in the United States by the end of the twentieth century.

When Japan conquered the Philippines in 1942 and Filipinos joined Americans in the struggle to defeat the rising Japanese empire, the U.S. government took a new look at Filipino Americans. A few Filipino veterans of World War I had been granted citizenship during the 1930s, a practice that expanded once the war began. Less than a month after the Japanese attack at Pearl Harbor, the Selective Service Act permitted Filipinos to serve in the U.S. Army, and eventually several hundred thousand fought on the side of the American forces.[65] Seven thousand volunteers served in two Filipino infantry regiments in the Pacific theater, and others fought in mostly non-Filipino units in Europe. Over a three-year period submarines landed 1,000 Filipinos in their homeland to gather intelligence and fight a guerrilla war.[66] Congress also extended the right of naturalization to Filipino soldiers, and in February 1943, 400 took the oath of citizenship at Camp Beale in California.[67]

After the end of the war, when the Philippines became an independent nation, Congress passed the Luce-Celler Act of 1946 granting the Philippines an annual quota of 100 and its immigrants the right to become American citizens. Naturalization proved to be very important for immigration, for immediate family members of U.S. citizens (defined as spouses and minor children, with parents added in 1965) were permitted to enter above the quota. A year after passage of the Luce-Celler Act, historian Elliott Barkan reported that more than 10,000 Filipinos became U.S. citizens and thus eligible to bring their immediate family members to America.[68]

Until the 1990s, the United States maintained a large naval base and airfield in the Philippines. Under the provisions of immigration law and special legislation passed for war brides and fiancées, Filipino women who married American GIs were eligible to immigrate to the United States, and more than 100,000 did so.[69]

Those soldiers who became citizens at Camp Beale in 1943 were entitled to full benefits as citizens and veterans. But what of those who served in the Philippines during the war and who remained there? Congress allowed them to become citizens but failed to provide the machinery in the Philippines to effect this change. A movement to alter this injustice partly succeeded in 1990 when Congress permitted the veterans to come forward to claim citizenship. Speaking for many, one veteran reported that he wanted citizenship to "petition his wife and ten children" for immigration to the United States.[70] These former soldiers had to come to the United States to naturalize. In 1992 Congress allowed the veterans to be naturalized in the Philippines and extended the deadline for two more years. However, new citizens were not entitled to full veterans' benefits.[71]

While veterans' status and the Luce-Celler Act opened the door for renewed immigration during the 1940s and 1950s, it was the 1965 immigration act that made substantial immigration from the Philippines possible. Within ten years of the legislation's passage, 230,000 Filipino immigrants entered the United States, and 900,000 were recorded from 1970 to 1990.[72] Congress also enacted Medicare and Medicaid programs at the same time, thus creating a need for a growing number of health professionals, and Filipino men and women were quick to use the occupational sections of their quota to immigrate to the United States.

The Americanization of Filipino education, including medical and nursing schools, led to many Filipinos' familiarity with American methods and English-language skills. Some nurses came to the United States for advanced training and then stayed; others entered through special provisions for nurses; still others eventually came by using the occupational categories of the new immigration system. Within a few years nearly half of the immigrant nurses entering the United States were from the Philippines.[73] In 1978 Congress restricted the number of medical professionals allowed to enter. After 1980 some nurses were still permitted to immigrate, but the most common route to enter for nurses was by temporary work visas. In 1995, for example, 5,306 Filipino nurses entered on temporary work visas, representing about 80 percent of all such entrants in that category.[74] Due to a shortage of nurses in inner-city hospitals, many of these temporary workers were able to extend their stay. In the 1970s critics contended that there was no real shortage, but rather a shortage of nurses willing to work for lower wages. The nursing shortage eased a bit in the 1980s, but hospitals found themselves short of staff again in the 1990s. In 2002, hospitals estimated that they needed nurses to fill 125,000 vacancies, and they looked to Asian nations such as the Philippines, India, and Korea to help fill the need.[75]

Most of the Filipino physicians migrating to the United States after 1965 were men graduating from medical schools in the Philippines that utilized American-style training. Within a decade of the enactment of the 1965 immigration law, 7,000 Filipino physicians were practicing in the United States; in 1970 they constituted one-quarter of the foreign physicians entering the United States.[76] But female doctors were almost as numerous as the males.[77] As was the case with nurses, health professionals in the United States became alarmed at the number of foreign physicians. In 1976 the American Medical Association convinced Congress to curtail the entrance of these foreign doctors, and the numbers dropped after that. It was still possible for foreign physicians to come to the United States to practice medicine, mainly in inner-city hospitals, but it was much more difficult to gain a visa for this occupation.[78] Many other Filipino health professionals entered as dentists, technologists, paramedics, and pharmacists, of whom a majority were women.

Opportunities existed for other Filipino professionals to work in the Philippines, but these highly educated persons could not always find employment commensurate with their education where the working conditions were equal to those in the United States. "We have more than two hundred registered civil engineers in the city," said the mayor of Llucena City. "Where would I get them employed?"[79]

Most Filipinos entered through the family unification categories; no more than 10 percent of Filipino immigrants came under occupational preferences by the 1970s.[80] Filipino immigration was running nearly double the annual quota because so many were exempt as immediate family members of U.S. citizens. By the time of the 2000 census, the Filipino immigrant population numbered 1,222,000, slightly behind the Chinese, which was the largest Asian immigrant group in the United States.[81] Pressure to emigrate in the hopes of finding a better life was enormous. Because many Filipinos had absorbed American culture through the stationing of American military personnel in the Philippines after World War II, they had some knowledge of American life and were thus better prepared for such a transition. They had also learned of the United States from their Americanized educational system and from mass media, particularly television and movies.

Many Filipinos visited relatives or friends before deciding to emigrate. Immigration was running over 45,000 annually in the 1990s, but the number of visas for nonimmigrants (temporary visitors) was twice that figure. Long lines were reported outside the American embassy in Manila, which had to screen the applicants. Because the backlog in some immigrant preference categories was huge and the wait sometimes years, embassy officials suspected that many of the nonimmigrant visitors intended to overstay their visits and become illegal immigrants. As a result, many prospective visitors were turned down by officials in Manila, who had the last word on such applications. The Philippines and the Dominican Republic had the highest rejection rates for nonimmigrants.[82]

In 1992 the INS estimated that 90,000 Filipinos who entered as nonimmigrants overstayed to become undocumented aliens. The INS reported that of Asian nations, illegal immigrants from the Philippines were triple the next national group. Most, said the INS, were living in California.[83] During 1995–96, authorities deported only 159 Filipinos, of whom 66 were criminals, not an especially large part of the 54,632 criminal aliens deported in that year.[84]

One form of illegal immigration that particularly concerned American officials was marriage fraud, which prompted examinations by Congress and immigration officials. A 1999 study by the INS reported that an

American man wanting a foreign bride could easily find a mate. Women advertised through newspapers and e-mail, and immigration officials said that more than 100,000 women per year paid for ads seeking an American citizen willing to marry them. The Philippines provided the largest number of such Asian listings, but in the 1990s many women from Russia and the former Soviet Union nations also used such services. Moreover, the INS claimed that the agencies offering their services were very profitable.[85] While many of the women studied wanted an American husband as a way to reach America, other women maintained that Americans made better spouses than Filipino men, who were alleged to be unfaithful to their wives. The American men reported that they wanted women with traditional values, which they believed were held by immigrant women.[86]

As for the numbers, the report noted that a Filipino commission claimed about 10 percent of marriages of Filipino women and American men initiated relationships through the "mail-order" process.[87] These mail-order brides represented a small percentage of total Filipino immigration, but worried officials noted that once in the United States, some of these women quickly left their husbands, thus indicating that the marriage was fraudulent. A number of cases did come to the attention of authorities and the Filipino American community. In 1993 Emilia Clear sent her picture to *U.S.A. Tomorrow*, a mail-order magazine. She married an Ohio man, who turned out to be a different person from the one who found her photo in the magazine. The State Department and the INS found this case fraudulent; they deported her and barred her entry to the United States for ten years.[88]

The authorities were acting under a tough 1986 law on mail-order marriage, the Marriage Fraud Act, which aimed to combat fraudulent claims.[89] But the law might have left women subject to domestic abuse because it required them to live with their husbands for at least two years. Women who left abusive husbands in that period of time were subject to deportation.[90] The extent of domestic violence among Filipino immigrant families is not known. The Coalition for Immigrant and Refugee Rights and Services in San Francisco reported helping dozens of women who were abused by their husbands and afraid to leave for fear of deportation.[91] In addition, several scholars have stated that abuse of wives and sexual abuse of children had been increasing faster among Filipinos in the United States than in the Philippines.[92] One of the most sensational accounts of domestic violence among immigrant women was an incident involving a Filipino woman and a white American man. Timothy C. Blackwell found his bride, Rusana Remerata, by looking at the "Asian Encounters" catalog. After a brief correspondence, and even briefer acquaintance, they were married in the Philippines. The marriage lasted only three weeks, however, and was fraught with violence. She requested a divorce. After she revealed that she was pregnant by another man during the divorce proceedings, Blackwell shot and killed her along with the two friends with whom she was staying.[93]

The renewed Filipino migration to America after World War II was quite different from that of the pre-1930s, when 90 percent of the immigrants were men; now a majority were women.[94] In one respect, however, the latest newcomers resembled the "old-timers." The largest concentration in the continental United States was in California, the center of so much Asian immigration. The 2000 census reported that half of the Filipino population lived in California. About one-third resided in the San Francisco Bay Area, with Los Angeles being another popular destination.[95] Other settlements were in large cities such as New York and Chicago. The medical and technical professionals could be found living near their places of employment, and many settled in suburban regions outside large cities. Few lived in Philippine "ghettos." *Filipinas* magazine reported that three-quarters of the immigrants spoke English well and had little need for ethnic clustering. A 1990s Rand study of California discovered that more than 90 percent of Filipinos in that state spoke English, the highest figure among newcomers and greater than for white immigrants except those from the United Kingdom and Canada.[96] Compared with Chinese and Korean immigrants, Filipinos were much less apt to be running their own ethnic businesses, which often served to hold ethnic groups together. Filipinos' knowledge of English and possession of high school diplomas and college degrees have enabled them to find remunerative white-collar employment and avoid owning their own small businesses.[97] What held them together were the many organizations they created, common problems and experiences, cultural unity, and ties to the Philippines.[98]

The vast majority (85 percent) of the newcomers were Roman Catholic and attended Catholic services in America.[99] Others joined organizations to help immigrants or to promote Filipino culture in the United States, or patronized Filipino stores or read English-language Filipino magazines and newspapers. A major event was Philippine Independence Day, celebrated on June 12 to commemorate the proclamation of independence from Spain on that day in 1898.[100] Rizal Day was also a large event for the Filipino community. Begun before 1945, it celebrated Jose Rizal, a hero among Filipinos because he opposed Spanish imperialism in the Philippines and was killed during the 1896 insurrection against Spain.[101]

Contact with the Philippines was an important part of the new immigrants' experience. Some returned for visits or welcomed visitors from home. The immigrants also sent remittances back to the Philippines. These remittances, in addition to those from many temporary workers and immigrants in the Middle East and in other Asian nations, were important for the Philippine economy.[102]

Much of the political energy of Filipino immigrants concentrated on events at home rather than politics in the United States. Because Filipinos were subject to the violence and persecution of the Ferdinand Marcos dictatorship, they welcomed his replacement in 1986 by Corazon Aquino. They had somewhat scattered living patterns, making it nearly impossible to win election to American political offices based solely on a Filipino vote. Instead they worked with other Asian American groups on issues such as affirmative action, ethnic studies programs in universities, and local affairs that affected Filipino Americans.[103] At the local level Filipino Americans have won some offices in Hawaii and on the West Coast. The first Filipino elected governor was Ben Cayetano, who was chosen as governor of Hawaii in 1995 and reelected in 1999. Hawaii has a large Filipino population, but by no means a majority.[104] The size of the Filipino community promised future political clout, but citizenship was needed for the ballot and office holding, and about two-thirds of the Filipino American population was foreign born, many of whom had not become U.S. citizens.[105] Moreover, there were differences among Filipino Americans on particular issues such as affirmative action.

A few critics have suggested that lack of political unity is due to the fact that Filipinos in America are well educated, speak English, and are well-off economically. Except for the Japanese American group, they had the highest intermarriage rate of Asians, approaching one-half in some communities. The Rand study reported that the median years of schooling was higher for California's Filipino immigrants than for most immigrants. Among the most recent Filipino immigrants, about one-half had completed college, though outside of California the figure was lower.[106]

In 1989 the federal government reported that Filipinos had the third-highest median household income among Asian groups. However, Filipino families were more likely than other immigrants or native-born Americans to have two wage earners. In California they had the highest percentage of immigrant women in the paid labor force, and their educational levels were above the American average.[107] In 1989 almost 30 percent of Filipino households had three wage earners, compared to 13.4 percent of all U.S. families.[108] The high earners tended to be the well-educated professionals. While medical and technical professionals earned substantial incomes, not all Filipinos were so successful. Filipinos did not earn as much as similarly educated whites, in part because they were educated in the Philippines, and these degrees are sometimes not recognized in the United States. Professional certification was difficult to achieve with a Philippine education.[109] For Filipino immigrants at the bottom of the income pile, a lower proportion lived below the poverty line than the national averages.[110]

The extent to which ethnic prejudice created a "glass ceiling" that held Filipinos (and other Asians) back from higher incomes and top jobs is difficult to say. In the early 1990s Filipinos were underrepresented in top jobs of American firms. The Civil Rights Commission reported in 1992 that discrimination and violence against Asians had by no means been eliminated. The commission also noted that Asian women faced gender discrimination and sexual harassment in addition to ethnic bias.[111] English fluency, high levels of education, and mostly middle-class and upper-middle-class status and income did not exempt Filipino Americans from social conflicts within the community. Filipinos faced the traditional conflicts among themselves and their children, including disapproval if a child selected a spouse who was not a Filipino American.

Japan and Korea had to wait until the McCarran-Walter Immigration Act of 1952 to receive quotas, and even then, like the first quotas granted to Chinese and Filipinos, the allotments were small. The largest Asian American community in 1945 was Japanese, which did grow, but mainly by natural birth rates, not migration. Indeed, immigration from Japan was relatively small. Whereas 60 percent of Asians were foreign born in 2000, only 20 percent of Japanese Americans were. By the 1990s Japanese Americans were no longer the largest Asian American group in the United States. The rapid recovery of the Japanese economy after World War II enabled Japanese to find jobs and to enjoy a rising standard of living at home, at least until the 1990s, when Japan's economy slowed.

Some Japanese did come to the United States to run branches of Japanese corporations. Many others traveled to see America's sights, but these were not immigrants, only temporary visitors, though it was possible that some of these temporary migrants might remain after their permits expired.

Most of the approximately 5,000 annual immigrants from Japan, especially in the 1950s and 1960s, were the spouses of American servicemen stationed in Japan.[112] These Japanese women were often better educated than their American spouses, urban in background, and with some acquaintance with Western and American values and culture. They met their husbands in and around the many military bases that were set up during the occupation. Some of the women even attended "bride schools" to prepare themselves for American-style marriages when they went to the United States with their soldier-husbands.[113] The American government reserved the right to approve of marriages, and it discouraged and barred the marriage of GIs to prostitutes, criminals, and those with chronic diseases.

In fact, the military did little to encourage marriages between soldiers and foreigners, and liaisons between Japanese and Americans were not viewed favorably by the Japanese either. Some Japanese women "never bothered to introduce their families to their husbands."[114] When their husbands were reassigned to the United States, the young women found themselves living in army posts, especially in the American southern states, where there were few Japanese. Life was not always easy. "Theirs tended to be an isolated existence," as one scholar put it, and divorces were not uncommon under the new conditions.[115] Most American men, however, remained with their Japanese wives, and most Japanese women reported good marriages.[116]

During the 1990s a small wave of immigrants arrived for economic reasons.[117] Most of the increase was accounted for by entrepreneurs and their families. The most common businesses opened by these latest immigrants were restaurants. About 85 percent of Japanese-run restaurants in New York City served Japanese food. Restaurants also needed chefs and were able to sponsor Japanese on employment visas. The owners and cooks were usually men.[118]

Immigration from Korea also was revitalized after the passage of the 1952 immigration act, which specifically opened the United States to immigrants from Korea. Eventually more than 800,000 Koreans became residents of the United States.[119] Korea received a quota (only 100) in

1952, but Koreans married to American citizens were exempt. During the Korean War (1950–53) more than 500,000 American troops served in Korea, and tens of thousands of American soldiers have been stationed there since 1953. When they married Korean women, they began a new immigration channel. Korean "war brides" constituted the largest single share of the newcomers during the first years of renewed immigration; since that time, Korean women have continued to marry GIs and follow them when these soldiers were reassigned to the United States or elsewhere. Between the outbreak of the war and 1965, when a new immigration law was passed, more than 15,000 Koreans entered the United States, 40 percent of them married to U.S. citizens, mostly soldiers. Data are not precise, but working with American and Korean figures, Daniel Lee estimated that from 1950 to the mid-1990s "some 90,000 Korean women have immigrated to America as wives of U.S. soldiers." At least one scholar has used a higher figure of 100,000.[120]

The importance of wives of servicemen who became immigrants is not limited to their numbers alone. Under the 1965 Hart-Celler Act, Korean women entering as wives of U.S. military personnel were able to sponsor their parents and siblings after they became American citizens. The snowball effect of chain migration was now written into law. Daniel Lee estimates, for example, that military brides were directly and indirectly responsible for a significant number of immigrants, which he claims amounted to 40 to 50 percent of all Korean immigrants since the passage of the Hart-Celler Act.[121]

A smaller flow of immigrants, but also related to the stationing of American troops in Korea, consisted of Amerasian children and Korean orphans. Amerasians were children fathered by American servicemen and left behind by returning troops. In some cases they were abandoned. A few were later adopted by Americans. In addition, thousands of children lost their parents during the conflict, and American GIs adopted some of them. As Korea underwent industrialization and urbanization after 1950, some children, mostly girls, were abandoned. One of the first agencies to establish a Korean adoption program was founded by Harry Holt and his wife, who brought back eight orphans and Amerasian children to the United States. The couple then founded an organization specializing in the adoption of Asian children. From 1950 until the end of the twentieth century, approximately 80,000 such children were adopted by American couples, who were usually white Protestant middle-class Americans.[122] There are no figures on how many of these children were Amerasians.

In the early 1960s, children accounted for 40 percent of the total Korean immigration to the United States.[123] Between 1955 and 1977, roughly 13,000 such orphans were adopted by Americans; in the late 1970s and 1980s, about 3,000 Korean orphans were adopted annually by American citizens, amounting to 60 percent of all foreign-born children adopted by U.S. citizens during those years. The number of Korean adoptees peaked at 6,150 in 1986, after which the number and share of children who were Korean declined.[124] In 1991 the number of foreign-born children adopted by U.S. parents was 9,000; in 2000 it reached 18,000, of whom 1,794 were from South Korea. Only 62 Chinese children were adopted in 1991, but China quickly became the leading "exporter" of children adopted by American citizens, with Russia in second place.[125] Thus, overall, adopted children and military wives were the key segments of renewed Korean immigration for years after 1950, even when the changes from the 1965 law went into effect in 1968.

The Korean War made many American officials and citizens notice Korea, a country they had been only dimly aware of prior to the date. It also made Koreans more eager to learn about and study in the United States. Since the 1950s, the goods sold in the American PXs and American radio and television broadcasts could hardly be missed in South Korea. Many Koreans were employed by American firms and the military and had even closer contact with things American. In addition, in traditional immigrant fashion, those who went first encouraged and even financed relatives and friends to follow. At first, reports, letters, and visits encouraged many Koreans to immigrate to the United States.

Illsoo Kim reports that Koreans had their own sources of information about life in America. A series of newspaper articles were turned into a popular book, *Day and Night of Komericans: A Visit to Korea in the United States*; it became a best-seller in the late 1970s "not only because it dealt with the national issue of Korean emigration to the United States but also because it provided prospective emigrants with essential information as to how they might prepare themselves . . . in the new land."[126]

To learn more about the United States and upgrade their educations, hundreds of thousands of students have enrolled in American institutions of higher learning. From 1953 to 1980 more than 10,000 Koreans attended American universities, and a few eventually became immigrants.[127] The El Paso Korean community, for example, originated with Korean students studying at the University of Texas at El Paso and Korean military personnel who received training at Fort Bliss in El Paso.[128]

According to Pyong Gap Min, most of the first students arriving in the 1950s were sponsored and aided by American servicemen, and many of these students later stayed in the United States. As Min notes, "Many Koreans who came to the United States as students between 1950 and 1964 currently have professional occupations in the United States, including teaching positions at colleges and universities."[129]

Korean medical professionals joined other Asian physicians, nurses, and pharmacists in practicing their occupation in the United States after 1965. Between 1966 and 1979, when the rules were tightened by Congress for physicians, 13,000 Korean doctors, nurses, and pharmacists received green cards.[130] The migration of medical professionals to the United States was not simply a response to the lure of American money. Changes in Korean medicine, which prompted the migration, were not unrelated to the Korean War. Western medicine was introduced to Koreans by American missionaries in the late nineteenth century. Around the turn of the twentieth century, Horace Allen, a diplomat who was also a physician and Presbyterian minister, founded the Severance Hospital and the Severance Union Medical College, which eventually became major medical facilities in Korea.[131] The Korean War accelerated the development of Western medicine in Korea, and physicians and nurses were in great demand there during the violent war years. For example, it was in those years that antibiotics were first introduced in Korea. Moreover, exchange programs enabled some young Korean medical professionals to study in the United States at medical schools or hospitals. As Illsoo Kim relates, "Thus, once the United States Immigration Act of 1965 opened the door to the immigration of professional, skilled workers, South Korea was ready to send a large number of medical workers to the United States."[132] The share of Korean immigrants using the occupational preferences declined in the 1980s, but once medical professionals were established, they could send for their families under the family unification provisions of immigration law.[133]

Whether related to the Korean War or somewhat independent of the conflict, Korean immigration to the United States increased after 1950, especially after passage of the Immigration Act of 1965. Arriving between 1950 and 2001, more than 800,000 Korean immigrants were recorded by the INS, averaging over 30,000 annually in the 1980s. Unlike at the turn of the twentieth century, few of these more recent Korean immigrants have settled in Hawaii, and that state is no longer an important center for them. For those who choose the mainland, the West Coast is the main destination, as it is for so many Asian immigrants. California claims the greatest number, with Los Angeles's Korea Town being the largest single urban Korean settlement in the United States. About one-fifth of the entire Korean American population lives in the Los Angeles–Long Beach metropolitan region. But they have also dispersed throughout the United States, with important centers existing in both New York and Chicago.[134] Korean neighborhoods can also be found in Texas, Georgia, and New Jersey. In these areas Koreans are not segregated into distinct neighborhoods in spite of the existence of Korea Towns. Los Angeles's Korea Town, for example, is only 15 percent Korean.[135] Many of the economically successful Koreans live in predominantly white communities such as New Jersey's Bergen County or New York's Westchester County.

Like all Asian immigrants, Koreans have experienced both success and problems as new immigrants. Those married to American servicemen often began to have difficulties before the migration to America. Many women met American GIs while working for PXs or U.S. government agencies. Yet the initial contact with soldiers has often occurred in the "camptowns," close to military bases. Camptowns included small operations selling goods to the soldiers but also bars, clubs, and houses of prostitution, which gave them their unsavory reputations. Bruce Cummings has called the militarized prostitution of the camptowns the "most important aspect of the whole relationship (between the United States and South Korea) and the primary memory of Korea for generations of young Americans who have served there."[136] The American military's main concern was to keep venereal disease in check, not necessarily to close the brothels.

Given the reputation of the camptowns, many Koreans disapproved of the women who worked there and rejected Korean camptown women who married American military personnel as nothing more than prostitutes. Women who married African American soldiers had the additional problem of dealing with racism whether in Korea or later in the United States. Ji-Yeon Yuh's study of Korean women married to American soldiers revealed a difficult adjustment for the wives. Many did not have an adequate knowledge of English and were simply unprepared to cope with American culture. For these women, isolation on military posts was trying, as was dealing with American society generally. It is no surprise that some of these unions ended in divorce. The divorce rate among war brides is not known, but the rate is higher for Koreans in America than for those in Korea.[137] Nor is spousal abuse unknown to these women.

Such abuse was not limited to Korean women with non-Korean husbands, however; it also occurred when the husbands were Korean.[138]

Of the postwar Korean immigrants, medical professionals who arrived
before 1980 have had the most success in the United States. These are the
Korean immigrants who earn the highest incomes, own homes in high-
status, predominantly white suburbs, and purchase expensive American
consumer goods. They are also able to visit their homelands because they
have the funds to do so.[139] Yet they have generally entered low-paid medical practices and were often recruited by hospitals in inner cities; they
had to pass tough American language and licensing exams. Nurses, of
course, have not been as successful as doctors.[140] Other professionals
served the immigrant community by offering legal advice, selling real estate, issuing insurance, and providing banking.[141]

To look at the Korean American experience is to examine two distin-
guishing phenomena: self-employment and religion. Self-employment has
been the main economic feature of Korean immigrants and sets them
apart from most other immigrants. One study found that in Los Angeles,
53 percent of male and 36 percent of female Koreans were self-employed.
Another third of the men found jobs in Korean ethnic businesses, which
meant that only one-fourth of employed Koreans worked for non-Koreans.[142] A 1980s New York City survey found that 61 percent of the husbands and 51 percent of the wives were self-employed and that the businesses they ran employed other family members as well.[143] The most well-
known economic activities, of course, were the green groceries in
American cities. In Los Angeles alone, Koreans ran 2,800 grocery-liquor
stores in 1990.[144] Others place the figures even higher, and one source
claims that the number of Korean-owned grocery stores in the United
States in the 1990s was approximately 25,000.[145] A few were begun by
Korean immigrants who came from South America, but most were
started by immigrants fresh from Korea. Taking over fruit and vegetable
stores formerly run by Jews and Italians, often in predominantly black
neighborhoods, Koreans have found an economic niche; they have
pooled their funds and been willing to work the requisite long hours to
earn a profit from these enterprises.[146] Operators of groceries get up at
dawn, or in some cases earlier, head for centers of produce distribution,
return to their stores, and labor into the evening selling this produce.[147]

Although the Korean presence is especially noticeable in New York
City and Los Angeles, Korean entrepreneurs have opened stores in cities
and towns ranging from El Paso, Texas, to the Washington, D.C., area,

to Palisades Park, New Jersey; they have branched out as well, operating other small businesses. While Los Angeles claimed the largest number of Korean stores in its Korea Town, Palisades Park, a much smaller town, boasted several hundred Korean-run shops.[148] In 1999 the Annandale community just outside of the nation's capital reported that Korean-run businesses included "16 beauty salons, 10 weekly newspapers, nine acupuncturists, eight women's clothing shops and two bridal shops."[149] More recently, nail salons started by Korean women, but sometimes taken over by men, have appeared especially around New York City, Chicago, and Los Angeles.[150] The Korean-American Nail Salon Association estimated that 4,000 nail salons were run by Koreans in New York City and the surrounding suburbs in 2001.[151] Dry cleaners were at first shunned by Koreans as being too expensive to start and run. More recently, however, the advantages of dry cleaning establishments have attracted Koreans. As the *Atlanta Journal-Constitution* described the Atlanta area, "Drop off a load of dirty clothes at practically any dry cleaners and the business owner is likely to be Asian—Korean actually."[152] Such stores can be operated in safer suburban neighborhoods and with regular hours, not the seventy-two-hour week required in green groceries.

If they could not find fellow countrymen to employ, Korean entrepreneurs hired non-Koreans. In New York City and elsewhere, these additional employees were essential for keeping their businesses open twenty-four hours a day. These workers were mostly Latinos—primarily Mexicans in California and New York City. Conflicts have developed, and several Korean owners have faced union drives. Trade unions, insisting that Koreans violated labor laws concerning working conditions and pay, set up pickets in front of several stores. The owners claimed that they were not violating the law and said they had to stay open at all hours in order to make a profit.[153]

Ethnic disagreements involving Koreans and Latino employees were minor compared with those between owners and customers in predominantly African American neighborhoods. These conflicts have sometimes erupted into boycotts instigated by black leaders, who claimed that the green grocers were rude, unwilling to employ blacks in their businesses, and exploitative of the African American community. The first major boycott, which occurred in New York City in 1982, was organized by an African American nationalist group. Other boycotts followed, some ending in violence and forcing the closing of the stores.[154]

The greatest shock experienced by Korean American business owners came in the 1992 Los Angeles riot, which was sparked when a jury acquitted several white Los Angeles police officers of charges that they had beaten Rodney King, an African American man, in a traffic stop. According to Helen Zia, "Everything about life changed for Korean Americans on April 29, 1992. When the smoke cleared from the three-day uprising in Los Angeles, 54 people had died and some 4,500 shops were reduced to ashes."[155] Owners complained that police protection was lacking, that the loss of revenue forced them out of business, and that hundreds of Korean businesses were destroyed as a result of the rioting. The riots were not limited to blacks and Koreans; many Latinos were also involved in the violence. In spite of efforts to restore the Korean Los Angeles community, many merchants closed their doors because of the destruction. Four years after the upheaval, nearly one-quarter of Korean owners had ceased to conduct business in Korea Town, and Korean leaders claimed that they were continuing to leave, finding better locations elsewhere in the city.[156] Korean and African American leaders formed organizations to ease tensions between the two groups, but they had only mixed success.

Of course, in small Los Angeles shops as elsewhere, the owners were also subject to robbery, and several Korean merchants were killed.[157] But it was not violence, boycotts, and robbery alone that forced some Korean business owners to stop running their stores and return to Korea in the 1990s. Seventy-hour workweeks and the labor of both husbands and wives were required to return a profit, and in some cities there were simply too many stores competing with one another. In the early 1990s Korean leaders estimated that 1,600 Korean-run stores went bankrupt.[158] In New York City the number of green grocers dropped from 5,000 in 1993 to 4,000 just three years later.[159] Women who ran nail salons were also faced with the question, "Just how many nail salons can operate profitably in one neighborhood?"[160]

Overall, Korean women were more apt than women generally to work for wages. Studies in Chicago, New York City, and Los Angeles revealed that 75 percent of Korean immigrant wives worked for pay either in family businesses or for others, while the figure for American women generally was roughly 60 percent in 1993. Women, whether working in family enterprises or in garment shops or other positions, were still expected to run the family household. Educated women fared better than others in sharing household tasks with their husbands, but studies indicate that

Korean women generally had a larger burden of housework than American women.[161]

In spite of their high rate of self-employment or working for other Koreans, Koreans have also found low-wage employment working for non-Koreans. For Korean women, jobs were easy to obtain. In Los Angeles in 1980 many Korean women held jobs as operators in garment shops, where knowledge of English was not required and the pay was low.[162] Some of these shops were run by Koreans—an estimated 700 in Los Angeles and 350 in New York City—and they utilized cheap family labor or employed other Korean women. Most of the employees in the Korean-run garment factories were not Korean; rather, they were Latino.[163]

The adverse experiences of so many immigrants no doubt played a major role in discouraging immigration after 1990. After averaging more than 30,000 annually in the 1980s, Korean immigration dropped to 25,430 in 1991 and to 18,734 in 1992, the year of the Los Angeles riots. It dropped further during the rest of the decade, averaging about 17,000, or only half of the 1980s figures. Clearly Koreans were showing less desire to go to the United States.[164] Indeed, many returned home in the 1990s. According to the *Korea Times,* a Chicago newspaper, 6,487 Koreans returned to Korea in 1992.[165] Improved politics and a growing Korean economy after 1980 also played roles in inducing this return migration.[166] In the early 1990s the crisis triggered by North Korea's plan to manufacture nuclear weapons made many South Koreans uneasy, but what impact the announcement of North Korea's intentions would have on immigration to the United States was not clear. The crisis certainly provoked tensions and debate in Korean American communities.[167] The crisis was temporarily resolved in 1994 when North Korea halted its program, but then a new crisis erupted in 2002 when North Korea once again announced that it was producing atomic weapons.[168]

While earning a living required long working days, Koreans have nonetheless found time to form ethnic associations. Business organizations have provided one forum for pooling knowledge and even money, especially in view of the fact that Koreans are not necessarily ghettoized in housing. Cultural groups, newspapers, and Korean television have also served the Korean communities. But by far the most important immigrant institutions have been the churches, and to speak of Korean Americans is to speak of Protestant Christianity. Religious life is the second main feature of Korean immigrant life. About New York City Pyong Gap Min notes, "Go to any part of New York City where a sizable number of Koreans live and you are bound to find many Korean churches." *The Korean Churches Directory of New York* said that nearly 600 Korean churches served the metropolitan area in 2000. Min concluded, "In both their number and their social functions, Korean churches are the most important ethnic organizations in the New York Korean community."[169] In Chicago another survey found that there was one Korean minister "for every 69 Korean adult residents."[170] Korean churches were also found in the South. The *Atlanta Journal-Constitution* reported that Koreans had 100 churches in the Atlanta metropolitan area in 1997.[171] Two years later the *Fort Worth Star-Telegram* estimated that Texas had 180 Asian Baptist churches, including 80 where Koreans worshiped.[172]

Only 20 percent of Koreans in their homeland are Christians, but half of those coming to America are estimated to be Christians, mostly Methodists and Presbyterians. Authorities also believe that a considerable number of the others become members of Protestant churches after they settle in the United States; some surveys estimate that 70 percent of Koreans are members of churches.[173] The churches themselves provide not only a faith but also many programs to aid the newcomers; they remain vital for the cohesion of the Korean community.[174]

Like so many Asian immigrants, Koreans stressed education for their children. Because so many of the best schools in the United States were located in well-off suburbs, parents made special efforts to live in these communities. Children were also apt to take music lessons and to attend classes and programs designed to raise grades and SAT scores.[175] In 1995 the Korean-language yellow pages listed ten special "cram" schools in the New York City area.[176] Nancy Foner told about one extraordinary case of aiding children in their educational endeavors: "Chinese and Korean parents put intense pressure on their children to excel and often make enormous personal sacrifices to ensure that they get a good education. An extreme example is a Korean woman who believed that by fasting she would help her children get into a selective New York high school." In this case her wish was answered; each of two children won places in the city's Bronx Science High School.[177] In New York City, where Korean students constitute only 1 percent of the school population, they make up 15 percent of students at Stuyvesant and Bronx Science, both of which were among the city's elite high schools.[178] In short, the children were expected to be part of the controversial model minority.[179]

The future of Korean immigration depends on both the political and economic life of Korea and the opportunities available in the United States. However, there is not an absolute correlation with economic conditions in the United States. The good years of the American economy in the 1990s were a period of decreasing immigration from Korea. The difficulties of making a living in small business in the United States and the violence and prejudice Koreans experienced, even in a booming economy, served to prevent the large-scale immigration of the 1970s and 1980s from continuing. Of course, conditions at home, such as the crisis over North Korea's nuclear policy in 2002 and 2003, also play a major role in the migration process.

The Korean American community is slowly shifting into the hands of the children who came of age after the 1980s. The Korean community in the United States is still largely foreign born, but as the second generation and the "1.5 generation" (those born in Korea but migrating to the United States at an early age) mature, they will increasingly define the future of Korean Americans.

American society has become much more tolerant since World War II. While the post-1950 Koreans experienced prejudice and violence, they had many more opportunities than the first wave that arrived between 1903 and 1907. Yet ethnic tension remains a reality of American life. The Los Angeles riot of 1992 prompted some Koreans to return home and deterred others from migrating, but it also induced Koreans to organize politically. Thus far their small numbers and sometimes lack of citizenship have given them very limited political clout, although Jay Kim, a conservative California Republican, was elected to the U.S. House of Representatives in 1992. He served several terms in Congress, until he was defeated for renomination in 1998.[180] Koreans will no doubt begin to become more active and learn the value of coalitions in order to have more say over their lives.

In 1940 less than one-half of 1 percent of the American population was Asian. The 2000 census revealed that persons claiming to be Asian or part Asian numbered nearly 12 million, which was 4.2 percent of the U.S. population.[181] Ethnic Chinese, Filipinos, and Koreans constituted well over half of this figure. Most of them were immigrants who had arrived after immigration policy changed, especially the Hart-Celler Act of 1965. These three groups clustered along the West and East Coasts, but their presence was noticeable throughout the United States. Yet there remained the other half of the new Asians. Their story will be told in the next chapter.

7

Across the Pacific Again
South Asian Immigrants

The renewed non-European immigration also included South Asians, who had come in small numbers before World War II. The Asian Indian migration flow began with legislation in 1946 that permitted the entry of 100 Indian immigrants yearly and granted them the right to naturalization. Two decades later the Hart-Celler Act of 1965 gave India the same number as other nations—20,000, not counting immediate family members of U.S. citizens. In 1990 the allotment was increased slightly for all countries. While in the 1940s only 1,761 Indians came to America, by the end of the twentieth century India had become one of the largest source nations for new American immigrants. From 1994 to 1998, a total of 189,081 Indian immigrants arrived, making India fourth, after Mexico, the Philippines, and China, and by the late 1990s Indian immigration averaged about 40,000 annually; in 2001 it reached a high of 65,916. Only Mexico sent more immigrants to the United States in that year.[1] The census of 2000 counted more than 1.7 million Indians in the United States, and given the immigration figures for the 1990s, the number was sure to grow during the first decade of the twenty-first century.[2]

The Immigration and Naturalization Service reports differed from the census total because their immigration figures do not consider the fact that many Indians migrated from areas outside of India, such as Trinidad, Guyana, or England. Those entering from the Caribbean were descendants of the first wave of Indian immigrants who had been recruited as laborers in the nineteenth century. For example, Dayanand Bhagwandin, the first Indian to run for political office in New York City, was born in Guyana. In 1998 Guyana-born Michael Duvalle and England-born Faisal Sipra also ran unsuccessfully for the New York State Assembly. All three were Republicans.[3] Just before Memorial Day, 2003, some 50,000 Indians showed up in New York City to celebrate Phagwah, a traditional Hindu holiday. Those participating hailed from Guyana and were mostly Indian Hindus.[4]

Still other Asian Indians were expelled from Africa when Uganda's Idi Amin ordered the confiscation of Asian property in the 1970s. Most of the Ugandan Indians migrated to Canada and Great Britain. Only a few came directly to the United States, though some later settled in America. In the 1980s and 1990s about 7 percent of African immigrants heading for the United States were Asians. Settlement for some required second or even third moves. *Little India* reported of one such family's migration. First the Manu Lal family migrated from India to Afghanistan; when that country exploded in violence, they fled to Germany and finally to America. Another migrant, Ravina Advani, traveled from India to Hong Kong and from there to Sierra Leone. From Sierra Leone he finally came to America. Another family migrated from Kenya to England and finally the United States.[5] The flight from England to the United States was not unusual because substantial numbers of these immigrants came to the United Kingdom, especially in the 1940s and 1950s, and some then immigrated to the United States. Overall the second half of the twentieth century witnessed an Indian diaspora even greater than that of the nineteenth century. As the twentieth century came to an end, an estimated 18 million Indians lived outside their original homeland.[6] Although the number of undocumented Indian immigrants is unknown, most experts do not believe that figure is large.

Transnational Indians sometimes worked temporarily before moving on to the United States, Great Britain, or Canada. For example, many Asian Indians worked for months in nations such as Saudi Arabia or the United Arab Emirates before relocating to the United States. By and large Middle Eastern nations did not welcome Asians other than as temporary workers. Thus some Indians coming to America might have brothers, sisters, or other family members residing temporarily in the Middle East as well as kin in Canada and/or Great Britain.[7]

The movement of Indians to the United States was vastly larger than the number at the turn of the twentieth century, and the social and economic composition of the latest Asian Indian immigrants was considerably different as well. Although uneducated Sikh men dominated the first wave of immigration, the post–World War II migration was made up of families, with women and children becoming the majority, and most were Hindus. The new migration was also characterized by persons of high education and skills. Some of the first to arrive in the 1950s and 1960s were students, who found jobs after completing their studies. These students accounted for a significant number of Indian immigrants in those decades.[8] After 1980, study in America remained popular for Asian Indians. A case in point is Kalpana Chawla, the Indian American who was killed when the space shuttle *Columbia* exploded in February 2003. Chawla came to America as a young woman with an engineering degree. She earned a master's degree at the University of Texas, which enrolled the largest number of foreign students among southern colleges and universities. She then earned a doctoral degree at the University of Colorado before entering the space program.[9] In the 2001–2 academic year, Indians topped the list of foreigners in American colleges and universities. For the first time, in that year India's 66,936 students surpassed China's 63,211.[10]

The *Handbook for Asian Indians* reported in 1998 that 80 percent of Indian immigrant men possessed college degrees and that a large proportion, perhaps as high as one-half, held advanced degrees.[11] While students from India continued to study in American colleges and universities and then change their immigration status after 1970, many more were educated in India and elsewhere. It was the highly educated Indians who caught the public eye. Hardly a hospital in the nation's largest cities was without Indian medical professionals on staff. Dr. Pradeep Thapar, who specialized in child psychiatry and lived in the prosperous Chicago suburb of Flossmoor, remarked, "Go into any hospital in the United States and you'll find Indian doctors on the staff."[12] An estimated 33,000 Indians practiced medicine; in 1998 they accounted for about 5 percent of all U.S. physicians. Many entered specialities such as anesthesiology, where they amounted to 10 percent of the total. If they could not obtain high-paying medical jobs, they staffed inner-city hospitals, psychiatric wards, and rural clinics.[13] Indian physicians were so numerous that they formed an ethnically specific professional association: the American Association of Indian Physicians.

Karen Leonard reports that in addition to the doctors' organization, there were associations of Indian pharmacists and dentists.[14] Most of the doctors were men, but many Indian women also practiced medicine or worked in the health professions. In Bakersfield, California, forty of the ninety physicians from India were also married to a doctor.[15] A 1980 survey revealed that among Indian immigrants 11 percent of the men and 8 percent of the women were physicians. Another 7 percent of the women were nurses. After 1980, tighter immigration restrictions for medical professionals slowed the growth of Indians in these fields.[16]

Indians' professional employment was not limited to the practice of medicine. Engineering, computer science, and the sciences also attracted

Indian immigrants, who found employment in the nation's universities or in large companies such as IBM. The Entrepreneurs and Indian CEO High Tech Council boasted a Washington, D.C., membership of 165 Indian American CEOs, whose companies employed nearly 20,000 people.[17] The secretary of the New Jersey Asian-Indian Chamber of Commerce noted, "In the pharmaceutical industry much of the research staffs are Asian-Indians."[18] It was in Silicon Valley and in other centers of computing and high-tech industry that the Asian professionals, including Indians, made a major contribution. AnnaLee Saxenian, the author of a 1999 study of Asian entrepreneurs in Silicon Valley, noted that when technologists say Silicon Valley is built on ICs "they refer not to integrated circuits, but to Indian and Chinese engineers."[19]

In addition to immigration, the United States permitted tens of thousands of persons to work temporarily for periods ranging from several months to six years. The number varied from year to year depending on demand in the United States, and they included Caribbean agricultural workers and highly skilled persons who had special merit or training in fields such as computer programming or medicine. In 1999 the H-1B visas for these well-educated workers numbered 115,000. Of that number, nearly half went to Indians.[20] Indians also were granted the lion's share of L-1 visas, which were given to employers transferring employees from a foreign branch to the United States.[21]

In other cases, employers paid "headhunters" to find workers for their businesses. Maria Tray, owner of a small computer consulting company in Ohio, decided that regular hiring channels were inadequate to secure skilled workers, foreign or domestic. Rather than pay a headhunter to find workers, she and her husband flew directly to India to find them, and she returned with six new employees. She had to offer jobs to only eight Indians.[22]

Indians' educational training and ability to speak English gave them a head start among immigrants. In the 1990 census Indians topped the list for family income levels among immigrant groups. Family incomes were not the product of the men alone. More than half of Indian women were working for pay, many in highly paid professions.[23] Moreover, Asian Indians were not clustered in poverty-stricken immigrant ghettos.

Some of these successful immigrants sent cash remittances back to India to foster economic development in their home villages. One Indian cab driver, hardly a highly skilled or highly paid occupation, managed to send enough money to his home village to establish a school there for girls. He named it for his illiterate mother.[24] Still others returned to India as new opportunities opened there for those with high-tech skills.

Following the first professionals were the entrepreneurs, especially those owning and managing motels. The first Indian motel owner was reported to be Kanjibhai Desai, who purchased a motel in downtown San Francisco. Others followed, and by the 1960s the numbers had reached sixty or seventy nationally. One of the most successful owners is Hasmukh P. Rama, who arrived in the United States in 1969 and observed that many Indians were the purchasers of motels. Four years later he bought one himself, and by 1999 his company operated twenty-three motels in six states. He became the first Asian to head the American Hotel and Motel Association.[25]

A majority of Indian motel owners had the surname Patel and came from Gujarati Province. While some were related to each other, most were not. One owner in Huntsville, Alabama, explained to a visitor that fifteen miles down the road a cousin owned a motel, and an uncle operated another motel "somewhere in Georgia."[26] A substantial number of these individuals hailed from Uganda, as featured in the film *Mississippi Masala*. At first the Patels and other Indians purchased independent motels, which could be bought relatively cheaply. If the price was too high, friends and relatives could be counted on for financial assistance. Often in the red, these marginal motels required physical improvement and long hours to turn a profit; as Tunku Varadarajan put it, "The first generation of Indian hotel owners, in a manner consistent with many an emergent immigrant group, scrimped, went without, darned old socks and never took a holiday."[27] In the 1980s Indians began to operate individual concerns in large motel chains, such as Days Inn, and by 2000 they operated well over one-third of the nation's motels.[28]

Often families or friends provided capital to purchase enterprises, but being included in the Small Business Association (SBA) set-aside program for minorities also helped. It required lobbying by Indians and other Asians to win the SBA's favor. Among the Asians to receive assistance from the SBA were Indonesians. According to Hugh Graham, the Indonesian population in the United States in 1989 was only 20,000, most of whom were middle-class. Other small immigrant groups such as those from Nepal and Bhutan won SBA approval, but those from Middle Eastern countries did not. Graham remarks that apparently "the Khyber Pass" was the dividing line.[29] Indians were a major beneficiary of the SBA loans; as the *Atlanta Journal-Constitution* noted, "No immigrant group better takes advantage of the program than Indian-Americans."[30]

These programs were not uncontroversial, in particular, because Asians began to surpass blacks and Latinos in receiving loans. The *Wall Street Journal* reported that in 1984 Asians received only 2.6 percent of SBA loans in Alabama, while blacks' share was 88 percent. A decade later Asians secured roughly half of the loans, and blacks won only one-third. About Alabama, one SBA official noted, "Almost all of my firms are in high tech." Elsewhere the picture was little different.[31]

Asian Indians found niches in the American economy other than motels. In New York and other cities they obtained licenses to run newspaper stands and to drive taxi cabs. Some were college graduates who could not find other jobs.[32] The newspaper stands also provided employment for those who lacked education or financial resources. Indians also began to purchase and run gas stations and convenience stores. When he retired in India, Kirpal Mangat and his wife, Balvinder, followed their three sons from Punjab to America. Kirpal worked as bookkeeper before purchasing a gas station, using his own savings and borrowed funds from friends. While one son ran the New Jersey station, the Mangats moved to Lancaster, Pennsylvania, and leased a Getty Mart convenience store and gas station. Another son operated a similar store in Reading, Pennsylvania.[33]

Indians also opened restaurants to cater to fellow Indians and other Americans who began to enjoy Indian food. Still others opened stores selling electronics and appliances. In 1976 two Indian friends, both engineers, opened an electronics store in the New York City borough of Queens, the first such shop of its kind in the city to be owned by Asian Indians.[34] Branching out was Vjina Haridass, who started with one job and then became co-owner of two businesses. She was born in Newark, New Jersey, but was educated partly in India. She became president of the Newark-based Vee Emm Marketing, which ran two stores selling inexpensive items, and also ran Micro Computing Consulting in New York City.[35]

In Laredo, Texas, Indian merchants operated several jewelry shops that catered to that city's large Mexican population. "What brought me to the U.S.?" asked one merchant. "The Mexicans come and they buy gold from me."[36] One estimate claimed that in 1989 these jewelry stores accounted for $500 million in sales. Other Laredo Indians branched out into selling electronics and clothing. As a result of these prosperous activities, "more than a few Indians live in the fashionable Del Mar C and Regency Park neighborhoods on the city's north side."[37]

On occasion Indians' businesses were illegal. In 1999 a New Jersey businessman was arrested and charged with illegally transmitting money for clients who wanted to send cash to their families in India. He was caught attempting to influence his case and pled guilty.[38] When Congress passed legislation in 1996 making it easier to deport immigrant criminals, a few Indians were deported. In 1998, fifty-two Indians were deported but only seven of them for criminal activities.[39]

The financial success of many new Indian immigrants enabled them to locate in upscale urban neighborhoods or in the suburbs.[40] The major concentrations were in the New York–New Jersey area and California, but Indians could be found throughout the United States. The 2000 census found 129,465 Indians in Texas.[41] To be sure, some settled near the hospitals where they worked, and others settled in polyglot neighborhoods such as Queens, a borough of New York City, where an incredibly diverse group of immigrants lived.[42]

The economic picture was not uniformly upbeat. Professionals had spearheaded the new Indian migration, but once they began using the family preference system, Indians with less education arrived. The migrating brothers and sisters did not always have the high level of education of the first wave. As Karen Leonard put it, "Many of these later immigrants, who came under the Family Reunification Act [the Immigration Act of 1965] are not so well qualified and their arrival occurred during a recession in the U.S. economy."[43] Madhulika Khandelwal's study of New York City's Indian population notes that the "brain drain" to New York City was a product of the immigrant flow of the 1960s and 1970s, but the migration of Indians with less education after the 1970s made the New York City Indian community "multilayered," with class distinctions.[44] In fact, the post-1980 migration in part accounts for the entrepreneurial activities, for running such businesses required less education, and often the enterprises are only marginally profitable.

To be sure, as a group Indians were better off than Latinos or most other Asians, but success had its limits. To cope with inadequate family incomes, women and even children had to work. A reporter for *India Currents* noted many Indian students who attended high schools in Berkeley, California, worked at jobs after school hours: "Increasingly the children of the less affluent second and third wave of immigrants from South Asia are working long hours in violation of the child labor laws designed to protect their rights. They worked in family-owned gas stations, motels and Indian fabric shops—as well as taking jobs in other business to contribute to the family's income."[45]

Then, too, a number of Indian families lived below the official poverty line. Following his sister, who migrated to the United States in 1975, Vinvod Gupta came in 1987 to seek medical care and a better life. He returned to India to meet his future wife. After marriage, he brought his family to the United States in 1993. Yet bad health followed Gupta, and eventually he could no longer work. He was forced to live on public assistance and food stamps and the meager earnings from his wife's job, which brought home only $900 a month.[46]

For the most part, Asian Indians have been spared the tensions and violence that occurred between Koreans and blacks and Latinos, and Indians have not experienced a riot on the scale of the Los Angeles eruption of 1992. Yet Indians have been subject to discrimination and abuse. In Jersey City, New Jersey, in 1987, "Dotbusters" attacked several young Indians and sent them to the hospital. This term refers to the dot, or *bindi,* that Indian women often wear on their foreheads as a sign of marital fidelity. Resentful of the growth of Indian stores, one angry Dotbuster claimed, "The Hindus own everything." His friend said, "A lot of kids around here go Hindu hunting at night."[47] The 11,000 Indians in Jersey City were terrified; some did not let their children attend school until the violence lessened.[48] Other incidents followed elsewhere in New Jersey.[49] Similar attacks also occurred in New York City, where Rjishi Maharaj, whose family was from Trinidad, was beaten senseless by three men wielding baseball bats.[50]

Most Asian Indians did not experience such violence, but they nonetheless confronted American racial history, which could be a trial for these newcomers. Racism apart, even the highly educated had to deal with different mores and customs. For women, the new society represented a special challenge, which weakened the traditional authority of men and impacted the family world of these immigrants.[51] Back home, elite women had an immediate and extended family network, along with servants. If they worked in a highly paid American profession, conflicts were less acute because money was available for household help. Less educated women, however, often had to work in family enterprises and were utilized as cheap labor. As one authority noted, "The woman who is running a grocery or restaurant in L.A. would not have done this back in India or Pakistan or Bangladesh."[52] One critic noted that the educated

elites were eager for work in a new environment, but that the less educated were "resentful about having to work since the kinds of jobs in re-
tailing, factory work or service jobs they are likely to get bring them little prestige."[53] Moreover, first-generation immigrant women, Indians included, were still expected to cook, tend to the children, and clean the
house, while at the same time their relative status rose because their earnings were crucial to the family income. Cooking traditional ethnic food,
essential to immigrant identity, required considerable time. In addition,
there was the task of raising children in a whole new environment. This
immigrant generation, like so many others, did not fully understand their
children, who faced a high-pressure youth culture in school, on television,
among peers, and in shopping malls. The generational conflict was especially evident in battles over arranged marriages, with many of the second
generation rejecting their parents' notions about dating and marriage.[54]

Maintenance of traditional culture was not limited to food or family
roles. The new Indian immigrants, unlike those of the early twentieth century, were mostly Hindus. To be sure, a number of Sikhs arrived, as did
Muslims and even some Christians and smaller groups. The newcomers
came to a predominantly Christian culture but one that was becoming
more tolerant and pluralistic. For the Christians, of course, there are
ample churches and denominations, and Christian leaders from India
have been known to visit America.[55] Before 1920 Sikhs had already established themselves, but their numbers were small and temples few.
Their numbers expanded rapidly as new Sikh immigrants arrived. At a
1999 gathering of Sikhs, Dr. I. J. Singh, a professor of dentistry, declared,
"When I came to the United States in 1960, there were two Sikhs in Manhattan and one was me. Then I went to Oregon, where I was the only one.
Now I am seeing so many familiar faces that I can't find my friends
here."[56] Sikhs were apparently among the most highly educated of the Indian community and had funds to build their religious institutions.[57]
They even ran summer camps for their children, to instruct them in the
ways of their ancestors' religion.[58]

Hindus arrived from a country where they were the majority, but now
they were only a small fraction of America's religious population. Like
Sikhs they had to build their religious structures and customs from the
bottom up. In areas where Hindus were few in number, religious worship
took place in the home until enough followers arrived to build their own
temples.[59] One of the first to be built was the Ganesha Temple in New
York City, which was founded in 1977 and became "the most inclusive

and welcoming of the city's Indian religious centers." On the facade were symbols of Hinduism, Islam, Christianity, Judaism, and Buddhism, thus "signifying this temple's recognition that all religions seek a common end."[60] The largest temple was the Hindu Temple of Greater Chicago, which cost $7 million to build in the 1980s.[61] Hindu temples expanded during the last decades of the twentieth century, with religious life becoming an important mechanism for maintaining traditional culture. Indeed, some believed that Indians were more religious in America than in India; such was the need for familiarity in a new country.[62]

The new South Asian Indians also formed a variety of secular organizations, such as professional or business associations, to maintain their culture. In New York and California, Indians held annual parades celebrating their heritage and the independence of India from British rule. The 1998 New York City parade was the concluding event of a year-long celebration of the fiftieth anniversary of India's independence.[63] Various associations were sometimes brought together in celebration of Indian traditions. Such was the case in January 1998, when the Indian Cultural Society of New Jersey sponsored events in that state, and Indians hosted a major celebration of Indian culture at New York City's Lincoln Center, featuring music and dance.[64] Bhartati Mukherjee was probably the best known of Indian writers telling of the immigrant experience, and by the late 1990s a number of younger novelists and poets were making their mark writing ethnic literature.[65]

The rapidly growing Indian community and the problems it encountered prompted several leaders to urge their fellow immigrants to become politically active so that their concerns would be addressed by politicians. Several candidates ran unsuccessfully for Congress. Others ran for local office, but they had neither a major impact nor a record of winning elections.[66] Indian groups also lobbied Congress to express their worries about conflicts between Pakistan and India, especially regarding the fate of Kashmir.[67] The ongoing Pakistani-Indian conflict over Kashmir periodically aroused the Indo-American community. In 1999, for example, when the controversy heated up, Indians lobbied Congress and raised funds to send to Kashmir.[68]

If the Indian community is to be effective, Indians will have to close ranks, become American citizens, and acquire the skills needed for political success. The 2002 Democratic primary in Georgia's Fourth Congressional District illustrated both the strengths and the weaknesses of Indian political efforts. In that contest Indians rallied with other groups to defeat

Congresswoman Cynthia McKinney, whom they believed to be anti-India. Her opponent, Denise Majette, defeated McKinney, who partly blamed Indians for her loss. Some Indians agreed, but without the support of other groups that targeted McKinney, Majette would not have been successful. Indian voters were few in the district.[69] The rapid growth of the community and the increasing number of Indians who were becoming American citizens pointed to greater political involvement, but the process was a long and slow one.[70]

While not as impressive as the Indian diaspora, a growing number of immigrants from Pakistan, Bangladesh, Afghanistan, Thailand, Sri Lanka, Nepal, and Tibet came to America following the 1965 changes in immigration law and special legislation enacted later. The 2000 census reported 153,533 Pakistanis in the United States.[71] The United States was not the only destination for Pakistani immigrants; Africa, Canada, and especially the United Kingdom were favorite receiving countries. When Congress passed the 1946 law granting the Philippines and India small quotas, persons from Pakistan and Bangladesh were included in that quota. However, when Pakistan became independent the next year and Bangladesh received its independence from Pakistan in 1971, each got a separate number. From 1954 to 1964 Pakistan recorded only 1,310 newcomers to the United States, but the number grew to a high of 20,355 in 1991, only to drop off in the next few years; it was 16,448 in 2001.[72] Of course some ethnic leaders believed the official figures were inaccurate. The Triennial Comprehensive Report on Immigration, using data supplied by the INS, estimated that undocumented Pakistanis living in the United States in 1996 numbered 41,000.[73] This number was greater in 2000, which led to large estimates of unauthorized persons. By the end of the 1990s, fewer than 31,000 Pakistani immigrants lived in New York City, but some sources say as many as 120,000 lived there, with 15,000 just in Brooklyn's "Little Pakistan."[74]

Among the first persons to arrive from Pakistan were students, who majored in engineering, business, and economics.[75] Like so many other foreign students, these pioneers often became immigrants after finishing their studies.[76] Others were professionals who studied at home or in other countries before coming to America. For example, one of the elite was Dr. Abdus Saleem, who left Pakistan in 1971. He located first in Pennsylvania, then moved to Houston in 1975. His wife was also a doctor. Abdus became chief of hematology at Methodist Hospital and a professor of pathology at Baylor College of Medicine. These elite migrants were numerous enough to form groups such as the Association of Pakistani Physicians.[77]

Others tried their hands at running small businesses. In 1994 it was estimated that half of the newspaper stand licenses in New York City were held by Indians and Pakistanis and that 90 percent of the new applicants were from those groups.[78] The Midwest also attracted Pakistanis. When Ali Khoja arrived from Pakistan, a friend advised him to purchase a Dunkin' Donuts outlet in Waukegan, Illinois. His friend, Armit J. Patel, encouraged other Indian and Pakistani immigrants in Chicago to buy Dunkin' Donuts shops. Patel himself was running a convenience store in 1973 when he happened to drop into a doughnut store in Skokie, Illinois, a Chicago suburb. To his amazement, "The guy making doughnuts was speaking Gurarati." Patel believed that operating a doughnut shop was better than managing his small store. He used his savings and money borrowed from friends to purchase a Dunkin' Donut shop in Skokie. While these South Asian immigrants had probably never heard of doughnuts in their native lands, by 1999 Indian and Pakistani immigrants allegedly owned a large number of Chicago's Dunkin' Donuts outlets.[79]

Like Indians, Pakistanis ran convenience stores or opened small businesses to support their growing ethnic community. Pakistani immigrants also became limousine drivers and drove cabs in New York and other cities. A Pakistani business group, the Pak Brothers Yellow Cab Drivers, began to buy New York City cab medallions in the 1990s and then hired Pakistanis as drivers. When the city offered 400 new medallions for sale in 1995, Pak Brothers was first in line.[80] In addition to the long hours driving a cab required to make a living, on several occasions drivers were robbed and even killed. Still other Pakistanis worked in construction. Those lacking adequate English skills and higher education often had little choice in jobs. One occupation open to Pakistani Muslim women was in Islamic schools, where they became teachers.[81] South Asian women also ran ethnic grocery stores.[82]

Although their community was not large, enough Pakistanis had come to the United States by 2000 to have an impact on the nation's religious groups. Islam appears to be the fastest-growing religion in America, and Pakistanis were overwhelmingly Muslims. Their growing presence is especially felt in cities that have mosques. The San Francisco area alone reported having thirty mosques in 1998.[83] Pakistanis have joined with other

Muslims in worshiping and in sending their children to Islamic schools. The growth of Islam was part of the general proliferation of diverse cultures in the United States due to the new immigration.

Among the new secular organizations were associations for professionals and the Pakistani Veterans Association. By the 1990s four Pakistani newspapers were being published. Written mainly in Urdu but also in English, these papers aimed to keep their readers informed about events at home. Some were sold in South Asian restaurants. One paper, the *Pakistan News*, edited by Irshad Hussain, boasted that it had a circulation of 25,000 across the country.[84]

The Pakistani community was not entirely removed from the conflicts between India and Pakistan. At New York City's India Day parade in 1993 a Pakistani man was arrested for harassing the parade. One of the organizers insisted that Pakistani immigrants "have no business to be here."[85] The next year Pakistanis held their own parade, which coincided with the anniversary of India's independence from British rule.[86] Both Indians and Pakistanis were uneasy when their countries carried out nuclear tests in 1998.[87] And, of course, the dispute over Kashmir was still alive in 2003. While one can exaggerate the conflicts between the Pakistani American and Indian American communities, they nonetheless point to the difficulties of developing a larger Asian American identity and movement.[88]

Bangladesh's independence did not come easily but the bloodshed in that struggle was only one of the nation's problems. Plagued by natural disasters, poverty, and overcrowding, many Bangladeshis were only too willing to leave their homes. Bangladesh's 123 million people live in one of the most crowded nations in the world, with about 1,800 persons per square mile. As one immigrant noted about the advantages of living overseas, "In our country, job opportunities are very poor. If they come here, they can help their families."[89] Some newcomers did not bring their families but only hoped to save enough to return home. As one commented, "If I get enough money, I will say goodbye to this [American] place."[90] Although the 1965 immigration act gave Bangladesh the same quota as all other nations, Bangladesh lacked the close connections required for immigration under this new system, which emphasized skills and family unification. As a result, immigration grew slowly, amounting to only a few hundred annually in the 1970s and early 1980s.

Beginning in the 1990s, however, the number of migrants from Bangladesh increased; this immigration peaked in 1991, when more than

10,000 persons obtained immigrant visas.[91] Buttressed by a 1990 law that included a provision for "diversity visas" for those nations that had not sent many to the United States before that time, Bangladeshis found a new way to enter the United States. The word was out that the lottery would help not only the Irish, for whom it was intended, but other nations as well, including Bangladesh.[92] From the time of the first lottery until 1998, Bangladesh won more than 20,000 such visas. In 1996, 3,753 of Bangladesh's 8,221 immigrants used the diversity visas. In 1999 it was reported that 1.3 million Bangladeshi were applying for the diversity visas, even though Bangladesh was allotted only 3,850 of the 55,000 slots for the next drawing. During the 1990s Bangladeshi postal officials opened extra counters and extended their hours of operation to twelve per day to handle the flood of applications. With several million applications sent from around the world to the United States, the chances of winning were slim, but as one Bangladeshi said, he was going to apply for "the DV-1 [diversity visa] even it if costs me that last piece of my land. Why should I rot in Bangladesh and starve almost every day if I have a place in America?"[93] The number of DV-1s dropped after 1996, but Bangladesh won 1,509 of the diversity visas in 2000 and 1,720 the next year.[94] An additional advantage of the lottery was that it made it possible for immigrants to come to America and then use the family preference system to bring their family members.

Not all arrived as a result of the lottery or family connections. A small number of well-educated professionals came under the preferences for those with certain skills. One of the highly educated was Iqbal Z. Quadir, a member of the faculty of Harvard University's Kennedy School of Government who held two degrees from the University of Pennsylvania's Wharton School. Quadir remembers that when his brother was ill in Bangladesh in 1971, he walked an entire day without success trying to find medicine. The memory prompted him to found Graemeen Phone, a small cell phone company, in 1997, in his native land. By 2002 it had become a profitable enterprise.[95] Other professionals were able to find a niche in the American economy, making the community somewhat bipolar.

Like so many other immigrants, many of those not using their professional skills sought employment as taxi drivers.[96] Bangladeshi immigrants also opened "Indian" restaurants. As one New York City restaurant owner said, "If we called them Bangladeshi only Bangladeshi immigrants will come. Americans don't know about our food; they come only to eat

Indian food. So we serve them South Asian food and call it Indian—so they do not get confused."[97] A few others opened food stores and real estate agencies. In New York City a number of such small stores in one block prompted residents to tag a portion of Sixth Street in Manhattan "Mini-Bangladesh."[98]

Bangladeshi immigrants settled in urban areas, such as Washington, D.C., Los Angeles, and New York City, with New York claiming the largest concentration. Figures are not precise, and some authorities believe that a number of the Bangladeshi were illegal immigrants. The presence of unauthorized immigrants made it difficult to know the exact size of the Bangladesh population in the United States. The New York president of the Bangladeshi Society claimed, for example, that the New York area housed more than 100,000, which was certainly an inflated figure.[99] Following enactment of the 1996 immigration act, which provided for more INS agents and tougher procedures for deportation of undocumented aliens and criminals, the INS deported increased numbers of illegal Bangladeshi immigrants. Eighty-one were deported in 1998, compared with sixty-one the year before, and an additional eleven were sent home from the nation's jails and prisons.[100]

In the late 1990s, some New York Bangladeshis moved to Detroit, the home to many of the nation's rapidly growing Muslim population. The immigrants found that smaller Detroit factories had jobs, and rents were considerably lower in the Detroit area than in New York City.[101]

Like so many other newcomers, the Bangladesh American community formed organizations and published newspapers. The Los Angeles Bangladesh Association dates to 1971, while the Texas Bangladesh Association claimed nearly 500 members in 1997.[102] A theater group was formed about the same time and newspapers published in Bengali, the language of Bangladesh. The Dallas area Bangladesh population was reported to be 5,000 in 1997 and was large enough to hold an annual Baishaki Mella (Spring Festival). A New York City school responded to its growing Bangladesh population by establishing a bilingual program in Bengali and English.[103] While trying to preserve their cultural traditions, Bangladesh immigrants also added to the growing Muslim population, helping to diversify both religion in general and Islam in particular in America.

Immigrant women, including those from Bangladesh, were confronted with the usual adjustments required of nearly all immigrants, in addition to domestic violence. How common domestic violence was to the

Bangladesh American community is unknown both to the Department of State, which monitored it in Bangladesh, and to local American police. The State Department reported wife beating to be widespread; a South Asian advocacy group for South Asian women, called Sakhi, also claimed that violence was not uncommon.[104] Few women came forward to make charges. Moreover, immigrant women lacking English and familiarity with local and immigrant laws were at a distinct disadvantage in confronting violence.[105] The spokeswoman for a New Jersey domestic violence group added that 70 percent of Asian Indian women arriving after 1970 came as dependents, with their husbands sponsoring them, and "this dependency on husbands for legal residency, loss of traditional family support as well as unfamiliarity with the laws and services of their adopted land keep many South Asian women captive within their abusive situations."[106]

Nor were new immigrants subject to violence limited to the poor and uneducated or those from Bangladesh. As Anita Govindarajan, founder of the South Asia Women's Empowerment and Resource Alliance in Portland, Oregon, put it, "The truth is domestic violence knows no boundaries of class, creed, religion, educational, or economic level. Victims have included members of every region, culture, and community found in the South Asian subcontinent."[107] In the 1990s in Fremont, California, the Federation of Indo-American Associations (FIA) sponsored a domestic violence shelter through a program called Aasra, which means "shelter" in Hindi. Most of the women involved in founding this project were Hindu immigrants, highly educated and from upper Indian castes, and many of the caste tensions of India were reproduced here. A staff member who was hired was a Pakistani Muslim woman, which created tension just below the surface in this organization.[108]

Afghanistan, one of Pakistan's neighbors, also sent immigrants to America after 1970, but under somewhat different circumstances. Most Afghans were exiles from their native land, even if they were unable to obtain refugee or asylee status. Few Afghans had settled in the United States prior to the Soviet invasion of Afghanistan in 1979. Most post-1945 refugees came to the United States to escape communism, and the Afghans were no different. As long as Soviet troops remained in their country (1979–89), millions fled Afghanistan. Most ended up in refugee camps in neighboring Pakistan, though some managed to go to other Asian nations or to Europe. Life in the camps was often brutal, especially for the women. The Soviet Union struggled for a decade, trying to control Afghanistan and support the Marxist government there; during the strife the United States supported anticommunist forces and accepted several thousand Afghan refugees annually.[109]

After the withdrawal of Soviet troops, Afghanistan still experienced turmoil and violence until the Taliban finally was able to control most of the country in the late 1990s and establish a radical Islamic regime. The United States gave refugee status to some Afghans wanting to flee during these violent years, but immigration officials were reluctant to grant large numbers of Afghans asylum or refugee status in the United States. In the 1980s, for example, the INS jailed several dozen Afghans who entered illegally and applied for asylum, keeping them in detention for more than a year and a half. Some of these detainees resorted to a hunger strike to dramatize their claims.[110]

Yet Afghans continued to flee in the 1990s, and some heading for the safety of Europe or the United States encountered long journeys, crossing rough terrain and eluding border guards. In May 2000, for example, Turkish soldiers were reported to have killed nine Afghans at the Turkish-Iranian border. Those not killed were detained by the Turkish authorities.[111] In 2000, a total of 1,561 Afghans were granted refugee status; another 269 received asylum.[112] Prospects for increased refugees were not bright after September 2001. Tighter rules for all refugees by the United States following the destruction of the World Trade Center on September 11, 2001, led to a drop from an average of 76,000 annually in the late 1990s to 68,400 in 2001. Further screening left thousands waiting after 2001 and limited the total to only 26,000 in 2002.[113]

Scholars believe that the official number of Afghans living in the United States is an undercount and that their numbers could be as be as high as 75,000, although considerably fewer were tallied in the 1990 census.[114] Whatever the exact number, these immigrants represented a variety of languages and cultures, but as two scholars noted, "Nearly all Afghans are Muslims, although a small number of Sikhs, Hindus, Christians and Jews live there as well."[115] The population in America is not representative; it is disproportionately middle-class or elite, consisting of those who could acquire the funds for the exodus. David Yaar, an economics professor in California, insisted, "The cream of the crop of Afghan society migrated to the U.S. or Europe."[116]

The largest concentration of Afghans is in the San Francisco Bay Area, with Fremont, the fourth-largest city in that area, hosting a neighborhood known as "Little Kabul" because of its Afghan shops and restaurants.[117]

The second-largest U.S. community of Afghans is located outside of Washington, D.C.[118] Nearly all Afghans faced financial struggle, but some managed, in immigrant fashion, to open small, successful businesses. Zia Nasery, the former head of Afghanistan's drug enforcement agency, arrived in 1984 and opened the Kyber Pass Restaurant in San Diego. Nasery was not unusual in his flight to America. He migrated first to Pakistan, then to India and Germany, and finally to California.[119] Others struggled. In one observer's words, "I've seen medical doctors driving taxis. I've seen former governors selling hot dogs from a cart."[120] Women have found that they entered a society that had more opportunities for them than the patriarchal one they had fled. But female Afghans were less educated than the men, although they could easily find low-level jobs.[121]

The destruction of the World Trade Center and its aftermath shook the Afghan American community.[122] President George W. Bush's military response—destroying the Taliban and terrorist camps based in Afghanistan—suddenly changed their homeland. Nearly all were concerned about the violence and widespread destruction at home, even if they welcomed the quick military defeat of the Taliban, which opened the possibility of the exiles returning to help rebuild their nation of origin. For those who emigrated in the 1980s and built new lives in America, thoughts of going home had less appeal. As Sheila Jahan, a physician practicing in the Washington, D.C., area said, she had to go home, at least for several months, but she also noted, "I am torn between two countries."[123]

Other Afghans were confused by the implications of the turmoil in their native land. At one mosque in New York City, the *New York Times* reported a division of opinion over the Taliban and the terrorist leader Osama bin Laden, who had claimed responsibility for the World Trade Center attacks of September 11 and was alleged to be in Afghanistan. The divisions were aggravated by the ethnic divisions within the Afghan community in the United States, which reflected those in Afghanistan. One scholar noted that such divisions were not limited to New York City: "The Afghan community is extremely divided, largely along ethnic lines. There are pro-Taliban factions and there are anti-Taliban factions."[124]

Unlike Afghans, the initial wave of Thai immigrants consisted of either professionals, students who remained in the United States, or women married to American military personnel who had been stationed in Thailand during the Vietnam War. Thais were bombarded with American culture during that era, triggering a desire by many to move to the United States.

With high rates of unemployment at home, even among medical professionals, the lure of America became stronger. The number of Thai immigrants grew, and several thousand were immigrating to the United States annually in the 1990s.[125] The center of Thai growth was in southern California, where so many other Asians settled. The 2000 census indicated that 112,969 Thais were in the United States, with one-third of them living in California.[126] While some of the latest Thais were professionals, the entrepreneurs among them often opened restaurants; in 1994 they reportedly ran 550 restaurants in California in addition to many auto repair services, beauty salons, hotels, travel agencies, and liquor stores.[127]

Many were not so fortunate, because they lacked English language skills and the education necessary for economic success. Some were illegal immigrants who worked as street merchants, and for those newcomers unskilled employment at low wages became the norm. Many of the women could find jobs only in low-paying garment shops. The most sensational employment that came to light involved Thai women who were working in a sportswear shop under conditions resembling a prison. In a second case the companion of a Thai diplomat was indicted for holding two illegal Thai women as virtual indentured servants.[128]

The Thai presence was also attested to by their Buddhist temples, cultural fairs, weekly radio and televisions in California, and newspapers. The Wat Thai Temple in Los Angeles was a Buddhist temple that counted more than 1,000 members in 1998.[129] In 1993, when students at the University of California at Los Angeles requested a course on the Thai American experience, the university agreed, establishing the first such course in American colleges and universities.[130]

From elsewhere in South Asia, small numbers of Sri Lankans, Tamils, Nepalese, and Tibetans arrived after the changes in immigration law.[131] Tibetans did catch the eye of Congress when their uprising against China's communist rule in 1959 was brutally suppressed by the Chinese. The teaching of Buddhism, the religion of Tibet, was banned, and several hundred thousand Tibetans fled to neighboring India or Nepal. Among those seeking a safe haven was the Dalai Lama, Tibet's spiritual leader. Only a handful of Tibetans managed to settle in the United States.[132]

At first, in spite of the fact that Tibetans were fleeing China's domination of their homeland, the U.S. government was unwilling to include them in refugee programs because George H. W. Bush's administration feared doing so would displease China. Finally, in 1990 Congress provided for the admission of 1,000 Tibetans over a three-year period. It required extensive lobbying and avoiding the refugee act to admit and aid them financially. Instead, these Tibetans came from third countries and were settled by private groups.[133] After these initial refugees arrived, others followed, and an estimated 9,000 lived in the United States in 2000.[134]

With only a few thousand being admitted to the United States, it was hard to determine who would receive the limited number of green cards. The Tibetan government in exile picked the recipients by lottery, granting preference to those few who had families already in the United States, who were educated, or who were government employees.[135] The newcomers were scattered throughout the United States, in communities such as San Francisco, Boston, Minneapolis, and Portland. In San Francisco, for example, 100 new arrivals tripled the city's earlier Tibetan population of only 50.[136] The new migrants faced the usual immigration problems: learning English, finding jobs and housing, and dealing with the differences between their own and American culture.[137] At the same time they wanted to keep pressure on China to change its policy toward Tibet. With such small numbers it was difficult to have much influence, and even hard to meet collectively. Connecticut's 100 Tibetans were scattered, and it was "difficult for Tibetans to get together."[138] However, they had American friends, and their plight was dramatized by demonstrations, Hollywood movies, several high-profile Hollywood actors, and the popularity of the Dalai Lama himself when he visited the United States.[139] His appeal reached far beyond the Tibetan community.

Of the South Asian immigrants, the Indian community is clearly the largest and is already established, with 1.7 million counted in the 2000 census, most of whom were born in India. Using the networks created through immigration law, Asian Indians were in a position to expand their population by migrating directly from India or places in Africa, the Caribbean, and even Great Britain. Of the other South Asian nations, Pakistan is in the best position to increase the number of visas to the United States by using family unification, while Bangladeshis have utilized the diversity lottery. The remaining South Asian groups are small and do not yet have networks to rapidly increase immigration. Yet world conditions can change, and so can American immigration laws. Future changes might increase flows from countries whose connections are small at the turn of the twenty-first century. What will happen to Bangladesh and other nations remains an open question.

While the east and south Asian communities, especially Filipino, Chinese, Korean, Vietnamese, and Indian, dominated immigration statistics from Asia, the changing immigration polices after World War II opened new channels of immigration from the nations of the Near East. Middle Easterners are the subject of the next chapter.

8

Middle Easterners

Few Middle Easterners came to the United States before the 1880s. When they did, the immigrants traveled from ports in the Mediterranean Sea on the journey to America. Mainly from the Ottoman Empire, they consisted of a variety of groups and cultures, just as Asians and European immigrants differed. Among them were Chaldeans from Telkaif (in present-day Iraq), most of whom were family farmers. They numbered only a few thousand. Unlike most Middle Easterners, Chaldeans were Roman Catholics. The first known Telkaif immigrant was Zia Attala, who arrived in 1889. Attala worked in a Philadelphia hotel before acquiring one of his own. Returning to Telkaif, he opened a hotel there and spread the news about America. Most of those following him were young men. In spite of initially intending to work only a few years in America, the majority remained and sent for their families. The center of Chaldean culture in America was Detroit.[1]

Armenians had appeared before 1890, but their numbers substantially increased in the following decades. Bitter because they lived under Turkish (and Russian) rule, they were looking for a haven from violence and persecution. Armenians were always fearful that new massacres would be perpetrated by Turks. Some 12,000 fled Turkey in the 1890s, and a greater number came to America before World War I—13,000 in 1913 alone.[2] Immigration authorities counted 51,000 in the fifteen years before World War I and 65,950 from 1889 to 1914.[3] Economic factors also played a role in their migration. Roughly three-quarters of Armenian immigrants were young men with meager futures in the Ottoman Empire. It helped that the journey was made cheaper; the cost of steerage from the Black Sea and the Mediterranean to New York City dropped after 1900.[4]

In the early twentieth century the Armenian church played a key role not only in aiding Armenian immigrants in the United States but also in disseminating information about America to Armenians thinking of escaping Turkish rule. American Protestant missionaries, who had founded churches and schools in the Middle East, persuaded Armenian youths to go to America to study religion.[5] Moreover, the Armenian Apostolic Church was the center of social life in the United States, and it kept ties with Armenia alive.[6]

Armenian immigrants settled in the Mid-Atlantic states and the Northeast, but they were also found in Fresno, California. At first they worked as unskilled laborers in manufacturing, but eventually many moved up into skilled positions and opened businesses such as tailor shops, groceries, and shoemaking establishments. The Fresno immigrants became successful farmers. And, of course, Armenians moved into the Oriental rug trade in all cities where they settled.[7] The newcomers utilized their contacts in the rug business in Armenia to their advantage. Some sold rugs while "the rug business . . . also fostered an important sideline for ambitious Armenian immigrants, who lacked the capital but who possessed strong arms and sturdy backs[:] the oriental rug cleaning and repairing business."[8]

Armenians faced social and economic discrimination in their new land, and they encountered barriers in joining clubs and in schools. Moreover, violence against them was not unknown. Americans hostile to immigrants also wanted to bar them from immigration. These Americans considered Armenians nothing more than inferior "Asiatics" ineligible for citizenship.[9] Were they "white," which entitled them to become U.S. citizens and to own land? Geographically Armenia was partly in Europe, but mostly in Asia. Given the widespread racism of the day it was possible that courts would consider them dark, non-European, and therefore not "white." Such rulings would limit their immigration and access to citizenship. A government commission reported that some Armenians had naturalized before the issue reached the courts in 1909. In that year a federal judge held that they had always been classified as "white" and adaptable to European and Western standards; therefore Armenians were "white."[10] A few years later Lebanese/Syrians were also declared "white" and hence eligible for naturalization as opposed to immigration exclusion.[11]

The largest number of Middle Eastern immigrants were Arabic speakers from Lebanon/Syria, which were districts in the Ottoman Empire; these individuals often identified themselves as Syrians. Because they did not come from an independent nation, scholars and immigration officials had difficulty counting them precisely, but at least 100,000 entered the

United States between 1880 and World War I.[12] Most of those in this Syrian first wave were Christian Maronites or members of other Eastern Orthodox churches. Only a small minority were Muslims. Indeed, some had been exposed to the missions and schools founded by Protestant missionaries in the Middle East.[13] These contacts stimulated interest in migration to America, but so did economic conditions. Most of the early immigrants were poor men with few skills who came to America to make money and then return home.[14]

In the United States, Lebanese/Syrian immigrants quickly fanned out into all regions and states as peddlers. Historian Alixa Naff notes that in search of wealth "no region was to prove too remote or forbidding."[15] They carried their goods on their backs and sold items in villages all over the United States. The networks of suppliers were fellow Syrians operating out of New York City or midwestern places such as Fort Wayne, Indiana.[16] Peddling did not require an education or even fluent English. These were mostly Christian networks, although a few Muslims peddled, too.[17] The practice was so common that a few women peddled, even though their culture dictated that women should stay home.

Eventually many peddlers opened their own businesses and settled in communities with their own institutions. None was so important as the churches, and if the newcomers did not establish their own, many joined existing Catholic parishes. Muslims joined with others of their faith. Because most Arabs were Christian and geographically scattered, Alixa Naff believes that they assimilated easily into mainstream American society. Economic success also helped the process of assimilation. Certainly the shortage of women forced the men to look elsewhere for partners, and many married non-Syrians.[18] The drop in immigration after World War I cut the flow of new arrivals so important for maintenance of immigrant and ethnic culture. That picture would not change until the post–World War II era, when new waves of immigrants entered and altered Arab America.

The restrictions of the 1920s, the Great Depression, and World War II all combined to curtail Middle Eastern migration. After the war, however, new immigration policy made it possible for persons from the Middle East once again to enter the United States in substantial numbers. But the Middle Easterners' share of the nation's population was not large, nor were nations from that area among the top sending countries. In 2000 the 2.5 million immigrants from the Middle East constituted about 1 percent of the American population and approximately 5 percent of the foreign born.[19] In 2000 and again in 2001, the Immigration and Naturalization Service reported no Middle Eastern nation among the top twenty nations sending emigrants to America.[20] No Middle Eastern country, according to immigration authorities, had as many as 30,000 estimated unauthorized immigrants in 1996.[21] The new immigration was considerably different from the old. To be sure, Armenians still came to America, as did persons from Lebanon and Syria, but these were not the only Middle Eastern nations experiencing an outflow of people. Immigrants also entered from Turkey, Iraq, Iran, Israel, Palestine, and North Africa. While Egypt is part of Africa, Egyptians have many social and economic characteristics in common with their Arab neighbors. For example, Egypt has been intensely involved with affairs in Israel and Palestine and is a member of the Arab League. Many Americans identify Egypt as part of the Middle East, and thus Egyptians in America are usually perceived as Middle Eastern.

Many Middle Easterners arrived as refugees, and many others were refugees in fact, if not in legal status. The Refugee Relief Act of 1953 included several thousand refugees from the Middle East, and subsequent 1950s legislation permitted more such refugees to enter. The Immigration Act of 1965 set aside 10,200 places for refugees from the Eastern Hemisphere, and the Refugee Act of 1980 set 50,000 as the "normal flow" from all parts of the globe. Some Middle Easterners entered under these laws. Others arrived in the United States as visitors or students and successfully pursued their claims of asylum. However, most post-1980 refugees were from Cuba, East Asia, and the former Soviet Union, not the Middle East.[22]

Middle Eastern immigrants represent a variety of religious, linguistic, and cultural groups. A case in point is the immigration of Arabs to America. Many Americans automatically assume that all Middle Easterners are Arabs, whom they believe to be Muslims. Particularly after the terrorist attacks in the United States on September 11, 2001, Muslims and Arabs were often conflated in the eyes of many Americans, in part because the terrorists were known as fundamentalist Muslims, or "Islamists." Arabs are overwhelmingly Muslim, but most of the early immigrants from that region were not Muslims, and it has only been in the last two decades that Muslims represent a majority (more than 70 percent) of Arab immigrants. Many Arabs who came to the United States were Lebanese Christians. Another Christian group, Egyptian Copts, among the oldest of Christian groups, also left for America.

In addition, a small number of Jews have immigrated, from both Israel and Arab nations. Many Jews from North Africa and Iraq went to Israel, but a few found their way to America. In 2000, Zoroastrianism, a religion originating in Iran, included only 200,000 adherents worldwide. Yet roughly 10 percent of Zoroastrians lived and worshiped in North America, including several thousand located in the United States.[23] After a revolution in Iran in 1978 and 1979, members of the Baha'i faith also found their position untenable in a Muslim nation ruled by fundamentalist religious leaders, and they left for the United States as well. Moreover, Christian Armenians who lived under Iranian rule quickly discovered the new regime was less tolerant than the old; they, too, emigrated to the United States.[24] The breakup of the Soviet Union after 1989 led to the creation of a new Armenian state and resurgence of migration by Christian Armenians to the United States.

Religious diversity was not the only characteristic of these latest newcomers. Quite a few hailed from Arabic-speaking nations, but others did not speak Arabic. Yet again, many American citizens assumed they all spoke the same language. Rather, they spoke a variety of languages, were members of many cultures, and represented a diverse group of social classes, including an educated elite as well as those without technical skills. Middle Easterners as a group have a higher proportion of college degrees than the U.S. population generally. However, unskilled workers and farmers from Yemen are also part of the migrant flow.[25]

Iran, which sent more people to America after 1945 than any other Middle Eastern nation, is a good example of the complexity of this diverse immigration. Immigrants from Iran are not Arabs. Rather, they spoke Persian or Farsi, not Arabic, and they represented several religious faiths, and were not especially involved with the wars between Israel and its Arab neighbors. Of greater concern to Iranians was the eight-year war against Iraq during the 1980s, as well as economic issues within Iran itself.

Iranian migration to the United States occurred in two distinct phases: the first before 1978 and the second after the Islamic revolution of 1978–79.[26] Of the quarter million Iranians who immigrated to the United States after World War II, the vast majority came after the 1978 coup. Until the Iranian religious revolution, American involvement in Iran centered around the production of oil and support of an anticommunist regime run by Mohammed Reza Shah, whom the American Central Intelligence Agency (CIA) had helped install in a 1953 coup. The Iranian economy did grow after 1945, but the prosperity created by oil production aided mainly the upper classes, who could now afford a higher standard of living, which included travel and the ability to send their children abroad for higher education. The United States was the main destination for Iranians seeking to elevate their educational skills. Overwhelmingly the children sent were male; because of the "patriarchal nature of Iranian society, females were less likely than males to be sent to study abroad unsupervised."[27] The students were able to study in the United States because they spoke English, which had become the main second language of Iran's high schools. Students in America could acquire the technical skills needed for the oil industry and industries allied to it. As a result, a growing number of Iranian students received their training in American colleges and universities.[28] Nearly half of those studying in the United States majored in engineering, followed by the humanities and business.

As did many students from other nations, Iranians found employment after completing their studies, obtained green cards, and worked in the United States. Some had returned first to Iran and then decided to emigrate. Overall the pre-1979 movement was relatively small, but it was growing decade by decade. More than 2,000 Iranians entered in the 1950s, another 8,895 in the 1960s, and 23,000 more before the Islamic Revolution. As a result, the Iranian exodus prior to 1979 consisted of many college graduates, who were able to find white-collar and professional employment in the United States. In addition, as was the case with Asians, some of these new immigrants were physicians.[29] Although small in numbers, the pre-1979 immigrants formed groups to maintain their culture.[30]

The Islamic Revolution of 1978–79 changed life for many Iranians who decided to move to either Europe or the United States if they could obtain a visa. In Mehdi Bozorgmehr's words, "More than any other factor, the Iran Revolution of 1978–79 and its aftermath have contributed to the growth of the Iranian diaspora population worldwide."[31] About half of those leaving Iran settled in the United States, with others going to Western Europe or Asia. The numbers going to America rapidly increased. In the 1980s, a total of 116,172 were recorded by the INS, with another 100,000 counted from 1990 to 1998, after which the numbers dropped. In 2001 Iran was not among the top sending nations.[32]

A number of those entering after 1979 came as refugees and were accorded the aid granted in refugee programs. Following the seizure of the American embassy by young radicals 1978, the United States and Iran became adversaries, and the American government was willing to receive some Iranians as refugees. Not a few were families of students already in the United States. California received the largest number, but exile and immigrant communities also developed in New Jersey, Georgia, Florida, and Virginia.[33] Still others managed to get to the United States and then applied for asylum. Asylum was difficult to gain even though the United States and Iran were at odds after 1979, for asylum was approved only on a case-by-case basis. Nevertheless, after the revolution, Iranians had one of the highest approval rates, and more than 85,000 Iranians managed to stay in the United States by winning refugee status or asylum.[34]

Refugees were eligible for federal programs geared to help them adjust to the United States. Such aid was welcomed by many because they had difficulty leaving with funds adequate for adaptation to American life. Refugees were less apt to come alone, and religious minorities in particular were likely to migrate in groups. Religious Iranians, if they did not share the dominant religious faith of the new Iran, were apt to suffer persecution, but such persecution did not automatically guarantee them asylum or refugee status in the United States even though the American government was hostile to post-1979 Iran.[35]

Economically, post-1979 Iranian exiles were similar to earlier immigrants in social and economic status. On the whole, they were well educated, with more than half of these immigrant men in Los Angeles holding a bachelor's degree or beyond.[36] Based on 1990 data, Mehdi Bozorgmehr's study of Los Angeles, which contains the largest Iranian community in the United States, indicates that Iranians were the third most highly educated immigrants, behind Asian Indians and Taiwanese.[37]

As new immigrants, Iranians sometimes had difficulty transferring their occupational skills to fit American patterns. Like some Asian groups, Jews, and Armenians, Iranians chose self-employment in part because they had access to the capital of others.[38] Iranian women were generally less well educated than the men, but the Los Angeles data indicate that 42 percent held a bachelor's degree or higher. Female participation in the paid workforce was not common in Iran, yet many immigrant women sought remunerative work in the United States.[39] In the 1990s only 15 percent of women in Iran worked for pay, but in the same period 48 percent of Iranian women in the United States participated in the paid workforce.[40] Some were well-educated professionals, and others operated their own businesses. Some men resisted working wives and returned to Iran to find a "proper" wife. "They think a woman who has been exposed to

214 I *Middle Easterners*

Western culture is too independent," said one Iranian psychologist. "They think," he continued, "women in Los Angeles have become too selfish, that they are not as loving and sacrificing and giving. That a woman from Iran will be more obedient."[41] Such changes were by no means limited to Iranian immigrants, for similar shifts in attitudes and behavior of women occurred for many women from traditionally conservative cultures.

Iranians, as relatively new immigrants, attempted to maintain their own cultures by forming institutions to keep alive their language and foster intraethnic communities for their children. Some of these were expressions of their religious faith, but others were more secular. Ethnic associations include newspapers, and in Los Angeles a twenty-four-hour Iranian television station began operation in 2000. It joined some other stations in broadcasting in Farsi, the modern dialect of Iran, and it was the first such station to operate all day, attempting to reach those persons in Iran who owned illegal satellite receivers.[42] Because many Iranians were minorities, such as Armenians and Jews, within the larger Iranian migration, their communities were important in settling the newcomers and helping them become integrated with prior waves of Armenians and Jews. One scholar has suggested that if the Iranian Jews and Armenians assimilate, it will occur within the American Armenian and Jewish communities, and not with other Iranians.[43] Those who are Muslims found themselves confronting religious diversity in America.

With the American embassy gone—once diplomatic ties were severed, it was closed—it was hard to obtain a visa in Iran, a situation that forced some exiles to leave for another country first and then come to America. The explosive political situation in the Middle East in the early twenty-first century made predictions risky. Relations between the United States and Iran had been improving until the destruction of the World Trade Center on September 11, 2001; after that time, President George W. Bush linked Iran to a dangerous "axis of evil," a group of nations allegedly fomenting anti-American terrorism that also included Iraq and North Korea.

The continued struggles and wars between Israel and its Arab neighbors prompted many Jews to move to Israel.[44] Syrian Jews are a case in point. Amid the violence, Jews in Arab lands "became separated from their non-Jewish neighbors more than in the past, resulting ultimately in their emigration."[45] For a time, Syria would not allow Jews to leave, but in the 1990s the government switched policy, and as a result Jews joined with others in North Africa to find homes elsewhere. In Egypt, for example, the Jewish population was virtually expelled after the 1956 war.[46] Many Syrian Jews went to Israel, but others immigrated to the United States, South America, England, or elsewhere in Western Europe. In the United States the latest immigrants found a Syrian Jewish community that had originated around the turn of the twentieth century.[47] These first arrivals had settled primarily in Brooklyn, New York, where they established a variety of ethnic organizations to serve their communities. A few of these new Syrian Sephardim also went to Chicago.[48]

A larger migration of Middle Eastern Jews came from Israel. Steven Gold has remarked that the actual number "of Israelis in the U.S. has been a subject of intense controversy."[49] Some officials of Jewish organizations have placed the figure as high as half a million; others said it was nearly 200,000 in 1990.[50] Census and official immigration figures cited lower numbers, so that it is necessary to insist upon counting many undocumented immigrants to justify using the higher figure. Immigration from Israel ran between 2,000 and 4,000 in the 1980s and 1990s; the number of nonimmigrant visitors and scholars was higher, and many believe that some of them overstayed their visas in order to remain in the United States. However, those arriving were not necessarily permanent immigrants; instead, some returned to Israel after stays in the United States.[51]

The Israeli immigrants congregated in several cities; New York, Chicago, and Los Angeles hosted the largest Israeli populations. To some extent they mingled with other American Jews by joining Jewish organizations, but many American Jews believed that Jews should not leave Israel. The newcomers were sometimes labeled *yordim,* a pejorative name given to those who leave the Jewish state. As a result, some Jews were reluctant to have social contacts with the Israelis.[52] There is less controversy about the social and economic status of the immigrants themselves. Mehdi Bozorgmehr's study of Los Angeles Israelis revealed that they had higher education levels and greater earnings than most other Middle Easterners, a picture confirmed by Steven Gold and Bruce Phillips's study.[53]

Turkish immigration was not directly related to the violence of the Middle East. It began around the turn of the twentieth century but fell when the 1920s restrictions, the Great Depression, and World War II served to decrease all immigration to the United States. Of the Turkish immigrants recorded from 1900 to 1930, many were Armenians and Kurds. Barbara Bilge's study of Michigan Turks found that nearly half were Kurdish speakers.[54] Another group was Spanish-speaking Jews, who left during the turmoil and destruction of World War I. These Jews settled mainly within the Sephardic Jewish enclave.[55] The non-Jews were mostly young single men, who often were illiterate peasants with few skills fitting for an urban industrial society. According to Bilge, the overwhelming majority of these men never married.[56]

After World War II, immigration resumed. More than 13,000 persons entered in the 1970s and another 23,233 in the 1980s. According to the 1990 census, 83,850 persons in the United States claimed Turkey as their ancestral land.[57] Because prior immigration had been low, Turks were eligible for the "diversity" visas that became part of the immigration admission system in 1990. Turkey received only 614 such visas in 2001, but the number helped Turkey's immigration to grow from 906 in 1988 to 3,477 in 2001.[58] The largest Turkish communities were in New York, New Jersey, and California, with a fast-growing one in Philadelphia.[59] In 1999 Turkey sent more persons to America than any other Middle Eastern Muslim nation, but that figure included students and other nonimmigrant visitors.[60]

How many additional Turkish immigrants were undocumented and living in the United States is impossible to determine. In 1996 the INS estimated that there were fewer than 30,000.[61] In 1990 Turkish leaders in New York City said that the number of undocumented aliens could easily be three times the official count of 9,500.[62] Certainly some Turks have tried to reach the United States illegally. In April 2002 several jumped ship in Norfolk, Virginia; a more common approach is to enter on a visitor's visa and then stay on without immigration papers.[63]

The post-1945 newcomers differed substantially from the earlier immigrants. Like many Asians, Turks came to pursue graduate studies in American colleges and universities. These students were usually young men between the ages of twenty and thirty-five, some from well-off secular families who admired the West. Those who were married sent home for their spouses if they intended to remain in the United States. On the whole, they did rather well economically in American society.[64] Another group of students came to study under the auspices of the North Atlantic Treaty Organization (NATO). Barbara Bilge reports that a number married American women and eventually stayed in the United States. The students were followed by Turks with more diverse social and economic origins.[65]

The newcomers followed the path of those who had gone before to build ethnic organizations, to see familiar faces, and to speak Turkish.[66]

According to the *Bergen (County) Record*, approximately 20,000 Turks lived in Passaic County, New Jersey, with the largest contingent in Paterson. In 1993 the mayor of Paterson proclaimed a Turkish American Day and ordered the Turkish flag to be flown over city hall. This was the second time such a day had been declared in Paterson. The mayor said the city has many Turkish "mosques, stores, coffee houses—everything."[67]

World War I disrupted travel between Turkey and America, but between 1919 and 1924, 30,000 Armenians came to America, including some who were "picture brides." Then the quotas, the Great Depression, and World War II brought Armenian immigration virtually to a standstill. Armenians began to arrive again right after the war as displaced persons, entering from Turkey, Lebanon, and the Soviet Union.[68] The largest concentration of these newcomers was in Los Angeles, with important communities in New York; Worcester, Massachusetts; Detroit; and Fresno, California. With the end of the cold war, the breakup of the Soviet Union, and the creation of the Republic of Armenia, opportunities once again beckoned to those wanting to come to the United States. From 1992 to 1998, about 30,000 did so, and in all, the post-1945 migrations doubled the size of the Armenian community in America.[69]

About 300,000 persons wrote "Armenian" in response to the ancestry question on the 1990 census, but Anny Bakalian believes that this figure is an undercount. She suggests that 800,000 to 1 million Armenians lived in the United States in 1996, which was the largest number outside the Republic of Armenia. Yet reliable figures are not available.[70] Some of the postwar immigrants in the late 1970s and early 1980s had "barely a shirt on their backs," but others tended to be well-off, with excellent educational backgrounds, skills, and capital; many spoke English.[71] The first to arrive settled in Los Angeles and opened small groceries and other shops to cater to the growing Armenian community. The Armenian-run Hye Mart was founded there in 1980, when practically no Armenian competition existed. By the mid-1990s, however, fifty Armenian markets had opened, catering to Armenian and Middle Eastern tastes generally. Because of the rapid growth of stores, some had difficulty surviving.[72]

Mehdi Bozorgmehr and others demonstrated that one-quarter of Los Angeles's Armenians were college graduates in 1990, but that figure was lower than for other Middle Easterners. Of the Middle Easterners in that city, Armenians had the lowest labor force participation and lowest income level. Compared with other Middle Easterners, the city's Armenian workers were more apt to be blue-collar workers.[73] Anny Bakalian argues that the second generation has been relatively successful nationally, with many becoming professionals. From her research based on Los Angeles and New York–New Jersey in the 1980s, Bakalian concludes, "For the most part, Armenian Americans are solid members of the middle class, with a significant segment being in the upper middle class."[74]

Like practically all refugees, the Armenians created institutions to serve their needs and help incoming immigrants. The most important was the Armenian Apostolic Church, but Armenians have also organized dozens of day schools and put out a phone book listing 40,000 household businesses.[75] It is important to remember that Armenians who have come to America after 1970 represent a recent group, and they "arrived in the United States with a highly developed ethnic identity." Out-marriage was relatively rare in the 1990s. Moreover, Bozorgmehr notes, "They feel a stronger bond to their symbolic homeland, the newly established state of Armenia in the former Soviet Union."[76]

However, as the American-born Armenian community began to grow, it faced pressure to assimilate. One issue was language, and like most second-generation ethnic groups, younger Armenians became bilingual but with little ability to read and write Armenian. Bakalian noted, "The quantitative and qualitative data presented here [indicate] that there is a generational decrease in maintenance of traditional Armenian culture. . . . In the final analysis the Armenian-American community is not a speech community; if it is to survive it cannot afford to alienate those who do not speak Armenian."[77] Once there were ten major Armenian-language newspapers, but by 2000 only one survived.[78] To many older Armenians the role of their language in the Armenian American community is critical, and some of them believe that loss of language was merely the first step on the path to assimilation.

Iraq has also witnessed turmoil that sent exiles abroad in search of peace and a better life. The long war with Iran in the 1980s contributed to upheaval in Iraq. Then came the Gulf War of 1991, when under the American-led military coalition Iraq suffered considerable bombing and destruction and was forced to withdraw from Kuwait. During the brief military conflict, those Iraqis already in the United States were alarmed at the television images and news reports of the widespread destruction in their homeland. One Chaldean priest summarized their concerns: "At the least, people need to know who is still alive and who is dead. If people died, they need to mourn the dead. Those are very primary needs. You can see the sorrow on their faces everyday."[79]

Iraq's economy partly recovered after Saddam Hussein's 1991 debacle in Kuwait, but the violence and tension between the United States and Iraq did not end. When Hussein refused to permit the United Nations (UN) to inspect locations alleged to be producing weapons of mass destruction, the United States retaliated with air strikes in the late 1990s. As a result, many Iraqis fled to neighboring nations and eventually to the United States if they could gain entrance. From 1989 to 1991, a total of 8,405 Iraqi immigrants entered the United States; after the Gulf War of 1991, during the 1990s more than 15,000 Iraqis entered the United States, most of whom were accepted as refugees.[80] Overall from 1986 to 2002, out of a total of 49,000 Iraqi immigrants, 32,187 entered as refugees or asylum seekers. The 2000 census reported that 89,892 Iraqis resided in the United States, with this population almost equally divided between the foreign and native born.[81] They were mainly Shiite Muslims from southern Iraq, who had originally fled to refugee camps in Saudi Arabia. They had suffered when the Iraqi military crushed a revolt in their towns. They were also generally rural folk, not well prepared for settlement in the United States.[82] In 2003, after another U.S. war against Iraq, American troops uncovered mass graves of Shiites who had been part of this uprising.[83]

The Iraqis were sometimes aided by a prior migration of their countrymen. Like many Asian immigrants, some of the early Iraqi Muslims were professionals or those who had come to study in the United States and then became immigrants either through finding employment or marriage.[84] Mary C. Sengstock notes that the number of Iraqi Christian immigrants increased rapidly after 1965, with many heading for Detroit. Chaldeans formed a tight-knit community built around churches, families, and economic enterprises. "The Chaldean community in Detroit is centered around the religious tradition that was brought from the homeland and in the northern part of Iraq, the modern-day descendant of the ancient land of Mesopotamia," wrote Sengstock in a book published before the Persian Gulf War.[85] Besides Detroit, other centers of Iraqi settlement were Chicago, San Diego, Los Angeles, and Phoenix.[86]

Once the second Gulf War broke out with the American invasion of Iraq in March 2003, many American Iraqis were faced with a new crisis. Some welcomed the overthrow of Saddam Hussein and vowed to return to their native land to help build a new Iraq. "The first thing I want to do when I put my feet on the ground, I just want to kiss it," remarked one Iraqi living in Dearborn, Michigan.[87] Many others, however, had begun to sink roots into America soil, building business and ethnic organizations. They realized the difficulties of returning to their homeland to begin a new life.[88]

Another smaller group of exiles from Iraq were Kurds from northern Iraq and eastern Turkey. Some had come right after World War I, and a second group migrated when the Kurdish rebellion against Iraq was defeated in the 1970s. Tens of thousands of Kurds were killed by Iraq's military forces, and poison gas was used against several villages during the 1970s. When Kurds rebelled again at the time of the Gulf War, the American government gave them only halfhearted support and admitted only a few refugees. Even then, the admission of Kurdish refugees was difficult because agencies trying to settle them lacked staff who could speak Kurdish.[89] For those remaining in Iraq, the creation of a "no-fly zone" by American and British aircraft "kept Iraqi troops at bay" for ten years, which allowed the Kurds to live in peace, and as a result they developed their own quasi-nation.[90]

Other Kurds suffered under the regime of Turkey. They found that the Turkish government was not sympathetic to their desire for an independent state, and a virtual civil war existed in eastern Turkey, where many of the Kurds settled. Those who managed to get to the United States formed a small community in San Diego, where an estimated 1,000 lived. They owned many small businesses there, "including trucking companies and driver education companies." Their dream for an independent homeland was far from being realized at the end of the twentieth century.[91]

During the 1990s the CIA backed northern Iraqis, who were trying to overthrow Saddam Hussein's dictatorial rule, but when the American government decided not to intervene directly, the revolt was easily crushed, sending anti-Hussein leaders into exile. After CIA aid ended in 1996, the United States gave 6,700 Kurds resettlement if they wanted. They were admitted as refugees, which entitled them to refugee benefits. The federal government also scattered the Kurds, with some joining earlier Kurdish immigrants who had been previously settled in places such as Fargo, North Dakota.[92]

A few other Iraqis reached the United States but found themselves being detained by the INS while their claims for political asylum were decided. One objected, "The worst thing was prison here. I was an opponent of Saddam Hussein, but now the government of the United States has betrayed me. If somebody invites you to come to their home and then arrests you, what is that called?"[93] A former CIA agent claimed that

Iraqis should be granted asylum and objected to the use of secret evidence against them, asserting, "It's not just a little bit like Kafka's 'The Trial'—it's exactly like Kafka's 'The Trial.'"[94] Just before leaving office in 2001, Attorney General Janet Reno released five of them from jail to work in a midwestern community while awaiting their appeals.[95] The federal government admitted 6,000 additional exiles from Iraq who had managed to get to camps in Turkey or who had been airlifted to Guam.[96] Others who had traveled to Mexico were accepted as immigrants into the United States to apply for asylum. They had support from politicians, who noted that the approval rate for cases from Iraq was high, due to the oppressive regime of Saddam Hussein. This particular group, estimated to be composed primarily of Christian Chaldeans, found a warm welcome from San Diego's Iraqi community.[97]

Whether Christian or Muslim, many Iraqi Americans who had friends and relatives remaining in Iraq were uneasy about the ongoing conflict between the United States and their homeland. After Hussein expelled the UN arms inspectors, Presidents Bill Clinton and George W. Bush ordered periodic air attacks, but the conflict did not lead to a large number of Iraqis finding a haven in the United States. Federal officials began to monitor Iraqis as tension between the United States and Iraq grew in the fall of 2002.[98] As war neared in 2003, the FBI stepped up its efforts to keep track of Iraqis who had "gone missing" since their arrival in the United States. They were estimated to number some 3,000 persons.[99]

The ongoing conflict between Israel and its Arab neighbors—Lebanon, Syria, Jordan, and Egypt—prompted many Middle Easterners to seek a new life in the United States or Europe. Even if they were not individually displaced by the wars involving Israel and Arab nations, for the better-educated elites conditions looked far better in the West than at home. Arabs and Jews have contested Palestine's terrain from the days when Israel first became a nation. Many Arabs rejected the UN vote in 1947, which divided the region into a Jewish state and an Arab one. Jews established their own nation of Israel, but many Arabs still refused to accept the new state, and instead Arabs from neighboring states invaded Israel. The truce in early 1949 led to Jews proclaiming Israel as their homeland, but it left hundreds of thousands of Arabs with no place to go. They either left voluntarily or were expelled by Israeli forces; they eventually ended up in refugee camps in the Gaza Strip, the West Bank, or in Arab states, thus setting the stage for further conflict.[100]

Israel joined forces with France and Great Britain in 1956 and seized control of the vital Suez Canal. The intervention of President Dwight D. Eisenhower forced the invaders to back down. Eleven years later, in a bold preemptive strike, Israeli forces destroyed Egyptian aircraft before they could become airborne and successfully defeated the Jordanian and Syrian military to the north. By the end of hostilities (1967), Israel controlled the West Bank, Gaza, the Sinai, the Golan Heights, and Jerusalem. Arabs within the borders of these areas were now under Israeli control. The confident Israelis then began to build settlements in the West Bank.

Although defeated, the Arabs surrounding Israel by no means had given up the fight to take back their lands and destroy Israel. Arabs organized the Palestinian Liberation Organization (PLO) two years after the 1967 war and at a time when the first settlements were being built. In October 1973, on Yom Kippur, the Jewish Day of Atonement, Egypt and Syria attacked a surprised Israel. After initial defeats, Israel rallied and won yet another war. President Anwar el-Sadat of Egypt responded by going to the diplomatic table, and in 1979, under the leadership of President Jimmy Carter, Israel and Egypt negotiated a peace for Israel's southern border. However, the northern border remained insecure, and in 1982, after attacks from PLO-led forces operating out of Lebanon, Israel attacked Lebanon and occupied the southern part of that country. Lebanon itself was badly divided by a civil war that began in 1975 and did not end until the 1990s. After the 1982 war, conflict shifted to the occupied territories. Israel ceded some villages and land to Palestinian authority, but efforts to fully resolve the future of the West Bank failed. After suicide bombers killed a number of Israelis in 2002, Israel's prime minister Ariel Sharon ordered a new assault on Palestinian villages and suspected places of terrorism.[101]

In the wake of continued violent conflicts, many Arabs (and some Israelis) decided to become exiles. Estimates on how many Palestinians immigrated to the United States vary because so many entered with Jordan, Syria, or Lebanon listed in their passports as their country of origin. Palestinians were also estimated to constitute 15 percent of travelers with Israeli passports coming to America from 1949 to 1979, which amounted to 25,600 persons. The census of 1990 recorded 44,651 persons of Palestinian origin, of whom 25,399 were foreign born. The INS had reported only a few thousand Palestinian immigrants.[102] For those coming prior to the 1967 war, immigration limits posed a real problem, but after the 1965 immigration act, Palestinians and other Arabs found it much easier to migrate to the United States.

If they could not obtain resident alien cards, Palestinians and Israelis were reported to be willing to become unauthorized immigrants. After witnessing months of violence during an intifada (uprising) that erupted in 1988, one Palestinian woman declared, "We are suffering too much here. . . . We need relief. We want to leave."[103] Increased numbers lined up at the American embassy in East Jerusalem for visitors' permits. Officials believed that these nonimmigrants would stay on after the expiration of their visa and simply become unauthorized immigrants.[104]

If scholars disagree on how many Palestinians arrived, they are in agreement about other characteristics of this postwar wave of Palestinian immigrants. At the turn of the twentieth century, the vast majority of rural immigrants were Christians who were not especially well-off. In the post-1970 era, a majority of Arab immigrants have been Muslims, though Christians have still migrated. Michael W. Suleiman, a leading scholar of the Arab experience in America, noted that the constant violence drove many from their home, especially middle-class and elite persons: "Whereas the early Arab immigrants were mainly uneducated and relatively poor, the new arrivals included large numbers of relatively well-off, highly educated professionals: lawyers, professors, teachers, engineers, and doctors." More than a few had originally come to the United States as students.[105] Suleiman and others also believe that the 1967 war was especially traumatic for Palestinians and nearly all Arab Americans, and that even the descendants of the immigrants from the turn of the twentieth century felt a heightened sense of being Arab.[106]

Two other studies drew similar conclusions. Daniel Pipes, who is critical of aspects of Islam, insists: "In socioeconomic terms, Muslims have little to complain about. They boast among the highest rates of education of any group in the United States, with a 1999 survey finding that 52 percent have a graduate degree."[107] A study by the sociology department of Queens College in New York City yielded similar results and noted that Muslims had incomes higher than U.S. average. It is important to remember that such studies include all ethnic components of Islam in America, that Middle Easterners are only a minority of Muslims, and that these findings included the native born as well as immigrants.[108]

The post-1945 Palestinian immigration, regardless of nationality, usually followed a chain migration, with many settling where earlier Arabs

TABLE 4

American Cities with the Largest Numbers of Arabs (2000)

City	Arab Residents
New York	70,965
Dearborn, MI	29,344
Los Angeles	25,937
Chicago	14,971
Houston	11,322
Detroit	8,300
San Diego	7,448
Jersey City	6,764
Boston	5,955
Jacksonville	5,861

SOURCE: Bureau of the Census, 2000.

had. As before, the center for the new Arabs was the Detroit metropolitan area, but they have also settled in New York, California, and in other states with large immigrant populations. (See Table 4.) Those displaced by the 1940s wars, and above all the 1967 war, saw their lands taken by Israel and decided to leave. They often went to Jordan and Lebanon before migrating to the United States. But the conflict between Jordan and Israel and the raging civil war in Lebanon gave them no peace; hence many took the next step and came to the United States.[109] Their lives in America were built around families, community groups, churches, and mosques.[110] Especially important for these immigrants were events in the Middle East, which hardly improved after 1967.

Like Palestinians, Lebanese (and Syrians) included both Muslims and Christians. The numbers were not large, amounting to only a few thousand annually. Christians encountered a Christian Lebanese community that was assimilating into American society but willing to help them. Many Lebanese Maronites had joined the Roman Catholic Church, moved up socially and economically, and even intermarried.[111] Included in the Lebanese immigration were Druze, who represented an offshoot of Islamic Shiism. The center of their settlement was Los Angeles. Their numbers are not known.[112]

The continuing Middle Eastern violence kept many immigrants' attention centered on their homelands. When an uprising (the intifada) of Palestinians against Israeli occupation of Gaza and the West Bank took place in 1988, it brought pride to a Long Island Palestinian community. The Reverend Paul Tarazi said, "For the first time, it was an expression of the full-fledged reality that Palestinians have been trying to express—

indeed to their Arab neighbors, too—that the Palestinians are an entity and a people."[113] Yet, as noted, the intifada also prompted many Palestinians to leave the region.

Egypt reached an accommodation with Israel in 1979, but before that date some Egyptians left for the United States. While the number of immigrants from the Arab nations of northern Africa grew, Egyptians outnumbered those by far. Generally northern African Arab nations watched their peoples migrate to Europe, not the United States. And Egyptians continued to migrate to the United States after the 1979 peace with Israel, numbering about 4,000 annually in the 1990s.[114] The Egyptian educational system produced more educated persons than the economy could usefully accommodate. Those with university degrees often traveled to the United States for graduate training; many had no intention of returning home. Finishing their advanced education gave them skills that could bring higher wages in the United States than in their own land. The 1990 census showed that nearly half were in professional, technical, and managerial fields and that 60 percent of them had graduated from a college or university. This was the highest level of education for Middle Easterners.[115] They joined the educated elites of Iran and Palestine in seeking skilled positions in the United States.[116]

Other Egyptian immigrants included the middle-class Copts, who found their minority status a strain in the postcolonial world of Egypt. Dating to the fifth century, Copts were among the earliest Christians, although they had their own traditions and forms of worship. On the whole, they were well-off by Egyptian standards, but when Gamal Abdel Nasser swept into power in 1952, their economic status was threatened. They were also a small minority of Christians in a Muslim nation. In the 1950s Copt families began to send their children, mostly single males, abroad for advanced education, and some of them stayed in the United States, settling in New York, New Jersey, and California. After the 1967 war, conditions worsened for Copts, and more began to emigrate. In 1972 some Copts received refugee visas, coming by way of Lebanon. These first immigrants in turn became U.S. citizens and sponsored their relatives in coming to America.[117] Their exact numbers are not known, but one scholar has suggested that in New Jersey, a center of Copt life, they might account for 80 percent of the early post-1945 immigration from Egypt.[118] By 1988 another scholar estimated that their churches in America had 50,000 members. Copt leaders put the figure much higher.[119]

Yemeni immigrants were quite different from most other Middle Easterners, who had often had religious and political reasons for migration. They were removed from the violence of 1948 to 2002 and mainly had economic reasons for leaving home. The young men faced a limited economic future in their own land. A few came around the turn of the century, but most date from the 1960s, when young single men began to search for employment in the auto plants of Detroit, especially Chrysler's Hamtramack Assembly Plant. Largely unskilled, the workers were able to find automobile and other industrial jobs in Detroit until the downturn in auto production. Many had intended to be sojourners, to work for only a few years and return with their pockets full of money. When industrial jobs disappeared, they found work as "busboys, dishwashers, and janitors in numerous restaurants and hotels scattered throughout the Detroit area."[120] Their all-male societies tended to be isolated from mainstream American society, but when hope for returning home dimmed, they began to send for their families.[121]

Another colony of Yemeni immigrants located in the borough of Brooklyn in New York City. Along that borough's Atlantic Avenue a number of Middle Eastern restaurants, grocery shops, bakeries, and spice stores had opened their doors before the post-1970 immigration from the Middle East, and in the 1940s the neighborhood had earned the name "Arab New York." Arabs from Lebanon and Syria ran most of these enterprises. As the older businesses moved to other locations in New York City, Yemenis, Palestinians, and other Muslim Arabs moved in and opened shops of their own.[122] Yemeni owners of the new businesses offered employment for workers and also provided a place for socialization. Many of the workers were single men or had migrated without their families in the expectation that they would make enough money to enable them to return to Yemen "to begin building a house."[123] Often their expectations were not met.[124]

All Arabs, like Iranians and other non-Arab Middle Eastern immigrants, faced the task of rebuilding their lives in a vastly different world. Those going to preexisting communities in Michigan, California, New York, and New Jersey were assisted by those already in the United States. But for many others fleeing the violence of the Near East, resettlement was not an easy task. While the educated often spoke English, most of these newcomers did not, and some, like the Yemeni, had few skills suited for the high-tech economy emerging after the 1960s in the United States. For many Arab Muslims the relative freedom of American women was unacceptable. But economic necessity meant that many families had two wage earners. Then, too, there were different standards for rearing children.[125]

The diversity of Arab immigrants should not lead one to overlook a major trend after World War II. A study by the Council on American-Islamic Relations published in 2001 found that the number of mosques had increased greatly in the preceding decade, due largely to immigration. Indeed, the number was up 25 percent in a six-year period.[126] This study put the number of Muslims in America at between 6 and 7 million. Others disagreed, such as a report commissioned by the American Jewish Committee, *The American Religious Identification,* which suggested that the number of Muslims was at most 2.8 million.[127] Daniel Pipes has noted different opinions: "No one knows how many Muslims there are in the United States—the estimates range widely and are prone to exaggeration—but their number are clearly in the several millions."[128] Examining problems with the available data (such as the lack of governmental statistics), two reporters for the *Christian Science Monitor* wrote a column titled "How Many U.S. Muslims? Our Best Estimate." Their answer was around 2 million.[129]

On one subject scholars and religious leaders find agreement: Arabs make up only a minority of the nation's Muslims, somewhere between 20 and 25 percent. The largest group of American Muslims are African Americans, with South and East Asians also accounting for significant segments of Islamic America.[130]

The new religious mosaic of the United States emerging since the 1960s, which included the entrance of many Muslims, Sikhs, Hindus, and Buddhists, was not always greeted with open arms by Americans. In the past, many American schoolchildren had been told that Islam was a dark religion and that Arab lands had no culture worth knowing about. Scholars as well as the American-Arab Anti-Discrimination Committee have pointed out that in popular culture, as reflected by cartoons, news reporting, and movies, Arabs are portrayed as sinister people interested only in extracting oil profits from the West.[131] A 1995 survey of mosques throughout the United States revealed a number of attempts to destroy them, as well as attacks on individual Muslims.[132]

It did not help matters that some terrorism has been linked to Arabs and Muslims. For example, the 1993 bombing of the World Trade Center, which resulted in the destruction of the basement garage, six deaths, and the wounding of 1,000 others, was traced by officials to Egyptian

Sheikh Omar Abdel-Rahman, the spiritual leader of the bombers.[133] Two years later, when the bombing of the Murrah Federal Building in Oklahoma claimed 145 lives, some media officials were quick to blame Muslim-Arab extremists for the destruction that ultimately was demonstrated to be the work of Timothy J. McVeigh and Terry L. Nichols, both white, American born, and considered to be motivated by fanatical right-wing politics, not religion. They had no connection to Islam or the Arab world.[134]

Then came September 11, 2001, and the destruction of the World Trade Center. The hijackers were all young men from Arab nations, some here illegally; this sent a chill through Muslim and Arab communities in the United States. Arab Americans and Islamic leaders quickly condemned the attacks, and in the days that followed, Arab and Muslim military personnel were involved in the U.S.-led retaliatory attacks in Afghanistan. Later, in 2003, they fought in the Second Gulf War; they were served by Abdul-Rasheed Muhammad, the first Muslim chaplain in the armed forces.[135]

Nevertheless, the destruction of the World Trade Center immediately led to violent incidents against Arabs and Muslims.[136] In May 2002 the Council on American-Islamic Relations said that incidents of bias had increased since September 2001. As reports of workplace bias grew, the Equal Employment Opportunity Commission (EEOC) became alarmed and met with a variety of groups to deal with such discrimination. EEOC spokesman David Grinberg noted, "The Sept. 11th backlash continues."[137] National polls of Arabs and Muslims also revealed that they experienced increased prejudice after September 11.[138] The Justice Department and local law enforcement groups arrested several persons for their attacks on Arabs and Asians and for attempts to burn down mosques.[139] Even Christian Arabs reported harassment. Fakry Gai, a Copt, said that his store was defaced with graffiti.[140] A Sikh, mistaken for an Arab terrorist because he wore a turban and sported a beard, was shot to death in Arizona. Sikhs reported other incidents of violence.[141]

To combat such incidents, President Bush made a point of assuring Americans that American Muslims should not be blamed for the World Trade Center's destruction, and he hosted an *iftaar* (a Ramadan break-the-fast dinner) in the White House. The president declared, "We send our sincerest wishes to Muslims in America and around the world for health, prosperity, and happiness during Ramadan and throughout the coming year."[142] Arab Americans and Muslims reported other acts of acceptance and tolerance amid the turmoil. Only hours after the destruction of the World Trade Center, the chairman of the Ford Motor Company called a meeting to talk to Arab American leaders in Detroit about what could be done to ease their fears. In response Ismael Ahmed reported, "What that phone call meant is that Arab-Americans are part of the fabric of the entire country."[143]

There can be no doubt, however, that the September 11 incidents led to increased governmental suspicion of and action against Arab Americans and Muslims. To begin with, Attorney General John Ashcroft took a hard line against suspected terrorists. The INS, joined by other federal agencies, began a campaign to deport Arabs who lacked proper immigration papers. The number of foreign-born Arabs expelled to their native lands increased more rapidly than for nationals of non-Arab lands. According to the *Atlanta Journal-Constitution,* the largest increases for deportation were to Tunisia, Morocco, Egypt, Yemen, Jordan, Lebanon, Pakistan, Algeria, and Saudi Arabia.[144] Pakistan is an East Asian nation, but it is also a Muslim country.[145] The total was not large—only 1,627 over a year's time—and the INS admitted that it did not know what had happened to 314,000 unauthorized persons who had been ordered to leave.[146]

In the immediate aftermath of September 11, the Justice Department rounded up and detained more than 762 men, mostly from Arab or Islamic countries. Some were held for months without being able to consult a lawyer, while others were released shortly after being seized by federal authorities. Most were eventually deported, but a number found themselves incarcerated for months, some under appalling conditions, without specific charges of wrongdoing. An internal investigation by the inspector general of the Justice Department criticized the department for civil liberties violations, such as picking up men with little or no evidence that they were connected to terrorism. Furthermore, the investigation revealed that the men were hindered and delayed in their attempts to obtain lawyers.[147] The American Civil Liberties Union (ACLU) initiated a class action suit aimed at freeing the others.[148]

Federal officials also asked several thousand Arab men to come in for questioning. In addition, the government raided several Muslim charities and seized the assets of several groups. In a plea bargain Enaam M. Arnaout, the director of one of the largest Islamic charities, agreed that his efforts had aided military forces. Arnaout, director of the Chicago-based Benevolence International Foundation, acknowledged that he had funneled funds for military uses to Muslims in the Balkans during the 1990s. He did not agree that he had connections to Al Qaeda, the terrorist organization headed by Osama bin Laden, which claimed responsibility for the September 11 attacks.[149] In another case, an Arab from Lackawanna, New York, pleaded guilty to contributing funds and services to terrorists.[150] In June 2002, Attorney General Ashcroft added to the anti-Islam mood when he announced that Abdullah al-Muhakir, an American-born Latino who converted to Islam, was involved in a plot to set off a "dirty bomb" in the United States. It was left unclear how valid the government's allegation was, but it certainly did not help the cause of those who believed that Muslims were unfairly blamed for terrorism.[151]

In the fall of 2002 the FBI and other federal officials admitted that they were closely monitoring young Arab men, looking for connections to the terrorist group Al Qaeda. The FBI was using wiretaps authorized under the Foreign Intelligence Surveillance Act.[152] That fall, immigration authorities began a program that required men (over age sixteen) from Arab and Muslim nations temporarily residing in the United States to appear before an INS agent to be interviewed, fingerprinted, and photographed.[153] Initially the INS applied the new regulations only to Iranians, Iraqis, Libyans, Sudanese, and Syrians. INS authorities at portals of entrance to the United States claimed the power to require registration.[154] At the same time, immigration officials overseas began to step up interviews of those wanting to visit America and increase the rejection rate of those applying for visas.[155]

Federal officials arrested several Yemenis and prosecuted them for connections to Al Qaeda in Afghanistan. In a plea bargain one Yemeni admitted his connections to Afghan camps and agreed to give testimony against others.[156] In June 2003 two other Arabs from Morocco were found guilty of a terrorist plot against the United States.[157] In addition, several imams and mosques came under suspicion for alleged connections to terrorism.[158]

With the outbreak of the second Gulf War against Iraq in 2003, federal officials announced new procedures for persons seeking asylum. Asylum seekers now faced detention while their requests were being heard. Tighter rules on asylum were put into effect, especially for persons from the Middle East.[159] Special registration was required of persons from Iran, Iraq, Libya, Sudan, and Syria, to be followed by similar procedures for those from other nations, slated to go into effect in January 2004.[160] Civil liberties organizations joined Muslim groups protesting these actions. Many of the new restrictions were not limited to aliens but included American citizens as well.[161] There was no doubt that the events of September 11, 2001, had a deep impact on the nation's Arabs and Muslims. The terrorism issue, events in the Middle East, and the detention of Arabs convinced many Arab Americans to become more politically active. Yet even before 2001 some leaders had urged more direct political involvement. As noted, bias against Arabs predated September 11, 2001. In addition, the turmoil of the Middle East has prompted many to organize. The 1967 war, as one spokesman said, "was a turning point."[162] Several groups were founded soon afterward, leading to the 1980 formation of the American-Arab Anti-Discrimination Committee (ADC) under the leadership of former U.S. senator James Abourezka. The ADC compiled data on discrimination and hate crimes and "was a milestone in political activism on behalf of creating a space for Arabs as American citizens."[163] In 2000 the ADC merged with the National Association of Arab Americans (NAAA) to play a more active role in politics.[164]

It was clear to many Arab leaders that better organization was required to offset the generally positive view that most Americans held toward Israel. But more important after September 2001 was dealing with the civil liberties crisis in the United States. Arab Americans had been winning elections long before 2001, but now there was a new urgency.[165] It would no doubt be necessary to work with other organizations. Those calling themselves of Arab ancestry numbered only 1,202,871 in the 2000 census; such a limited number, although growing, was only a small segment of the nation's population.[166]

9

The New Black Immigrants

Since the end of the World War II, more black immigrants have entered the United States than during the slave era, when 450,000 black slaves were forced to migrate from their homes to America. Of course slaves were hardly immigrants with legal rights; neither did they arrive of their own volition. For eighty years after the Civil War, free blacks did migrate to the United States, but even adding their numbers to those of the slave era would leave the total well short of the numbers experienced during the last fifty years. According to the Immigration and Naturalization Service, Caribbean immigration to the United States increased steadily after 1970; more than 900,000 Caribbean immigrants, most of whom were black by American racial classification, arrived during the 1990s. Even some Spanish-speaking Dominicans and Cubans, both major categories of immigrants, were considered black. In 2001 Jamaica and Haiti were among the top sending nations. In that year Haiti was eighth on the list, with 27,120, and Jamaica was nineteenth, with 15,393. So many black immigrants went to New York City that it retained its position as the city with the nation's largest foreign-born black population in 2000.[1]

Immigration from Africa also increased after 1970. The INS reported that during the last five years of the twentieth century, Africa was sending about 40,000 immigrants annually to America, and the number reached 50,209 in 2001. (See Table 5.) More than 400,000 Africans arrived in the 1990s, the highest figure since any decade after the Civil War.[2] The figure was small compared with the numbers from the Caribbean, but it represented a large increase from the 1950s and 1960s. The combined totals of the new black immigrants now make up roughly 5 percent of the black population in the United States, considerably more than the less than 1 percent reported in 1940.[3]

The exact number of black immigrants from Africa is unknown. Some refugees fleeing African nations, such as Uganda in the 1970s, were Asians.

TABLE 5
Immigration from Selected African Nations (1991–2001)

Country of Birth	1991	1992	1993	1994	1995	1996	1997	1998	1999	2000	2001
Africa	36,179	27,086	27,783	26,712	42,456	52,889	47,791	40,660	36,700	44,731	53,948
Ethiopia	5,127	4,602	5,191	3,887	5,960	6,086	5,904	4,205	4,272	4,061	5,106
Ghana	3,330	1,867	1,604	1,458	3,152	6,606	5,105	4,458	3,714	4,344	4,031
Liberia	1,292	999	1,050	1,762	1,929	2,206	2,216	1,617	1,358	1,575	2,285
Morocco	1,601	1,316	1,176	1,074	1,726	1,783	2,359	2,410	2,971	3,626	4,968
Nigeria	7,912	4,551	4,448	3,950	6,818	10,221	7,038	7,746	6,769	7,853	8,291
Senegal	869	337	178	213	506	641	435	373	370	555	665
Somalia	458	500	1,088	1,737	3,487	2,170	4,005	2,629	1,710	2,465	3,026
South Africa	1,854	2,516	2,197	2,144	2,560	2,966	2,093	1,904	1,580	2,833	4,100

SOURCE: Immigration and Naturalization Service, Statistical Yearbook, 2001.

Until recently nonrefugee immigration from the continent was dominated by individuals from Egypt and other parts of northern Africa, most of whom the federal government called "white." Among those leaving South Africa before the end of apartheid, whether entering as refugees or as regular immigrants, an estimated 70 percent were whites who could no longer tolerate apartheid or who saw little future in their native land. A number of these were highly educated and constituted a "brain drain."[4] One New York doctor, who left because he did not wish to see his children raised under apartheid, said, "The politics was embarrassing to me. At times I was ashamed to mention to people that I'd been a South African."[5] A few other whites left Zimbabwe when blacks took control of that country.[6]

After 1980 the vast majority of immigrants leaving from other African countries were black. Among the regular immigrants after 1970, black nations such as Ethiopia, Nigeria, Kenya, and Ghana contributed the largest number.[7] The Urban Institute's Jeffrey Passel believed that only half of the more than 360,000 Africans counted in the 1990 census were black.[8] But other officials put this figure at 70 percent or even higher. The growth of immigration from the sub-Saharan region in the 1990s doubled the number of African-born individuals in the United States. In 1999 the *Journal of Blacks in Higher Education* estimated that "perhaps 70 to 75 percent" of the African immigrants to the United States were black as defined by U.S. standards.[9] The most careful estimates, based on the 2000 census, are by John Logan, who estimates that the sub-Saharan African population in the United States is more than 537,534, of whom 80 percent were foreign born.[10]

These African newcomers with black skins faced a society with a long and continued racist history, but in many ways they differed sharply from one another, just as Asian, Latino, and European immigrants represented a variety cultures. Among the new black immigrants were Protestants, Catholics, Muslims, and followers of many African religions; sometimes they blended various religious practices. Some were refugees fleeing domestic violence; others were political refugees fleeing war or persecution. Others were extraordinarily poor and sought better economic opportunities in America. But among the newcomers were highly educated men and women, especially Nigerians with doctoral degrees who sought employment in American universities and hospitals. Many Africans, such as these Nigerians, spoke English, but their accents differed, and the Senegalese spoke French. Others spoke only their own African or creole languages. Quite clearly, these newcomers were adding to the ethnic mix of the United States and diversifying the African-ancestry population.

African immigration increased only after American policy changed. As mentioned in an earlier chapter, the African continent had few slots for immigration to the United States when the national origins system went into effect in 1929. After World War II, as newly independent nations emerged in Africa, they had the same status as independent Ethiopia, which was given a quota of 100 in the 1920s. The McCarran-Walter Act of 1952 removed race as a condition for citizenship, but it did not increase African quotas. It was not until the 1965 immigration act that Africans were finally placed on the same footing as all others. Prospective immigrants had to enter within the quota of 20,000 (excluding immediate family members of U.S. citizens) for their country under the new system of preferences. Until the 1970s, educated Africans migrated primarily to Europe rather than the United States. When European nations tried to stem this flow, Africans found fewer opportunities in Europe and instead looked to America.

Like many Asians, Africans entered first to study in the United States. Indeed, some African leaders of the new nations had been educated in the United States. Among those studying before 1940 was Nnamdi Azikiew, the first president of independent Nigeria, who was a classmate of Thurgood Marshall, future justice of the U.S. Supreme Court, and the writer Langston Hughes.[11] Moreover, African students often stayed in the United States after they finished their educations.[12] Such was the case of Funke Popoola, who came in 1977 to attend Texas Southern University. After completing his studies, he worked for others before finally opening his own business and eventually a restaurant catering to Houston's Nigerian community.[13] Popoola and many Africans enrolled at predominantly black colleges in the United States, but some Africans studied at white institutions as well. One scholar reported in 1991 that although many African émigrés came to America with college educations and advanced degrees, some 60 percent of his sample acquired additional education in the United States.[14] In the 1980s about 40,000 black Africans were studying at colleges and universities in the United States, and although the figures dropped after that, some 20,000 were still enrolled in the late 1990s. Asian students dominated the figures.[15]

Most of the early students were males, but a few women accompanied their husbands and also attended American colleges and universities. Astair Gebremariam, who became vice chairman of the Chicago Ethiopian Community Association, went to Clarkson University in Potsdam, New York. Her husband was a graduate of Harvard University and a professor at Northwestern University.[16] Zewditu Wondemu of Ethiopia completed her education, opened a restaurant in Washington, D.C., and settled permanently in the United States. She did not wish to return to a then-communist-dominated Ethiopia.[17] Marylander Patricia Okoye Igwebuike was born in England; after going to Nigeria, the land of her parents, she returned to London, where she became a lawyer. After she came to the United States with her family, she began her preparation to pass the New York bar exam.[18] The *Journal of Blacks in Higher Education* described the student-to-immigrant process: "Many of these college students end up staying on in the United States after graduation. African students who secure teaching positions after gaining their graduate degree may apply for legal alien status. Others who study here meet and marry U.S. citizens and are permitted to apply for U.S. citizenship."[19]

Kofi K. Apraku's 1991 study of several hundred African immigrants who were college professors, economists, physicians, accountants, and nurses found that many used their educations to become professionals in the United States. Men made up 88 percent of his sample, although the INS reported that African men outnumbered women only by a factor of three to two. The vast majority of Africans Apraku polled were married, even though some did not have their families with them.[20] It would not be an exaggeration to state that these post-1965 immigrants represented a brain drain to the United States.[21] Indeed, the 1990 census, without breaking down the figures by race, revealed that African immigrants had the highest levels of education among the foreign born, even greater than those for Asians. Almost one-half had college degrees, and fully one-fifth had at least a master's degree.[22] The fact that the elite came first was not unusual, for like Asian Indians and other educated immigrants, these highly trained immigrants could get green cards. Mulegeta Gerefa, executive director for the African Immigration and Refugee Resources Center in San Francisco, put it this way: "The first wave from anywhere tends to be people who have contacts in the United States often from having attended college here. They tend to be the best educated, people who were civil servants and so on in their home countries."[23]

These African elite were coming to the United States for better jobs and higher pay than they found at home, but political persecution and violence also convinced many to emigrate. Although they encountered racism and prejudice in the United States, many watched events in Africa with dismay. Nigerians witnessed a violent civil war between 1967 and 1970, which forced many ethnic Ibos to flee. One émigré, who first came to the United States in 1979 to study at Morgan State College (a black school), told the *Washington Post* about the violence and lack of democracy in Nigeria and commented, "If we had a good leader, most people would go home. I know that I would." Of the nullification of Nigerian elections in 1993 and the continuation of military rule, another émigré remarked, "I'm very disappointed. The elections were annulled for no reasons that any of them could prove."[24] These immigrants were obviously refugees just as much as economic migrants, even if they did not enter as official refugees. Democracy returned to Nigeria in 2000, but whether Nigerian immigrants would return home was an open question, for in spite of the racism they encountered in America, their incomes had been considerably greater than they would have been in Africa. Moreover, the 2003 election was once again contested by the losing candidates. The situation in Nigeria, the largest African nation in population, was duplicated in other African nations in the 1990s; civil wars and dictatorships hardly induced those living abroad to return home.[25] Even when Amadou Diallo, an unarmed Guinean immigrant, was killed in 1998 in a hail of bullets fired by four white New York City police officers, it did not appear to deter immigration from Guinea. One Guinean leader noted, "But I've talked to young people there in America who say that if they tighten their belts, they can eventually take care of their families better." He concluded by saying that life in New York was dangerous, but back home "there are no jobs."[26]

The 1965 law's preference for refugees benefited Africans little at first, for the United States used most of the annual numbers for persons fleeing communism, such as South Asians and Cubans, or persons from the former Soviet Union. Even after 1980 when the new Refugee Act defined refugees as persons fleeing from persecution generally and not simply from communism, refugee admissions were slow to change. Africa certainly had many refugees, but that continent received only a few of the refugee allotments. From 1960 until 1980, only 11,000 Africans were granted refugee status, a small proportion of the 1.5 million total for those years; for the period 1946 to 2000, 90,969 Africans entered as refugees.[27]

Among the first black refugees from Africa were Ethiopians fleeing a Marxist regime established in the 1970s; hence they were more acceptable to U.S. decision makers. Typical of the Ethiopian refugees was Tesvfa Awoke, who fled to the United States when his father was imprisoned and his brother killed. As he recounted, "It was a matter of survival, there was killing everywhere."[28] The cold war played a role, especially in view of the fact that the United States maintained a communications base in Ethiopia and provided Ethiopia with the lion's share of foreign aid for Africa. In 1983, for example, of the 2,450 refugees from Africa, 2,209 were Ethiopian. Other African nations began to send more refugees to the United States after 1983, but until the mid-1990s Ethiopian refugees accounted for more than half of the African total, and for the entire post–World War II period, Ethiopia sent 38,658 refugees to the United States.[29] Although turmoil seemed to abate in Ethiopia by the early 1990s, a war between Ethiopia and Eritrea erupted in 1998 and sent thousands of Ethiopians and Eritreans fleeing for their lives, some of whom gained entrance into the United States.[30]

After the American intervention in Somalia's civil war in 1991 and the debacle there, a connection was formed that lasted after U.S. troops withdrew in 1993.[31] Beginning in the 1990s, Somalia accounted for about one-third of all African refugees, sending more than 16,000 refugees to the United States.[32] In 1997, for example, the 4,974 Somali refugees were more than half of the continent's total. By comparison, Liberia had 231 and Ethiopia, 197.[33] Conflict emerged in other parts of Africa in the 1980s and 1990s. In Sierra Leone a civil war began in 1990 and was temporarily ended in 1999. The next year the peace agreement failed, and once again civil war broke out, producing refugees, as did events in the Sudan and elsewhere.[34]

In the Sudan civil war broke out in 1956, following independence, leaving almost 2 million dead from 1955 to 1999. In addition, tens of thousands of others were left homeless or living in fear of persecution. Some minorities caught up in the war found themselves seized and sold as slaves.[35] A military regime seized power in 1989, but it imposed a militant Islamic regime, which sent non-Muslims as well as many Muslims fleeing in the 1990s. Following the Gulf War of 1991, Sudanese who had worked in the oil-producing states were forced to leave, and some of them ended up in the United States as refugees.[36] Others arrived on temporary visas and requested asylum.[37]

Africa certainly had refugees aplenty. An estimated two-thirds of the victims of all wars during the 1980s and 1990s were Africans, and by the early 1990s Africa had replaced Asia as the largest source for refugees throughout the world.[38] African nations had more than 8 million persons living outside their borders in 2000, accounting for more than one-third of the world's total of refugees.[39]

In the face of the rising violence and flow of millions of refugees, the United States responded slowly, unlike in Kosovo, where the United States led a NATO effort to save Albanians in that war-wracked land. The United States did not intervene in Rwanda when a virtual genocide took place in 1994. The American response was to send some humanitarian aid and to increase the refugee allotment for Africa to 7,000 in 1997 and 1998, but this was only 10 percent of the total refugees admitted. As conditions deteriorated in several African countries, pressure mounted from the congressional Black Caucus to take in more refugees. Representatives John Conyers Jr. (D-MI) and Melvin L. Watt (D-NC) told President Bill Clinton via letter that although there were more refugees in Africa than anywhere else in the world, only 9 percent of the United States's refugee allocations went to Africa. The situation, they wrote, was "unconscionable."[40] President Clinton's historical trip to Africa in 1998 did lead to an announcement of an increase to 12,000 for African refugees, but the figure was still far short of the European numbers.

The president made another visit to Africa in 2000 during which he spoke out for human rights and boycotted Nigeria to protest its military dictatorship. Following a democratic election two years later, he visited Nigeria to encourage the elected government. President Clinton no doubt was aware of Nigeria's primary export: oil. In 2000 the United States needed Nigerian oil because of the production cutbacks by other oil-producing nations. Thus in 1999 the administration increased the number of

African refugees, and in July 2000, it announced that 20,000 of the 80,000 refugees for the next year were to be African. Although only one-fourth of the total, the African figure was the highest ever and more than double that of 1998.[41] In 2001 the George W. Bush administration increased the allotment to 22,000, but refugee admissions were temporarily slowed after the destruction of the World Trade Center in September 2001.[42] Immigration authorities grew cautious about granting refugee status in the wake of this attack; Africans were not the only ones affected by this desire to tighten immigration policy. In 2001 the United States admitted only 68,000 refugees. Of this total the Sudan contributed 5,959; Somalia, 4,951; Ethiopia, 4,454; and Sierra Leone, 2,004.[43] In spite of concerns about terrorism, in March 2003 the United States agreed to accept 12,000 Somali Bantu refugees who had been living in camps in Kenya.[44]

The Bantus had a long history of persecution in Somalia, and they were glad to be able to find a safe home in the United States. The first to arrive did so during the summer of 2003. As refugees they were entitled to assistance from the federal government; most of them had little experience with modern culture, including the wide range of consumer items available in the United States. Moreover, some of the Bantu were sent to upstate New York and Burlington, Vermont, which had climates quite different than in the camps of Kenya, which meant the refugees faced major challenges in adjusting to a new world.[45] The admission of these latest Africans was a sign that the George W. Bush administration was continuing the policies of the Clinton administration in increasing the number of African refugees. The Bush administration planned to admit 21,000 Africans in 2002. However, the number of refugees dropped after the destruction of the World Trade Center in September 2001, and it dropped again the next year.[46]

President George H. W. Bush had granted Liberians temporary protected status, a status authorized by the 1990 immigration act. Because the United States created Liberia, Liberians had a special connection to the United States. When their TPS was about to expire in 1999, the Rhode Island congressional delegation expressed its wish to halt any deportation of Liberians because of the civil war in their home. Rhode Island's Liberians made up the largest Liberian settlement in the United States. President Clinton extended TPS in 1999. At the eleventh hour in September 2000, when the new deadline for deportation neared again, Clinton gave Liberians deferred enforced departure status, similar to TPS, for another year. The supporters of TPS noted that although the civil war in Liberia had ended in 1997, violence had once again erupted. These temporary measures might have kept Liberians, estimated at between 10,000 and 15,000 persons, in the United States, but they did not give them the right to become immigrants. A bill to make them resident aliens was put forth by Patrick J. Kennedy, a Democrat of Rhode Island; it received support but did not pass. Nonetheless, the INS had the authority to hold off deportation.[47] By avoiding deportation, those with TPS or deferred enforced departure status had the potential for gaining an immigrant visa either by finding employment acceptable to the INS or by marrying an American citizen.[48] TPS was by no means limited to Liberians. In addition to Central American nations such as Honduras, El Salvador, and Nicaragua (see chapter 5), African nations such as Rwanda, Sierra Leone, Somalia, and the Sudan have received TPS at one time or another.[49]

Among the refugees were young men and boys from Sudan, many of whom had fled that country's violence only to live in refugee camps in Kenya for up to eight years. These orphans had suffered considerable trauma in their country's civil war and as survivors in refugee camps. Lack of adequate food and exposure to natural dangers added to their woes. "A lot of them were eaten by wild animals. A lot of them starved," noted one camp official.[50] In 2000, when it became clear that it was impossible to find their families, the United States, working with the United Nations High Commissioner for Refugees (UNHCR), agreed to admit several thousand of the Sudanese. Being safe in the United States was welcome, but how these unfortunate refugees would deal with American culture was an open question. In Fargo, North Dakota, where some were settled, they confronted a whole new way of life.[51]

In addition to the few thousand refugees admitted each year, there was another way for one to find refuge in the United States: enter as a visitor or illegally cross the American border and then claim asylum. In 2000, 7,269 Africans won asylum, and 6,330 did so in 2001. The largest groups came from Somalia and Ethiopia.[52] The most sensational African cases involved women faced with genital mutilation. In the 1990s physicians began to report seeing immigrant women from Asia, Africa, and the Middle East who had endured genital mutilation.[53] In 1995 Meserak Ramsy, a nurse from Ethiopia who had been in the United States for twenty years and was an American citizen, organized a campaign against the practice, and later other women's groups took up the cause. Also in 1995 a woman from Sierra Leone won asylum on grounds of escaping such mutilation, which she would undergo if forced to return home, but another Sierra Leone woman lost her case. The following year, Fauziya Kasinga, who fled her homeland of Togo, found herself in jail and claimed asylum on the grounds that she was escaping mutilation and an arranged marriage to become "the fourth wife of a man nearly three times her age." Her case reached the Board of Immigration Appeals, the highest immigration tribunal in the nation, where she won. In August 1999 Adelaide Abankwah became the third woman to win asylum on the grounds that she would be subjected to genital mutilation if she returned to Ghana.[54] Amid other cases being reported, the issue reached national attention in the late 1990s, when several states and Congress banned the practice, and the INS announced that it would consider the fear of mutilation valid grounds for winning asylum in the United States.[55]

In a few cases women claimed that they were entitled to asylum on the grounds of violence by their husbands. In August 1999 a Moroccan woman won asylum when the U.S. Board of Immigration Appeals agreed that she was entitled to asylum from religious persecution rather than domestic violence. Yet a year later a Guatemalan woman who had suffered abuse was denied asylum because she could not demonstrate religious or political persecution. Clearly the board was reluctant to see domestic abuse alone as a reason for receiving the right to live in the United States.[56]

These individual victories required each woman to convince the INS authorities and judges that she was speaking the truth and that her case fell within guidelines.[57] Doctors continued to report cases. Dr. Nawal M. Noour, who grew up in the Sudan, Egypt, and Great Britain and was educated at the Harvard Medical School, said she was shocked when she first encountered cases of genital mutilation. Subsequently, she devoted part of her Boston practice to caring for immigrant women who had undergone mutilation, establishing a clinic specifically to treat them.[58]

Another way to become a legal immigrant was through the diversity program begun in 1986 and made a permanent part of the immigration process four years later. Because so few Africans had arrived either before or after the 1965 law was passed, African nations were eligible to apply for visa slots to be determined by a lottery. As noted in chapter 7, the lottery was originally intended to assist the Irish in immigrating to the United States. Many Latino and Asian groups had criticized the lottery provision when the 1990 immigration act was being debated. Nonetheless, the lottery or diversity program became part of immigration policies during the 1990s.[59] Of the 55,000 annual slots available in the late 1990s, Africa received 20,000. In the late 1980s a U.S. post office in Virginia, where the applications were to be sent, was overwhelmed by the sheer volume of applicants from around the world, and millions continued to apply when the lottery was made part of immigration law. In 1997 the INS received more than 7 million applicants for the coveted visa.[60] From Africa, Nigeria headed the visa lottery for 2001, with 2,664 of the continent's allotment. The black nations of Ethiopia, Sierra Leone, and the Sudan also gained slots.[61]

If they could not qualify for visas, eager Africans entered illegally or overstayed their visitors' permits and found jobs and housing in the United States. Observers believe that Senegalese men were the most numerous of undocumented Africans, with many getting their start in New York City. For those who entered before the Immigration Reform and Control Act (IRCA) deadline of 1982, there was an amnesty to legalize their status. Eventually 39,006 Africans who were in the United States before 1982 adjusted their status under the law. This figure represented only 1 percent of the total receiving an amnesty.[62]

Africans entering under the amnesty program, as winners of the lottery, as refugees, and as immigrants with skills needed in the United States formed the core of the immigration chain. By the 1990s, however, those holding green cards or becoming U.S. citizens were beginning to sponsor their relatives. In 1995, for example, 3,403 Africans entered under the occupational categories, but 4,232 arrived under the family preferences, and 11,734 came as spouses, minor children, or parents of U.S. citizens who were exempt from the quotas. The remainder were refugees or asylum seekers.[63] In 2001 half of Africa's 53,948 immigrants were exempt from quotas, and roughly 18,000 were immediate family members of U.S. citizens.[64] These figures will continue to grow as additional Africans become eligible to sponsor the migration of their relatives. As more family members have arrived, the average skill level of the new immigrants has begun to drop, as it did for other groups whose first migrants came to take jobs requiring high levels of education.[65]

Even after the IRCA amnesty, many Africans were willing to come without authorization. The preferred way was to enter with a temporary visa and then simply remain. For example, Senegalese, reportedly the largest group of undocumented immigrants from Africa, first appeared in the 1980s. The number of Senegalese certainly ran into the thousands, and some were quite visible as street vendors.[66] The 2000 census revealed that nearly 9 million aliens resided illegally in the United States. If the same ratio of IRCA's amnesty prevailed, about 100,000 Africans without "papers" lived in the United States in that census year. The new African immigrants of the second half of the twentieth century have settled in nearly all areas of the United States. New York City reportedly contained the largest settlement of Africans; some African community observers placed the number as high as 90,000 in the late 1980s, with 50,000 more arriving between 1900 and 1994. Siddique Wai, a native of Sierra Leone and head of the United African Congress, put the number at 200,000, a figure much too high.[67] Andrew Beveridge, a sociologist at Queens College in New York City, said the number was about 100,000 in the late 1990s. The 2000 census placed the number in New York City at 122,400. The largest groups were from English-speaking Nigeria and Ghana, which accounted for one-half of the sub-Saharan immigrants settling there between 1900 and 1994. Immigrants from the former French-speaking colonies Guinea and Senegal also had established communities in the nation's largest city, and a community of Liberians could be found in the borough of Staten Island.[68]

The state of California claimed 113,255 Africans in 2000, with the San Francisco Bay Area housing 29,930. After Ethiopia the next highest numbers were from Nigeria, Egypt, and South Africa.[69] These figures were not separated into racial categories, and some of the immigrants were either white or Asian. Washington, D.C., was the home of Ethiopians, but the capital area has also claimed African immigrants from a number of other countries, including Ethiopia's rival Eritrea. In the mid-1990s an estimated 75,000 Ethiopians lived in the Greater Washington area, with one-third living in Washington, D.C., proper.[70] While New York City claimed the largest actual number, a 2001 Brookings Institute report noted that 16.2 percent of Greater Washington's immigrants were Africans.[71] Los Angeles claimed to be the second-largest community of Ethiopians, with 45,000, in addition to 6,000 Eritreans. Smaller communities of Ethiopians could also be found in Seattle, Tampa, and St. Louis.[72] In the Midwest an estimated 4,500 Ethiopians and 3,000 Eritreans lived in Columbus, Ohio, and another 5,000 Africans settled in Minneapolis.[73] In 1993 a journalist estimated that 50,000 Nigerians lived in Chicago. Most of these estimates were guesses, made in the absence of factual knowledge about the number of illegal immigrants from Africa. The center of Somali life was in the St. Paul–Minneapolis area, where refugee organizations helped them settle. Overall John Logan found from the 2000 census that Africans were widely dispersed throughout the United States.[74]

Because many of the Africans are refugees, the federal government and private groups had the right to disperse them. San Diego was selected as one site, and Boston was another.[75] Nonrefugees had more freedom to settle. In the mid-1990s Colorado ski resorts, short of help during the ski season, recruited West Africans. Some were only temporary workers recruited on visas allowing them to be employed for a specified period; others were in the United States illegally and were eager to work. As one immigrant remarked, "We have a lot of relatives in Africa who don't have anything. We can't live the life of America. We can't go to nightclubs, go to restaurants, go to basketball games. We eat together. We send money home."[76]

A small group, the Nuer from southern Sudan, have been the subject of a careful study. The civil war in Sudan, which became particularly intense in the 1980s, drove the Nuer to seek refuge abroad. Many first lived in Ethiopian camps established by the UNHCR, but as their situation deteriorated, they moved to refugee camps in Kenya before coming to the United States in the mid-1990s. About 400 settled in Minnesota's Twin Cities area, but a few left to live in Nebraska, Iowa, and South Dakota.[77]

The federal governmental and voluntary agencies (VOLAGs) settled refugees in particular communities, but they could not control secondary migration. In 2001 and 2002 Somalian refugees, many of whom lived in Atlanta, began to move to Lewiston, Maine, where housing was cheap and where the city's welfare policy made the Somalis eligible for benefits. When 1,000 of these Africans went to Lewiston, a community of 36,000, their presence was not always welcome. Some residents did not like the fact that the newcomers were black and Muslim. The mayor and others protested that welfare programs required taxes for support and that the city's budget was being stretched.[78] As the number of new Somalian refugees dropped in late 2002, the city's tension eased.[79]

While some of the first African immigrants were the highly educated elite who found employment in the professions after completing their educations, many of the refugees and regular immigrants of the 1980s and 1990s had to seek nonprofessional occupations to make a living in their new land. They opened restaurants, gift shops, export businesses, and stores catering to their fellow immigrants. Small businesses were operated mostly by men.[80] They were enterprising, opening African restaurants or small businesses that catered to non-Africans as well. Although the vast majority of the vendors were men, some women came as well, such as those who opened African hair-braiding stores on 116th Street in New York City.[81] For these immigrants, hours were long and rewards few. Some Africans operated their own shops, but many sold merchandise on the streets of American cities. Senegalese men first peddled in New York City, selling watches or umbrellas on rainy days along the sidewalks. The *New York Times* reported in 1985 that the Senegalese were almost certain to appear on midtown corners with bags full of umbrellas as soon as the "first raindrops fall."[82] African New Yorkers sold a variety of items, such as baseball caps, pirated video tapes, sunglasses, and watches with expensive names. It was relatively easy to purchase fake designer goods manufactured in Asia.[83] Merchants were able to buy such goods from Korean suppliers in lower Manhattan.[84] If skeptical buyers could not believe the low prices, at least one merchant claimed he told customers goods were falsely labeled. "They probably know anyway, from the price. I mean, it's hard to get a real Rolex for twenty-five dollars."[85]

While striving to making a profit by selling on the streets, the undocumented immigrants encountered the opposition of established businesses when they sold their goods in front of these shops. Responding to pressure by licensed merchants, New York's mayor, Edward Koch, sent the police to evict African street vendors; but a judge threw out the arrests, claiming that since almost all those arrested were Senegalese, the action violated laws against bias.[86] In 1996 mayor Rudolph Giuliani ordered 200 police officers to evict vendors along Manhattan's 125th Street in Harlem, forcing them to move to a different, less remunerative location.[87] Paul Stoller's account of Issifi Mayaki and other African merchants revealed a difficult life, endured because conditions at home were very bleak. Issifi set up shop in Harlem's Malcolm Shabazz Market, where he sold both African and non-African goods.[88] Between 1996 and 1998, Issifi shifted from his New York City base and mainly peddled his wares at cultural events outside of the city.[89]

Many of the street merchants doubled up in living accommodations so that they could save on housing and send money home. Certain apartments and single resident occupancy hotels (SROs) earned reputations as being inhabited almost entirely by West Africans.[90] With green cards and a mastery of English, their opportunities for advancement improved. Many West Africans worked as stock clerks and security guards, but for those who remained undocumented, low-skill work such as delivering groceries was available. Other Africans crossed the Hudson River to sell in New Jersey on their way to Detroit's annual Afro-American Music Festival. Journalist Joel Millman estimates that in the 1990s these modern-day peddlers attended about 200 black events around the country to hawk their goods.[91]

Another visible occupation for Africans, here both legally and illegally, has been driving cabs. With little capital and willing to work long hours, Africans, especially Ethiopians, drove cabs in the nation's capital. African cab drivers could be found in other cities such as Atlanta, Saint Louis, New York City, and Chicago. Driving was sometimes a dangerous occupation. A Senegalese, Elhadji Gaye, was among the thirteen cab and livery drivers killed in 1997 in New York City.[92] West Africans claimed that fifty African drivers had been killed in the city between 1986 and 1999.[93] Only a handful of Senegalese women worked in this high-risk occupation.[94]

In 1990 the census revealed that 88 percent of African immigrants had finished high school and, as noted, nearly half had a college degree. Scholars found from the 2000 census that Africans still had high levels of education.[95] Using that census, John Logan found that African immigrants on average had 14.5 years of education, which was higher than the years reported by Caribbean blacks and African Americans.[96] Incomes for African immigrants were higher than for native-born African Americans but lagged behind those of whites and Asians.[97] Exactly why incomes were lower is not clear. Some of the immigrants might have had language difficulties or lacked skills that would secure better employment in the United States. Delivery men in New York City, for example, lacked "legal status and fluent English," and hence held one of the lowest-paying jobs in New York.[98] Moreover, it was not uncommon for newly arrived professional immigrants to work in jobs below their skill levels for years before they were able to find more remunerative employment. Using the 1990 census, F. NII-Amoo Dodoo looked at a number of variables affecting earnings of men. He noted that language was not a major issue but recency of arrival did depress the overall earnings of African immigrants.[99]

The issue of racism cannot be avoided. Like Caribbean black immigrants, Africans entered a society with a long history of racism, and although progress had been made since the civil rights movement of the 1960s, discrimination remained. Commenting on his reception in America compared with in his home, Eritrean Takle Gabriel, who ran a restaurant in Chicago, remarked, "We were the same homogenous people, and when you come to a society where most things are divided along racial lines, it takes a while to grasp things like discrimination. I have never experienced anything like racism until I came here."[100] Africans also have higher rates of poverty than Americans generally.[101] A New York City African immigrant agreed: "If you are foreign and black and looking for a job in New York, you will very likely receive low pay."[102] However, it should be kept in mind that the figures for sub-Saharan African immigrants also included whites and Asians; just what proportion were black was not revealed by the 1990 or 2000 census.[103]

Facing a racism different from that found in their home countries, where in most cases blacks were in the majority, many newcomers felt a kinship with native-born blacks in the United States. Yet their experiences were not the same; Africans, as immigrants, at times confronted problems that were different from those that faced native-born blacks. Language was one difference for those whose primary language was not English. Another was the immigrants' connection to their homelands. They kept in contact with relatives and friends by letter, phone, and e-mail about the conflicts and economic needs of their homeland. Like many newly arrived immigrants, they sent money home. In the Apraku study of an elite group, only 12 percent did not send remittances to their immediate families or other relatives or friends in Africa.[104] Somalis in Minneapolis–Saint Paul were estimated to have sent at least $75 million home in 2000.[105] When war erupted again in Sierra Leone in 1999, Sierra Leoneans in Washington, D.C., held a demonstration to express their concern and called for a more positive role for the U.S. government to end the violence.

In the past, immigrant groups such as Italians have sent money home not only to support their relatives but also to build homes in their native villages. Mexicans and Central Americans have continued these practices, and so have Africans. An organization called Ghana Homes appeared in New York City to assist in house building in Ghana. One immigrant noted, "You can own a home here, but no one's going to know about it, so you have to own a home in Ghana."[106]

For migrants such as the Senegalese, immigrant status was a large issue. At the beginning of the twenty-first century, just how an effective alliance could be built to include African-born and native-born blacks was not clear. But given the growing immigration from Africa (and the Caribbean as well), these communities may work together at least on certain occasions.[107]

If Africans found life in the United States challenging, they were not without friends in American communities. Official refugees were entitled to refugee programs, which included medical support and English classes. In Los Angeles, the African Community Refugee Center provided instruction in English as a second language for the newcomers.[108] In Boston the Somali Development Center also conducted English-language classes, and a TV channel produced a Somali-language program. Voluntary organizations that had traditionally aided immigrants included Africans in their programs.[109]

In the tradition of earlier immigrants, Africans have begun to publish their own newspapers; the best-selling paper was the *African Sun Times*, published in New York City.[110] Millman reports that *Xabaar*, a Senegalese newspaper, is printed in French, Wolof, English, and Arabic.[111] Africans hailed from different cultures, and like previous waves of immigrants, they sought to maintain their traditions in America. In Seattle, which had a small community of Africans, the Ethiopian Community Mutual Association was created as early as 1983 to help incoming Ethiopians. Wherever Africans settled, they formed organizations to deal with immigrant problems and focus political attention on affairs at home.[112] Women have been prominent in associations to help the newcomers. Immigrant-run stores catered to the newcomers' desire for familiar clothes and food, and local television stations contained special programs for the new immigrants. Festivals featured food, dancing, and sports events.[113]

Perhaps no other institution has been as important as the immigrant churches, although, again, there is a broad range of religious organizations. In Allentown, Pennsylvania, Africans founded the Christ Assembly Church to aid all Africans, especially those displaced by the Liberian civil war.[114] The new Liberty Evangelical Church in Philadelphia also sought to bring Africans together.[115] The Coptic Christians of Ethiopia, who date back to the third century, have developed their own style of Christian worship. For example, these Christians celebrate Christmas on January 6. While most Copts came from Egypt and Ethiopia, some came from the Sudan, where militant Islam forced them to seek a new home in the United States.[116] Some Ethiopians established the Holy Trinity Ethiopian Orthodox in New York City, and by the late 1990s the Washington, D.C., area had four Ethiopian churches.[117] In Tampa, Florida, an Ethiopian church opened its doors in 1998.[118] In other cases local Protestant churches invited the new immigrants to worship with an eye to reviving declining congregations and also to aid the immigrants in adjusting to the United States. These efforts were not always successful. The Nuer of Minnesota were mostly Christian, but the effort to recruit them and allow them to have their own services ended in failure, even though some still attended Protestant churches in the area.[119]

Some of the newcomers were Roman Catholic, and the Catholic Church began to recruit them. In Los Angeles, Saint Cellulase Catholic Church used Spanish in worship and then opened the door to the Ibo of Nigeria, who spoke their own language in services. Nigerians celebrated Lent with lively events, including "centrums and African music" and women wearing traditional clothing.[120] Elsewhere, in Madison, Wisconsin, Paul Ugochukwu Arinze became the first Nigerian to be ordained a priest in that diocese, and in 1998 the Archdiocese of Boston opened the African Pastoral Center to minister to African immigrants.[121] To further complicate the matter, many Africans were Muslims. The Somalis and the Senegalese practiced Islam and were generally more conservative than other Americans in their social attitudes. Neither did Islamic Africans always follow the same traditions. The Senegalese had a community center of their own in New York City.[122]

Exactly how the new Africans will accept American-style religion or American customs was another open question. African parents, for example, perceive American society as being "very wild." It was not unknown for immigrant parents to leave their children at home with the grandparents to avoid exposing them to American culture.[123] But like so many immigrants, the new Africans had to make accommodations to American culture, with its more liberal attitudes toward gender and children. Moreover, women are taking on new roles in American society, whether in organizations, the family, or the economy. On the whole, African women were less educated than men and were often unable to attain professional careers. Nonetheless, for many families the income of wives was vital to maintaining their desired standard of living, a situation that can have a far-reaching impact on family roles.

Jon Holtzman's study of the Nuer community in Minnesota offers some clues about the changing gender roles. The strict gender-determined divisions of labor the Nuers practiced in Africa could not be maintained in the United States, where women have joined men in the workforce. Holtzman did not discover major shifts from the roles observed in Africa; rather, changes were more subtle, with the men and women sharing more household tasks than they did in the Sudan. He also noted violence against women in some of the marriages, which was not unknown in Africa.[124] Obviously, the recency of African immigration makes it hard to generalize. Clearly all immigrants had to face unfamiliar conditions in their new homes, which often meant more independence for women and children.

The largest numbers of new black immigrants after World War II came not from Africa but from the Caribbean. (See Table 6.) During World War II, the federal government recruited Jamaicans to cut cane in Florida and work in the cranberry fields of Wisconsin. Some of these workers stayed on. Prior to 1952, British colonial residents could migrate under the large national origin quota of Great Britain. But in 1952 Congress changed the law and provided colonies such as Jamaica with an annual quota of only 100. Furthermore, when some Caribbean colonies became independent, as Jamaica did in 1962, they kept their limit of 100, unlike other independent nations of the Western Hemisphere, which had no numerical ceiling. Such a provision obviously restricted immigration from these colonies and new nations, and many Jamaicans headed for Great Britain during these years.

The situation changed again when Great Britain restricted West Indian immigration in 1962 and the American immigration act of 1965 gave Jamaica and other newly independent countries the same status as all Western Hemisphere nations. In the 1970s, as noted, Congress provided for a worldwide system, with each nation receiving 20,000 visas, not counting immediate family members of U.S. citizens. These post-1965 changes made it possible once again for newly independent Caribbean countries to send growing numbers of immigrants to the United States.[125] Jamaica sent 8,659 immigrants to America during the 1950s; in the 1960s it sent 71,011, and that figure doubled in the 1970s. In the 1980s more than 200,000 Jamaican immigrants came to the United States, followed by another 169,227 in the 1990s.[126] Except for Latino nations, Jamaica, Bar-

TABLE 6
Immigration from Jamaica and Haiti (1971–2001)

Country of Last Residence	1971–80	1981–90	1991–2000	1998	1999	2000	2001
Haiti	56,335	138,379	179,644	13,316	16,459	22,004	22,535
Jamaica	137,577	208,148	169,227	14,819	14,449	15,654	15,099

SOURCE: Immigration and Naturalization Service, Statistical Yearbook, 2001.

bados, and Trinidad and Tobago headed the list of Caribbean countries exporting people, but immigrants came from the other Caribbean nations as well. Most were Anglophone, but Francophone Haiti, Guadeloupe, and Martinique were also sources for immigrants.[127] These figures were for those with proper documents; only guesses can predict the number of undocumented immigrants. Under the terms of the IRCA's 1986 general amnesty and that for agricultural workers, 123,000 Caribbean immigrants gained an amnesty out of the total of nearly 3 million successful applicants.[128]

On Labor Day, West Indian immigrants hold a huge carnival in Brooklyn, New York. In 2000 more than 1 million turned out for this growing celebration. Organizers claimed that the event was a recognition of the rising influence of West Indians in New York City. At the same time, it must recognized that Caribbean peoples have a variety of interests and represent different cultures. What, for example, ties dark-skinned Dominicans to others in the Caribbean?[129] Their Spanish language sets them apart, and they are a relatively new group, which also has a different history than that of many Anglophones. The vast majority of Dominicans are not considered black, and those who are black often identify with other Spanish-speaking Dominicans. In New York City, which has the largest settlement of Dominicans, Dominicans generally live among their compatriots. If language is the most obvious division, individuals from the region are also connected to their particular homeland by kinship ties and political interest. Their remittances, visits, and communications are to their homelands, and if they are dissatisfied with American education, they may even send children home to live with grandparents or other kin to be schooled.[130]

West Indian immigrants have settled mostly on the East Coast, which is in keeping with the practice of pre–World War II days. The largest settlements are in New York City and its surrounding suburbs and cities. Nancy Foner pointed out that New York is "the significant destination, by far, for Caribbean immigrants to the United States."[131] Indeed, about half of the Anglophone migrants from the Caribbean live in New York or New Jersey. In the South, Florida, especially Miami, accounts for the largest number. In Miami foreign-born blacks amounted to about one-third of the city's black population. Concentrations of West Indians are also found in Atlanta, Richmond, and the suburbs of Washington, D.C., where black immigrants live in areas overwhelmingly populated by other blacks.[132] In Connecticut, earlier Jamaican immigrants helped harvest tobacco, but they no longer did this type of labor by the 1990s. Instead, Connecticut's Jamaicans moved to cities such as Hartford.[133]

Like most immigrants of recent years, women outnumber the men in the migration flow, though historically Caribbean immigration has been "traditionally male dominated."[134] Family unification partly accounts for the gender difference; as immigrant men become established, they use the family preferences to bring their wives and children to America. Yet women have often taken the lead in immigration, for they were able to find employment as nurses, child care providers, or domestics, occupations in demand in the United States. Regardless of whether they came first or later, West Indian women participate in the workforce at a higher level than do American women generally. The rapid development of the service industry opened many, usually low-paying, jobs for English-speaking women.[135]

Anglophone West Indians have won a reputation for being well educated, skilled, "hard workers," and, consequently, economically successful.[136] Economist Thomas Swell is the most outspoken proponent of this view, and some scholarly studies have reported evidence to support it. West Indians overall have incomes that are higher than those of American-born blacks and many Hispanics.[137] Scholars and even West Indians themselves suggest that white employers prefer West Indians, believing they are more willing than black Americans to work hard and stay off welfare.[138] Some scholarly studies have refuted beliefs about West Indian success, showing that when education, their knowledge of English, and skills are held constant, West Indians lag behind white Americans in income.[139] John Logan's data for 2000 revealed that West Indians fared better than native-born blacks and Latinos but had incomes below those of whites and Asians.[140]

West Indians have also won a reputation for becoming entrepreneurs who find economic "niches." Many have opened their own businesses in retail trade, at times with the help of rotating credit associations. In New York, for example, in the 1980s West Indians drove gypsy cabs and jitney buses, some legal, some not, which supplemented the city's regular cabs, buses, and subways. These jitneys filled a niche as public transportation declined in some neighborhoods.[141]

In actuality, West Indians have participated in such enterprises at lower rates than native-born Americans generally and most other immigrants. Suzanne Model's examination of 1990 New York City census data shows that West Indians were less likely to be self-employed than other New

Yorkers.[142] The service industries employed most of these immigrants, and in some occupations their knowledge of English was an advantage. Health care institutions—hospitals, nursing homes, and medical clinics— became important sources of employment for West Indians. Roger Waldinger reported that in the 1990s health care occupations accounted for more than one-fifth of West Indian employment in New York City.[143] Network hiring was important in health care, and Mary Waters's study of a food service company also revealed the importance of network hiring in that industry.[144] Networks aided the newcomers, but so did employer preferences for Caribbean blacks.[145]

West Indians have joined existing American institutions, such as Catholic and Protestant (usually Episcopal) churches. Their presence has not always been welcome, and like other immigrants they have also created their own organizations. These range from church groups to sporting clubs and benevolent societies. Notes sociologist Philip Kasinitz about New York City, "By the mid-1980s literally hundreds of new West Indian voluntary organizations had sprung up in the New York metropolitan area. They vary in size, function, and nation of origin, but nearly all are associated with a particular Caribbean nation or territory."[146] The "Caribbean Guide" in *Everybody's* magazine listed 158 such groups. Like other ethnic organizations, they helped recent immigrants adjust to their new environment. Sometimes this aid was financial.[147] The professionally elite West Indians in Washington, D.C., frequently associated with the predominantly black Howard University. They aided the students at Howard who had come from the Caribbean and helped the students maintain close relations with their countries of origin. While Ransford Palmer found the Howard group somewhat loosely connected, he reported that the community of Hartford, Connecticut, was tightly knit.[148]

Coming from nations where blacks were in a majority, West Indians were unprepared for the racism they encountered in the United States. Mary Waters reported, "The expectations that the immigrants have about race relations in the United States do not prepare them well for their experiences. Most respondents [in her study] report surprise at the racial situation they encounter; many report deep shock."[149] The newcomers find limits on available housing, which is rigidly segregated, and in employment. Segregated neighborhoods often meant that the schools their children attended were in need of repair, overcrowded, and periodically violent. The parents expected the schools to be rigorous, and some believed in corporal punishment for unruly children.[150] If it was difficult or even impossible to find housing in a neighborhood with high-quality schools, some parents elected to send their children home to be educated.

Scholars and community observers have noted that West Indians were often reluctant to identify with native-born black Americans. A few black leaders said that the immigrants believed themselves to be superior.[151] The same charge has been made about Africans.[152] Yet the encounter with American racism has forced many immigrants to work with black Americans to deal with racial issues; black immigrants clearly supported the goals of the civil rights movement of the 1960s, and they have joined with American blacks to concentrate on other racial issues.[153] West Indians have also seen the need for representatives in local, state, and federal governments to respond to their needs. As a result, a growing number have been become citizens, especially in New York City, where their presence is large.[154]

The experience of Haitian immigrants has been different than that of other Caribbean migrants. It will be recalled that when Congress passed the Johnson Reed Act in 1924, the Western Hemisphere was left without numerical limits, though immigrants had to satisfy general restrictions such as the literacy requirement and not be deemed likely to become a public charge. Ira De Reid's 1940 study of black immigrants located about 500 Haitians in New York City, largely a well-educated group who had migrated in the 1920s during the era of American occupation of Haiti. In the 1930s few Haitians came to America. Nor was World War II conducive to immigration. Until 1960 only a few hundred Haitians immigrated annually to the United States, along with several thousand students, visitors, or persons on business.[155] But then the circumstances changed in Haiti. A struggling economy that made Haiti the poorest nation in the Caribbean that was ruled by a brutal dictator prompted thousands of Haitians to leave. Many went to other Caribbean islands, as Haitians had done for generations, but increasingly they looked to the United States.

The 1965 immigration act and its 1970s amendments, which brought the Western Hemisphere into a uniform system, gave Haiti a quota of 20,000 (not counting immediate family members of U.S. citizens). On the surface, the allotment was generous in that Haiti had the same quota as the world's most populous nation, China. However, the preference system within the numerical limit made it difficult for Haitians to come to the United States. They lacked the skills that the INS said were needed, and many Haitians lacked family connections for immigration.

There also existed the possibility that because Haiti was a violent and politically oppressive nation, Haitians might qualify as refugees. The reign of Francois Duvalier ("Papa Doc") as dictator, beginning in 1957, prompted many Haitians to leave. Papa Doc's rule lasted until 1971, and during that period 35,000 persons left, most of whom settled in the United States. Upon his death in 1971, his son Jean-Claude ("Baby Doc") succeeded him and stayed in power until 1986. At first the middle classes, professionals, and intellectual leaders fled to the United States and elsewhere in the Caribbean, but as the violence continued and the economy deteriorated, poor Haitians joined the exodus. Because many could not satisfy immigration regulations, they fled by boat, hoping to enter even without proper documents and find work in America. During the period of the dictatorship the United States ignored human rights violations in Haiti because the American government saw Haiti as an ally in the cold war and was unwilling to admit that the Duvaliers' rule was one of violence and oppression. Haitians who tried to enter illegally by boat first appeared in the early 1970s, but they were turned back by the INS and the Coast Guard. These desperately poor people braved the seas to get to Florida, and hundreds drowned in the process.[156] The numbers continued to grow in the 1970s. Haitians were not without friends in the United States. Church, black, and civil rights groups challenged governmental rulings and achieved some success in slowing deportation, gaining entrance, and forcing the government to set up procedures for hearing Haitian claims. However, the judicial and political victories gradually caused the U.S. government to change its procedures. Winning asylum on a case-by-case basis continued to be difficult. The IRCA granted those in the United States before 1982 the right to adjust their legal status to immigrant. From 1991 to 1994, a total of 80,857 Haitians, including those covered by the amnesty, were admitted as resident aliens. Haitian immigration to the United States numbered 22,364 in 2000 and 27,120 in 2001.[157]

But unauthorized Haitians continued to make the perilous trip by sea after 1982. The Reagan and Bush administrations sent the Coast Guard and navy to pick up those attempting to sail to America and return them to Haiti. Under President Bush a partial shift occurred. Haitians were plucked from the sea and sent to Guantánamo Bay in Cuba to have their applications screened. This process took time, and the refugees were not allowed to consult properly with lawyers. As more Haitians fled and were caught and sent by American vessels for screening at Guantánamo, the camp quickly became overcrowded and disease ridden, prompting President Bush to order that all fleeing Haitians be returned to Haiti, by force if necessary. This meant a virtual blockade of any boats leaving Haiti with potential refugees. In 1992 presidential candidate Bill Clinton criticized these actions, but he maintained the same policy during the first years of his presidency.[158]

Following the end of Duvalier rule, Haitians experienced an elected government headed by Father Jean-Bertrand Aristide. However, the military removed him in a 1991 coup, prompting an estimated 40,000 to flee during the 1990s. The Clinton administration interned some Haitians at Guantánamo Bay in Cuba while they were pursuing their applications for asylum.[159] Ten thousand of them were considered potential refugees and were sent to the United States while their claims were being considered, but the U.S. government returned others to Haiti. Complicating the issue was the fact that some Haitians had the AIDS virus and were deemed ineligible for admission. As the number of Haitians seeking to come to America rose in 1994, the Clinton administration decided to use military force to return Aristide to power. In the fall of 1994 American troops landed to oust the military dictatorship and install Aristide once again as Haiti's president. While employing the rhetoric of restoring democracy, the president made it clear that the new occupation of Haiti was also driven by immigration issues. Said Clinton: "As long as Cedras [the military] rules, Haitians continue to seek sanctuary in our nation. This year, in less than two months, more than 21,000 Haitians were rescued at sea by our Coast Guard and Navy. Today more than 14,000 refugees are living at our naval base in Guantanamo." He concluded with a warning about the future: "Three hundred thousand more Haitians—more than 5 percent of their entire population—are in hiding in their own country. If we don't act, they could be the next wave of refugees at our door. We will continue to face the threat of a mass exodus of refugees and its constant threat to stability in our region and control of our borders."[160]

Political stability lasted a few years, but after Aristide retired, the situation remained precarious. Aristide returned to power once again, but the economic status of Haitians continued to decline, and after the removal of American and other troops the economy continued its downward path. In 2000, 80 percent of Haitians lived in poverty. With a per capita income of $250—less than one-tenth of the Latin American average—Haiti was the hemisphere's poorest nation.[161] Some fled to the Bahamas, while others crossed into the Dominican Republic to find work. Neither the Dominicans nor the Bahamians wished to see a large number of refugees streaming into their country. Thus many Haitians were willing to run the risk of escaping in overcrowded, rickety boats in order to land in Florida. Commented one Haitian official in 2000, "We fear an upsurge of boat people departures this year. First there is drought in the north; second if elections aren't held as anticipated, international aid will be held up and the economic situation will worsen."[162] Such conditions made smugglers happy, for desperate Haitians were willing to pay to take the dangerous trip, packed together and hoping to elude American vessels that were ready to send them back home.[163]

Friends of the Haitians insisted that they were political refugees and were no different from Russian and South Asian refugees. They suggested that racism explained why so few Haitians won refugee status or asylum. Even Central Americans were treated more generously. In 1997 Congress granted an amnesty to Cubans and Nicaraguans who entered the United States before 1995; it also allowed Salvadorans and Guatemalans to remain in the United States while processing their claims for asylum. Finally, in 1998, Congress did pass legislation permitting Haitians to remain while pursuing their asylum claims if they had entered before 1995. In 1999 the INS established guidelines for an estimated 50,000 Haitians who had arrived before 1995.[164] But the conditions were harsher than those imposed upon Central Americans. Those who arrived with a phony passport, if Haitian, were not included in the amnesty. In addition, there remained the plight of Haitians who landed after the cutoff date.[165]

In spite of these difficulties and inconsistent policies, Haitian immigration grew. Exact figures are lacking because many Haitians were residing in the United States without proper papers. Undocumented aliens settling in New York City were more apt to arrive on a temporary visa rather than by boat. But the number of those arriving with immigrant visas grew. From 1900 to 1995, a total of 85,000 Haitian legal immigrants were counted by the INS, and a similar number arrived in the last five years of the twentieth century.[166] The 1990 census revealed that nearly 300,000 claimed Haitian ancestry, but this was no doubt an undercount.[167] The 2000 census revealed that 569,000 Haitian immigrants lived in the United States.[168]

Those settling before the 1970s, generally educated professionals, had an easier time adjusting to their new society. A majority of the post-1980 immigrants were single and young. Some were college graduates, but nearly two-thirds lacked a high school diploma. Moreover, many

Haitians spoke only Haitian creole, which put them at a disadvantage in finding employment. Educated Haitians also spoke French.[169] Haitians, like most black Americans whether foreign or native born, lived in largely segregated neighborhoods. In New York City, Haitians settled among other immigrants from the Caribbean and native-born black Americans in several of the city's boroughs. In Miami the majority were found in a ghetto east of the large native-born black community, called "Liberty City" or "Little Haiti."[170]

Given their skin color and educational and language backgrounds, it is not surprising that Haitians were generally employed in low-paying occupations. Those arriving illegally along the Florida coast are especially likely to be poor, with limited prospects in the United States. According to Alex Stepick, "Their employment situation compares unfavorably to any other immigrant population in the country."[171] Even so, in 1994 Haitians were no more apt to use welfare than the American population generally.[172] A middle class has emerged, consisting of those professionals who migrated before the large-scale movement began in 1970 and those who operated the many small businesses that Haitians developed, especially in New York City.[173] In Florida the middle class, whose members usually arrived as regular immigrants, was reported by Alex Stepick to look down upon the "boat people."[174]

The growth of the Haitian community prompted Florida and New York officials to call for reimbursement to local communities for their aid given to Haitian immigrants. Government personnel said crowded schools and the lack of interpreters in hospitals and courts caused problems in conducting judicial proceedings and providing health care. In Miami, for example, a trial of four Haitians who were alleged gang members was postponed in September 2000 because of a shortage of creole-speaking interpreters in the judicial area where the four were to be tried; this was not the only area lacking interpreters.[175] The search for bilingual creole speakers and reimbursement for educational and medical expenses had only limited success.

While Haitians encountered the same racism experienced by black Americans and received some help from black groups such as the Black Caucus in Congress, they have not always worked with native-born blacks to deal with their situation in the United States. Most observers point out that as immigrants Haitians have different political concerns than black Americans. Not only has winning asylum been important but prospective Haitian immigrants had to fight an image that they were especially prone to have had

AIDS or be HIV positive. The Centers for Disease Control (CDC) in Atlanta designated them as one of the groups to be at prime risk for AIDS. As a result of the CDC's statement, Haitians found it more difficult to find jobs. The INS joined the attack because it now had an additional reason to deny Haitians entrance. Eventually the CDC withdrew the designation, and the INS stopped denying Haitians entry on the grounds that they were liable to be carriers of the AIDS virus or to be HIV positive.[176]

As a result of these differences, Haitians formed their own organizations—social, religious, and political. They wanted their own organizations that would tie them to other Haitians, deal with their problems, reinforce Haitian culture, and pay particular attention to events in Haiti. For example, Haitians rented time on a local radio station in Miami, with much of the programming focusing on events in Haiti. Like other immigrant groups that arrived not knowing English, Haitians published foreign-language newspapers. Indeed, language has become an important factor in the creation of Haitian American identity. The vast majority of these new immigrants were Christian, divided almost evenly between Protestant and Catholic, although because of the influence of voodoo on their religious practices some Americans have seen Haitians as "carriers" of a strange and exotic religion.[177]

The existence of a vibrant, distinct culture set Haitians apart from black Americans and most other Caribbean migrants. Because relations between Haitians and black Americans have not always been smooth, it was not clear at the turn of the twenty-first century what the future would hold for Haitian–black American relations. Nor was it clear what was in store for Haitians themselves, but if Haiti's economic situation continues to deteriorate and violence continues, many desperate Haitians will likely migrate to the United States illegally.

The asylum issue became public again in October 2002, when a ship carrying 200 Haitians reached Florida's shores. Once in the United States they were eligible to request asylum, which many did. The Bush administration placed them in detention while their cases were being heard. Immigrant advocates claimed that detention was unique to Haitians because in other cases asylum seekers were allowed to remain free and work.[178] However, the Department of Justice also announced a new policy. In the future, illegal aliens requesting asylum would be kept in custody while their cases were being decided.[179]

The Bush policy once again confirmed that the difficulties that Haitians experienced stand in sharp contrast to those of several other nationalities arriving as official refugees after World War II. Both Cubans and South Asians were fleeing communism; hence their reception was readily accepted by the U.S. government. Yet even entering the United States as refugees, with special programs to aid them, did not necessarily make their adjustment to a new land easy, as we shall see in the next chapter.

10

The Refugees
Cubans and Asians

During the 1930s and World War II, few refugees seeking a haven in the United States were able to settle in America. After World War II, with America's emergence as a superpower and the influence of the cold war, immigration and refugee policy shifted, and the United States admitted several million persons as refugees or displaced persons (DPs). With an eye toward the postwar situation in Europe, the Truman administration urged Congress to admit some of the hundreds of thousands of persons in displaced persons camps. After intensive lobbying, Congress provided for 400,000 DPs, but the legislators did not substantially overhaul the national origins provisions of prevailing immigration law.[1] Following enactment of the Displaced Persons acts, Congress passed the Refugee Relief Act of 1953, admitting another 200,000 immigrants.

An important step in widening the door occurred when Hungarians took up arms against the Soviet Union in 1956. The defeated revolutionaries fled into neighboring Austria. Austria did accept 200,000 of the "freedom fighters," as the West called them, but insisted that other sympathetic powers share the burden of caring for these refugees. Because the Hungarian quota was small, President Dwight D. Eisenhower used the parole power of the McCarran-Walter Immigration Act of 1952, which had been intended only for individual cases, to admit more than 30,000 Hungarians. The use of this power was later expanded to admit thousands of other refugees even after Congress finally passed refugee laws meant to be a permanent part of the immigration system.

Refugees other than Europeans had a more difficult time until the 1960s, when 2 million were admitted from Cuba and Southeast Asia. Of the 200,000 admitted under the Refugee Relief Act of 1953, Congress included several thousand Palestinians and 5,000 East Asians.[2] This was the first time that U.S. legislation admitted persons other than Europeans as refugees. Congress then authorized the admission of several thousand

Chinese scholars and students who were caught in America after the Communists won control of China.[3]

President John F. Kennedy used the parole power in 1961 to accept another 14,000 Chinese refugees who had fled to Hong Kong. At the time, the cold war reigned supreme, and the United States backed the overthrow of the left-leaning Chilean government in 1973 in which President Salvador Allende was assassinated and replaced by a right-wing regime more acceptable to Washington. The federal government was none too eager to accept persons associated with Allende and was willing to overlook human rights violations in noncommunist nations, but the National Security Council did recommend modest quotas for dissenters in both Argentina and Chile. As Gil Loescher and John Scanlan note, "The administration responded to this advice by establishing parole programs for Chileans and Argentineans." However, ideological concerns, including a desire to refrain from being too visibly critical of pro-American, anti-Soviet regimes in Central America and the Caribbean, ensured that no similar programs were established closer to home. The numbers from Argentina and Chile were small. Only 1,323 Chileans eventually came to the United States; most settled in Europe or Latin America.[4]

The United States was not opposed to Latino, black, and Asian refugees per se; they simply had to be the right kind of refugees. The parole power, along with new legislation, demonstrated the tie between refugees and foreign policy most clearly when 800,000 Cubans and more than 1 million Vietnamese, Cambodians, and Laotians eventually migrated to America under these provisions. (See Table 7.)

For years Cuba was racked by political turmoil that temporarily ended with the dictatorship of Fulgencio Batista in 1952. During the reign of Batista nearly 70,000 Cubans immigrated to the United States. For a number of reasons they chose not to live under Batista's dictatorship, even though the previous turmoil had ended. Then under assault by Fidel Castro's revolutionary movement, Batista's regime fell from power; Castro's small army entered Havana on January 8, 1959. At first the charismatic Castro had wide support among the Cuban people, who for the most part did not wish to continue living under Batista's dictatorship. However, as Castro moved to the left politically and eventually proclaimed himself to be a communist, many Cubans no longer supported him. From 1959 to 2001 more than 800,000 Cubans chose exile, immigrating mostly to the United States but also to Spain and other Latin American countries.[5]

TABLE 7
Selected Refugees and Asylees
Granted Permanent Resident Status (1946–2001)

Country of Birth	Total	1946–50	1951–60	1961–70	1971–80	1981–90	1991–2000	2000	2001
Cambodia	128,266	—	—	—	7,739	114,064	6,388	36	75
China	47,744	319	12,008	5,308	13,760	7,928	7,608	487	813
Cuba	663,746	3	6	131,557	251,514	113,367	144,612	14,362	22,687
Iran	73,182	118	192	58	364	46,773	24,313	956	1,364
Iraq	40,257	—	130	119	6,851	7,540	22,557	3,483	3,060
Laos	202,439	—	—	—	21,690	142,964	37,265	708	520
Vietnam	691,936	—	2	7	150,266	324,453	206,857	5,576	10,351

SOURCE: Immigration and Naturalization Service, Statistical Yearbook, 2001.

The Cuban exodus came to the United States in waves. The first to arrive, just before Castro's march into Havana, were Batista and several hundred of his immediate advisers and family, who fled in December 1958. The United States granted refugee status to 500 of these émigrés. Others did not wait long, for members of the economic and political elite began to leave in the early days of the successful Castro revolution. These were mostly highly "educated, wealthy landowners, sugar barons, industrialists, entrepreneurs, professionals, and former employees of U.S.-owned companies." From January 1959 to October 1960, 10,000 Cubans entered the United States. Following the precedent of the Hungarians, they were quickly settled.[6]

The Eisenhower administration accepted these latest refugees in part because of humanitarian concerns and in part because it wished to embarrass Fidel Castro's communist state. Thus President Eisenhower called upon the American people to "open their homes and hearts" to the fleeing Cubans. The president sent Tracy S. Voorhees, who had run the Hungarian program, to coordinate refugee efforts in Florida.[7]

President Kennedy continued the Eisenhower policy of welcome, and just behind the top elite came Cubans who were relatively well-off. In 1961, 56,000 fled to America, most being professionals and technicians.[8] In the cold war atmosphere of the early 1960s the United States broke off diplomatic relations with Cuba in January 1961, after the Cuban seizure of American assets in Cuba. A more serious rupture followed the failed Central Intelligence Agency's Cuban exile attempt to overthrow Castro in April 1961, in which 1,500 Cubans landed at the Bay of Pigs in Cuba with no air cover or offshore support from the American navy. The outnumbered invaders were quickly defeated, and those who were not killed surrendered. Years later the prisoners were exchanged for commodities badly needed in Cuba. The Bay of Pigs fiasco also slowed the exodus to the United States, but the airlifts from Havana to Miami continued nonetheless. They came to a halt with the Cuban missile crisis in the fall of 1962. For the next three years some Cubans escaped by boat, and a few managed to get to the United States by going to a third country first, which was the only way they could legally leave Cuba.[9]

Among those leaving were more than 14,000 children who came under "Operacion Pedro Pan." Many parents, who did not wish to see their children raised under the new regime or who had heard rumors that children would be sent to Moscow for indoctrination, decided instead to send them into exile. Most intended to follow their children, and many did, but some had difficulty leaving Cuba, and the children had to be placed with American or Cuban American families living in the United States. Consequently, some children and parents waited twenty years for a reunion. This divided exodus was not unprecedented, for children had come alone as part of the Hungarian settlement in the United States after the failure of the Budapest uprising in 1956.[10]

In September 1965 Castro indicated that he would once again permit disaffected Cubans and those with relatives in the United States to leave. Clearly he wanted to rid the island of his opponents. When President Lyndon Johnson signed the new immigration law at the Statue of Liberty in October 1965, he took up Castro's suggestion and said that the United States would accept all Cubans who desired to come. He could do so by using, or misusing, as critics insisted, the parole power, as had been done for Hungarians. Congress responded the next year by passing the Cuban Adjustment Act, granting refugee status to any Cuban reaching American soil. The legislators also granted Cubans special aid as refugees. And, of course, refugees could become resident aliens and citizens if they chose to do so. At first Cubans left through the port of Camarioca, where they were picked up by boats rented, borrowed, or owned by Cuban Americans. This unsatisfactory arrangement was soon replaced by regular airlifts, once again through agreement between the United States and Cuba. From then until the early 1970s, more than 200,000 mostly middle-class Cubans traveled by air to Florida. In 1973 the airlift ended once again.[11] A few thousand continued to arrive via a third country or by escaping from Cuba by boat.

It was not simply occupation, education, or social class that divided the Cubans. Most Cubans were Roman Catholics, but among those coming in the 1960s were Cuban Jews. By the 1980s nearly all of the 16,000 Jewish Cubans had left the island nation. The new regime's anticapitalist dogma made many of Cuba's Jews believe they had little future in Cuba. Because so many of them were engaged in business, they were threatened by Castro's leftward drift. Moreover, there was the question of religion. Some of the Cuban Jews had fled to Cuba decades earlier to escape anti-Semitism in Europe. The Castro government was not particularly anti-Semitic, but Castro was hostile to religion in general, especially the Catholic Church; thus his rhetoric "evoked memories of Jewish oppression and suffering in the twentieth century, and so provided a greater impetus for many [Cuban] Jews to go into exile in the United States."[12] Castro was careful not to advocate an open break with Catholics because he was well aware of the hold that Catholicism had among the Cuban people; in the late 1990s he even permitted a visit from the pope, who received an enthusiastic welcome by Cubans.

Relations between the United States and Cuba improved in the late 1970s, and Castro once again surprised Washington when he permitted Cuban Americans to travel to Cuba to visit relatives still there. More than 100,000 visited in 1979, bringing with them stories of their success in America and material goods to share with Cuban friends and relatives. These visits added to the unrest in Cuba, which was plagued by economic and social problems. In April 1980 six Cubans crashed a bus into the Peruvian embassy in Havana and demanded political asylum. Others followed, and the grounds were soon crowded with 10,000 persons making similar pleas.[13] Castro responded by proclaiming that any Cuban who wished to leave could do so through the port of Mariel. Cuban Americans quickly answered by using their boats to pick up the refugees, known as Marielitos. President Jimmy Carter and his administration were caught off guard and consequently pursued a policy that flip-flopped between allowing the boats to bring in Cubans and trying to seek a more controlled policy. As the Marielitos arrived, so did stories that Castro was filling the boats not simply with disaffected Cubans but also with mentally ill persons and hardened criminals. The subsequent chaotic boat lift was not halted by the U.S. Coast Guard and U.S. Navy until 125,000 Cubans had arrived in the United States.[14]

Once here, Cubans were entitled to refugee status under the 1966 Cuban Adjustment Act. Although the act gave them special status, they still had to satisfy other parts of immigration law. Dangerous criminals were barred, as were persons with specific diseases. In addition, some of the Marielitos later committed crimes in the United States, for which they were incarcerated. Washington wanted to ship these undesirables back to Cuba, but Castro gave no indication that he was willing to accept them. As a result, several thousand from the 1980 flotilla found themselves in American jails and prisons apparently for an indefinite period or at least until the United States and Cuba reached an agreement regarding their fate. Those incarcerated at the Atlanta prison and at the INS-run Oakdale, Louisiana, facility rioted, demanding to be set free or that the federal government consider their cases for asylum. The Oakdale facility was destroyed in the upheaval. An agreement was finally reached whereby the Cuban government agreed to take "the excludables." Some but not all were returned.[15]

Cubans continued to reach the United States by boat after 1980, but the numbers were not large until 1994. As Cuba struggled with economic problems, including the loss of aid from the former Soviet Union, these boat trips increased again in 1994. As many as 25,000 "rafters," as they were called, arrived during the summer of 1994. Officially 37,139 Cubans arrived during 1994.[16] Once they reached the United States, they were entitled to political asylum. The Clinton administration was clearly aware of how the Mariel crisis developed, and it did not wish to see that episode repeated when it appeared that the United States had lost control of its immigration policy. The number of Haitians sailing for America increased during the same period, which complicated matters further.

President Jimmy Carter had failed to negotiate with the Castro government, but President Bill Clinton moved to prevent another Mariel. The two governments agreed to regulate the migration flow. The United States was willing to take 20,000 Cubans annually, while the Cuban government committed itself to halting the boat exodus.[17] Those to be admitted were either political dissenters, prisoners who opposed the regime, or those with relatives in America. After that agreement, some Cubans still tried to leave clandestinely by boat, but the U.S. Navy and Coast Guard halted most of them at sea and returned these "boat people" to Cuba. Some were housed temporarily at the American base on Cuba at Guantánamo Bay, where their claims for asylum could be processed. Cuban "rafters" were unhappy at being housed at the American base; some agreed to return to Cuba, while others rioted to protest their conditions in the base's tent city. Many eventually were screened and allowed into the United States, but others found themselves being deported to Cuba.[18] Clinton was trying to avoid an uncontrolled immigration flow, for if the

Cubans landed on American soil, they were covered by the Cuban Adjustment Act and entitled to political asylum.

Angry Cubans in Florida and elsewhere condemned the U.S. administration for what they saw as a virtual repeal of the Cuban Adjustment Act, but Clinton's action had the support of a number of Florida's community leaders and politicians. They believed their state had enough problems trying to support, aid, and educate so many immigrants. Of the few Cubans still managing to get to the United States by boat, the most sensational case was that of six-year-old Elian Gonzalez, whose mother had drowned attempting to reach Florida in 2000. The boy had managed to survive by clinging to a raft. Many Cubans in Florida and some of his relatives demanded that he be given asylum, but in the end the INS and the Clinton administration ruled that he should be returned to Cuba to live with his father. The Elian episode was an explosive one, and the Clinton administration had to remove the boy by force to return him to his Cuban father. The case filled news headlines across the United States.[19]

To talk of Cuban immigrants and the Cuban American generation is to speak of Florida, especially Miami and the surrounding area. Florida, only ninety miles from Cuba, was the natural destination of those coming by boat and air. The rafters and Marielitos mostly stayed near their place of landing. The airlift left from Havana to Miami's international airport. To be sure, those coming from a third country might enter the United States in other cities, but Miami quickly became the home of these exiles.

Beginning in the early 1960s the U.S. government made efforts "to resettle anti-Castro exiles away from Miami."[20] The Cuban Refugee Program under President Kennedy centered on resettling them across the country. The federal government made this effort to disperse refugees being processed in Florida because officials feared that if too many concentrated in one city or county, they would strain the resources of that community and possibly fuel anti-immigrant sentiments.[21] Important Cuban communities did develop in New Jersey, especially in Union City and West New York, just across the Hudson River from New York City, which attracted 20 percent of the refugees. Cubans had been coming to Union City since as early as the 1940s. One scholar notes that by 1959 Union City had as many as 2,000 Cubans, and thousands more came in the 1960s to work in local industry. Once settled, Cubans opened small businesses and by 1975 made up 75 percent of the population of Union City, which became known as "Havana on the Hudson."[22] But it was small by comparison to Miami's "Little Havana." Cubans also settled in New York City and indeed in small numbers throughout the United States.

By the 1990s more than half of the Cubans in the United States lived in the greater Miami area, and in 2000 it was estimated that about two-thirds resided in Dade County alone.[23] Proximity alone does not explain the attraction of Florida; many Cubans were already aware of and had traveled to Miami. Florida had a long history of Cuban settlers, including cigar makers and revolutionaries dating from the late nineteenth century who had organized to overthrow Spanish domination of Cuba. Later, when General Gerardo Machado, an elected president, tried to "stay indefinitely in power, he triggered a new flow of exiles going to Miami and New York." When his regime came to an end in 1933, his friends eventually ended up in Miami "with bags of gold."[24] During the Batista regime the growing Cuban middle class found Miami to be "a popular vacation spot." In addition, Cubans traveled to the city to shop for "the latest fashions and consumer goods" and, in the process, partake of the glitter of Miami Beach's Gold Coast. Pan American Airlines began when it inaugurated service to Cuba. Prerevolutionary businessmen also came to the city on business.[25] Also important is the fact that Floridian Cubans were willing to aid the latest immigrants. Moreover, Florida's climate is similar to that of Cuba, making it comfortable and familiar. And once the Cuban American community was established by the first refugees, others traveled there to see family and familiar faces. This process of chain migration may have been somewhat extreme in the case of Cubans, but it has been common throughout the history of immigration to America.

The congregation of so many Cubans in one geographic region gave the Miami area a distinct Latino and Cuban air. The schools quickly had to develop special bilingual programs to teach English to the children of the émigrés. In addition, Miami suddenly had many businesses with employees speaking Spanish, and Spanish was heard everywhere on the streets. The *Miami Herald* responded with a Spanish-language edition in 1976, and radio and television stations added Spanish programs to their offerings.[26] Many of the exiles chose to live and shop in the city's emerging Little Havana, where stores, coffee shops, and restaurants were recast with a Cuban flavor. The older refugees found the enclave comforting, for unlike the many school-age children, they were not as eager or as able to learn English. As noted, after 1980 other Latinos, from Nicaragua and elsewhere in Latin America, reinforced the Spanish flavor of Little Havana, and expanded its geographic and ethnic boundaries.

Many non-Latino Miamians were uneasy about the sudden influx of the new refugees. They countered with proposals to make English the official language of the city, but in 1973 the Dade County Board of County Commissioners declared the county to be bilingual and bicultural. Following the arrival of the Marielitos in 1980, a citizens' initiative proclaimed the county's official language to be English and declared that all governmental business should be conducted in English. In another reversal thirteen years later, voters repealed this English-only county ordinance. But in 1988 Florida voters rebuffed the vote by referendum and declared Florida to be an official English state. Yet the inroads of the Spanish language could not be ignored, and the ordinance quickly became a dead letter. Businesses did not suddenly switch to English if their customers were Spanish speakers, and Spanish did not disappear from the streets. One scholar maintains that the effect of the proposal was to create more confusion and ethnic tension. These conflicts were partly responsible for Cuban and Latino groups organizing, and in 1989 they elected Lleana Ros-Lehtinen, a Cuban exile, to Congress. She was the first Cuban American sent to Congress. She was followed a few years later by a second Cuban American congressional representative.[27]

By the 1990s Miami's public officials could hardly ignore the growing Latino influence, which was no longer so dominated by Cubans. Nicaraguans, Puerto Ricans, and South and Central Americans also began to arrive after 1980. In 1998, Miami's school board, recognizing the power of Latino voters in the city, endorsed a plan to increase bilingual teaching for all students and not simply those with limited English. The goal was to immerse all children in both English and another language, which would be Spanish. The board was acting to educate all its students for a world in which both English and Spanish were required for success. In fact, there was much praise and little criticism in the city for the program.[28] This direction stands in sharp contrast to that of the state of California, where the voters restricted bilingual education in 1998.

The different waves of the Cuban exodus were diverse socioeconomically. As noted, the first few hundred Cubans to leave were politically and economically elite members of the Batista regime. Then came business professionals, landowners, professional workers, and technicians. Some of those coming before the missile crisis of 1962 left with few possessions, but because they were well educated, they brought with them human capital. Indeed, some of these newcomers knew English because they had received part of their schooling in the United States.[29] This does not mean that they immediately resumed their careers in the United States. Indeed, many took whatever jobs were available, including low-paid positions formerly held by African Americans. Physicians and lawyers discovered that they would not be able to practice their professions; they either lacked English or could not immediately satisfy American licensing standards. To prepare Cuban doctors for an American practice, the University of Miami's Medical School established a special program, and eventually several thousand Cubans received licenses to practice in the United States.[30] Similar programs were run for dentists and engineers.[31] The federal government and local governments responded to the exodus by developing bilingual education programs and other services for the refugees. These programs were mostly carried out through cooperation between the federal and local government and voluntary agencies, such as the Church World Service (Protestant), the U.S. Catholic Conference, the Hebrew Immigrant Aid Society, and the International Rescue Committee. Voluntary agencies had already been assisting refugees and other immigrants for a number of years, and they continued to play an important role when new groups of refugees arrived. Altogether, when the Cubans were finally settled, the federal government had expended more than $2 billion to assist them.[32] The aid for Cubans sometimes prompted black leaders to be extremely critical of these efforts, and general resentment of Cuban émigrés played a role in the riots that rocked Miami in 1968 and again in 1980.[33]

Those coming in the "freedom flights" after 1965 were also disproportionally white and well educated, and in fact many were related to the pre-1964 exiles. They were apt to be older men, because Castro refused to allow the departure of men of military age, women, and children. One-third of the pre-1965 refugees were professionals and managers, compared with only one-fifth of those coming from 1965 to 1973.[34] By 1970 more than half of the refugees were blue-collar, service, or agricultural workers.[35] White-collar workers and small-business operators were also common on the post-1965 flights, but as the exodus continued into the 1970s, eventually only 12 percent were professionals or managers.

The Mariel group was considerably different. They were younger, and 79 percent were male. They were disproportionally black or mulatto and working class, and, as noted, included criminals and the mentally ill. The undesirable immigrants received considerable press coverage and account for the cool reception this group received throughout the United States, including Miami.[36] While some of the first to arrive had already been to Miami or knew of its life and culture, the Marielitos had been raised in Castro's communist Cuba and had little knowledge of life in America. Their adjustment proved to be more difficult than that of the earlier arrivals, in part because housing was scarce. Even some members of the Cuban exile community were not overwhelmingly enthusiastic about these latest arrivals. In time they generally became integrated into the Cuban American community, though at a slow pace, lagging behind other Cubans.[37] Moreover, the fact that so many working-class immigrants were entering raised the issue of whether they were truly refugees fleeing persecution or people simply looking to better themselves economically. Many in Miami did not trust anyone who had lived "most of their lives under communism." The old-timers asked, "Aren't these just opportunists leaving Cuba because the Soviet Union isn't around to subsidize the revolution?"[38] Of course, the motives of many of the pre-1980 émigrés were often a combination of politics and economics. Whatever their motives, when they arrived, the need for unskilled labor was less than it was in the 1960s and 1970s.

The advantages of knowing English, having a good education, possessing contacts, receiving governmental assistance, and having been to Florida before fleeing Cuba were of enormous importance to these refugees as they struggled to rebuild their lives in Florida and elsewhere. While government aid helped, so did the changing pattern of Cuban families. In Cuba married women did not usually work for pay, but not so in the United States. Alejandro Portes and Alex Stepick have noted, "A typical mid-sixties Cuban household in Miami featured a husband who had been a member of an anti-Castro organization and now strained to find employment and a wife who had never worked outside the home before but now sewed full time in a Hialeah factory."[39] Clearly, the employment of women became essential for success.

The entrepreneurs became prominent as they opened many small businesses and rose in banking, trade, and construction. Their activities quickly enabled a "Cuban enclave" to emerge, and Miami surpassed New Orleans as the trade outlet with Latin America. By the 1980s the city's airport had become one of the nation's largest and a major international hub.[40] The Cuban enclave certainly boosted not only Miami but also the immigrants themselves, for they provided important contacts for employment. By the mid-1980s Latinos (mostly Cubans) owned 40 percent of the city's banks, and in 1995 Dade County reported that 45,000 Latino businesses operated in the county. To be sure, many were family enterprises and small—restaurants and coffee shops—but they attested to the vitality of Cuban entrepreneurship and offered employment to new immigrants. Moreover, Cuban-run banks stood ready to extend credit to their fellow countrymen and countrywomen.[41]

Success stories about Cuban refugees abound. Perhaps the most notable was that of Roberto Boizueta, who was born in Cuba, was educated at Yale University, and worked for Coca-Cola in Cuba before fleeing to the United States. When he arrived in the United States, he was hired by Coca-Cola and eventually worked his way up to become the company's chairman of the board and chief executive. By the time of his death in 1997, he was one of the richest men in America.[42]

Clearly Boizueta was exceptional, but the general success of many Cuban Americans was notable. The news media repeated stories of the "golden exiles" and how they emerged to become the dominant group in Dade County's economy. In construction, for example, despite discrimination by local trade unions, the Cubans "undeterred . . . created their own home repair businesses by buying a truck and going door-to-door seeking work." By 1979 Cubans owned half of the county's construction companies.[43] In the early 1990s, 11 percent of Cubans who came before 1980 had incomes of $75,000, compared with only 9 percent of the general U.S. population.[44]

Cubans escaping to America did not automatically find success. While they moved into the garment business and ran many small shops, they mostly relied on cheap Cuban labor to make their profits. These were struggling enterprises: "Cuban garment 'factories' usually started in the owner's garage, with the wife, the mother, and other women in the family as the operators."[45] Others were old, did not speak English, or had difficulty adjusting to America. Moreover, dark-skinned Cubans could not avoid the realities of racism. Racism was different and considerably less common in Cuba than in Florida. In a series of articles on how race is lived in America, a *New York Times* reporter followed two Cubans, one black and one white. In black Joel Ruiz's "new world, whites, even white Cubans, have become a race apart, and while they are not necessarily to be avoided, they must be watched and hardly ever trusted." Ruiz commented that he can no longer see himself in a serious relationship with a white woman. "Not for marriage. Not for marriage," he said.[46] Having a black skin was one of the handicaps that many of the Marielitos found when they sought to rebuild their lives in America. Marielitos, generally working-class, entered the Florida market as low-wage workers. Reporter Roberto Suro pointed out that a decade after the Marielitos arrived, 40 percent had annual household incomes of less than $15,000, compared with 30 percent of Salvadorans and 37 percent of Mexicans who arrived in the United States during the same period.[47]

By the 1990s Cubans or persons of Cuban origin had higher incomes than most Latinos. The 1990 census reported that Cubans in the United States had an average family income of $41,469, but the figure for Guatemalans, who had been in the United States for only a short time, was $25,923, and for Mexicans it was $25,829.[48] Overall, while 23.3 percent of Latinos were listed as living below the poverty line in 2000, the figure for Cubans was 17.3 percent, but this was higher than for non-Hispanic whites.[49]

In 1993 the average educational attainment of Cubans in the United States was 16.5 years, compared with 9 for all Latinos. As noted in chapters 4 and 5, only a minority of Central Americans and Mexicans were high school graduates, but in 2000 roughly three-quarters of Cubans were. Cuban educational level was higher than for all Latinos, and was about the same as for South Americans.[50] What can be said is that while Cubans did especially well since their first arrival in 1959, they still lagged behind persons of European origin in income.[51] Moreover, Afro-Cubans did not fare as well as white Cubans with similar educations. One scholarly study concluded: "Nonwhite Cuban immigrants also have lower returns to education than whites."[52]

As Cubans prospered, they moved, in immigrant fashion, from Little Havana to better houses and schools in the surrounding suburbs. Taking their places in low-wage employment such as garment factory work were incoming Latinos. Two scholars wrote in 1991, "But middle-class Cubans, and especially professionals, are now hard to find in Little Havana. Their upward mobility has taken them to more suburban areas to the west. The current residents of Little Havana are likely to be blue-collar and service workers, the elderly, the poor, and recent immigrants, including non-Cuban Latinos."[53] In New Jersey, a similar suburbanization process occurred. Union City's Cuban population dropped from 80,000 to 60,000 after 1970. One sociologist commented, "Anyone who can afford a house in [more prosperous] Bergen County these days seems to be moving."[54] Union City's Bergeline Avenue shops, once Cuban owned, were increasingly run by other new Latinos, although many Cubans returned to shop there and attend social and cultural events.[55]

The flourishing economic enclave in Miami spawned a host of organizations responding to the social and cultural life of the Cuban émigrés.[56] The Catholic Church was one of the leading groups to welcome the exiles, providing spiritual assistance and helping them to find jobs and housing. The émigrés built "a shrine in Miami to house a statue of *La Virgen* that was brought out of Cuba in September 1961." There were also bookstores serving both writers and the reading public. Special groups staged Cuban and other Latino events. In addition, the local community college and Florida International University (founded in 1972) catered to the exiles as they pursued their educations.[57] Even the Cuban Jews created their own religious and cultural organizations, in part because American Jewish groups were not especially welcoming in the early days of the exodus.[58] The creation of an entire range of Cuban institutions in the Miami area was partly responsible for the resettlement of Cubans to Miami who had originally gone to other cities.

The formation of cultural, social, and economic organizations and the creation of an immigrant ethnic economy was not unique to Cubans, of course. It was part of the experience for most immigrants coming to America. Yet for Cubans the exile mentality was a crucial factor in their organizations and culture. The first refugees assumed that their stay in America would be only temporary, and that when Castro fell they would return home. They built organizations around the politics of return and worked with the CIA in anti-Castro activities. Under both President Eisenhower and President Kennedy the United States was eager to use the Cubans against Castro. The most ardent male exiles joined the regiment that failed to remove Castro in the Bay of Pigs fiasco of 1961.[59] Although the invasion failed and the prisoners were not immediately repatriated to the United States in exchange for vital goods, many of the exiles continued their efforts to destroy communism in Cuba. They were, as one said, "not immigrants. We were exiles . . . somebody who doesn't want to leave his country. He expects to come back."[60]

Cubans and the U.S. government beamed radio programs to Cuba, picked up those escaping at sea, favored a tight American embargo against Cuba, and backed those politicians who took a hard line against Cuba.[61] As late as 2000, exiles asserted themselves in the case of Elian Gonzalez, attempting to block his return to his Cuban father. In 2000 a poll by a Miami TV channel found that 88 percent of Cubans in Miami wanted Elian to stay in Florida. Another poll found the number to be 83 percent. The hard-line position was clear. As one woman put it, "He should stay [in Florida]."[62]

Cubans also realized that they needed something more than CIA money and a strong desire to return home. They turned to politics and especially the Republican Party, with its staunch anticommunist platform, for support. In 1997, encouraged by special efforts on the part of the federal government to get immigrants to become citizens, 53,753 Cubans naturalized; they were a third of Florida's immigrants in that year to become American citizens.[63] Florida's Cuban voters cast their ballots overwhelmingly for George W. Bush in the 2000 election in part, as one expert said, "to avenge the Clinton administration's handling of the Elian Gonzalez case, the shipwrecked boy at the center of an international custody battle."[64] Growing numbers of Cubans also naturalized and voted because of local issues. The thrust toward politics grew steadily as Cubans naturalized and elected Cubans to local, state, and federal office. Two sat in Congress when President George W. Bush appointed a Cuban, Mel Martinez, to become the secretary of housing and urban development.[65]

By the turn of the twenty-first century, however, Castro had been in power for forty years, and even though he lacked Russian aid and faced a host of economic problems, it did not appear that the exiles would be able to return to Cuba. Moreover, the second generation was taking center stage and looked to become Americans or Cuban Americans, and not exiles. The younger Cubans did not necessarily share the views of the immigrant generation. The children of immigrants moving into adulthood were beginning to challenge the leadership of the older Cuban Americans. The second generation organized Cambia Cubano and the Cuban Committee for Democracy, urging that the boycott of Cuba come to an end. Now that the most ardent anticommunist leaders have died or are aging, anti-Castro politics might lose its influence among the second-generation Cubans.[66]

Another generational dispute erupted in 2001 over the location of the Latin Grammy Awards. Some exiles in Miami feared that pro-Castro artists might appear and make the ceremony a favorable forum for the Cuban leader. Noting that younger Cubans were not as concerned about exile politics, one observer remarked, "The younger generation has Cuba somewhat lower on their agendas. They do feel strongly about Cuba but it is not the first thing on their minds."[67]

At first glance Southeast Asians refugees resemble those from Cuba.[68] Both groups entered because of the cold war, as part of American anticommunist policy. Like the Cubans, the Asian refugees came in waves. Moreover, diversity characterized these waves, and some individuals in both groups, mostly the first to arrive, fared better than others. Finally, the United States was caught by surprise in both cases and did not anticipate that large numbers of Southeast Asians and Cubans would eventually migrate to the United States.

Yet in many significant ways Asian refugees differed from the Cubans and, for that matter, from other Asians as well. During the Vietnam War, American refugee policy focused on aiding those Vietnamese who had been made homeless by the fighting. Only 603 Vietnamese found their way to the United States by 1964.[69] A few others were women married to American servicemen. In 1975, a total of 918 such women were recorded, not a large number. During the same year 1,727 women came as wives of Americans stationed in Thailand.[70]

Few American officials predicted the rapid fall of South Vietnam to the communists in 1975. Suddenly the United States was confronted with hundreds of thousands of Vietnamese who feared for their lives because they had fought against the communists, worked for American companies, or were connected to the American war effort. State Department officials told U.S. senators that the precise number of those to be evacuated was unknown, but it could be as high as 200,000. During the final days before the communists occupied Saigon, frantic Vietnamese were brought from that city by helicopters to American aircraft carriers and then to Guam and the Philippines. On April 18, 1975, President Gerald Ford established the Interagency Task Force for Indochinese Refugees. Congress was at first reluctant to finance the needs of those escaping, but the legislators finally agreed to set up programs for them.[71] Some of those not removed by helicopters simply crossed the border into Thailand, while other desperate people escaped by boat, hoping to find refuge in Hong Kong, Malaysia, the Philippines, or any other Asian nation that would accept them, or possibly to be picked up at sea by American naval craft in the hope of eventually being resettled in the United States. Many were fleeing on their own, but most came with their families. Overall, American aircraft and ships brought 130,000 Southeast Asian refugees to safety by the end of 1975, and thousands more crossed the border or joined the exodus of the boat people later.[72]

Then, in 1978, several new crises developed that sent a second wave fleeing Vietnam. Political repression and unstable economic conditions forced thousands more to leave, and their numbers were swelled by ethnic Chinese Vietnamese who found themselves the object of persecution. Smugglers operating boats were eager to collect funds from the fleeing refugees. But lacking sufficient money was not the only problem they faced. Historian Ronald Takaki reports, "The second wave Vietnamese refugees took their wives and children and boarded crowded, leaky boats, risking their lives at sea where storms threatened to drown them and pirates waited to rob them and rape the women. Two thirds of the boats were attacked by pirates."[73] Pirates were not content with robbery or rape; they sank the boats or left the refugees adrift without food or water. Overall, beginning in 1978, the flight eventually included several hundred thousand new refugees. Many who escaped ended up in camps, living in crowded, unsanitary conditions. Not a few died or decided to return home. Nearly 900,000 Vietnamese ended up in camps, but they were eventually resettled or returned to Vietnam.[74] Ethnic Chinese not only escaped to the United States, but a quarter of a million also crossed the northern border of Vietnam to live in China.[75]

Wishing to bring order into the refugee flight in Southeast Asia, the United States opened negotiations with the United Nations High Commissioner for Refugees and various European and Asian nations, including the Vietnamese government. From these discussions an agreement emerged to permit disaffected Vietnamese and ethnic Chinese Vietnamese to migrate under the Orderly Departure Program (ODP). Those with family connections or who were considered especially vulnerable to repression were expected to register with the UN or with American and Vietnamese officials to immigrate in an orderly arrangement. The agreement, however, did not entirely halt the exodus to Thailand or to other Asian nations by boat.[76] Nations besides the United States and China accepted refugees, but several Asian countries worried that they would still be left supporting and running refugee camps unless the aliens were moved directly from Vietnam and the camps to nations willing to give them sanctuary.[77]

The consensus to halt the boat or border migrations lacked specific procedures, and the high hopes for orderly departure were not always realized. Vietnamese still tried to escape by sea or across borders as the ODP was unable to place all of those who wanted to flee. Not until 1984 did those leaving through the program exceed the number escaping by sea. United States officials believed that Vietnam was unwilling to move more quickly; the Vietnamese, in turn, thought the Americans were hindering the process. Vietnam briefly suspended the ODP in 1986. Thailand, unhappy about maintaining so many camps, even if they were supported financially by the UN and Western powers, began to "push back" those crossing its border. Thailand was not the only Asian nation to reject the Vietnamese migrants. Opposition also arose in Malaysia, Hong Kong, and Indonesia.[78]

Thus throughout the 1980s and 1990s, while some refugees left directly from Saigon (renamed Ho Chi Minh City), others were picked up at sea or brought from the various camps throughout Southeast Asia. Many Vietnamese had suffered political "reeducation" and could be considered refugees as defined by American immigration law. Working with the Vietnamese government, Americans also accepted some directly from Vietnamese political prison camps. Yet many others wanted to leave because of poor economic conditions or to join families and friends overseas. Until the 1990s the United States considered virtually all of those it accepted as being refugees and entitled to benefits provided by law. In spite of the confusion surrounding the ODP and the continuation of refugee camps outside of Vietnam, a steady stream of emigrants left Vietnam in the 1990s. The camps themselves closed in 1996. Those choosing emigration, if they could, more than outnumbered the thousands of Vietnamese who decided to return home after several months in the camps.[79]

One other group deserves mention: Amerasian children, thousands of whom were left behind in Vietnam when their American soldier fathers left. They were by no means unique, as troops stationed in Korea and the Philippines also departed without taking their Asian wives and Amerasian children with them when they were reassigned to other duties.[80] In fact, many of Vietnam's Amerasian children did not know who their fathers were. Adding to their woes was the fact that they were looked down upon by the Vietnamese and called "dust of life," the equivalent of "trash."[81] They often lived on the margins of society, begging and accepting whatever housing was available.[82] A first attempt in 1975 to rescue orphans ended in disaster when a plane crashed during "Operation Baby Lift," killing 150 children.[83] About 2,000 children were flown to America for adoption before Operation Baby Lift ended.[84] As for Amerasian children, they were then generally ignored by American officials, and not until 1983 did the United States began to bring a few of these children to the United States. Under the ODP 4,500 such children and 7,000 of their relatives managed to migrate to America.

Adverse publicity in the media about the Amerasians finally convinced Congress to enact the 1987 Amerasian Homecoming Act. This act permitted children and their mothers to settle in the United States, provided they could demonstrate their fathers were Americans, even if the fathers' identities were unknown.[85] United States officials were even willing to accept the children if they looked half "American." While several thousand children and their mothers eventually found their way to the United States, in many cases it was impossible to find their fathers, and many of the children, now teenagers, arrived with psychological scars that made their transition to the United States difficult. Some Vietnamese in America looked down on them, and the children faced an American public uneasy and even hostile to those whose fathers were African American.[86] The program was meant to end in two years, but it was extended, and by 1994 a total of 69,168 children had been settled in the United States. Further extensions brought a few thousand more to the United States, including 902 in 1999.[87] In addition, a few hundred Vietnamese orphans were being adopted by American families at the beginning of the twenty-first century.[88]

Vietnam accounted for the vast majority of Asian refugees arriving between 1975 and 2003, but important groups also came from neighboring Cambodia and Laos. Cambodia reluctantly became part of a widening war in the 1960s. When the North Vietnamese began to use Cambodia for smuggling troops and supplies into neighboring South Vietnam, the United States retaliated with military strikes against alleged communist troops and supply stations. In addition, a radical communist movement—the Khmer Rouge—fought a war against Cambodia's government. In 1975, when communist forces captured Saigon and South Vietnam, the radical Khmer Rouge, under the leadership of Pol Pot, seized power in Cambodia, now renamed Kampuchea. Pol Pot's regime relocated urban populations to the countryside and slaughtered at least hundreds of thousands in the "killing fields" if they had any connection to the American-backed forces formerly in power. To add to the woes of the Kampuchean people, troops from Vietnam invaded in 1979. During this invasion about one-half of the Kampuchean people found themselves without homes, adequate food, or medical supplies. Desperate Kampucheans crossed the border between their nation and Thailand. They settled in camps without adequate facilities, but their choices were limited. British journalist William Shawcross described these refugees: "Daily, awful spindly creatures, with no flesh and with wide vacant eyes stumbled out of the forests and the mountains into which the Khmer Rouge had corralled them. They had malaria, they had tuberculosis, they had dysentery, they were dehydrated, they were famished, they were dying."[89]

The government of Thailand accepted these refugees but wanted an international effort to resettle them, return them to their home, and pay for their upkeep. But as the numbers swelled, Thailand responded and closed the border.[90] Working with various nations, the UNHCR delivered food and other necessities and worked to end the camps through settlement elsewhere. The camps nonetheless received more Cambodians, who after several years of Vietnamese occupation were losing their welcome as a buffer against the Khmer Rouge. Many of the refugees also settled temporarily along their border, ready, if necessary, to cross into Thailand or return home if conditions improved.[91] The UN was able to repatriate many Cambodians, but others found a haven in the West, including the United States. The State Department worked with state and voluntary agencies to settle them. In the end 150,000 Cambodians came to the United States, which was the largest number coming to any one country. Their numbers declined in the 1990s, as they did for all Southeast Asian refugees.

The third group of Southeast Asians to come to the United States as the result of the Vietnam War were Laotians. Laos also underwent a civil war in the 1960s and 1970s, and when Saigon fell, the communists also came to power in Laos. Thousands fled, but others waited to see what would happen. Eventually many Laotians believed that they, too, had no future in their native land, and they sought a haven in Thailand, hoping to be settled in the United States or some other nation. They represented different tribes, with the Hmong being the most prominent. About 300,000 Laotians fled across the border to live temporarily in the overcrowded camps. Most were able to come to the United States, although several thousand still lived in the camps in the early 1990s as the trickle of refugees from Laos continued. The Hmong, an ethnic group living in the mountains, was especially vulnerable and knew that their future was limited at home. When the United States took over the war in Vietnam from the French after 1954, the CIA recruited the Hmong to fight against the communists in both Laos and Vietnam. About 36,000 of these tribesmen rescued downed American flyers, fought against the communists, and assisted American planes in locating targets; thousands were killed. With the shift in power in 1975, they found that being on the losing side in the war made them especially vulnerable to persecution.[92]

By the late 1990s the Thai refugee camps were being closed and the refugee flows were down to a trickle. The UNHCR reported that 1,440,000 refugees from the three countries had been assisted in the camps and provided resettlement, most of them in Western countries. In addition, 130,000 had been rescued by the United States through its frantic airlifts from Saigon during the closing days of the war or picked up at sea. In the 1990s the numbers dropped, and resettlement aimed more at family unification under the regular immigration laws rather than aiding those allegedly seeking freedom from political persecution. Of the 30,000 or so (mostly Vietnamese) arriving at the turn of the twenty-first century, most entered as regular immigrants, not refugees.[93] Those few entering as refugees were men and women who had been imprisoned in "reeducation" camps.[94] But whatever the motive of individuals and the fits and starts of resettlement, by 2003 the United States had received more than 1 million refugees from the Asian nations of Vietnam, Cambodia, and Laos. As a result, new ethnic communities developed in America.[95]

American officials feared that the development of ethnic enclaves with distinct cultures would lead to cultural conflict and have an adverse economic impact on local host communities. The government wanted to "avoid another Miami," as one authority put it.[96] Officials therefore pursued a policy of dispersal of the refugees throughout the United States. Those coming in the chaotic days of 1975 first went to Guam or the Philippines and were then were processed into the United States. The government set up four camps to receive the Vietnamese, the first opening at Camp Pendleton in California. Refugees coming through these camps were given an orientation to help them live in American society. They received English-language instruction, medical care, and vocational training. Christian and Buddhist services were provided for those who belonged to those religions.[97]

The dispersal policy was carried out in cooperation with the voluntary agencies, which found families, churches, and local communities to receive the refugees. Later Asian refugees did not go through American camps but came directly to the communities that sponsored them. The dispersal policy was a mixed success. Once out of the camps and in the United States, the refugees could move, and as a result California became the center of Vietnamese and Cambodian life. Another center for

Cambodians was Lowell, Massachusetts, which became home to the second-largest Cambodian community, behind Long Beach, California. Not unusual was Tony Roun, who fled Cambodia and lived for five years in a Thai refugee camp. He then immigrated to Chicago but resettled in Lowell.[98]

About half of the Vietnamese ended up in California, and Texas received the second-largest influx. Yet many refugees remained in or near their primary place of settlement. Minneapolis–Saint Paul, for example, had the largest Hmong community; pockets of Vietnamese appeared in the Washington, D.C., area, and many Cambodians settled in Massachusetts.[99]

After going through the camps, all refugees received aid from the federal government, but lawmakers did not want them to become permanent wards of the state. Congress placed restrictions on how long the refugees could receive aid, including cash grants and medical assistance. Eager to limit aid, the federal government funded projects to follow the refugees' progress. As the federal role diminished, states began to aid the newcomers, but the amount of assistance rendered through programs such as Aid to Dependent Children (ADC) varied, being higher in California than in Texas, for example. As part of the welfare reforms of 1996, Congress withdrew food stamps from Laotians who had fought in the CIA's secret war, and that community, especially enraged, protested.[100] Laotians had their supporters in Congress, and in March 1998, the legislators restored food stamps to 20,000 of these refugees who had aided the U.S. military.[101]

The Southeast Asian immigrants and refugees came from distinct cultures, and even within the nationality groups themselves there were major differences. These variations in turn help to explain their differing adjustment patterns in American society. Among the first Vietnamese to leave were an elite, many with connections to American firms or governmental agencies, including service with the military. They were disproportionately urban and better educated than most Vietnamese, and a number were Roman Catholic. Roughly 40 percent of the first cohort had some knowledge of English.[102] They were clearly an advantaged group in comparison to those who followed. As a result, they moved quickly from receiving government assistance to taking jobs, and in time had relatively low unemployment rates. Their early arrival gave them an additional advantage, for the longer the refugees were in the United States, the better were their prospects for advancement.[103] The ethnic Chinese who arrived in significant numbers between 1978 and 1981 also had business skills that they could utilize.

But life was not always easy even for the first to arrive in 1975. A sluggish economy in many of the communities of settlement left few of these immigrants with immediate economic opportunities. Like so many other immigrants, they took whatever jobs were available even if below their level of education and work experience.

Vietnamese who came after 1981 had a more difficult time learning English, finding employment, and adjusting to the mores of American society.[104] Although the first Vietnamese were earning almost as much as other Americans by the 1990s, by no means did all Indochinese refugees achieve this status.[105] Many Vietnamese found the culture of their new land hard to master and struggled to make a living, even one well below the standards of other Americans. Yet Vietnamese as well as Cambodian and Laotian children were doing reasonably well in the public schools and even pursuing higher education, which scholars believe is best explained by a strong family structure, desire to work hard, and commitment to education.[106] The educational achievement prompted some observers to see them as part of the Asian "model minority," a term that greatly distorts their progress. One can hardly overlook the horrible conditions that many arriving after 1979 faced at sea or in the Asian refugee camps. Some children had seen their fathers beaten and mothers raped by pirates, and others lingered for months in camps that scarcely provided necessities. It is too soon to assess the progress of those coming under the family unification provisions of the 1990s immigrant laws.

While the upward mobility of the Vietnamese was certainly apparent, individual experiences varied. In April 2000 the *Washington Post* reported on the fate of three individuals, all of similar background, and all graduates of the elite air force academy. Xuan Pham escaped in 1975 as Saigon fell to the communists. Starting a new life at age twenty-seven, he became a prosperous research engineer living in a large house "that architects designed for him." Hai Van Chu was not able to leave until the 1980s, and his stay in Vietnam was marked by five years in a "reeducation" camp. He managed to live in the United States as a translator. Giau Nguyen, of the same background, reached America in the 1990s after spending years in a "reeducation" camp. Residing in the large Washington, D.C., Vietnamese community, he was barely making ends meet when interviewed.[107]

Along the Texas coast, Vietnamese fisherman found scratching out a living to be difficult. The Vietnamese who settled in Seadrift, Texas, quickly set out to establish themselves in the shrimp industry. Because their customs were different from those of American-born fisherman, conflict erupted, which led to violence and an appearance by the Ku Klux Klan. One white fisherman angrily remarked, "There's too many gooks and too few blue crabs."[108] Although tensions lessened and both sides continued to fish, the days of Vietnamese Texas fishermen appeared to be nearly over by 2000.[109] Women who used to cull shrimp and men who did the actual fishing were seeking other employment. The younger generation saw little future for Gulf fishing. The daughter of a fisherman, who was a nursing home administrator, noted, "Our community is changing dramatically. People are getting out of shrimping. There are just too many rules and regulations, and it doesn't pay."[110]

As Vietnam and the United States normalized relations and permitted travel, trade, and investment, the more prosperous Vietnamese returned to visit, sponsor their relatives to become immigrants, and conduct business. Approximately 100,000 were making the journey yearly by the late 1990s.[111] If unable to visit, many Vietnamese sent remittances home, amounting to an estimated $2 billion annually. The remittances and growing numbers of people coming to the United States through family unification were signs that the refugee phase was ending in Vietnam and that regular immigration would characterize the future.

Among the first Cambodians were well-educated and urban leaders, who had quickly become aware that the Khmer Rouge were out to exterminate them. Yet rural folk were also eager to get out, and they dominated the flow. Whereas the numbers of men and women were approximately equal among the Vietnamese and Laotians, about one-quarter of Cambodian households in the United States were female headed. A San Diego study found that only 49 percent of Cambodian youth lived in a family with both parents present.[112] The men had been killed by the Khmer Rouge. In contrast to the Vietnamese in the first years, Cambodians, as well as Laotians, were not highly educated; only one-third of Cambodians and Laotians in the United States had at least a high school diploma according to the 1990 census.[113]

Life in the camps tested the physical conditions of even the hardiest survivors, leaving many in poor health when they arrived in America. Moreover, many survivors of the Cambodian "killing fields" carried with them serious mental problems as well as poor physical health. When they arrived in America, they often found that the United States's cultural views of proper health care were considerably different from their own, and it was not always possible to reach an easy accommodation between the two cultures. More than 100 Indochinese, mainly Hmong, died from sudden unexpected nocturnal death syndrome. The refugees claimed this was caused by evil spirits, but American officials attributed their deaths to culture shock.[114] Government surveys revealed that the refugees suffered stress when they arrived, but their emotional condition improved over time.[115] Similar conflicts occurred within the judicial system.[116] Some refugees claimed that opium, which a few grew in the United States, was used for medicinal purposes, but in the United States growing and using opium was illegal.[117] It is not surprising that compared with the Vietnamese, the Hmongs' incomes were lower, and their unemployment rates, reliance on public assistance, and poverty rates were all higher.[118] Based on 1990 data, one scholar concluded, "The Hmong stood out clearly in the 1990 Census data as the immigrant group with lowest average educational attainment, lowest average earnings, lowest average employment rate, and the heaviest average reliance on public assistance."[119]

Most Hmong and many Cambodians had been in the United States only a few years, but they did make social and economic progress. The longer they remained in America, the greater chance for finding adequate employment to avoid poverty. Enterprising Cambodians, for example, entered the doughnut trade in California. The success of Ted Ngoy in opening Christie's Donut Shop caught the eye of other refugees. As one put it, "Before opening this doughnut shop in 1984, I was working 10 hours a day as a janitor at a public school. . . . This business also requires hard work, but we are our own boss. We don't have to speak much English. And the money is better than working as a janitor."[120]

Most Cambodian and Laotian men and women generally did not own and operate doughnut shops. With aid from their sponsors and their countrymen, they usually found jobs in low-wage manufacturing or the service economy. Cambodians in Boston, for example, were mostly rural people with little training and education for urban society. One scholar noted, "Their employment opportunities have been limited to unskilled factory jobs, minimum-wage service employment, or piecework with poor benefits or security."[121]

The traditional crafts made by Hmong women did provide income and were a way for them to hold on to their traditional culture.[122] In a study of the Hmong community of Wausau, Wisconsin, the author found that these immigrants struggled to make ends meet and labored in variety of low-paid jobs. There as elsewhere, Hmong worked in light manufacturing that required little knowledge of English, or in food service positions.[123] The men in Wausau also worked for others at low-wage jobs, but one of the enterprises they dominated was driving taxicabs. Wausau Hmong women were flexible in their work habits. During the ginseng season, they grew this herb in an area that produced 95 percent of all ginseng grown the United States. This was not year-round work, and in the off-season they labored as peddlers and traders and did needlework for sale. Making and selling "Asian" clothes also supplemented the family income.[124]

Low-wage employment, mental stress, and lack of access to health care all taxed the resourcefulness of Southeast Asian refugees. The hostility they encountered in some communities also challenged their ability to survive. The Seaport, Texas, fishermen episode was not the only instance of violence. In the 1980s dozens of Hmong found themselves under attack by blacks in Philadelphia.[125] Cities such as Denver also reported incidents of prejudice against the refugees.[126] In Boston in 1985 it was reported that two Cambodians were beaten and several homes were the target of arsonists.[127] Jeremy Hein's 1995 study reported widespread incidents of violence against Indochinese refugees, of which the Gulf Coast controversy was only one. He concluded, "Although hostility and aggression against the refugees are commonly attributed to divisiveness of the Vietnam War, they are in fact the result of racial prejudice."[128]

Except for the first Vietnamese, who were disproportionately Roman Catholic, most of the Southeast Asian refugees were Buddhists. To be Khmer is to be Buddhist, one scholar has noted, because Buddhism had such a powerful influence on the family life and culture of Cambodians. But refugees were settling in a predominantly Christian nation, without many Buddhist centers. Buddhist temples had to be built in America, which was difficult because of the lack of resources available.[129]

The creation of Buddhist temples was part of the ongoing immigrant saga, to duplicate institutions of the old world in the new. Religion was by no means the only way for newcomers to feel at home in America. Along the Merrimack River in Massachusetts, for example, Cambodians created a water festival much like those in Cambodia. The Merrimack "reminded me of the Mekong River," one refugee said. In August 2002, some 50,000 refugees gathered along the Merrimack for the annual Southeast Asian Water Festival, which celebrated the regional cultures they had left behind.[130]

The roles of women in Southeast Asian communities were different than in America, where women had higher status and considerable more social, political, and economic independence. Like Cubans, Vietnamese began to depend on working women to increase the family income. Such income might have raised the standard of living of families, but it did not come without conflict in many cases. Women now wanted the men to share in household tasks, which was difficult for some husbands to do.[131] The refugees also watched their children being exposed to a permissive culture that they did not fully accept. They wanted their children to do well in school, but they also wanted them to be mindful of strong traditional family cultures that at times were out of step with American ones.[132]

Catholic Vietnamese, about one-third of the refugees, found adjustment somewhat easier. Catholic agencies that helped settle the refugees often placed them in communities with a high proportion of Catholics. New Orleans was one such location: "New Orleans is a very Catholic city. Catholic charities were involved in the resettlement. The fact that Louisiana is a heavily Catholic area was an appeal to heavily Catholic Vietnamese."[133] The refugees joined existing Catholic parishes in Louisiana and also formed new ones. Other important Vietnamese Catholic centers were in Houston, Texas, and San Jose, California.[134] The refugees, in turn, influenced American Catholicism. While considerably fewer in numbers than Latino Catholics, they were disproportionately becoming nuns and priests and helping to change the social composition of American Catholicism. A Georgetown University study from 2000 concluded that while the refugees represented only 1 percent of Catholics, their young men accounted for 3 percent of those studying for the priesthood.[135]

Clustering in ethnic residential enclaves helped these newcomers deal with American society. The largest enclaves were found in Orange County, California, especially Westminster, which was labeled "Little Saigon." Westminster's streets were lined with Vietnamese restaurants and shops owned and operated by Vietnamese. It was also a city that Vietnamese from all over the United States visited. They could be assured of hearing Vietnamese spoken on the streets and could find a radio station and TV programs in their native tongue. Westminster became the first American city to elect a Vietnamese official, Tony Lam, as a city council member. Voters in Saint Paul, Minnesota, had elected Choua Lee, a Hmong woman, to the school board a few years earlier (1992).[136]

Many Southeast Asian refugees did not live in ethnic enclaves; instead they lived on different blocks scattered throughout their towns and cities. The newcomers knew one another and helped mind each other's children, find housing and jobs, and assist with problems of adjustment. Twenty-five years after their initial settlement, Vietnamese who could afford better housing moved from Westminster to surrounding towns, and their children were leaving home to attend nearby community colleges or California's state colleges and universities.[137]

Poll data on the Vietnamese indicated a growing satisfaction with American society and less interest in returning to Vietnam in the event of the collapse of communism.[138] Vietnamese immigrants and their children exhibited interest in the politics of their native land, but not on a scale equal to that of Cubans. There was no single leader to hate such as Fidel Castro, and Vietnam was an ocean way, not the mere ninety miles from Florida to Cuba. Yet many Vietnamese hated communism and were bitter about what had happened to them. When Truong Van Tran, who owned an electronics store in Westminster, put up a picture of Ho Chi Minh, he was physically abused and faced angry crowds demonstrating outside his store.[139] This was but one of several incidents involving anti-communist sentiment.[140]

Whether Vietnamese, Cambodian, or Laotian, many immigrants saw their children do well in school and leave home to work elsewhere or attend institutions of higher learning. They watched the children learn English rapidly and accept American values and institutions but worried about retention of their own heritage. The generation gap was part of the immigrant experience, and the Southeast Asians were not exempt from it. How they and other immigrants, including the large number of Asians and their children who arrived after 1965, would adapt to American culture was not clear as the twentieth century ended, but many signs pointed in the direction of second-generation success.[141]

Epilogue

The surge of immigration of "people of color" in the last three decades can scarcely be missed. The majority of immigrants have settled in six states (California, New York, Texas, New Jersey, Florida, and Illinois) and in large metropolitan areas such as New York City, Washington, D.C., Los Angeles, Miami, and Houston. But they have also been spreading across the United States to states and communities with little prior history of contact with Asian, black, or Hispanic immigrants. One can find Asian Indians running motels in Mississippi; Hmong refugees in Minneapolis; Somalian refugees in San Diego and in Lewiston, Maine; Vietnamese along the coast of Texas; Mexicans and Central Americans working along the "chicken trail" in North Carolina, Missouri, and Iowa; and Koreans in the nation's cities, running small ethnic enterprises.

Yet it is important to remember that black, Latino, and Asian immigrants have always been part of American immigration history, though their numbers in the past were much smaller than in the early twenty-first century. First-generation slaves in colonial America were essential for the development of the nation's economy. Later Chinese and Japanese migration to California and Hawaii provided those states with agricultural laborers. After the United States annexed the Southwest, the nation incorporated a population of Mexicans, and immigrants from Mexico have been settling in the United States ever since.

When numbers of blacks, Latinos, and Asians appeared to grow, Americans decided to limit or exclude them. The Chinese Exclusion Act was only the first of federal actions to stem the flow of Asians. While Mexicans were not included in the restrictions on Asians (and Europeans), Mexican newcomers nonetheless faced intense discrimination in California and Texas, the two states with the largest Mexican populations. Moreover, several hundred thousand Mexicans and their children were deported during the 1930s. Blacks could still enter from the

Caribbean, even after the restrictions of the 1920s, but these newcomers encountered a society characterized by intense racism.

The large-scale immigration of non-Europeans since the 1960s has changed America and is continuing to do so. Immigrants constitute more than 11 percent of the population, and they provide 12 percent of American workers. It took a long time for the nation's Protestants to accept Catholics and Jews, but now religious pluralism also includes Buddhists, Hindus, Muslims, Sikhs, and members of other small sects. And today, Catholics and Protestants are undergoing a growth of immigrants in their congregations as Korean Protestants and Latino and Asian Catholics join existing churches or form new ones. American radio, newspapers, and television inform readers, listeners, and viewers in a variety of languages, just as the theater, music groups, restaurants, and dance reflect the latest wave of immigration. Yellow page phone books are not published solely in English. There is no doubt that the latest newcomers have made the United States a more pluralistic and interesting society.

Some people view the trends since the liberalization of immigration laws after 1943 with alarm. They point out that in 1940 the Asian and Latino populations were very small, and that foreign-born blacks were found mainly in Florida and New York City. Outside of the descendants of African slaves, the vast majority of Americans had their origins in Europe. Those uneasy about the current trends of immigration note that the Bureau of the Census has projected that whereas roughly 85 percent of the American population was "white" (meaning of European origin) in 1940, by 2050 only a slight majority (52.8 percent) of the population will be white. In 2050, a quarter of the American people will be Hispanic, 10 percent will be Asian, and a rising proportion of black Americans will be foreign born or the children of black immigrants.[1]

It is important to recognize several points about the changes. First, terms such as "Asian" and "Hispanic" are social constructions that government officials, scholars, and the media use to cover a great variety of groups. Often the subgroups within these large categories have little in common; they do not form a monolithic bloc. Cubans are better off than Mexicans, and whereas Mexicans who are citizens tend to vote Democratic, Cubans are solidly Republican, to cite one example.

Moreover, the new immigrants do not threaten American core values or burden the nation economically. During the Gulf War of 2003, the media noted that Asians, blacks, and Hispanics were among the troops, and a number of these soldiers were immigrants.[2] This should not be surprising because immigrants have always served the nation well in times of war. As for the economic and social impact of current immigration, Frank D. Bean and Gillian Stevens note, "Thus, the weight of the evidence indicates that present levels and patterns of U.S. immigration, if maintained in the future and if not overridden by other forces, will continue to generate what are, on balance, a favorable ratio of benefits to costs for American society."[3]

Although racism still stains the American present and ethnic tension and violence are not unknown, American society has been undergoing an increase in tolerance and an enormous degree of social and economic mixing. At the turn of the twentieth century, most immigrants did not marry outside their ethnic group, but at the turn of the twenty-first century, intermarriage among European-origin Jews, Protestants, and Catholics is common. The same trend is noticeable among non-Europeans. The children and grandchildren of black, Asian, and Hispanic immigrants learn English and frequently marry outside their group. Almost half of Japanese and Filipinos marry spouses from other groups, and third-generation Chinese frequently seek partners who are not Chinese. Overall, about one-quarter of Asians marry non-Asians. At the turn of the twenty-first century, there were nearly 2 million marriages between "non-Hispanic whites and Hispanics" and 700,000 white-Asian couples.[4] Commenting on projections of the Census Bureau and demographers, one writer said in 1999, "As a new millennium looms, America is set to become more a nation of blended races and ethnic groups than it has ever been."[5] Even whites and blacks are intermarrying in increased numbers.[6]

What will it mean in a decade or so that one's mother is Mexican and father part German, Irish, and Italian? Clearly such terms as "Asian" and "Hispanic" will not have a precise meaning or the same meaning they have today. The entrance of so many people from beyond Europe is a major factor changing the very meaning of race and ethnicity in the United States. This may not signal the end of racial or ethnic conflict, but certainly important changes are under way. Predictions about the long-range future are risky at best. But in the short run, the present patterns of immigration will continue to make America a more global society.

Notes

NOTES TO THE INTRODUCTION

1. Kenneth M. Stampp, *The Peculiar Institution: Slavery in the Ante-bellum South* (1956; New York: Knopf, 1961). For Phillips, see Ulrich B. Phillips, *American Negro Slavery* (New York: D. Appleton, 1918).

2. Eugene D. Genovese, *Roll, Jordan, Roll: The World the Slaves Made* (New York: Pantheon Books, 1974); Herbert G. Gutman, *The Black Family in Slavery and Freedom, 1750–1925* (New York: Pantheon Books, 1976); John Blassingame, *The Slave Community: Plantation Life in the Antebellum South* (New York: Oxford University Press, 1979); Ira Berlin, *Many Thousands Gone: The First Two Centuries of Slavery in North America* (Cambridge, MA: Harvard University Press, 1998); Berlin, *Generations of Captivity: A History of African American Slaves* (Cambridge, MA: Harvard University Press, 2003);

3. Walter Johnson, *Soul by Soul: Life inside the Antebellum Slave Market* (Cambridge, MA: Harvard University Press, 1999).

4. Steven Hahn, *A Nation under Our Feet: Black Political Struggles in the Rural South from Slavery to the Great Migration* (Cambridge, MA: Harvard University Press, 2003).

5. Leon F. Litwack, *Trouble in Mind: Black Southerners in the Age of Jim Crow* (New York: Knopf, 1998).

6. Marilyn Halter, *Between Race and Ethnicity: Cape Verdean American Immigrants, 1860–1965* (Urbana: University of Illinois Press, 1993).

7. John A. Arthur, *Invisible Sojourners: African Immigrant Diaspora in the United States* (Westport, CT: Praeger, 2000); Jon D. Holtzman, *Nuer Journeys, Nuer Lives: Sudanese Refugees in Minnesota* (Boston: Allyn and Bacon, 2000); Rogaia Mustafa Abusharaf, *Wanderings: Sudanese Migrants and Exiles in North America* (Ithaca, NY: Cornell University Press, 2002); Paul Stoller, *Money Has No Smell: The Africanization of New York City* (Chicago: University of Chicago Press, 2002).

8. Ira De A. Reid, *The Negro Immigrant: His Background, Characteristics, and Social Adjustment* (New York: AMS Press, 1970).

9. Winston James, *Holding Aloft the Banner of Ethiopia: Caribbean Radical-*

ism in Early Twentieth-Century America (New York: Verso, 1998); Philip Kasinitz, *Caribbean New York: Black Immigrants and the Politics of Race* (Ithaca, NY: Cornell University Press, 1992); Milton Vickerman, *Crosscurrents: West Indian Immigrants and Race* (New York: Oxford University Press, 1999); Irma Watkins-Owens, *Blood Relations: Caribbean Immigrants and the Harlem Community, 1900–1930* (Bloomington: Indiana University Press, 1996); Mary Waters, *Black Identities: West Indian Dreams and American Realities* (Cambridge, MA: Harvard University Press, 1999).

10. See Nancy Foner, ed., *Islands in the City: West Indian Migration to New York* (Berkeley: University of California Press, 2001).

11. See Ransford Palmer, *Pilgrims from the Sun: West Indian Migration to America* (New York: Twayne, 1995).

12. George M. Stephenson, *A History of American Immigration, 1820–1924* (Boston: Ginn and Co., 1926).

13. Marcus Lee Hansen, *The Atlantic Migration, 1607–1860* (Cambridge, MA: Harvard University Press, 1940).

14. Carl Wittke, *We Who Built America* (Cleveland: Press of Case Western Reserve University, 1964), 472.

15. Oscar Handlin, *The Uprooted: The Epic Story of the Great Migrations That Made the American People* (Boston: Little, Brown, 1952). John Bodnar's *The Transplanted: A History of Immigrants in Urban America* (Bloomington: University of Indiana Press, 1985) also neglects Asian, black, and Hispanic immigration.

16. Maldwyn Jones, *American Immigration,* 2nd ed. (Chicago: University of Chicago Press, 1992).

17. John Higham, *Strangers in the Land: Patterns of American Nativism, 1860–1925* (New Brunswick, NJ: Rutgers University Press, 1955); Andrew Gyory, *Closing the Gate: Race, Politics, and the Chinese Exclusion Act* (Chapel Hill: University of North Carolina Press, 1998).

18. Mary Roberts Coolidge, *Chinese Immigration* (New York: Holt, 1909).

19. Roger Daniels, *The Politics of Prejudice: The Anti-Japanese Movement in California and the Struggle for Japanese Exclusion* (Berkeley: University of California Press, 1962). For some of his other important works, consult *Asian America: Chinese and Japanese United States since 1850* (Seattle: University of Washington Press, 1988); *Prisoners without Trial: Japanese Americans in World War II* (New York: Hill and Wang, 1993); *Coming to America* (New York: Perennial Press, 2002). The latter is a general history of immigration that incorporates much of his own work and that of others on Asians.

20. Gary Okihiro, *Margins and Mainstreams: Asians in American History and Culture* (Seattle: University of Washington Press, 1994). See also the collection of essays on Asians, Pyong Gap Min, ed., *Asian Americans: Contemporary Trends and Issues* (Thousand Oaks, CA: Sage, 1995).

21. Gary Okihiro, *Cane Fires: The Anti-Japanese Movement in Hawaii, 1865–1945* (Philadelphia: Temple University Press, 1991); Evelyn Nakano Glenn, *Issei, Nisei, War Bride: Three Generations of Japanese American Women in Domestic Service* (Philadelphia: Temple University Press, 1986); Yuji Ichioka, *The Issei: The World of the First Generation of Japanese Immigrants, 1885–1924* (New York: Free Press, 1988); Akiko S. Hosler, *Japanese Immigrant Entrepreneurs in New York City: A New Wave of Ethnic Business* (New York: Garland, 1998).

22. Judy Yung, *Unbound Feet: A Social History of Chinese Women in San Francisco* (Berkeley: University of California Press, 1995); Erika Lee, *At America's Gates: Chinese Immigration during the Exclusion Era, 1882–1943* (Chapel Hill: University of North Carolina Press, 2003).

23. See Xiaolan Bao, *Holding Up More Than Half the Sky: Chinese Women Garment Workers in New York City, 1948–92* (Urbana: University of Illinois Press, 2001); Hsiang-Shui Chen, *Chinatown No More: Taiwan Immigrants in Contemporary New York* (Ithaca, NY: Cornell University Press, 1992); Renqui Yu, *To Save China, to Save Ourselves: The Chinese Hand Laundry Alliance of New York* (Philadelphia: Temple University Press, 1992); Jack Kuo Wei Tchen, *New York before Chinatown: Orientalism and the Shaping of American Culture* (Baltimore: Johns Hopkins University Press, 1999).

24. Kenneth J. Guest, *God in Chinatown: Religion and Survival in New York's Evolving Immigrant Community* (New York: New York University Press, 2003).

25. Wayne Patterson, *The Ilse: First-Generation Korean Immigrants in Hawaii, 1903–1973* (Honolulu: University of Hawaii Press, 2000); Ji-Yeon Yuh, *Beyond the Shadow of Camptown: Korean Military Brides in America* (New York: New York University Press, 2002); Pyong Gap Min, *Changes and Conflict: Korean Immigrant Families in New York* (Boston: Allyn and Bacon, 1998); and Kyeyoung Park, *The Korean American Dream: Immigrants and Small Business in New York City* (Ithaca, NY: Cornell University Press, 1997).

26. Karen Isaksen Leonard, *Making Ethnic Choices: California's Punjabi Mexican Americans* (Philadelphia: Temple University Press, 1992); Madhulika S. Khandelwal, *Becoming American, Being Indian: An Immigrant Community in New York City* (Ithaca, NY: Cornell University Press, 2002); Johanna Lessinger, *From the Ganges to the Hudson: Indian Immigrants in New York City* (Boston: Allyn and Bacon, 1995).

27. Jeremy Hein, *From Vietnam, Laos, and Cambodia: A Refugee Experience in the United States* (New York: Twayne, 1995); Cathleen Jo Faruque, *Migration of Hmong to the Midwestern United States* (Lanham, MD: University Press of America, 2002); James M. Freeman, *Changing Identities: Vietnamese Americans, 1975–1995* (Boston: Allyn and Bacon, 1995).

28. Bruno Lasker, *Filipino Immigration to Continental United States and Hawaii* (1931; New York: Arno Press, 1969).

29. Yen Le Espiritu, *Home Bound: Filipino American Lives across Cultures, Communities, and Countries* (Berkeley: University of California Press, 2003); Dorothy B. Fujita-Rony, *American Workers, Colonial Power: Philippine Seattle and the Transpacific West, 1919–1941* (Berkeley: University of California Press, 2003); Barbara M. Posadas, *Filipino Americans* (Westport, CT: Greenwood Press, 1999).

30. Sucheng Chan, *Asian Americans: An Interpretive History* (New York: Twayne, 1991); Ronald Takaki, *Strangers from a Different Shore: A History of Asian Americans* (Boston: Little, Brown, 1989).

31. Carey McWilliams, updated by Matt S. Meier, *North from Mexico: The Spanish-Speaking People of the United States* (Westport, CT: Greenwood Press, 1990).

32. Alberto Camarillo, *Chicanos in a Changing Society: From Mexican Pueblos to American Barrios in Santa Barbara and Southern California* (Cambridge, MA: Harvard University Press, 1979); George Sanchez, *Becoming Mexican American: Ethnicity, Culture, and Identity in Chicano Los Angeles, 1900–1945* (New York: Oxford University Press, 1993); Douglas Monroy, *Rebirth: Mexican Los Angeles from the Great Migration to the Great Depression* (Berkeley: University of California Press, 1999); Arnoldo De León, *Mexican Americans in Texas: A Brief History* (Arlington Heights, IL: Harlan Davidson, 1993); Mario Garcia, *Desert Immigrants: The Mexicans of El Paso, 1880–1920* (New Haven, CT: Yale University Press, 1981); Juan R. Garcia, *Mexicans in the Midwest, 1900–1932* (Tucson: University of Arizona Press, 1996).

33. Vicki L. Ruiz, *From Out of the Shadows: Mexican Women in Twentieth-Century America* (New York: Oxford University Press, 1998).

34. Manuel G. Gonzales, *Mexicanos: A History of Mexicans in the United States* (Bloomington: Indiana University Press, 1999).

35. Roberto Suro, *The Strangers among Us: How Latino Immigration Is Transforming America* (New York: Knopf, 1998); Frank D. Bean and Gillian Stevens, *America's Newcomers and the Dynamics of Diversity* (New York: Russell Sage Foundation, 2003); Richard Alba and Victor Nee, *Remaking the American Mainstream: Assimilation and Contemporary Immigration* (Cambridge, MA: Harvard University Press, 2003).

36. Douglas S. Massey, Jorge Durand, and Nolan J. Malone, *Beyond Smoke and Mirrors: Mexican Immigration in an Era of Economic Integration* (New York: Russell Sage Foundation, 2002).

37. Sherri Grasmuck and Patricia R. Pessar, *Between Two Islands: Dominican International Migration* (Berkeley: University of California Press, 1991); Felix Robert Masud-Piloto, *With Open Arms: Cuban Migration to the United States* (Totowa, NJ: Rowman and Littlefield, 1988); Masud-Piloto, *From Welcomed Exiles to Illegal Immigrants: Cuban Migration to the United States, 1959–1995* (Lanham, MD: Rowman and Littlefield, 1996); Alex Stepick, Guillermo Grenier,

Max Castor, and Marvin Dunn, *This Land Is Our Land: Immigrants and Power in Miami* (Berkeley: University of California Press, 2003); Alejandro Portes and Robert L. Bach, *Latin Journey: Cuban and Mexican Immigrants in the United States* (Berkeley: University of California Press, 1985).

38. Ann Orlov and Reed Ueda, "Central and South Americans," in *Harvard Encyclopedia of American Ethnic Groups*, ed. Stephan Thernstrom (Cambridge, MA: Harvard University Press, 1980), 210.

39. Carlos B. Cordova and Paquel Pinderhughes, "Central and South Americans," in *A Nation of Peoples: A Sourcebook on America's Multicultural Heritage*, ed. Elliott Robert Barkan (Westport, CT: Greenwood Press, 1999), 117.

40. Terry A. Repak, *Waiting on Washington: Central American Workers in the Nation's Capital* (Philadelphia: Temple University Press, 1995); Sarah Mahler, *American Dreaming: Immigrant Life on the Margins* (Princeton, NJ: Princeton University Press, 1995); Maxine L. Margolis, *Little Brazil: An Ethnography of Brazilian Immigrants in New York City* (Princeton, NJ: Princeton University Press, 1994); Leon Fink, *The Maya of Morganton: Work and Community in the Nuevo New South* (Chapel Hill: University of North Carolina Press, 2003).

41. Anny Bakalian, *Armenian Americans: From Being to Feeling Armenian* (New Brunswick, NJ: Transaction, 1993); Robert Mirkak, *Torn between Two Lands: Armenians in America, 1890–World War I* (Cambridge, MA: Harvard University Press, 1983); Alixa Naff, *Becoming American: The Early Arab Immigrant Experience* (Carbondale: Southern Illinois University Press, 1985).

42. Mehdi Bozorgmehr and Alison Feldman, eds., *Middle Eastern Diaspora Communities in America* (New York: New York University Press, 1996).

43. *New York Times*, Nov. 9, 2003. See also Clara E. Rodriquez, *Changing Race: Latinos, the Census, and the History of Ethnicity in the United States* (New York: New York University Press, 2000).

44. See Darryl Fears, "The Roots of 'Hispanic': 1975 Committee of Bureaucrats Produced Designation," *Washington Post*, Oct. 15, 2003.

45. *Hispanic*, Dec. 2000, 40–42. See the Pew Hispanic Center/Kaiser Family Foundation, *2002 National Survey of Latinos* (Washington, DC: Pew Hispanic Center, 2002).

NOTES TO CHAPTER I

1. Michel Gannon, ed., *The New History of Florida* (Gainesville: University Press of Florida), 168.

2. Jane Landers, *Black Society in Spanish Florida* (Urbana: University of Illinois Press, 1999), 7–9.

3. Quoted in ibid., 8.

4. Ira Berlin, *Many Thousands Gone: The First Two Centuries of Slavery in North America* (Cambridge, MA: Harvard University Press, 1998), 25–26.

5. Ibid., 40.

6. Ibid., 25–28.

7. John Russell, *The Free Negro in Virginia, 1619–1865* (New York: Negro Universities Press, 1913), 24–29.

8. Alden T. Vaughan, "Blacks in Virginia: A Note on the First Decade," *William and Mary Quarterly* 29 (July 1972): 467–78. For examples of black indentured servants, see Russell, *Free Negro in Virginia*, chap. 2.

9. For a discussion of these early settlers, see T. H. Breen and Stephen Innes, *"Myne Owne Ground": Race and Freedom on Virginia's Eastern Shore, 1640–1676* (New York: Oxford University Press, 1980).

10. Marina Wikramanayake, *A World in Shadow: The Free Black in Antebellum South Carolina* (Columbia: University of South Carolina Press, 1973), 8.

11. Berlin, *Many Thousands Gone*, 123–24.

12. Aaron Spencer Fogelman, *Hopeful Journeys: German Immigration, Settlement, and Political Culture in Colonial America, 1717–1775* (Philadelphia: University of Pennsylvania Press, 1996), 132–34, 137, 146.

13. Berlin, *Many Thousands Gone*, 52.

14. For early slavery, see Berlin, *Many Thousands Gone*.

15. Daniel P. Mannix in collaboration with Malcolm Cowley, *Black Cargoes: A History of the Atlantic Slave Trade, 1518–1865* (New York: Viking, 1962), 121.

16. See Berlin, *Many Thousands Gone*; Ira Berlin, *Generations of Captivity: A History of African American Slaves* (Cambridge, MA: Harvard University Press, 2003).

17. Berlin, *Generations of Captivity*, 61.

18. Berlin, *Many Thousands Gone*, 106.

19. The best overall summary of slavery is Berlin, *Many Thousands Gone*.

20. See, for example, Leon F. Litwack, *North of Slavery: The Negro in the Free States, 1790–1860* (Chicago: University of Chicago Press, 1961).

21. James Horton, *Free People of Color: Inside the African American Community* (Washington, DC: Smithsonian Institution Press, 1993), 27.

22. Ira Berlin, *Slaves without Masters: The Free Negro in the Antebellum South* (New York: Pantheon Books, 1974), 47–48. In the lower South the number of manumissions was considerably fewer.

23. Michel S. Laguerre, *Diasporic Citizenship: Haitian Americans in Transnational America* (New York: St. Martin's Press, 1998), 64–68.

24. Berlin, *Many Thousands Gone*, 333–34; Shane White, *Stories of Freedom in Black New York* (Cambridge, MA: Harvard University Press, 2002), 29–32.

25. Gary Nash, *Forging Freedom: The Formation of Philadelphia's Black Community, 1720–1840* (Cambridge, MA: Harvard University Press), 142.

26. Horton, *Free People of Color*, 140.

27. Juliet E. K. Walker, "African Americans," in *A Nation of Peoples: A*

Sourcebook on America's Multicultural Heritage, ed. Elliott R. Barkan (Westport, CT: Greenwood Press, 1999), 23.

28. John E. Baur, "International Repercussions of the Haitian Revolution," *Americas* 26 (April 1970): 397; Berlin, *Slaves without Masters*, 116.

29. Alfred N. Hunt, *Haiti's Influence on Antebellum America: Slumbering Volcano in the Caribbean* (Baton Rouge: Louisiana State University Press, 1988), 42–43.

30. See the discussion in Hunt, *Haiti's Influence*.

31. Baur, "International Repercussions," 417.

32. Hunt, *Haiti's Influence*, 107–15.

33. Baur, "International Repercussions," 412–13.

34. Paul F. Lachance, "The 1808 Immigration of Saint-Dominque Refugees to New Orleans: Reception, Integration and Impact," *Louisiana History* 29 (spring 1988): 126.

35. Caryn Bell, *Revolution, Romanticism and the Afro-Creole Protest Tradition in Louisiana, 1718–1868* (Baton Rouge: Louisiana University Press, 1997), 38.

36. Hunt, *Haiti's Influence*, 58–73.

37. Bell, *Revolution*, 78. Both Roland McConnell and H. E. Sterkx give higher figures, but Sterkx includes all of Louisiana, not just New Orleans, while McConnell uses a slightly different time period. H. E. Sterkx, *The Free Negro in Ante-bellum Louisiana* (Rutherford, NJ: Fairleigh Dickinson University Press, 1972); Roland McConnell, *Negro Troops of Antebellum Louisiana: A History of the Battalion of Free Men of Color* (Baton Rouge: Louisiana State University Press, 1968), 47.

38. Bell, *Revolution*, 35.

39. Berlin, *Slaves without Masters*, 115–16.

40. Donald E. Everett, "Emigres and Militiamen: Free Persons of Color in New Orleans, 1803–1815," *Journal of Negro History* 38 (Oct. 1953): 394.

41. Quoted in Bell, *Revolution*, 55.

42. Bell, *Revolution*, 55.

43. Quoted in Bell, *Revolution*, 57.

44. Hunt, *Haiti's Influence*, 49–51, 74–83.

45. Ibid., 51–52.

46. Berlin, *Generations of Captivity*, 131.

47. James H. Kettner, *The Development of American Citizenship, 1608–1870* (Chapel Hill: University of North Carolina Press, 1978), 311–25.

48. Charles W. Tebeau, *A History of Florida* (Coral Gables, FL: University of Miami Press, 1971), 82–83, 90–91.

49. James S. Olson and Judith E. Olson, *Cuban Americans: From Trauma to Triumph* (New York: Twayne, 1995), 14–15.

50. Manuel G. Gonzales, *Mexicanos: A History of Mexicans in the United States* (Bloomington: Indiana University Press, 1999), 30–32.

51. Ibid., 36–37.

52. Ramon A. Gutierrez, *When Jesus Came the Corn Mothers Went Away: Marriage, Sexuality, and Power in New Mexico, 1500–1846* (Stanford, CA: Stanford University Press, 1991), is the best account of the conflict between Indians and the Spanish. See also James F. Brooks, *Captives and Cousins: Slavery, Kinship, and Community in the Southwest Borderlands* (Chapel Hill: University of North Carolina Press, 2003).

53. Gonzales, *Mexicanos*, 36–38.

54. Walter Nugent, *Into the West: The Story of Its People* (New York: Knopf, 1999), 29.

55. Thomas E. Sheridan, *Los Tucsonenses: The Mexican Community in Tucson, 1854–1941* (Tucson: University of Arizona Press, 1986), chap. 1.

56. James E. Officer, *Hispanic Arizona, 1536–1856* (Tucson: University of Arizona Press, 1987), 88.

57. Nugent, *Into the West*, 28.

58. See Arnoldo De León, *Mexican Americans in Texas: A History* (Arlington Heights, IL: Harlan Davidson, 1993), chap. 1.

59. Ibid., 8.

60. Armando C. Alonzo, *Tejano Legacy: Rancheros and Settlers in South Texas, 1734–1900* (Albuquerque: University of New Mexico Press, 1998), 40–41.

61. De León, *Mexican Americans*, 19–22.

62. Gonzales, *Mexicanos*, 38–40; Nugent, *Into the West*, 31–33; De León, *Mexican Americans*, 9–10; Alonzo, *Tejano Legacy*.

63. Gilbert C. Din, *The Canary Islanders of Louisiana* (Baton Rouge: Louisiana State University Press, 1988), chap. 2.

64. Ibid., chap. 5.

65. Ibid., 197.

66. This account relies on Leonard Pitt, *The Decline of the Californios: A Social History of the Spanish-Speaking Californians, 1846–1900* (Berkeley: University of California Press, 1966).

67. Gonzales, *Mexicanos*, 52–55.

68. See Martha Menchaca, *Recovering History, Constructing Race: The Indian, Black, and White Roots of Mexican Americans* (Austin: University of Texas Press, 2001).

69. Quoted in Gonzales, *Mexicanos*, 55. This figure is not universally accepted.

70. Gonzales, *Mexicanos*, 47–57.

71. De León, *Mexican Americans*, 29–33.

72. See Alonzo, *Tejano Legacy*.

73. See De León, *Mexican Americans*, chap. 3.

74. Gonzales, *Mexicanos*, 62–63. The standard treatment of decline of the ranchers of California is Pitt, *Decline of the Californios*.

75. Gonzales, *Mexicanos*, 64–65.
76. Ibid., 69.
77. Quoted in Sheridan, *Los Tucsonenses*, 13–14.
78. Officer, *Hispanic Arizona*, 106–10.
79. Ibid., 148–49.
80. Gonzales, *Mexicanos*, 65–68.
81. Ian F. Haney Lopez, *White by Law: The Legal Construction of Race* (New York: New York University Press, 1996), 240.
82. Ibid., 61.
83. See Pitt, *Decline of the Californios*.
84. Gonzales, *Mexicanos*, 86–90.
85. Ibid., 89–90. See the interesting discussion of Muerietta in Susan Lee Johnson, *Roaring Camp: The Social World of the California Gold Rush* (New York: Norton, 2000), 25–53.
86. For the gold rush generally, see Malcolm J. Rohrbough's excellent *Days of Gold: The California Gold Rush and the American Nation* (Berkeley: University of California Press, 1997).
87. Ibid., 224.
88. Carlos U. Lopez, *Chilenos in California: A Study of the 1850, 1852 (California) and 1860 Censuses* (San Francisco: R and E Research Associates, 1973), introduction.
89. Johnson, *Roaring Camp*, 63–67.
90. Ibid., 59–63.
91. Ibid., 195.
92. Ibid., chap. 4; Rohrbough, *Days of Gold*, 223–29.
93. Johnson, *Roaring Camp*, 216–18; Rohrbough, *Days of Gold*, 228–29. The tax was enforced against the Chinese.
94. See Pitt, *Decline of the Californios*, and Menchaca, *Recovering History*, for nativism against Latinos.
95. Johnson, *Roaring Camp*, 280.
96. Rohrbough, *Days of Gold*, 176–82.
97. Johnson, *Roaring Camp*, 294.
98. See Pitt, *Decline of the Californios*, and Albert Camarillo, *Chicanos in a Changing Society: From Mexican Pueblos to American Barrios in Santa Barbara and Southern California, 1848–1930* (Cambridge, MA: Harvard University Press, 1979).
99. Stephen J. Pitti, *The Devil in Silicon Valley: Northern California, Race, and Mexican Americans* (Princeton, NJ: Princeton University Press, 2003), 51
100. Ibid., 54–55.
101. Rohrbough, *Days of Gold*, chap. 18.
102. Richard Griswold del Castillo, *The Los Angeles Barrio, 1850–1890: A Social History* (Berkeley: University of California Press, 1979), 32–35.

103. Ibid., chap. 2.

104. Ibid., chap. 4.

105. Gonzales, *Mexicanos*, 87–88. See also Camarillo, *Chicanos in a Changing Society*.

106. George Sanchez, *Becoming Mexican American: Ethnicity, Culture, and Identity in Chicano Los Angeles, 1900–1945* (New York: Oxford University Press, 1993), 19.

107. Brian Godfrey, *Neighborhoods in Transition: The Making of San Francisco's Ethnic and Nonconformist Communities* (Berkeley: University of California Press, 1988), 59–60.

108. Jay Monahan, *Chile, Peru, and the California Gold Rush of 1849* (Berkeley: University of California Press, 1973), 163–70; Lopez, *Chilenos*, xi–xiv.

109. Linda Gordon, *The Great Arizona Orphan Abduction* (Cambridge, MA: Harvard University Press, 1999), 20–33.

110. Sheridan, *Los Tucsonenses*, 77.

111. Gonzales, *Mexicanos*, 91–98; Sheridan, *Los Tucsonenses*, chap. 7.

112. De León, *Mexican Americans*, 50.

113. Ibid., 35–39.

114. Alonzo, *Tejano Legacy*, 271–84.

115. Gonzales, *Mexicanos*, 98–104.

116. Ibid., 101.

117. Ibid., 104–5.

118. Sarah Deutsch, *No Separate Refuge: Culture, Class, and Gender on an Anglo-Hispano Frontier in the American Southwest, 1880–1940* (New York: Oxford University Press, 1987), 19–22.

119. Ibid., 22–24.

120. Gonzales, *Mexicanos*, 102.

121. Gerald E. Poyo, *"With All, and for the Good of All"; The Emergence of Popular Nationalism in the Cuban Communities of the United States, 1848–1898* (Durham, NC: Duke University Press, 1989), 1–2.

122. Ibid., 2–3.

123. Ibid., chap. 2. See also Susan D. Greenbaum, *More Than Black: Afro-Cubans in Tampa* (Gainesville: University Press of Florida, 2002), for a lengthy discussion of the Cuban exiles' activities.

124. Tebeau, *History of Florida*, 310–15.

125. Louis A. Perez Jr., "Cubans in Tampa: From Exiles to Immigrants, 1892–1901," *Florida Historical Quarterly* 57 (Oct. 1978): 129–31.

126. Poyo, *"With All, and for the Good of All,"* 52–55; Sharon Wells, *Forgotten Legacy: Blacks in Nineteenth Century Key West* (Key West: Key West Preservation Board, 1982), 1–35.

127. Greenbaum, *More Than Black*, chap. 7.

128. Silvio Torres-Saillant and Ramona Hernandez, *The Dominican Americans* (Westport, CT: Greenwood Press, 1998), 104–5.

129. Ibid., 105.

130. *Filipino Express*, May 12, 1996.

131. See Marina E. Espina, *Filipinos in Louisiana* (New Orleans: A. F. Laborde and Sons, 1988); Barbara M. Posadas, *The Filipino Americans* (Westport, CT: Greenwood Press, 1999), 13–14.

132. See Espina, *Filipinos in Louisiana,* for a discussion of the early villages and New Orleans.

133. Jack Chen, *The Chinese of America: From the Beginnings to the Present* (New York: Harper and Row, 1981), 3.

134. Ibid., 4.

135. Ibid.

136. Betty Lee Sung, *The Story of the Chinese in America* (New York: Macmillan, 1967), 21.

137. Ronald Takaki, *Strangers from a Different Shore: A History of Asian Americans* (Boston: Little, Brown, 1989), 21–24; Clarence E. Glick, *Sojourners and Settlers: Chinese Migrants in Hawaii* (Honolulu: University of Hawaii Press, 1980), 1–4.

138. Chen, *Chinese of America*, 5.

139. John E. Van Sant, *Pacific Pioneers: Japanese Journeys to America and Hawaii, 1850–80* (Urbana: University of Illinois Press, 2000), chap. 1.

140. Ibid., 44.

141. Yuji Ichioka, *The Issei: The World of the First Generation of Japanese Immigrants, 1885–1924* (New York: Free Press, 1988), 7–8; Van Sant, *Pacific Pioneers*, chap. 2.

142. Ichioka, *Issei*, 23–28.

143. Van Sant, *Pacific Pioneers*, 87–89.

144. Ibid., chap. 5.

145. Robert Mirak, *Torn between Two Lands: Armenians in America, 1890–World War I* (Cambridge, MA: Harvard University Press, 1983), 36–41

146. Ibid., 40–44.

NOTES TO CHAPTER 2

1. Ronald Takaki, *Strangers from a Different Shore: A History of Asian Americans* (Boston: Little, Brown, 1989), 79.

2. Betty Lee Sung, *The Story of the Chinese in America* (New York: Collier Books, 1967), 22–23.

3. Malcolm Rohrbough, *Days of Gold: The California Gold Rush and the American Nation* (Berkeley: University of California Press, 1997), 228.

4. Craig Storti, *Incident at Bitter Creek: The Story of the Rock Springs Chinese Massacre* (Ames: Iowa State University Press, 1991), 4.

5. See Sung, *Story of the Chinese,* for the early years of immigration.

6. Takaki, *Strangers from a Different Shore,* 80.

7. Rohrbough, *Days of Gold,* 228.

8. Storti, *Incident at Bitter Creek,* chaps. 3–4.

9. Ibid., chaps. 7–8; Sucheng Chan, *Asian Americans: An Interpretive History* (New York: Twayne, 1991), 49.

10. Sucheng Chan, *This Bittersweet Soil: The Chinese in California Agriculture, 1860–1910* (Berkeley: University of California Press, 1986), 79–81.

11. Ibid., 81–88.

12. Ibid., chap. 3.

13. Ibid., 106–19.

14. Ibid., chap. 11.

15. Jack Chen, *The Chinese of America* (New York: Harper and Row, 1981), chap. 6, is especially good on the Chinese building the railroad.

16. Quoted in Andrew Gyory, *Closing the Gate: Race, Politics, and the Chinese Exclusion Act* (Chapel Hill: University of North Carolina Press, 1998), 7.

17. Chan, *Asian Americans,* 31.

18. Quoted in Takaki, *Strangers from a Different Shore,* 85.

19. Chan, *Asian Americans,* 31.

20. Chen, *Chinese of America,* 75–76.

21. Gyory, *Closing the Gate,* 18–19.

22. Ibid., 24–26.

23. Gyory, *Closing the Gate,* is especially good on labor opposition to the Chinese.

24. Quoted in ibid., 60.

25. Ibid., 50–53.

26. Lucy E. Salyer, *Laws Harsh as Tigers: Chinese Immigrants and the Shaping of Modern Immigration Laws* (Chapel Hill: University of North Carolina Press, 1995), 208–9.

27. George Anthony Peffer, *If They Don't Bring Their Women Here: Chinese Female Immigration before Exclusion* (Urbana: University of Illinois Press, 1999), 6–11.

28. Sucheng Chan, "The Exclusion of Chinese Women," in *Entry Denied: Exclusion and the Chinese Community in America, 1882–1943,* ed. Sucheng Chan (Philadelphia: Temple University Press, 1991), 97–105.

29. Peffer, *If They Don't Bring Their Women,* 9.

30. Quoted in ibid., 76.

31. For agriculture generally, see Chan, *Bittersweet Soil*; Huping Ling, "Family and Marriage of Late Nineteenth and Early Twentieth Century Chinese Immi-

grant Women," *Journal of American Ethnic History* 19, no. 2 (winter 2000): 43–46.

32. For New York, see John Kuo Wei Tchen, *New York before Chinatown: Orientalism and the Shaping of American Culture* (Baltimore: Johns Hopkins University Press, 1999).

33. See Charles J. McClain, *In Search of Equality: The Chinese Struggle against Discrimination in Nineteenth-Century America* (Berkeley: University of California Press, 1994).

34. See the excellent account of the enactment of exclusion in Gyory, *Closing the Gate.*

35. Chan, "Exclusion of Chinese Women," 114–18.

36. Salyer, *Laws Harsh as Tigers*, 43.

37. Takaki, *Strangers from a Different Shore*, 235. See Erika Lee, *At America's Gates: Chinese Immigration during the Exclusion Era, 1882–1943* (Chapel Hill: University of North Carolina Press, 2003), for a careful and informative account of Chinese immigration during the exclusion era.

38. See his account in Tung Pok Chin, *Paper Son: One Man's Story* (Philadelphia: Temple University Press, 2000).

39. Salyer, *Laws Harsh as Tigers*, 44–45. See Lee, *At America's Gates*, for a detailed account of how Chinese immigrants managed to enter the United States.

40. Salyer, *Laws Harsh as Tigers*, 67.

41. Lee, *At America's Gates*, 75.

42. Ibid., 117–19.

43. Takaki, *Strangers from a Different Shore*, 233–39.

44. Quoted in ibid., 231.

45. McClain, *In Search of Equality*, 173–78.

46. Chen, *Chinese of America*, 109–10.

47. Ibid., 110–15.

48. Chan, *Asian Americans*, 33; Renqui Yu, *To Save China, to Save Ourselves: The Chinese Hand Laundry Alliance of New York* (Philadelphia: Temple University Press, 1992), 9.

49. Takaki, *Strangers from a Different Store*, 240–46; Yu, *To Save China*, 24–28.

50. Yu, *To Save China*, 31–36.

51. Ibid., chaps. 3–4.

52. Quoted in Takaki, *Strangers from a Different Shore*, 251.

53. See Yu, *To Save China*, for a thorough account of the political struggles in New York City's Chinatown.

54. Judy Yung, *Unbound Feet: A Social History of Chinese Women in San Francisco* (Berkeley: University of California Press, 1995), 69–77.

55. Ibid., 57–58.

56. Ibid., 86–92.

57. Ibid., 94–99.

58. See Madeline Yuan-yin Hsu, *Dreaming of Gold, Dreaming of Home: Transnationalism and Migration between the United States and China, 1883–1943* (Stanford, CA: Stanford University Press, 2000). See also Erika Lee, "The Chinese Exclusion Example: Race, Immigration and the American Gatekeeping, 1882–1924," *Journal of American Ethnic History* 21 (spring 2002): 36–62.

59. Clarence E. Glick, *Sojourners and Settlers: Chinese Migrants in Hawaii* (Honolulu: University Press of Hawaii, 1980), 12.

60. Ibid., chap. 2.

61. Ibid., chap. 3.

62. Ibid., chap. 5.

63. Lucy M. Cohen, *Chinese in the Post–Civil War South* (Baton Rouge: Louisiana State University Press, 1984), chap. 1.

64. Ibid., 49–81.

65. Ibid., chap. 6.

66. Ibid., chap. 7.

67. See ibid. for social conditions and education of Chinese in the South.

68. Yuji Ichioka, *The Issei: The World of the First Generation of Japanese Immigrants, 1885–1924* (New York: Free Press, 1988), 7–8.

69. Ibid., 23–28.

70. Quoted in ibid., 11. See also Mitziko Sawada, *Tokyo Life, New York Dreams: Urban Japanese Visions of America, 1890–1924* (Berkeley: University of California Press, 1996).

71. See Ichioka, *Issei,* and Evelyn Nakano Glenn, *Unequal Freedom: How Race and Gender Shaped American Citizenship and Labor* (Cambridge, MA: Harvard University Press, 2002), chap. 6.

72. Glenn, *Unequal Freedom,* chap. 6.

73. Takaki, *Strangers from a Different Shore,* 133.

74. Ibid., 132–42.

75. Ibid., 142–55; Gary Okihiro, *Cane Fires: The Anti-Japanese Movement in Hawaii, 1865–1945* (Philadelphia: Temple University Press, 1991).

76. Takaki, *Strangers from a Different Shore,* 148–55.

77. Ibid., 157–62.

78. Chan, *Asian Americans,* 35–37.

79. Masakazu Iwata, *Planted in Good Soil: A History of the Issei in United States Agriculture,* vol. 2 (New York: Peter Lang, 1992), 514–29.

80. Ibid., 546–602.

81. See ibid.

82. Ichioka, *Issei,* 146–56.

83. Takaki, *Strangers from a Different Shore*, 192.

84. Ibid., 186.

85. Edna Bonacich and John Modell, *The Economic Basis of Ethnic Solidarity: Small Business in the Japanese American Community* (Berkeley: University of California Press, 1980), chap. 3.

86. Sawada, *Tokyo Life,* 19.

87. Ibid., 22–24.

88. Ibid., 28. See also Akiko S. Hosler, *Japanese Immigrant Entrepreneurs in New York City: A New Wave of Ethnic Business* (New York: Garland, 1998), 47–50.

89. Mei T. Nakano, *Japanese American Women: Three Generations, 1890–1990* (Berkeley: Mina Press, 1986), 45–48.

90. Ichioka, *Issei,* 28–40.

91. Quoted in Takaki, *Strangers from a Different Shore*, 191.

92. Nakano, *Japanese American Women,* 44–45.

93. Ibid., 46. See especially Evelyn Glenn, *Issei, Nisei, War Bride: Three Generations of Japanese American Women in Domestic Service* (Philadelphia: Temple University Press, 1986).

94. Ichioka, *Issei,* 165–68.

95. Ibid., 168–71.

96. Ibid., 173–74.

97. Commission on Wartime Relocation and Internment of Civilians, *Personal Justice Denied* (Washington, DC: Government Printing Office, 1982), 30–34. The standard work on Japanese exclusion is Roger Daniels, *The Politics of Prejudice* (Berkeley: University of California Press, 1962).

98. Takaki, *Strangers from a Different Shore*, 202–4.

99. Ibid., 202–3.

100. Ian F. Haney Lopez, *White by Law: The Legal Construction of Race* (New York: New York University Press, 1996), chap. 4; Eileen H. Tamura, "Japanese," in *A Nation of Peoples: A Sourcebook on America's Multicultural Heritage,* ed. Elliott R. Barkan (Westport, CT: Greenwood Press, 1999), 322.

101. Ichioka, *Issei,* 153–56.

102. David Yoo, "A Religious History of Japanese Americans in California," in *Religions in Asian America: Building Faith Communities,* ed. Pyong Gap Min and Jung Ha Kim (Walnut Creek, CA: AltaMira Press, 2002), 129–33.

103. Quoted in Roger Daniels, *Prisoners without Trial: Japanese Americans in World War II* (New York: Hill and Wang, 1993), 21; Takaki, *Strangers from a Different Shore,* 220–25.

104. Takaki, *Strangers from a Different Shore*, 220–22.

105. Ibid., 399–405.

106. See Daniels, *Prisoners without Trial.*

107. Takaki, *Strangers from a Different Shore*, 380–86.

108. Wayne Patterson, *The Korean Frontier in America: Immigration to Hawaii, 1896–1910* (Honolulu: University of Hawaii Press, 1988), 8–11.

109. Takaki, *Strangers from a Different Shore*, 53–57.

110. Ibid., 54.

111. Patterson's *Korean Frontier* gives a detailed account of the negotiations leading to emigration from Korea.

112. Patterson, *Korean Frontier*, chapters 11–14.

113. Takaki, *Strangers from a Different Shore*, 270–71.

114. Ibid., 273–79.

115. Mary Paik Lee, *Quiet Odyssey: A Pioneer Korean in America* (Seattle: University of Washington Press, 1990), 12.

116. See Lee, *Quiet Odyssey*.

117. Quoted in Takaki, *Strangers from a Different Shore*, 293.

118. Chan, *Asian Americans*, 52.

119. Roger Daniels, "History of Indian Immigration to the United States: An Interpretive Essay" (paper presented to the conference "India in America: The Immigrant Experience," Asia Society, New York, April 17, 1986), 11.

120. An excellent account of South Asian immigration is Karen Isaksen Leonard, *The South Asian Americans* (Westport, CT: Greenwood Press, 1997). See also Leonard, *Making Ethnic Choices: California's Punjabi Mexican Americans* (Philadelphia: Temple University Press, 1993), and Joan Jensen, *Passage from India: Asian Indian Immigrants in North America* (New Haven, CT: Yale University Press, 1988)

121. Quoted in Leonard, *South Asian Americans*, 45.

122. Jensen, *Passage from India*, 45–52.

123. Takaki, *Strangers from a Different Shore*, 297.

124. Jensen, *Passage from India*, 108–20, chap. 7.

125. The best treatment of the Punjabis' attempt to maintain their culture is Leonard, *Making Ethnic Choices*.

126. Lopez, *White by Law*, 86–92.

127. Ibid., 91.

128. Leonard, *South Asian Americans*, 45.

129. Jensen, *Passage from India*, 172–73.

130. Elliott Barkan, *And Still They Come: Immigrants and American Society, 1920s to the 1990s* (Wheeling, IL: Harlan Davidson, 1996), 97.

131. Saund's story is told in his autobiography, D. S. Saund, *Congressman from India* (New York: Dutton, 1960).

132. Jensen, *Passage from India*, chap. 8.

133. Takaki, *Strangers from a Different Shore*, 313–14.

134. Ibid., 313.

135. Jon Cruz, "Filipinos," in Barkan, *A Nation of Peoples*, 203–4.

136. Barbara M. Posadas and Roland L. Guyotte, "Unintentional Immigrants: Chicago's Filipino Foreign Students Become Settlers, 1900–1941," *Journal of American Ethnic History* 9 (spring 1990): 28–32.

137. Ibid., 42. For general conditions, see Bruno Lasker, *Filipino Immigration to Continental United States and Hawaii* (New York: Arno Press and the *New York Times*, 1969), 58–64; Barbara M. Posadas, "Crossed Boundaries in Interracial Chicago: Pilipino American Families since 1925," *Amerasia Journal* 8, no. 2 (1981): 31–54.

138. Dorothy Fujita-Rony, *American Workers, Colonial Power: Philippine Seattle and the Transpacific West* (Berkeley: University of California Press, 2003), 57–68.

139. Takaki, *Strangers from a Different Shore*, 57.

140. Ibid., 58–62.

141. Robert N. Anderson with Richard Coller and Rebecca F. Pestano, *Filipinos in Rural Hawaii* (Honolulu: University of Hawaii Press, 1984), 165–75. The best account of labor movements in Hawaii is Okihiro, *Cane Fires*.

142. See Anderson, *Filipinos in Rural Hawaii*, for working conditions.

143. Ibid., 41–45.

144. Takaki, *Strangers from a Different Shore*, 318–24; Lasker, *Filipino Immigration*, chaps. 6–7.

145. *Filipino Express*, May 5, 1996.

146. Lasker, *Filipino Immigration*, 43–47.

147. Fujita-Rony, *American Workers*, is especially good on working conditions of Filipinos in the Pacific Norwest.

148. Yukiko Kimura, *Issei: Japanese Immigrants in Hawaii* (Honolulu: University of Hawaii Press, 1988), 200; Posadas, *Filipino Americans*, 22–23.

149. Posadas, "Crossed Boundaries," 41.

150. Lasker, *Filipino Immigration*, chap. 8; Takaki, *Strangers from a Different Shore*, 324–25.

151. Takaki, *Strangers from a Different Shore*, 326–28.

152. Quoted in Lasker, *Filipino Immigration*, 92.

153. Takaki, *Strangers from a Different Shore*, 325.

154. Quoted in ibid., 327.

155. Quoted in ibid., 332.

156. Takaki, ibid., 328–34.

NOTES TO CHAPTER 3

1. Ira De A. Reid, *The Negro Immigrant: His Background, Characteristics and Social Adjustment, 1899–1937* (New York: AMS Press, 1970), 42–44.

2. Quoted in Mae M. Ngai, "The Architecture of Race in American Immigration Law: A Reexamination of the Immigration Act of 1924," *Journal of American History* 86 (June 1999): 81.

3. Quoted in Desmond King, *Making Americans: Immigration, Race, and the Origins of Diverse Democracy* (Cambridge, MA: Harvard University Press, 2000), 153.

4. Ibid., 229.

5. Reid, *Negro Immigrant*, 239–40. Reid gives only a few thousand, but his figures are certainly an undercount.

6. Ransford W. Palmer, *Pilgrims from the Sun: West Indian Migration to America* (New York: Twayne, 1995), 7.

7. Quoted in Rogaia Mustafa Abusharaf, *Wanderings: Sudanese Migrants and Exiles in North America* (Ithaca, NY: Cornell University Press, 2002), 21.

8. Abusharaf, *Wanderings*, 26–32.

9. Quoted in Abusharaf, *Wanderings*, 35.

10. Marilyn Halter, *Between Race and Ethnicity: Cape Verdean American Immigrants, 1860–1965* (Urbana: University of Illinois Press, 1993), 36–39.

11. Ibid., 7.

12. Ibid., 45–47. Neither official federal immigration figures nor Census Bureau data are accurate. Both tend to underestimate the number of immigrants.

13. Ibid., chap. 3.

14. Ibid., 143.

15. Ibid., 7.

16. Ibid., 148.

17. Ibid., 60 n. 8; Ngai, "Architecture of Race," 74.

18. Philip Kasinitz, *Caribbean New York: Black Immigrants and the Politics of Race* (Ithaca, NY: Cornell University Press, 1992), 25–26; Winston James, *Holding Aloft the Banner of Ethiopia: Caribbean Radicalism in Early Twentieth-Century America* (New York: Verso, 1998), 355–56. James's figures differ somewhat from those of Ira De A. Reid, Philip Kasinitz, and those of Marilyn Halter (for the Cape Verdeans). James's figures are certainly an undercount, and the exact number of black immigrants is unknown.

19. James, *Holding Aloft the Banner*, 13–14. See also Michael L. Conniff, *Black Labor in a White Canal, Panama, 1904–1981* (Pittsburgh: University of Pittsburgh Press, 1985).

20. James, *Holding Aloft the Banner*, 36–41.

21. Irma Watkins-Owens, *Blood Relations: Caribbean Immigrants and the Harlem Community, 1900–1930* (Bloomington: Indiana University Press, 1996), 15.

22. Ibid., 14.

23. Quoted in King, *Making Americans*, 153.

24. James, *Holding Aloft the Banner*, 21–44.

25. Watkins-Owens, *Blood Relations*, 23–25.

26. Philip Kasinitz and Milton Vickerman, "West Indians/Caribbeans," in *A Nation of Peoples: A Sourcebook on America's Multicultural Heritage*, ed. Elliott Robert Barkan (Westport, CT: Greenwood Press, 1999), 524.

27. Reid, *Negro Immigrant*, 73–76.

28. Raymond Mohl, "'Black Immigrants: Bahamians in Early Twentieth-Century Miami," *Florida Historical Quarterly* 65 (January 1987): 272–73.

29. Marvin Dunn, *Black Miami in the Twentieth Century* (Gainesville: University Press of Florida, 1997), 16.

30. Ibid., 126.

31. Mohl, "Black Immigrants," 73–74.

32. Ibid., 273.

33. Ibid., 275.

34. Quoted in ibid., 286.

35. Mohl, "Black Immigrants," 282.

36. Ibid., 293–97.

37. Dunn, *Black Miami*, 106–17.

38. Mohl, "Black Immigrants," 287.

39. Quoted in Reid, *Negro Immigrant*, 189.

40. Mohl, "Black Immigrants," 287–90; Dunn, *Black Miami*, 117–24.

41. Dunn, *Black Miami*, 117–24.

42. James, *Holding Aloft the Banner*, 12.

43. Quoted in ibid., 12.

44. James, *Holding Aloft the Banner*, 78.

45. Ibid., 82–83.

46. Watkins-Owens, *Blood Relations*, 127–35; Kasinitz, *Caribbean New York*, 90–96.

47. James, *Holding Aloft the Banner*, 83.

48. Kasinitz, *Caribbean New York*, 42.

49. Watkins-Owens, *Blood Relations*, 57–63.

50. Ibid., 67–70.

51. Reid, *Negro Immigrant*, 94–97.

52. Ibid., 97–98.

53. Watkins-Owens, *Blood Relations*, 79.

54. Ibid., 79.

55. James, *Holding Aloft the Banner*, chap. 5.

56. Watkins-Owens, *Blood Relations*, chap. 7; James, *Holding Aloft the Banner*, 134–57, chap. 6.

57. James, *Holding Aloft the Banner*, 137–56.

58. Ibid., 122–34.

59. See ibid., chap. 7.

60. See the discussion in ibid.

61. Watkins-Owens, *Blood Relations*, chap. 5; Reid, *Negro Immigrant*, 167–69.

62. Kasinitz, *Caribbean New York*, 24–25.

63. Erika Lee, *At America's Gates: Chinese Immigration during the Exclusion*

Era, 1882–1943 (Chapel Hill: University of North Carolina Press, 2003), 157–75.

64. Emilio Zamora, *The World of the Mexican Worker in Texas* (College Station: Texas A&M University Press, 1993), 16.

65. Lawrence A. Cardoso, *Mexican Emigration to the United States, 1897–1931* (Tucson: University of Arizona Press, 1980), 34; Mark Reisler, *By the Sweat of Their Brow: Mexican Immigrant Labor in the United States* (Westport, CT: Greenwood Press, 1976), 13.

66. Figures are based on the Immigration and Naturalization (INS), *Annual Reports*.

67. Manuel G. Gonzales, *Mexicanos: A History of Mexicans in the United States* (Bloomington: Indiana University Press, 1999), 112.

68. Reisler, *By the Sweat of Their Brow*, chap. 2.

69. Gonzales, *Mexicanos*, 114–24.

70. Cardoso, *Mexican Emigration*, 2–9.

71. Gonzales, *Mexicanos*, 114–25.

72. Cardoso, *Mexican Emigration*, 12–14.

73. Ibid., 14.

74. Reisler, *By the Sweat of Their Brow*, 4–5.

75. Carey McWilliams, updated by Matt S. Meier, *North from Mexico: The Spanish-Speaking People of the United States* (Westport, CT: Greenwood Press, 1990), 167–69.

76. Cardoso, *Mexican Emigrants*, 14; Reisler, *By the Sweat of Their Brow*, 3.

77. Quoted in Roberto R. Calderon, *Mexican Coal Mining Labor in Texas and Coahuila, 1880–1930* (College Park: Texas A&M University Press, 2000), 169.

78. Ibid., 204.

79. Ibid., 116–34.

80. Ibid., chap. 5.

81. Sarah Deutsch, *No Separate Refuge: Culture and Gender on an Anglo-Hispanic Frontier in the American Southwest, 1880–1940* (New York: Oxford University Press, 1987), 87–92.

82. George Sanchez, *Becoming Mexican American: Ethnicity, Culture, and Identity in Chicano Los Angeles, 1900–1945* (New York: Oxford University Press, 1993), 67.

83. McWilliams, *North from Mexico*, 196–97.

84. Quoted in Reisler, *By the Sweat of Their Brow*, 5.

85. Reisler, *By the Sweat of Their Brow*, 7–10.

86. Camille Guerin-Gonzales, *Mexican Workers and American Dreams: Immigration, Repatriation, and California Farm Labor, 1900–1939* (New Brunswick, NJ: Rutgers University Press, 1994), chap. 2.

87. Reisler, *By the Sweat of Their Brow*, 49–55.

88. Guerin-Gonzales, *Mexican Workers*, 61–64.

89. Gonzales, *Mexicanos*, 133–34.

90. Juan R. Garcia, *Mexicans in the Midwest, 1900–1932* (Tucson: University of Arizona Press, 1996), 14–18.

91. Gonzales, *Mexicanos*, 133–34.

92. Neil Foley, *White Scourge: Mexicans, Blacks, and Poor Whites in Texas Cotton Culture* (Berkeley: University of California Press, 1997), 30–38.

93. Ibid., chap. 4.

94. Mario Garcia, *Desert Immigrants: The Mexicans of El Paso, 1880–1920* (New Haven, CT: Yale University Press, 1981), 65.

95. Ibid., 68.

96. Ibid., 70–71.

97. Ibid., 74–75.

98. Quoted in ibid., 101–6.

99. Quoted in Reisler, *By the Sweat of Their Brow*, 97.

100. Reisler, *By the Sweat of Their Brow*, 97.

101. Sanchez, *Becoming Mexican American*, 67.

102. Ibid., 190–95.

103. Richard Griswold del Castillon and Arnoldo De León, *North to Aztlan: A History of Mexican Americans in the United States* (New York: Twayne, 1996), 61; Garcia, *Mexicans in the Midwest*, 5–10.

104. Zaragosa Vargas, *Proletarians of the North: A History of Mexican Industrial Workers in Detroit and the Midwest, 1917–1933* (Berkeley: University of California Press, 1993), 60.

105. Ibid., 86.

106. Garcia, *Mexicans in the Midwest*, 38–41.

107. Vargas, *Proletarians of the North*, 92–96.

108. Garcia, *Mexicans in the Midwest*, 45–48.

109. Ibid., 58–60.

110. Vicki L. Ruiz, *From Out of the Shadows: Mexican Women in Twentieth-Century America* (New York: Oxford University Press, 1998), 11–12.

111. Garcia, *Mexicans in the Midwest*, 89–90.

112. Douglas Monroy, *Rebirth: Mexican Los Angeles from the Great Migration to the Great Depression* (Berkeley: University of California Press, 1999), 121.

113. Garcia, *Mexicans in the Midwest*, 98–100.

114. Ruiz, *From Out of the Shadows*, 19.

115. Garcia, *Desert Immigrants*, 76–78.

116. Ibid., 78.

117. Garcia, *Mexicans in the Midwest*, 92.

118. Ruiz, *From Out of the Shadows*, 74–77.

119. Quoted in Garcia, *Mexicans in the Midwest*, 94.

120. Quoted in ibid., 96.

121. Ruiz, *From Out of the Shadows*, chap. 3.
122. See McWilliams, *North from Mexico*.
123. Ian F. Haney Lopez, *White by Law: The Legal Construction of Race* (New York: New York University Press, 1996), 61.
124. Gonzales, *Mexicanos*, 129.
125. Lopez, *White by Law*, 145.
126. Garcia, *Desert Immigrants*, chap. 6; Monroy, *Rebirth*, 130–34; and David Montejano, *Anglos and Mexicans in the Making of Texas, 1836–1986* (Austin: University of Texas Press, 1987), 168–69, 191–93, 242–44.
127. Monroy, *Rebirth*, 133–34.
128. Guadalupe San Miguel Jr., *Brown, Not White: School Integration and the Chicano Movement in Houston* (College Station: Texas A&M University Press, 2001), 33, 75, 78, 82, 86. Later some whites in Texas welcomed the naming of Mexicanos as white, for it was then possible to place Mexicans and African Americans in the same schools and declare that the schools were integrated.
129. Evelyn Nakano Glenn, *Unequal Freedom: How Race and Gender Shaped American Citizenship and Labor* (Cambridge, MA: Harvard University Press, 2002), 163.
130. Benjamin Marquez, *LULAC: The Evolution of a Mexican American Political Organization* (Austin: University of Texas Press, 1993), 15–27.
131. For the debate about "whiteness," immigration, and citizenship, see Clare Sheridan, "Contested Citizenship: National Identity and the Mexican Immigration Debates of the 1920s," *Journal of American Ethnic History* 21 (spring 2002): 3–35.
132. Marquez, *LULAC*, 32–33.
133. Montejano, *Anglos and Mexicans*, 242–44.
134. There had been protests against Mexican schools before LULAC was founded. See Arnoldo De León, *Mexican Americans in Texas: A Brief History* (Arlington Heights, IL: Harlan Davidson, 1993), 87–90, 90–101.
135. Ibid., 103–7.
136. Gonzales, *Mexicanos*, 150–58. For the role of women, see Ruiz, *From Out of the Shadows*, 84.
137. Guerin-Gonzales, *Mexican Workers*, 123.
138. Zamora, *World of the Mexican Worker*, 92–93.
139. Gonzales, *Mexicanos*, 97–98; Ruiz, *From Out of the Shadows*, 88–90.
140. Guerin-Gonzales, *Mexican Workers*, chap. 4.
141. Sanchez, *Becoming Mexican American*, chap. 10.
142. Garcia, *Mexicans in the Midwest*, 223.
143. Vargas, *Proletarians of the North*, 169–70.
144. For a recent account, see Carlos B. Cordova and Raquel Pinderhughes, "Central and South Americans," in Barkan, *A Nation of Peoples*, 97–98, 100–103. Stephan Thernstrom, ed., *The Harvard Encyclopedia of American Eth-*

nic Groups (Cambridge, MA: Harvard University Press, 1980), also has little information on the pre–World War II era.

145. Brian Godfrey, *Neighborhoods in Transition: The Making of San Francisco's Ethnic and Nonconformist Communities* (Berkeley: University of California Press, 1988), 139.

146. Ibid., 139.

147. Ibid., 140.

148. Ibid., 59, 111, 148.

149. James, *Holding Aloft the Banner*, 235–36.

150. Ibid., 239.

151. Ibid., chap. 8.

NOTES TO PART 2

1. *New York Times*, July 4, 2000.

2. *New York Times*, Jan. 2, 1998.

3. *Christian Science Monitor*, Mar. 26, 2001.

NOTES TO CHAPTER 4

1. For an excellent summary of the importance of Mexican immigration, see Frank D. Bean and Gillian Stevens, *America's Newcomers and the Dynamics of Diversity* (New York: Russell Sage Foundation, 2003), chap. 3.

2. *Dallas Morning News*, Sept. 19, 1999.

3. *USA Today*, Jan. 2, 2004.

4. *Washington Post*, March 18, 2001.

5. Frank D. Bean, Rodolfo Corona, Rodolo Tuiran, Karen A. Woodrow-Lafield, and Jennifer Van Hook, "Circular, Invisible, and Ambiguous Migrants: Components of Difference in Estimates of the Number of Unauthorized Mexican Migrants in the United States," *Demography* 38 (August 2001): 411–22.

6. Bean and Stevens, *America's Newcomers*, 60–65.

7. Steve A. Camarota, *Immigrants in the United States—2000: A Snapshot of America's Foreign-Born Population* (Washington, DC: Center for Immigration Studies, 2002), 8. Camarota based his figures on data from the Census Bureau.

8. Jeffrey Passel, *New Estimates of the Undocumented Population in the United States* (Washington, DC: Pew Hispanic Center, 2002).

9. Immigration and Naturalization Service (INS), *Statistical Yearbook*, 2000, 21. Germany recorded 7,176,071.

10. Manuel G. Gonzales, *Mexicanos: A History of Mexicans in the United States* (Bloomington: Indiana University Press, 1999), 165.

11. Ronald Takaki, *Double Victory: A Multicultural History of America in World War II* (Boston: Little, Brown, 2000), chap. 5; Gonzales, *Mexicanos*, 161–64.

12. Maurice Mazon, *The Zoot Suit Riots: The Psychology of Symbolic Annihilation* (Austin: University of Texas Press, 1984); and especially Edward J. Escobar, *Race, Police, and the Making of a Political Identity: Mexican Americans and the Los Angeles Police Department, 1900–1945* (Berkeley: University of California Press, 1999), chaps. 8–12.

13. Stephen Pitti, *The Devil in Silicon Valley: Northern California, Race, and Mexican Americans* (Princeton, NJ: Princeton University Press, 2003), 125–27.

14. David M. Reimers, *Still the Golden Door: The Third World Comes to America,* 2nd ed. (New York: Columbia University Press, 1992), chap. 2; Gonzales, *Mexicanos,* 170–78.

15. Dionicio Nodín Valdés, *Barrios Norteños: St. Paul and the Midwestern Mexican Communities in the Twentieth Century* (Austin: University of Texas Press, 2000), 131–33.

16. Douglas S. Massey, Jorge Durand, and Nolan J. Malone, *Beyond Smoke and Mirrors: Mexican Immigration in an Era of Economic Integration* (New York: Russell Sage Foundation, 2002), 34–41. For recent discussion about illegal immigrants in agriculture, see B. Lindsay Lowell and Roberto Suro, *How Many Undocumented: The Numbers behind the U.S.-Mexico Migration Talks* (Washington, DC: Pew Hispanic Center, 2002), 8–10.

17. *Los Angles Times,* Apr. 20, 1999.

18. Gonzales, *Mexicanos,* 224–29.

19. Many workers easily found fraudulent documents to satisfy growers that they were legally entitled to work. The 1986 law that made it a crime to employ illegal aliens was simply not enforced on large-scale American farms. *Los Angeles Times,* Dec. 16, 1998.

20. *Los Angeles Times,* Aug. 26, 1999. Increased mechanization in the 1990s lessened the demand for cane laborers.

21. *Charlotte Observer,* Oct. 30, 1999.

22. Bart Jansen in Associated Press, Dec. 2, 2000.

23. *Dallas Morning News,* Nov. 27, 2000.

24. See Ramon Eduardo Ruiz, *On the Rim of Mexico: Encounters of the Rich and Poor* (Boulder, CO: Westview Press, 1998), chap. 4.

25. California Rural Legal Assistance Foundation, press release, Nov. 1, 2000.

26. *New York Times,* Aug. 24, 1997.

27. *Los Angeles Times,* Jan. 31, 1998.

28. *San Francisco Chronicle,* Oct. 13, 1998.

29. Ibid.

30. *New York Times,* Oct. 31, 2000. The new Bureau of Customs and Border Protection used somewhat different figures in 2003, but the difference was small. See *USA Today,* May 19, 2003.

31. *New York Times,* May 25, 2001; May 26, 2001.

32. *New York Times*, Oct. 16, 2002. This was not the first incident of illegal aliens being found in railroad cars, alive or dead.

33. *USA Today*, May 15, 2003.

34. For immigration into California, see William A. V. Clark, *The California Cauldron: Immigration and the Fortunes of Local Communities* (New York: Guilford Press, 1998), chaps. 2–3.

35. Arnoldo De León, *Ethnicity in the Sunbelt: A History of Mexican Americans in Houston*, Mexican American Studies Monograph Series No. 7 (Houston: University of Houston Press, 1989), 147.

36. *Dallas Morning News*, Sept. 20, 1999.

37. Valdés, *Barrios Norteños*, 214–26.

38. Ibid., 216–22.

39. *Time*, June 11, 2001, 79. See the discussion in Bean and Stevens, *America's Newcomers*, 56–60.

40. *New York Times*, May 6, 2003.

41. *Dallas Morning News*, Sept. 20, 1999; *Los Angeles Times*, Feb. 19, 1999.

42. *Dallas Morning News*, Sept. 20, 1999.

43. *Atlanta Journal-Constitution*, May 7, 2001.

44. *Burlington Free Press*, Aug. 15, 1999.

45. *Migration News* 5, no. 2 (Feb. 1998).

46. *Los Angeles Times*, Dec. 29, 1999.

47. Leon Fink and Alvis Dunn, "The Maya of Morganton: Exploring Worker Identity with the Global Marketplace," in *The Maya Diaspora: Guatemalan Roots, New American Lives,* ed. James Loucky and Marilyn M. Moors (Philadelphia: Temple University Press, 2000), 178–79.

48. *U.S. News and World Report*, Sept. 23, 1996; *New York Times*, Jan. 29, 1998; *St. Louis Post-Dispatch*, Dec. 28, 1997.

49. *U.S. News and World Report*, Sept. 23, 1996; *New York Times*, Jan. 29, 1998; *St. Louis Post-Dispatch*, Apr. 2, 2000.

50. *St. Louis Post-Dispatch*, Dec. 28, 1997.

51. *New York Times*, June 16, 2000.

52. *Fort Worth Star-Telegram*, July 4, 1999.

53. *New York Times*, Aug. 31, 2000.

54. *Los Angeles Times*, Nov. 28, 1997.

55. *Fort Worth Star-Telegram*, July 4, 1999.

56. *Atlanta Journal-Constitution*, Nov. 20, 2000.

57. *Austin American-Statesman*, Sept. 16, 1999.

58. *Fort Worth Star-Telegram*, July 4, 1999.

59. Ibid.

60. *Los Angeles Times*, Sept. 23, 1999.

61. *Atlanta Journal-Constitution*, Nov. 18, 2000; Roberto Suro, "Latino Re-

mittances Swell Despite US Economic Slump," *Migration Information Source*, Feb. 1, 2003.

62. *San Diego Union-Tribune*, Oct. 31, 1999; *Atlanta Journal-Constitution*, Nov. 18, 2000; *New York Times*, July 6, 2002.

63. Kevin O'Neil, "Consular ID Cards: Mexico and Beyond," Migration Information Source, Apr. 1, 2003. For further information, see www.migrationinformation.org.

64. *New York Times*, Mar. 15, 2003.

65. Massey, Durand, and Malone, *Beyond Smoke and Mirrors*, 145.

66. INS, *Statistical Yearbook*, 1998, 62. For a view critical of U.S. policy toward Mexican immigration, see Massey, Durand, and Malone, *Beyond Smoke and Mirrors*.

67. *New York Times*, June 7, 1992.

68. INS, *Statistical Yearbook*, 2001, 59.

69. Data are found in the annual reports of the INS. For example, only 804 Mexicans entered as managers or executives and 623 as professionals in 2001. Canada, which sent only one-eighth as many immigrants as Mexico, had figures of 3,769 and 623, respectively, in these categories. INS, *Statistical Yearbook*, 2001, 36.

70. *Los Angles Times*, Mar. 11, 1999.

71. *San Francisco Examiner*, Aug. 14, 1999.

72. *Los Angeles Times*, July 10, 1999.

73. *New York Times*, May 21, 2000; *Washington Post*, Mar. 2, 1999.

74. *New York Times*, Nov. 28, 1999.

75. *New York Times*, Apr. 11, 2003. The full report is Abel Valenzuela Jr. and Edwin Melendez, *Day Labor in New York: Findings from the NYDL Survey*, New School University, Apr. 11, 2003.

76. *San Jose Mercury News*, Nov. 27, 1999.

77. *New York Times*, Sept. 24, 2000. The white men were later caught and arrested.

78. *New York Times*, Nov. 28, 1999.

79. Ibid.; *Hispanic*, Oct. 31, 1997.

80. *New York Times*, May 27, 2001.

81. *New York Times*, July 18, 1997; July 22, 1997; Aug. 8, 1997; May 21, 2000.

82. *New York Times*, Dec. 23, 1997.

83. *Asheville Citizen-Times*, June 28, 1999.

84. Vilma Ortiz, "The Mexican Origin Population: Permanent Working Class or Emerging Middle Class?" in *Ethnic Los Angeles*, ed. Roger Waldinger and Mehdi Bozorgmehr (New York: Russell Sage Foundation, 1996), 251–57.

85. Ibid., 251–56.

86. Ibid., 273.

87. U.S. Census Bureau, Current Population Reports, *The Hispanic Population in the United States*, Mar. 2000. For data on the loss of foreign languages by Mexicans and other immigrants, see Alejandro Portes and Ruben G. Rumbaut, *Legacies: The Story of the Immigrant Second Generation* (Berkeley: University of California Press, 2001), chap. 6.

88. Ortiz, "The Mexican Origin Population," 251–57. See also Wayne Carroll, "Strangers in a Strange Land: The Status of the Hmong Immigrants in the United States in 1990" (unpublished paper, carrolwd@uwec.edu).

89. *Jersey Journal*, Mar. 24, 2001.

90. R. Rodriguez, *The Emerging Latino Middle Class* (Los Angeles: Pepperdine University Institute for Public Policy, 1996); R. Rodriguez, *From Newcomers to New Americans* (Washington, DC: National Immigration Forum, 1999).

91. Clark, *California Cauldron*, chap. 5. Other immigrants had higher rates of home ownership and higher incomes.

92. *New York Times*, Oct. 24, 2000.

93. Samuel O. Regalado, *Viva Baseball! Latin Major Leaguers and Their Special Hunger* (Urbana: University of Illinois Press, 1998), 17.

94. Ibid., 172–74; *New York Times*, Aug. 19, 1996.

95. *Los Angeles Times*, Mar. 1, 2000.

96. *New York Times*, Apr. 14, 2003.

97. *New York Times*, Nov. 15, 2000.

98. *Los Angeles Times*, Mar. 1, 2000.

99. Ibid.

100. *San Antonio Express-News*, June 30, 2000.

101. Ibid.

102. *Washington Post*, Feb. 19, 1999; quoted in Helen Rose Ebaugh and Janet Saltzman Chafetz, *Religion and the New Immigrants: Continuities and Adaptations in Immigrant Congregations* (Walnut Creek, CA: AltaMira Press, 2000), 125–52.

103. *USA Today*, Dec. 12, 2002.

104. Gonzales, *Mexicanos*, 196–202.

105. *Los Angeles Times*, May 26, 2000.

106. *Los Angeles Times*, Oct. 12, 1999; May 26, 2000; *New York Times*, Feb. 17, 2001; May 21, 2001. The history of organized labor's response to immigration is covered in Vernon Briggs, *Immigration and American Unionism* (Ithaca, NY: Cornell University Press, 2001).

107. *Los Angeles Times*, May 26, 2000.

108. *Third Force*, Feb. 28, 1998.

109. Gonzales, *Mexicanos*, chap. 8; Vicki O. Ruiz, *From Out of the Shadows: Mexican Women in Twentieth-Century America* (New York: Oxford University Press, 1998), chap. 5.

110. Ruiz, *From Out of the Shadows*, chap. 6.

111. See ibid. for a discussion of Mexican American women.

112. Richard Griswold del Castillo and Arnoldo De León, *North to Aztlan: A History of Mexican Americans in the United States* (New York: Twayne, 1996), 119–24; Gonzales, *Mexicanos*, 248–59.

113. *Lexington (Ky.) Herald-Leader*, Dec. 20, 1998.

114. *Los Angeles Times*, Feb. 14, 1999.

115. *Dallas Morning News*, Sept. 23, 1999.

116. Ibid.

117. *News and Record* (Piedmont Triad), Apr. 17, 2000.

118. Ibid.

119. *New York Times*, June 4, 1998; Dec. 18, 2000; Oct. 23, 2002. Californians in favor of bilingual education unsuccessfully challenged the demise of bilingual programs in federal court.

120. *New York Times*, Oct. 17, 2000.

121. *Los Angeles Times*, May 25, 1998.

122. See David M. Reimers, *Unwelcome Strangers: American Identity and the Turn against Immigration* (New York: Columbia University Press, 1998), 119–25; Raymond Tatalovich, "Official English as Nativist Backlash," in *Immigrants Out! The New Nativism and the Anti-immigrant Impulse in the United States,* ed. Juan F. Perea (New York: New York University Press, 1997), 78–102.

123. Ignacio M. Garcia, *Viva Kennedy: Mexican Americans in Search of Camelot* (College Station: Texas A&M University Press, 2000), 14–16.

124. Ibid., 31–32.

125. Ibid., 92. See Garcia for a discussion of Mexican American politics in the 1960s.

126. Garcia, *Viva Kennedy*, chaps. 6–7.

127. *New York Times*, Mar. 8, 2001.

128. U.S. Census Bureau, Current Population Survey, *The Hispanic Population in the United States*, Mar. 2000. Only one-fourth of all foreign-born Hispanics were citizens in 2000.

129. *New York Times*, Sept. 13, 1996.

130. Steve Sailer, "GOP-California Dream," *VDARE*, Nov. 21, 2000.

131. *New York Times*, July 5, 1999; *Los Angeles Times*, June 14, 1999; *Washington Post*, Oct. 15, 1999.

132. *Washington Post*, Nov. 20, 2000.

133. U.S. Department of Justice, INS, News Release, Nov. 15, 2000.

134. *Houston Chronicle*, Nov. 26, 2000.

135. *Dallas Morning News*, Sept. 19, 1999.

136. Lourdes Cue, "Election 2000: The Latino Factor," *Hispanic*, Jan./Feb. 2001, 25–26; *USA Today*, Aug. 27, 2002.

NOTES TO CHAPTER 5

1. *New York Times*, July 6, 2001; May 6, 2003; John Logan, *Immigrant Enclaves in the American Metropolis, 1990–2000* (Albany, NY: Lewis Mumford Center for Comparative Urban and Regional Research, 2001), 4.

2. Roberto Suro, *Counting the "Other Hispanics"* (Philadelphia: Pew Hispanic Center, 2002).

3. See Elizabeth Grieco, "Foreign-Born Hispanics in the United States" (Migration Information Service, 2003); U.S. Bureau of the Census, *The Hispanic Population of the United States, 2000* (May 2001).

4. Carlos B. Cordova and Raquel Pinderhughes, "Central and South Americans," in *A Nation of Peoples: A Sourcebook on America's Multicultural Heritage,* ed. Elliott Robert Barkan (Westport, CT: Greenwood Press, 1999), 106.

5. Alejandro Portes and Alex Stepick, *City on the Edge: The Transformation of Miami* (Berkeley: University of California Press, 1993), 151.

6. Ibid., 151–52.

7. *Miami Herald*, Apr. 11, 1987.

8. Associated Press, Sept. 7, 2001.

9. David E. Lopez, Eric Popkin, and Edward Telles, "Central Americans: At the Bottom, Struggling to Get Ahead," in *Ethnic Los Angeles,* ed. Roger Waldinger and Mehjdi Bozorgmehr (New York: Russell Sage Foundation, 1996), 281.

10. David M. Reimers, *Still the Golden Door: The Third World Comes to America,* 2nd ed. (New York: Columbia University Press, 1992), 202–3.

11. Ronald Fernandez, *America's Banquet of Cultures: Harnessing Ethnicity, Race, and Immigration in the Twenty-First Century* (Westport, CT: Praeger, 2000), 85.

12. Reimers, *Still the Golden Door*, 201–2.

13. Portes and Stepick, *City on the Edge*, 159–60.

14. Cordova and Pinderhughes, "Central and South Americans," 107; U.S. Bureau of the Census, *The Hispanic Population, Census 2000 Brief*, May 2001.

15. According to the Cuban Adjustment Act of 1966, practically any Cuban who reached American soil was considered to be a refugee. No other nationality had such an advantage.

16. Immigration and Naturalization Service (INS), *Annual Report*, 2001, 6.

17. Portes and Stepick, *City on the Edge*, chap. 7; *Daily News*, June 30, 1997.

18. Portes and Stepick, *City on the Edge*, 168–69.

19. Ibid., 154–55.

20. Ibid., 164.

21. Ibid., chap. 8.

22. Juan Gonzalez, *Harvest of Empire: A History of Latinos in America* (New York: Viking, 2000), 135–38.

23. Terry A. Repak, *Waiting on Washington: Central American Workers in the Nation's Capital* (Philadelphia: Temple University Press, 1995), 45–47.

24. Catherine L. Nolin Hanlon and W. George Lovell, "Flight, Exile, Repatriation, and Return: Guatemalan Refugee Scenarios, 1981–1998," in *The Maya Diaspora: Guatemalan Roots, New American Lives,* ed. James Loucky and Marilyn Moors (Philadelphia: Temple University Press, 2000), 35.

25. Ibid., 35–55.

26. See Gonzalez, *Harvest of Empire,* 138–39.

27. Associated Press, Dec. 30, 2000.

28. Data are from INS, *Annual Reports* and *Statistical Yearbooks.*

29. *Washington Post,* Feb. 9, 2000.

30. *Fort Lauderdale Sun-Sentinel,* Dec. 16, 2000. Reno said that in the future such cases should be decided when new rules were drafted.

31. Sarah J. Mahler, *American Dreaming: Immigrant Life on the Margins* (Princeton, NJ: Princeton University Press, 1995), 39.

32. Cordova and Pinderhughes, "Central and South Americans," 104.

33. Cecilia Menjívar, *Fragmented Ties: Salvadoran Immigrant Networks in America* (Berkeley: University of California Press, 2000), 104–5.

34. Data are from INS, *Annual Reports* and *Statistical Yearbooks.*

35. Gonzalez, *Harvest of Empire,* 143.

36. INS, *Statistical Yearbook,* 2001, 89.

37. *New York Times,* May 5, 1999.

38. Menjívar, *Fragmented Ties,* 84–89. The new TPS was granted only to those who had remained in the United States since that date. INS, *News Release,* Nov. 2, 2002.

39. *Washington Post,* May 26, 1999.

40. INS, *Statistical Yearbook,* 2001, 89–90.

41. *Los Angeles Times,* Oct. 31, 2000.

42. *USA Today,* May 1, 2001; *New York Times,* Mar. 23, 2001; Apr. 26, 2001.

43. *Los Angeles Times,* Oct. 31, 2000.

44. *Washington Post,* Jan. 2, 2001; *New York Times,* May 1, 2001.

45. *Migration News* 8 (Jan. 2001); *Sacramento Bee,* Dec. 19, 2000.

46. *The Modesto (CA) Bee,* Jan. 1, 2001; *Washington Post,* Jan. 2, 2001; *New York Times,* Feb. 20, 2001.

47. Associated Press, Dec. 15, 2000. For a detailed account of the struggle for legality, see Susan Bibler Coutin, *Legalizing Moves: Salvadoran Immigrants' Struggle for U.S. Residency* (Ann Arbor: University of Michigan Press, 2000).

48. Agencia EFE, Jan. 16, 2001.

49. INS, *Statistical Yearbook,* 2001, 19.

50. *New York Times,* Mar. 3, 2001; *Christian Science Monitor,* May 21, 2001; *Washington Post,* May 21, 2001.

51. INS, *Annual Report,* 2000, 6. As of May 2003, nationals of Burundi, El

Salvador, Honduras, Liberia, Montserrat, Nicaragua, Sierra Leone, Somalia, and Sudan were covered by TPS. Bureau of Citizenship and Immigration Service, May 8, 2003.

52. INS, *Statistical Yearbook*, 2001, 13.

53. Guillermina Jasso, Douglas S. Massey, Mark R. Rosenzweig, and James P. Smith, "The New Immigrant Survey Pilet (NIS-P): An Overview and New Findings about U.S. Legal Immigrants at Admission," *Demography* 37 (Feb. 2000): 136.

54. *Wall Street Journal*, Nov. 22, 2002. Eighty percent of the funds came from the United States.

55. Abel Valenzuela Jr. and Edwin Melendez, *Day Laborers in New York: Findings from the NYDL Survey*, New School University, Apr. 11, 2003. The authors found few women in the New York region, but many more in Los Angeles.

56. See the results by Valenzuela and Melendez, *Day Labor in New York*.

57. *New York Times*, May 21, 1999.

58. Ibid.

59. Mahler, *American Dreaming*, chap. 4.

60. Bureau of the Census, *Hispanic Population. 2000*. The INS no longer keeps records of where immigrants settle, but it does note the "intended" residence of newcomers. Throughout the 1990s, California claimed the largest number of Central Americans who indicated that their intended residence was California.

61. Lopez, Popkin, and Telles, "Central Americans," 283.

62. Associated Press, Jan. 3, 2001.

63. Repak, *Waiting on Washington*, 50.

64. *Washington Post*, Dec. 6, 1999.

65. Ibid.

66. Repak, *Waiting on Washington*, 3.

67. Ibid., 112.

68. Ibid., 58–61.

69. Ibid., 90–110.

70. Ibid., 122–24.

71. Ibid., chap. 7.

72. *Bergen (County) Record*, Mar. 27, 2000.

73. *Bergen (County) Record*, Aug. 24, 1998.

74. Menjívar, *Fragmented Ties*, 89–101.

75. Brian J. Godfrey, *Neighborhoods in Transition: The Making of San Francisco's Ethnic and Nonconformist Communities* (Berkeley: University of California Press, 1988), 112–13, 136–48.

76. *Washington Post*, Nov. 29, 1999.

77. Menjívar, *Fragmented Ties*, 59.

78. *New York Times*, Dec. 25, 2000.

79. *New York Times*, Jan. 1, 2001.

80. Associated Press, Mar. 9, 1999.

81. *Los Angeles Times*, Feb. 10, 1999.

82. *Washington Post*, Nov. 14, 1998; *New York Times*, Jan. 18, 1990.

83. *Washington Post*, May 1, 2002. Persons covered had to be in the United States before December 30, 1998.

84. *Washington Post*, Feb. 9, 1999.

85. *New York Times*, Jan. 18, 1999.

86. See Coutin, *Legalizing Moves*, for organizational life among Central Americans.

87. *New York Times*, Aug. 24, 1995.

88. Ibid.

89. Leon Fink, *The Maya of Morganton: Work and Community in the Nuevo New South* (Chapel Hill: University of North Carolina Press, 2003), 170–71.

90. Roberto Suro, *The Strangers among Us: How Latino Immigration Is Transforming America* (New York: Knopf, 1998), 31–32.

91. Fink, *Maya of Morganton*, 157.

92. Suro, *Strangers among Us*, 32–50; Nestor Rodriguez and Jacqueline Maria Hagan, "Maya Urban Villagers in Houston," in Loucky and Moors, *Maya Diaspora*, chap. 13.

93. See the essays in Loucky and Moors, *Maya Diaspora*.

94. Allan F. Burns, *Maya in Exile: Guatemalans in Florida* (Philadelphia: Temple University Press, 1993), chap. 4.

95. Leon Fink and Alvis D. Dunn, "The Maya of Morganton," in Loucky and Moors, *Maya Diaspora*, 175–93.

96. The history of the Maya in Morganton is told in Fink, *Maya of Morganton*.

97. James Loucky, "Maya in a Modern Metropolis: Establishing New Lives and Livelihoods in Los Angeles," in Loucky and Moors, *Maya Diaspora*, chap. 15.

98. INS, *Statistical Yearbook*, 2001, 62.

99. Burns, *Maya in Exile*, 94.

100. Ibid., chap. 5.

101. John Bowe, "Annals of Labor: Nobodies, Slavery in South Florida," *New Yorker*, Apr. 21, 28, 2003, 124. The plight of these Indian immigrants is covered graphically in Bowe's article.

102. Burns, *Maya in Exile*, 118–20.

103. *Cultural Survival Quarterly* 10 (Apr. 30, 1995).

104. Figures based on INS, *Annual Reports* and *Statistical Yearbooks*.

105. *Los Angeles Times*, Aug. 13, 1998.

106. *New York Times*, Oct. 4, 1998.

107. Associated Press, Dec. 30, 2000.

108. Silvio Torres-Saillant and Ramona Hernandez, *The Dominican Americans* (Westport, CT: Greenwood Press, 1998), 33; Eugenia Georges, *The Making of a Transnational Community: Migration, Development, and Cultural Change in the Dominican Republic* (New York: Columbia University Press, 1990), 28.

109. Figures based on INS, *Annual Reports* and *Statistical Yearbooks*.

110. For a view that focuses on the rural migration, see Glenn Hendricks, *The Dominican Diaspora: From the Dominican Republic to New York City—Villages in Transition* (New York: Teachers College Press, Columbia University, 1974). See a broader view in Torres-Saillant and Hernandez, *Dominican Americans*, 34–36; Sherri Grasmuck and Patricia R. Pessar, *Between Two Islands: Dominican International Migration* (Berkeley: University of California Press, 1991), chap. 4.

111. Torres-Saillant and Hernandez, *Dominican Americans*, chap. 2.

112. *New York Times*, Dec. 17, 1986; Dec. 13, 1992.

113. Hendricks, *Dominican Diaspora*, chap. 4.

114. Grasmuck and Pessar, *Between Two Islands*, chap. 6.

115. Suro, *Strangers among Us*, 179.

116. John Logan, "Immigrant Enclaves in the American Metropolis, 1990–2000," Lewis Mumford Center for Comparative Urban and Regional Research, July 3, 2001.

117. *New York Times*, Nov. 19, 1986.

118. Patricia Pessar, *A Visa for a Dream: Dominicans in the United States* (New York: Allyn and Bacon, 1995), 39.

119. *New York Times*, July 30, 2002.

120. Ramon Hernandez, Francisco Rivera-Batiz, and Roberto Agodini, *Dominican New Yorkers: A Socioeconomic Profile*, Dominican Research Monographs (New York: City University of New York, 1995), 46–48; Grasmuck and Pessar, *Between Two Islands*, chap. 7.

121. Hernandez, Rivera-Batiz, and Agodini, *Dominican New Yorkers*, 50.

122. See ibid., 25–41.

123. For data, see ibid., 33–41.

124. *New York Times*, Nov. 10, 1997

125. Ibid.; *New York Times, Dec. 16, 1997*; Torres-Saillant and Hernandez, *Dominican New Yorkers*.

126. *New York Times*, May 4, 2000.

127. Pessar, *Visa for a Dream*, 38.

128. *New York Times*, July 10, 1992; July 13, 1992.

129. *New York Times*, Oct. 17, 1993.

130. Pessar, *Visa for a Dream*, 38–39.

131. *New York Times*, Sept. 4, 1993. See Samuel O. Regalado, *Viva Baseball! Latin Major Leaguers and Their Special Hunger* (Urbana: University of Illinois Press, 1998), for a discussion of Latin Americans and baseball.

132. Patricia R. Pessar and Pamela M. Graham, "Dominicans: Transnational

Identities and Local Politics," in *New Immigrants in New York,* ed. Nancy Foner (New York: Columbia University Press, 2001), 258–59. Because of dual citizenship, New York Dominicans have also voted in Dominican elections and had an impact there.

133. *Newsday,* July 2, 1990.

134. Associated Press, Oct. 2, 1998. A one-year lottery was created as part of the IRCA. After it was renewed, the diversity visas became part of general immigration law in 1990.

135. U.S. Dept. of Justice, INS, and U.S. Dept. of Labor, Bureau of International Labor Affairs, *The Triennial Comprehensive Report of Immigration* (Washington, DC: Government Printing Office, 1999), 57.

136. INS, *Annual Report,* 2001, 19.

137. U.S. Bureau of the Census, Current Population Reports, *The Foreign Born Population in the United States,* Mar. 2000, issued January 2001.

138. Cordova and Pinderhughes, "Central and South Americans," 107.

139. U.S. Bureau of the Census, Current Population Reports, *Foreign Born Population in the United States.*

140. See Adriana Marshall, "Emigration of Argentines to the United States," in *When Borders Don't Divide: Labor Migration and Refugee Movements in the Americas,* ed. Patricia R. Pessar (New York: Center for Migration Studies, 1988), 129–31.

141. Gil Loescher and John A. Scanlan, *Calculated Kindness: America's Half-Open Door, 1945–Present* (New York: Free Press, 1986), 101.

142. Judith Laik Elkin, "Latin American Jewry Today: The Demography of Latin American Jewry," *American Jewish Yearbook* 85 (1985): 70.

143. *San Francisco Chronicle,* June 2, 2002.

144. *St. Petersburg Times,* June 19, 2001.

145. Ibid.

146. Associated Press, Aug. 12, 2002.

147. *San Francisco Chronicle,* June 2, 2002.

148. *Washington Post,* June 7, 2001.

149. Nancy Foner, *From Ellis Island to JFK: New York's Two Great Waves of Immigration* (New Haven, CT: Yale University Press, 2000), 72–73, 100–101.

150. Ibid., 94.

151. David Kyle, *Transnational Peasants: Migration, Networks and Ethnicity in Andean Ecuador* (Baltimore: Johns Hopkins University Press, 2000), 64–71.

152. William Kleinknecht, *The New Ethnic Mobs: The Changing Face of Organized Crime in America* (New York: Free Press, 1996), 258–59.

153. Latin American and Caribbean Center, *The Colombian Diaspora in South Florida* (Miami: Florida International University, 2001), 3.

154. Ibid.

155. Ibid., 4.

156. Gonzalez, *Harvest of Empire*, 156–58.

157. *New York Times*, July 15, 2002.

158. Hiram Ruiz, "Colombians Flee War without End," Migration Information Sources, Dec. 1, 2002, 2.

159. Ibid.

160. Ibid., 3.

161. *New York Times*, Apr. 10, 2001.

162. Gonzalez, *Harvest of Empire*, 159–60.

163. *Bergen (County) Record*, Sept. 5, 1999; *Los Angeles Times*, Oct. 13, 1999; *New York Times*, Apr. 10, 2001.

164. *Los Angeles Times*, Oct. 13, 1999.

165. *Fort Lauderdale Sun-Sentinel*, July 20, 1999.

166. *Miami Herald*, July 21, 1999.

167. *Bergen (County) Record*, Nov. 4, 2003.

168. *Houston Chronicle*, July 21, 1999; *New York Times*, Mar. 5, 2000; INS, *Statistical Yearbook*, 2001, 89.

169. *Boston Globe*, Nov. 1, 2000.

170. Latin American and Caribbean Center, *Colombian Diaspora*, 6–8.

171. Maxine L. Margolis, *Little Brazil: An Ethnography of Brazilian Immigrants in New York City* (Princeton, NJ: Princeton University Press, 1994), 13; INS, *Statistical Yearbook*, 1998, 27; INS, *Statistical Yearbook*, 2001, 49. Over half entered as immediate family members of U.S. citizens.

172. Margolis, *Little Brazil*, 15–16.

173. *The San Diego Union-Tribune*, Aug. 2, 2002.

174. *News from Brazil*, Mar. 31, 1996.

175. Margolis, *Little Brazil*, chap. 11.

176. *Miami Herald*, May 6, 1991.

177. *Los Angeles Times*, July 13, 1995.

178. *San Francisco Chronicle*, Feb. 21, 1988.

179. *Atlanta Journal-Constitution*, Sept. 18, 2000.

180. Margolis, *Little Brazil*, 31–42.

181. Ibid., chap. 4.

182. Ibid., chap. 5.

183. Ibid., 235–41.

184. Ibid., chaps. 8–9.

NOTES TO CHAPTER 6

1. K. Scott Wong, "War Comes to Chinatown: Social Transformation and the Chinese of California," in *The Way We Really Were: The Golden State in the Second Great War*, ed. Roger W. Lotchin (Urbana: University of Illinois Press, 2000),

164. See also Ronald Takaki, *Strangers from a Different Shore: A History of Asian Americans* (Boston: Little, Brown, 1989), chap. 10.

2. Sucheng Chan, *Asian Americans: An Interpretive History* (New York: Twayne, 1991), 140. See also David M. Reimers, *Still the Golden Door: The Third World Comes to America,* 2nd ed. (New York: Columbia University Press, 1992), chap. 2.

3. Erika Lee, *At America's Gates: Chinese Immigration during the Exclusion Era, 1882–1943* (Chapel Hill: University of North Carolina Press, 2003), 242.

4. Reimers, *Still the Golden Door*, chaps. 1–2; Linda Gordon, "Asian Immigration since World War II" (paper presented at the Lehrman Institute Study Group, New York City, May 20, 1987), 6–7; Morrison G. Wong, "Chinese Americans," in *Asian Americans: Contemporary Trends and Issues,* ed. Pyong Gap Min (Thousand Oaks, CA: Sage, 1995), 65–66. The 10,000 number for Hong Kong was increased to 20,000 a few years later, giving ethnic Chinese a potential total of more than 60,000 slots.

5. Dept. of Commerce, U.S. Bureau of the Census, *Current Population Survey (CPS)*, Feb. 2002.

6. Wong, "Chinese Americans," 58–70.

7. Ibid., 77.

8. A few Taiwanese also entered as spouses of American servicemen.

9. Immigration and Naturalization Service (INS), *Statistical Yearbook*, 2001, 51.

10. Hsiang-shui Chen, *Chinatown No More* (Ithaca, NY: Cornell University Press, 1992), 6–7.

11. Judy Yung, "Chinese," in *A Nation of Peoples: A Sourcebook of America's Multicultural Heritage,* ed. Elliott Robert Barkan (Westport, CT: Greenwood Press, 1999), 132.

12. *New York Times*, Nov. 18, 2002.

13. George Borjas, *An Evaluation of the Foreign Student Program* (Washington, DC: Center for Immigration Studies, 2002), 4. Some observers place the figure higher.

14. INS, *Statistical Yearbook*, 2001, 13.

15. Data from the INS, *Statistical Yearbooks*.

16. INS, *Statistical Yearbook*, 1998, 25; *Statistical Yearbook*, 2001, 18. The Immigrant Act of 1990 increased the quota for all nations by several thousand.

17. Min Zhou, "Chinese: Divergent Destinies in Immigrant New York," in *New Immigrants in New York,* ed. Nancy Foner (New York: Columbia University Press, 2001), 158–59.

18. John Horton, *The Politics of Diversity: Immigration Resistance and Change in Monterey Park, California* (Philadelphia: Temple University Press, 1995), 21–22.

19. Figures based on Dept. of Commerce, U.S. Bureau of the Census, 2000 (from American Fact Finder).

20. Jianli Zhao, *Strangers in the City: The Atlanta Chinese: Their Community and Stories of Their Lives* (New York: Routledge, 2002), 76–77.

21. U.S. Bureau of the Census, *Asian Population, 2000*; U.S. Bureau of the Census, *Foreign Born Population Living in the U.S., Regions by Sex and World Region of Birth, March, 2000,* Internet release, Jan. 3, 2001. The INS also reported similar patterns of settlement indicated by the "intended residence" of Asian immigrants in the 1990s. INS, *Statistical Yearbook, 1998,* 71–77.

22. Bernard Wong, *Ethnicity and Entrepreneurship: The New Chinese Immigrants in the San Francisco Bay Area* (Boston: Allyn and Bacon, 1998), 19–20.

23. Chen, *Chinatown No More,* 128–43.

24. AnnaLee Saxenian, *Silicon Valley's New Immigrant Entrepreneurs* (San Francisco: Public Policy Institute of California, 1999), 34.

25. Ibid., 16.

26. Wong, *Ethnicity,* 38.

27. Saxenian, *Silicon Valley's New Immigrant Entrepreneurs,* viii.

28. Wong, *Ethnicity,* 39.

29. Ibid., 40.

30. *New York Times,* Aug. 11, 2002.

31. Franklin Ng, *The Taiwanese Americans* (Westport, CT: Greenwood Press, 1998), 22–24; Chen, *Chinatown No More,* 68–74.

32. Chen, *Chinatown No More,* 105–27.

33. Wong, *Ethnicity,* 45–50.

34. Ibid., 54–55.

35. Ibid., 65–79; Chen, *Chinatown No More,* 104–27.

36. See Takaki, *Strangers from a Different Shore,* 427–29, for the difficulties of making a living in restaurants.

37. For an excellent account of New York's garment shops, see Xiaolan Bao, *Holding Up More Than Half the Sky: Chinese Women Garment Workers in New York City, 1948–1982* (Urbana: University of Illinois Press, 2001).

38. Ibid., chap. 7.

39. *New York Times,* Nov. 21, 2001.

40. See the report issued by the Asian American Federation of New York, *One Year after September 11th: An Economic Impact Study* (New York, Nov. 2002). Even parking became very difficult after the attack.

41. *New York Times,* Nov. 21, 2001; June 29, 2002. See the detailed study of the economic problems of the city's Manhattan Chinatown, Asian American Federation of New York, *One Year after September 11th.*

42. Wong, *Ethnicity,* 55–58.

43. Peter Kwong, *Forbidden Workers: Illegal Chinese Immigrants and American Labor* (New York: New Press, 1997), 1–3.

44. *New York Times*, Feb. 15, 1997. In addition to claims about political persecution in China, asylum could be obtained if an immigrant could prove he or she would be persecuted by the Chinese government for opposing the one child per family policy.

45. *New York Times*, Feb. 15, 1997; Apr. 21, 2000.

46. *Savannah Morning News*, Aug. 13, 1999.

47. *New York Times*, June 26, 2000; July 22, 2001.

48. See Kwong, *Forbidden Workers*, for a detailed account of how the system worked.

49. Yung, "Chinese," 132.

50. Ko-Lin Chin, *Smuggled Chinese: Clandestine Immigration to the United States* (Philadelphia: Temple University Press, 1999), 115–19.

51. Ng, *Taiwanese Americans*, 56–57.

52. Wong, *Ethnicities*, 18–32; Ng, *Taiwanese Americans*, 64–72; Saxenian, *Silicon Valley's Engineers*, chap. 3.

53. Min Zhou, "Social Capital in Chinatown: The Role of Community-Based Organizations and Families in the Adaptation of the Younger Generation," in *Beyond Black and White: New Faces and Voices in U.S. Schools*, ed. Maxine Seller and Lois Weiss (Albany: State University of New York Press, 1997), 202.

54. A number of scholars have criticized the use of this phrase. See, for example, Wong, "Chinese Americans"; Yung, "Chinese"; Harry H. L. Kitano and Roger Daniels, *Asian Americans: Emerging Minorities* (Englewood Cliffs, NJ: Prentice-Hall, 1988), 48–50.

55. *New York Times*, Mar. 20, 1999.

56. *New York Times*, Oct. 18, 1998.

57. Chan, *Asian Americans*, 176–78.

58. *New York Times*, June 18, 2002.

59. *New York Times*, Mar. 4, 1989; Oct. 4, 1993.

60. Yung, "Chinese," 134.

61. Ibid.

62. *New York Times*, Jan. 29, 2002.

63. For the struggle, see Horton, *Politics of Diversity*.

64. India received a similar quota in 1946.

65. *Northwest Asian Weekly*, Nov. 24, 1995; *Filipino Express*, Jan. 22, 1995.

66. *Northwest Asian Weekly*, Nov. 24, 1995.

67. Barbara M. Posadas, *Filipino Americans* (Westport, CT: Greenwood Press, 1999), 26–27.

68. Elliott R. Barkan, *Asian and Pacific Islander Migration to the United States: A Model of New Global Patterns* (Westport, CT: Greenwood Press, 1992), 201.

69. Posadas, *Filipino Americans*, 27–28.

70. Ibid., 43–44.

71. Ibid. By 2003 only 12,000 Filipinos veterans still lived in the United States and 35,000 in the Philippines.

72. INS, *Statistical Yearbook*, 2001, 19.

73. Posadas, *Filipino Americans*, 38.

74. Ibid., 39.

75. *USA Today*, Aug. 20, 2002.

76. Takaki, *Strangers from a Different Shore*, 434.

77. Antonio J. A. Pido, *The Philipinos in America* (New York: Center for Migration Studies, 1996), 77.

78. Reimers, *Still the Golden Door*, 88.

79. Quoted in Takaki, *Strangers from a Different Shore*, 433.

80. While the 1990 immigration act increased the occupational preferences, most of the slots still went for family unification, which were increased as well by the 1990 act.

81. U.S. Bureau of the Census, *Asians*, 2000.

82. *Filipino Reporter*, June 10, 1999.

83. *Filipino Reporter*, Feb. 6, 1997.

84. *Filipino Reporter*, Sept. 26, 1996.

85. INS, *The "Mail-Order Bride" Industry and Its Impact on U.S. Immigration*, Dec. 9, 1999.

86. Ibid., 2.

87. Ibid., 4.

88. *Wall Street Journal*, Sept. 2, 1999.

89. Posadas, *Filipino Americans*, 109.

90. INS, *The "Mail-Order Bride,"* 5.

91. *Wall Street Journal*, Aug. 28, 1989.

92. Posadas, *Filipino Americans*, 121.

93. *New York Times*, May 26, 1996.

94. Pido, *Philipinos in America*, 78–82. For example, in 2001 Filipino women outnumbered men by 33,642 to 22,773. INS, *Statistical Yearbook*, 2001, 59.

95. See the state summaries in Dept. of Commerce, Bureau of the Census, *Census, 2000* (from American Fact Finder).

96. Kevin F. McCarthy and Georges Vernez, *Immigration in a Changing Economy: California's Experience* (Santa Monica, CA: Rand, 1997), 38. See U.S. Bureau of the Census, CPS, *Foreign Born: Asians, 2000*.

97. Nathaniel S. Ramirez, *Philippine American Ancestry* (1999–2001), 8.

98. *Filipinas Magazine*, Oct. 31, 1994.

99. Steffi San Buenaventura, "Filipino Religion at Home and Abroad: Historical Roots and Immigrant Transformation," in *Religions in Asian America: Building Faith Communities,* ed. Pyong Gap Min and Jung Ha Kim (Walnut Creek, CA: AltaMira Press, 2002), 144, 171–74.

100. *Asian Week*, June 20, 1996. June 12, 1898, was the date that Filipino leader Emilio Aquinaldo declared independence following defeat of Spain in the Philippines.

101. For the 1930s, see Dorothy B. Fujita -Rony, *American Workers, Colonial Power: Philippine Seattle and the Transpacific West, 1919–1941* (Berkeley: University of California Press, 2002), 162–63.

102. *San Francisco Chronicle*, Mar. 23, 1998; Pido, *Filipinos in America*, 12; Posadas, *Filipino Americans*, 140–43.

103. Posadas, *Philipino Americans*, 84–89.

104. *Asian Week Archives*, Dec. 6–12, 2002; Posadas, *Filipino Americans*, 89–94.

105. Posadas, *Philipino Americans*, 90.

106. McCarthy and Vernez, *Immigration*, 38–39; *Filipinas Magazine*, Oct. 31, 1994.

107. McCarthy and Vernez, *Immigration*, 41; Posadas, *Filipino Americans*, 118–19. See also U.S. Commission on Civil Rights, *The Economic Status of Americans of Asian Descent: An Exploratory Investigation* (Washington, DC: Government Printing Office, 1988).

108. Posadas, *Philipino Americans*, 119.

109. Ibid., 111–19; Ramirez, *Philippine American Ancestry*, 1–9. For a particularly pessimistic view blaming racism for much of the difference between Filipinos and whites, see Pido, *Filipinos in America*, chap. 5.

110. *Filipinas Magazine*, Oct. 31, 1994.

111. *Filipinas Magazine*, Mar. 3, 1995.

112. Scott Rohrer, "Japanese War Brides" (paper in author's possession). Rohrer says the exact number of war brides is unknown but is estimated to be between 35,000 and 50,000 for the period from 1945 until 1960.

113. Ibid., 13–14.

114. Ibid., 12.

115. Paul R. Spickard, *Japanese Americans: The Formation and Transformation of an Ethnic Group* (New York: Twayne, 1996), 141; Evelyn Glenn, *Issei, Nisei, War Bride: Three Generations of Japanese American Women in Domestic Service* (Philadelphia: Temple University Press, 1986), 58–65, 231–41.

116. See the discussion in Rohrer, "Japanese War Brides."

117. See Akiko S. Hosler, *Japanese Immigrant Entrepreneurs in New York City: A New Wave of Ethnic Business* (New York: Garland, 1998).

118. Ibid., 63–76, 133–36. Many of these new businesses do not employ family members.

119. Gordon, "Asian Immigration," 7; INS, *Statistical Yearbook*, 2001, 19.

120. Quoted in Ji-Yeon Yuh, "Immigrants on the Front Line; Korean Military Brides in America, 1950–1996" (Ph.D. diss., University of Pennsylvania, 1999), xii, 237–38. Yuh herself uses a figure of 100,000 for the period from 1950 to 1989.

121. Daniel B. Lee, "Korean Women Married to Servicemen," in *Korean American Women Living in Two Cultures*, ed. Young In Song and Ailee Moon (Los Angeles: Academia Koreana, Keimyung-Baylo University Press, 1997), 97.

122. Figures from the INS provided by Marian Smith of the INS (e-mails to author, Oct. 14, 2001, Nov. 20, 2001). The Evan B. Donald Adoption Institute (*International Adoption Facts*, Mar. 6, 2003) reported in 2003 that from 1971 to 2001 Americans had adopted 265,677 overseas children. More than one-quarter of these children were from Korea.

123. Helen Zia, *Asian American Dreams: The Emergence of an American People* (New York: Farrar, Straus and Giroux, 2000), 265; Gordon, "Asian Immigration"; INS, *Statistical Yearbooks*; Illsoo Kim, *New Urban Immigrants: The Korean Community in New York* (Princeton, NJ: Princeton University Press, 1981), 42.

124. Gordon, "Asian Immigration," 19.

125. *USA Today*, July 12, 2001; Karen Koenig, "Asia's Precious Export: Americans Looking to Adopt Healthy Babies Are Flocking to China and Korea," *Asian Week*, Aug. 25, 1995; Zia, *Asian American Dreams*, 265–66. The most recent published figures given by the INS noted 1,705 children adopted in 1998. INS, *Statistical Yearbook*, 1998, 65.

126. Kim, *New Urban Immigrants*, 59–60.

127. Ibid., 37.

128. *New York Times*, Oct. 26, 1986.

129. Min, "Korean Americans," 204.

130. Kim, *New Urban Immigrants*, 147–48.

131. Ibid., 160–61.

132. Ibid., 162.

133. Min, "Korean Americans," 205.

134. Ibid., 206–8.

135. Pyong Gap Min, *Caught in the Middle: Korean Merchants in America's Multiethnic Cities* (Berkeley: University of California Press, 1996), 35.

136. Quoted in Ji-Ueon Yuh, "Immigrants on the Front Line," 15–16. Some of the "camptowns" dated to 1945, when the United States first occupied South Korea. Although they disappeared when American troops withdrew, they reappeared during the Korean War and have remained ever since.

137. See Siyon Rhee, "Separation and Divorce among Korean Immigrant Families," in Song and Moon, *Korean American Women*, 151–60.

138. See Yuh, "Immigrants on the Front Line," especially chaps. 3–5; Min, "Korean Americans," 219–20; Melissa London, "Korean Family Violence on the Rise," *Northwest Asian Weekly*, Aug. 1, 1997; Young I. Song and Ailee Moon, "Domestic Violence against Women in Korean Immigrant Families: Cultural, Psychological, and Socioeconomic Perspectives," in Song and Moon, *Korean American Women*, 161–73.

139. Kim, *New Urban Immigrants*, 169.

140. Ibid., 169–76.

141. Min, *Caught in the Middle*, 64–65.

142. Min, "Korean Americans," 209.

143. Pyong Gap Min, "Koreans: An 'Institutionally Complete Community' in New York," in *New Immigrants in New York*, rev. ed., ed. Nancy Foner (New York: Columbia University Press, 2001), 181.

144. Min, *Caught in the Middle*, 53.

145. Ibid., 57.

146. See Kyeyoung Park, *The Korean American Dream: Immigrants and Small Business in New York City* (Ithaca, NY: Cornell University Press, 1997).

147. Min, *Caught in the Middle*, 61.

148. *New York Times*, Oct. 26, 1986; *Washington Post*, May 16, 1999; *Bergen (County) Record*, Aug. 23, 1998.

149. *Washington Post*, May 16, 1999.

150. See Park, *Korean American Dream*; Min, *Caught in the Middle*, for overall views on these issue.

151. *New York Times*, Feb. 21, 2001.

152. *The Atlanta Journal-Constitution*, Sept. 13, 1999.

153. *New York Times*, Feb. 15, 2001.

154. *Washington Post*, May 7, 1995; Min, *Caught in the Middle*, 74–80.

155. Zia, *Asian American Dreams*, 171.

156. *New York Times*, Jan. 6, 1997.

157. Samuel R. Cacas, "Killings of Grocers in D.C. Prompts Concern over Asian-Black Relations," *Asian Week*, Oct. 29, 1993.

158. *Washington Post*, May 7, 1995.

159. *New York Times*, Mar. 11, 1996.

160. *Washington Post*, May 7, 1995.

161. Won Moo Hurh, *The Korean Americans* (Westport, CT: Greenwood Press, 1998), 92–93; Pyong Gap Min, "The Burden of Labor on Korean American Wives in and outside the Family," in Song and Moon, *Korean American Women*, 94–97.

162. Park, *Korean American Dream*, 118–21.

163. Min, *Caught in the Middle*, 59–61.

164. See Park, *Korean American Dream*; Hurh, *Korean Americans*, 131–36; INS, *Statistical Yearbook*, 2001, 19.

165. Hurh, *Korean Americans*, 46.

166. *New York Times*, May 16, 2003.

167. *New York Times*, Dec. 4, 2003.

168. *New York Times*, Apr. 16, 2003.

169. Min, "Koreans: An 'Institutionally Complete Community,'" 173–74.

170. Hurh, *Korean Americans*, 109.

171. *Atlanta Journal-Constitution*, Feb. 23, 1997.
172. *Fort Worth Star-Telegram*, Apr. 3, 1999.
173. Min, "Korean Americans," 14–15.
174. Hurh, *Korean Americans*, 108–15.
175. See, for example, *New York Times*, Oct. 10, 2001.
176. Nancy Foner, *From Ellis Island to JFK: New York's Two Great Waves of Immigration* (New Haven, CT: Yale University Press, 2000), 216.
177. Ibid., 215.
178. Pyong Gap Min, *Changes and Conflicts: Korean Immigrant Families in New York* (Boston: Allyn and Bacon, 1998), 67–68.
179. Hurh, *Korean Americans*, 94–96.
180. Michael Barone, *The New Americans: How the Melting Pot Can Work Again* (Washington, DC: Regnery Publishing, 2001), 272. Kim was also convicted of campaign finance violations.
181. U.S. Bureau of the Census, *Asian Population, 2000*.

NOTES TO CHAPTER 7

1. Immigration and Naturalization Service (INS) *Statistical Yearbook*, 2001, 19.
2. Figures from U.S. Dept. of Commerce, 2000 Census of Population, *The Asian Population*, 2000 (issued Feb. 2002), 8.
3. *New India-Times*, Feb. 26, 1999.
4. *New York Times*, Mar. 24, 2003.
5. *Little India*, Oct. 31, 1997.
6. Johanna Lessinger, *From the Ganges to the Hudson: Indian Immigrants in New York City* (Boston: Allyn and Bacon, 1995), 9–11; *New York Times*, Jan. 12, 2003.
7. Karen Isaksen Leonard, *The South Asian Americans* (Westport, CT: Greenwood Press, 1997), 75.
8. Ibid., 71.
9. *New York Times*, Feb. 3, 2003.
10. *New York Times*, Nov. 18, 2002.
11. A.T. & T., "Profile of Asian Indians in the USA," *Handbook for Asian Indians*, 1997–1998. For lower figures, see Madhulika S. Khandelwal, *Becoming American, Being Indian: An Immigrant Community in New York City* (Ithaca, NY: Cornell University Press, 2002), chap. 4.
12. *Chicago Tribune*, Sept. 10, 1998.
13. *Wall Street Journal*, Jan. 27, 1987.
14. Leonard, *South Asian Americans*, 78.
15. Ibid.
16. Ibid.; Khandelwal, *Becoming American, Being Indian*. 92–99.

17. *Washington Post*, Oct. 9, 1999.

18. *New Jersey Business*, Mar. 16, 1998.

19. *San Francisco Chronicle*, Oct. 6, 1999; AnnaLee Saxenian, *Silicon Valley's New Immigrant Entrepreneurs* (Los Angeles: Public Policy Institute of California, 1999), 9.

20. *India West*, June 25, 1999.

21. *New York Times*, May 30, 2001. Some firms have then contracted these employees to work for other firms. Such practices have resulted in controversies over the legality of using L-1 visas in this manner. L-1 visas numbered 57,700 in 2002.

22. *Wall Street Journal*, Oct. 5, 1999.

23. *Washington Post*, Oct. 9, 1999.

24. *New York Times*, Jan. 23, 2000; Jan. 27, 2000; Feb. 25, 2000; Feb. 29, 2000.

25. Tunku Varadarajan, "A Patel Motel Cartel?" *New York Times Magazine*, July 4, 1999, 36–37.

26. Ibid.

27. Ibid., 38.

28. See ibid., 36–38.

29. Hugh Davis Graham, *Collision Course: The Strange Convergence of Affirmative Action and Immigration Policy* (New York: Oxford University Press, 2002), 146–50.

30. *Atlanta Journal-Constitution*, July 2, 2002.

31. *Wall Street Journal*, Sept. 9, 1997; Small Business Administration, *Minorities in Business, 2002* (Washington, DC: Government Printing Office, 2001); *Atlanta Journal-Constitution*, July 24, 2002.

32. *India Currents*, Apr. 4, 1994.

33. *Central Penn Business Journal*, Oct. 1998.

34. Madhulika S. Khandelwal, "Indian Immigrants in Queens, New York City: Patterns of Spatial Concentration and Distribution, 1965–1990," in *Nation and Migration: The Politics in the South Asian Diaspora*, ed. Peter van der Veer (Philadelphia: University of Pennsylvania Press, 1995), 189.

35. *New Jersey Business*, Mar. 16, 1998.

36. "Indian Merchants Thriving in Enclave by Rio Grande," Associated Press, Sept. 4, 1989.

37. Ibid.

38. *Business News New Jersey*, Apr. 19, 1999.

39. *India West*, Jan. 22, 1999.

40. *Chicago Tribune*, Sept. 10, 1998.

41. See Bureau of the Census, *Asian Population*, 2000 (American Fact Finder).

42. *New York Times*, Nov. 7, 1999. See also Roger Sanjek's study of the Elmhurst-Corona neighborhood of Queens. Roger Sanjek, *The Future of Us All:*

Race and Neighborhood Politics in New York City (Ithaca, NY: Cornell University Press, 1998).

43. Leonard, *South Asian Americans,* 81–83.

44. Khandelwal, *Becoming American, Being Indian,* 7.

45. Anita Wadhwani in *India Currents,* Jan. 31, 1999.

46. *New York Times,* Jan. 11, 2003.

47. *Bergen (County) Record,* Oct. 2, 1987.

48. *Washington Post,* Nov. 16, 1992.

49. *New York Times,* July 10, 1988.

50. *New York Times,* Sept. 11, 1998; Oct. 7, 1998.

51. Michael Angelo, ed., *The Sikh Diaspora: Tradition and Change in an Immigrant Community* (New York: Garland, 1997), 172–74.

52. Quoted in Leonard, *South Asian Americans,* 85.

53. Lessinger, *From the Ganges to the Hudson,* 112.

54. Leonard, *South Asian Americans,* 159–68.

55. Ibid., chap. 4; Raymond Brady Williams, "Asian Indian and Pakistani Religions in the United States," *Annals of the American Academy of Political and Social Science* 558 (July 1998): 178–95.

56. *New York Times,* Apr. 5, 1999.

57. Angelo, *Sikh Diaspora,* 86–89.

58. *New York Times,* July 18, 1998.

59. Leonard, *South Asian Americans,* 110–14; Raymond Brady Williams, *Religions of Immigrants from India and Pakistan: New Threads in the American Tapestry* (New York: Cambridge University Press, 1988), 58–62.

60. Lessinger, *From the Ganges to the Hudson,* 49–51; *New York Times,* May 28, 2001.

61. *Chicago Tribune,* Sept. 10, 1998.

62. See Williams, "Asian Indian and Pakistani Religions," 178–90; Khandelwal, *Becoming American, Being Indian,* 78–86; Prema Kurien, "'We Are Better Hindus Here': Religion and Ethnicity among Indian Americans," in *Religions in Asian America: Building Faith Communities,* ed. Pyong Gap Min and Jung Ha Kim (Walnut Creek, CA: AltaMira Press, 2002), 99–120.

63. *Daily News,* Aug. 16, 1998.

64. *Asbury Park Press,* Aug. 10, 1997; Jan. 14, 1998; Khandelwal, *Becoming American, Being Indian,* chaps. 2–3.

65. *India Worldwide,* May 31, 1996.

66. *New India-Times,* Feb. 26, 1999; *Queens Tribune,* Oct. 12–20, 1999; Leonard, *South Asian Americans,* 90–91; Embassy of India, *Out of India,* 2002.

67. *Washington Post,* Oct. 9, 1999.

68. *New York Times,* July 6, 1999.

69. *USA Today,* Aug 15, 2002; Aug. 22, 2002; *Atlanta Journal-Constitution,* Aug. 22, 2002; *Times of India,* Aug. 23, 2002.

70. Embassy of India, *Out of India*, 2002.

71. See U.S. Bureau of the Census, *Asian Population by Group*, 2000.

72. Leonard, *South Asian Americans*, 172–73; INS, *Statistical Yearbook*, 2001, 22. Based on country of birth.

73. U.S. Dept. of Justice (Immigration and Naturalization Service), *The Triennial Comprehensive Report on Immigration* (Washington, DC: Government Printing Office, 2001), 40. Based on the 2000 census, government officials said the figures of 1996 were underestimated for unauthorized population. Jeffrey Passel, *New Estimates of the Undocumented Population in the United States* (Washington, DC: Pew Hispanic Center, 2002). Passel noted that best estimates from various federal government sources placed the figure at 8.5 million in the 2000 census.

74. *Washington Post*, May 29, 2003. In 1998 the *Daily News* of New York City noted that Pakistani leaders estimated that 30,000 of their nationals lived in New York. *Daily News*, Sept. 23, 1998.

75. *Houston Chronicle*, Oct. 28, 2001.

76. For the student generation, see Iftikhan Malik, *Pakistanis in Michigan: A Study of Third World Culture and Acculturation* (New York: AMS Press, 1989).

77. *Houston Chronicle*, Oct. 28, 2001.

78. *Newsday*, Feb. 10, 1994.

79. *Wall Street Journal*, Feb. 22, 1999.

80. Joel Millman, *The Other Americans: How Immigrants Renew Our Country, Our Economy, and Our Values* (New York: Viking, 1997), 41–42; *Newsday*, Nov. 11, 1998; Khandelwal, *Becoming American, Being Indian*, 108.

81. Leonard, *South Asian Americans*, 86.

82. *Houston Chronicle*, Mar. 21, 1993.

83. *San Francisco Examiner*, Aug. 23, 1998.

84. *Newsday*, Dec. 18, 1996.

85. *Newsday*, Aug. 16, 1993.

86. *Newsday*, Aug. 15, 1994.

87. *Newsday*, May 29, 1998.

88. Leonard, *South Asian Americans*, 94.

89. *Newsday*, Jan. 10, 1997.

90. *Newsday*, Mar. 29, 1992.

91. Leonard, *South Asian Americans*, 171–72; INS, *Statistical Yearbook*, 2001, 21, based on country of birth.

92. *Newsday*, May 27, 1998.

93. *New India-Times*, June 24, 1994; Reuters. Oct. 26, 1999.

94. Reuters, Oct. 26, 1999. Data on immigration is found in INS, *Statistical Yearbooks*. For 2000, *Statistical Yearbook*, 2000, 44; for 2001, *Statistical Yearbook*, 2001, 43.

95. *New York Times*, May 26, 2002.

96. *New York Times*, July 2, 1999.
97. Khandelwal, *Becoming American, Being Indian*, 20.
98. *Newsday*, Jan. 10, 1997.
99. *Daily News*, May 27, 1998.
100. *India West*, Jan. 22, 1999.
101. *New York Times*, Mar. 2, 2001.
102. *Dallas Morning News*, June 8, 1997; Leonard, *South Asian Americans*, 101.
103. *India in New York*, Oct. 10, 1998.
104. Margaret Abraham, *Speaking the Unspeakable: Marital Violence among South Asian Immigrants in the United States* (New Brunswick, NJ: Rutgers University Press, 2000), is based on detailed narratives of twenty-five South Asian women during the early 1990s.
105. *Newsday*, May 22, 1996.
106. *India in New York*, Jan. 2, 1998.
107. *Asian Reporter*, May 17, 1999.
108. Information provided by Kat Morgan, who worked at the shelter.
109. Juliene G. Lipson and Patricia A. Omidian, "Afghans," in *Refugees in America in the 1990s*, ed. David Haines (Westport, CT: Greenwood Press, 1996), 63–64.
110. *New York Times*, May 5, 1982; May 5, 1983; July 3, 1983; Jan. 11, 1986.
111. *Afghan News*, May 8, 2000.
112. INS, *Statistical Yearbook*, 2000, 82, 96.
113. *Washington Post*, May 30, 2003.
114. Lipson and Omidian, "Afghans," 64.
115. Ibid., 65.
116. *Los Angeles Times*, Oct. 11, 2001.
117. *San Francisco Chronicle*, Jan. 7, 2002; *New York Times*, Oct. 9, 2001.
118. *Washington Post*, Nov. 29, 1999.
119. *Los Angeles Times*, Oct. 11, 2001.
120. Ibid.
121. Lipson and Omidian, "Afghans," 74–76.
122. *New York Times*, Sept. 19, 2001; Oct. 11, 2001.
123. *New York Times*, Feb. 10, 2002.
124. *New York Times*, Sept. 19, 2001.
125. INS, *Statistical Yearbook*, 2000, 24.
126. U.S. Bureau of the Census, *Asian Population*, 2000 (American Fact Finder).
127. *Asian Week*, July 8, 1994.
128. *Los Angeles Times*, April 2, 1998; *Daily News of Los Angeles*, Aug. 29, 1995.
129. *Asian Week*, May 20, 1998.

130. *Asian Week*, May 14, 1993.

131. See Leonard, *South Asian Americans,* 91–126.

132. *Boston Globe*, Dec. 27, 1991.

133. *New York Times*, May 14, 1992; *Rocky Mountain News*, Apr. 10, 1992.

134. *New York Times*, Mar. 6, 2001.

135. *Asian Pages*, Oct. 14, 1995.

136. *Asian Week*, Jan. 10, 1992.

137. *Asian Pages*, Oct. 14, 1995; *New India-Times*, Sept. 13, 1996; *Boston Globe*, Mar. 8, 1998.

138. Associated Press, May 20, 2001.

139. *North Asian Weekly*, Aug. 30, 1996; *Asian Reporter*, Mar. 29, 1999.

NOTES TO CHAPTER 8

1. Mary E. Sengstock, *The Chaldean Americans: Changing Conceptions of Ethnic Identity* (New York: Center for Migration Studies, 1982), 42–43.

2. Robert Mirak, *Torn between Two Lands: Armenians in America, 1890–World War I* (Cambridge, MA: Harvard University Press, 1983), 44–59.

3. Ibid., 71–75.

4. Ibid., 52–53.

5. Robert Mirak, "Armenians," in *Harvard Encyclopedia of American Ethnic Groups,* ed. Stephan Thernstrom (Cambridge, MA: Harvard University Press, 1980), 138.

6. Mirak, *Torn between Two Lands*, chap. 10.

7. Ibid., chaps. 6–7.

8. Ibid., 110.

9. Ibid., 137–47.

10. Ibid., 282–83.

11. Sarah Gualtieri, "Becoming 'White': Race, Religion and the Foundations of Syrian/Lebanese Ethnicity in the United States," *Journal of American Ethnic History* 20 (summer 2001): 29–58.

12. Alixa Naff, *Becoming American: The Early Arab Immigrant Experience* (Carbondale: Southern Illinois University Press, 1985), 108–17; Najib E. Saliba, "Emigration from Syria," in *Arabs in the New World: Studies on Arab-American Communities,* ed. Sameer Y. Abraham and Nabeel Abraham (Detroit: Wayne State University Center for Urban Studies, 1983), 34–39.

13. Naff, *Becoming American*, chap. 2.

14. Ibid., 76–90.

15. Ibid., 128.

16. For the early Arab community in New York City, see Mary Ann Haick DeNapoli, "The Syrian-Lebanese Community of South Ferry from Its Origin to

1977," in *A Community of Many Worlds: Arab Americans of the City of New York,* ed. Kathleen Benson and Philip M. Kayal (Syracuse, NY: Syracuse University Press, 2002), 11–27.

17. Naff, *Becoming American*, chaps. 4–5.

18. Ibid., 237–38, chap. 7.

19. Steven A. Camarota, "Immigrants from the Middle East: A Profile of the Foreign-Born Population from Pakistan to Morocco," (Washington, DC: Center for Immigration Studies, 2002), 2–3. Camarota includes Pakistan and Bangladesh in his figures, which I do not. Hence, his figures are higher for Middle Easterners.

20. The Immigration and Naturalization Service (INS), *Annual Report*, 2000, 6; 2001, 6.

21. U.S. Dept. of Justice, INS, *The Triennial Comprehensive Report* (Washington, DC: Government Printing Office, 2002), 57. The figures based on the 2000 census are higher, but an exact breakdown is not yet available.

22. Data from INS, *Statistical Yearbooks* and *Annual Reports*.

23. Mehdi Bozorgmehr, "Misunderstood Minorities: Middle Easterners in the United States," in *Middle Eastern Diaspora Communities in America,* ed. Mehdi Bozorgmehr and Alison Feldman (New York: Hagap Kevorkian Center for Near Eastern Studies, New York University, 1996), 1–17.

24. Linda S. Walbridge, "Middle Easterners and North Africans," in *A Nation of Peoples: A Sourcebook on America's Multicultural Heritage,* ed. Elliott Robert Barkan (Westport, CT: Greenwood Press, 1999), 406–8.

25. See Camarota, "Immigrants."

26. The best introduction for Iran is Mehdi Bozorgmehr, "Iranians," in *Refugees in America in the 1990s,* ed. David Haines (Westport, CT: Greenwood Press, 1996), chap. 10.

27. Ibid., 215.

28. Ibid., 213–30.

29. Mabound Ansari, *Making of the Iranian Community in America* (New York: Pardis Press, 1992), 38. See Hossein Askari, John T. Cummings, and Mehmet Izbudak, "Iran's Migration of Skilled Labor to the United States," *Iranian Studies* 10 (winter–spring 1977), 3–32.

30. See Ansari, *Making of the Iranian Community.*

31. Mehdi Bozorgmehr, "From Iranian Studies to Studies of Iranians in the United States," *Iranian Studies* 31 (winter 1998): 5.

32. INS, *Annual Report*, 2001, 7; *Statistical Yearbook*, 2001, 19.

33. Ali Modarres, "Settlement Patterns of Iranians in the United States," *Iran Studies* 31 (winter 1998): 37–39.

34. See INS, Statistical Yearbook, 1998, 114.

35. Bozorgmehr, "Iranians," 221–22.

36. Ibid., 223.

37. Ibid.

38. Ibid., 224–25.

39. Ibid., 224.

40. *Los Angeles Times,* Dec. 10, 1998.

41. Ibid. See also Mehdi Bozorgmehr, Claudia Der-Martirosian, and George Sabagh, "Middle Easterners," in *Ethnic Los Angeles,* ed. Roger Waldinger and Mehdi Bozorgmehr (New York: Russell Sage Foundation, 1996), 345–78.

42. *New York Times,* July 24, 2000.

43. Bozorgmehr, "Iranians," 226–30..

44. For the Israeli-Arab conflicts, see Mark Tessler, *A History of the Israeli-Palestinian Conflict* (Bloomington: Indiana University Press, 1994); Michael Oren, *Six Days of War* (New York: Oxford University Press, 2002).

45. Walter P. Zenner, *A Global Community: The Jews from Aleppo, Syria* (Detroit: Wayne State University Press, 2000), 51.

46. Ibid., 177–78.

47. For the Syrians in Israel, see ibid., chaps. 5–6.

48. Ibid., chaps. 9–10.

49. Steven Gold, "Constructing an Israeli-American Identity," in Bozorgmehr and Feldman, *Middle Eastern Diaspora,* 35.

50. Ibid.

51. See Steven Gold and Bruce A. Phillips, "Israelis in the United States," *American Jewish Yearbook* (New York: American Jewish Committee, 1996), 51–101; Yindon Cohen and Vitchak Haberfeld, "The Number of Israeli Immigrants in the United States in 1990," *Demography* 34 (May 1997): 199–212; INS, *Statistical Yearbook,* 2001, 19.

52. See, for example, Moshe Shokeid, *Children of Circumstances: Israeli Emigrants in New York* (Ithaca, NY: Cornell University Press, 1988), chap. 2.

53. Bozorgmehr, Der-Martirosian, and Sabah, "Middle Easterners," 355–57; Gold and Phillips, "Israelis in the United States," 70–80.

54. Barbara Bilge, "Variations in Family Structure and Organization in the Turkish Community of Southeast Michigan and Adjacent Canada" (Ph.D. diss., Wayne State University, 1985), 72.

55. Scott L. Marks, "The Turkinos in America" *Turcoman Int,* www.turcoman.btineternet.co.uk/turkinos-in-america.htm (Apr. 18, 2002).

56. Bilge, "Variations," 103–4.

57. INS, *Statistical Yearbook,* 2001, 19. Figures on ancestry are from U.S. Bureau of the Census, *Ancestry of the Population in the United States,* 1990.

58. INS, *Statistical Yearbook,* 2001, 47.

59. *New York Times,* Apr. 2, 1996; *Philadelphia Inquirer,* Jan. 10, 2000.

60. *Detroit News,* Sept. 30, 2001.

61. U.S. Dept. of Justice, INS, *The Triennial Comprehensive Report,* 2002, 57.

62. *New York Times,* Apr. 2, 1996. The figures are based on the 1990 census.

63. *Norfolk Virginia-Pilot,* Apr. 19, 2002.

64. Barbara Bilge, "Turks," in *American Immigrant Cultures: Builders of a Nation,* ed. David Levinson and Melvin Ember (New York: Macmillan Reference USA, 1997), 213–14.

65. Ibid., 214.

66. For the development of Turkish communities, see Bilge, "Variations"; *New York Times,* Apr. 2, 1996; Walbridge, "Near Easterners," 408.

67. *Bergen (County) Record,* Jan. 27, 1993.

68. Anny Bakalian, "Armenians," in Levinson and Ember, *American Immigrant Cultures,* 42–51.

69. INS, *Statistical Yearbook,* 1998, 24.

70. Ibid. Before the breakup of the Soviet Union, there is no listing for Armenians as a separate people in the published INS yearbooks.

71. Bakalian, "Armenians," 44–47; *AIM: Armenian International Magazine,* July 31, 1993, 40.

72. *AIM: Armenian International Magazine,* July 31, 1993.

73. Bozorgmehr et al., "Middle Easterners," 356.

74. Bakalian, "Armenians," 47.

75. Anny Bakalian, *Armenian Americans: From Being to Feeling Armenian* (New Brunswick, NJ: Transaction, 1993), chap. 2; Bakalian, "Armenians," 45.

76. Bozorgmehr et al., "Middle Easterners," 373.

77. Bakalian, *Armenian Americans,* 311–12.

78. *New York Times,* July 6, 2000.

79. *New York Times,* Mar. 25, 1991. Tens of thousands of other refugees went to neighboring nations such as Kuwait, Saudi Arabia, or Jordan. Many temporary foreign workers lost their jobs because of the war.

80. Walbridge, "Middle Easterners and North Africans," 401.

81. U.S. Committee for Refugees, 2000, *Worldwide Refugee Information, Refugees Admitted to the United States by Nationality,* 2001, 86–99; Elizabeth Grieco, "Iraqi Immigrants in the United States," Migration Information Source, Apr. 1, 2003.

82. Walbridge, "Middle Easterners and North Africans," 401–3.

83. *New York Times,* June 2, 2003.

84. Mary C. Sengstock, "Iraqi Muslims," in Levinson and Ember, *American Immigrant Cultures,* 453–59.

85. Mary C. Sengstock, "Detroit's Iraqi-Chaldeans: A Conflicting Conception of Identity," in Abraham and Abraham, *Arabs in the New World,* 137.

86. Grieco, "Iraqi Immigrants in the United States."

87. *New York Times,* Apr. 11, 2003.

88. Ibid.

89. *New York Times,* Apr. 7, 1991; *Roanoke Times,* Aug. 11, 1992.

90. *New York Times,* July 28, 2002.

91. Sengstock, "Iraqi Muslims," 459.

92. *Rural Migration News*, Vol. 3 (July 1997).

93. *Washington Post*, Dec. 28, 2000.

94. Ibid.

95. *Washington Post*, Jan. 25, 2001. The administration feared that a sixth man who defected from Iraq's elite military unit might have been a spy.

96. *Washington Post*, Dec. 28, 2000.

97. *Los Angeles Times*, Dec. 22, 2000.

98. *New York Times*, Nov. 17, 2002.

99. *Washington Post*, Jan. 27, 2003.

100. For the Israeli-Palestinian conflict, see Tessler, *History of the Israeli Conflict,* and especially Michael Oren, *Six Days of War.*

101. See Oren, *Six Days of War.*

102. Gregory Orfalea, *Before the Flames: A Quest for a History of Arab Americans* (Austin: University of Texas Press, 1988), 140; Walbridge, "Middle Easterners and North Africans," 96–99.

103. *New York Times*, Aug. 29, 1989.

104. Ibid.

105. Michael W. Suleiman, "Introduction: The Arab American Experience," in *Arabs in America: Building a New Future,* ed. Michael W. Suleiman (Philadelphia: Temple University Press, 1999), 9.

106. Ibid., 10–11.

107. Daniel Pipes, *Militant Islam Reaches America* (New York: Norton, 2002), 157.

108. *New York Times*, Nov. 14, 2001. Data about religious affiliation are not always precise because governmental authorities, such as the Census Bureau, do not keep such figures.

109. Walbridge, "Middle Easterners and North Africans," 396–98.

110. May Seikaly, "Attachment and Identity: The Palestinian Community of Detroit" in Suleiman, *Arabs in America*, chap. 1.

111. May Ahdab-Yehia, "The Lebanese Maronites: Patterns of Continuity and Change," in Abraham and Abraham, *Arabs in the New World*, 147–62.

112. Walbridge, "Middle Easterners and North Africans," 398–99.

113. *New York Times*, Dec. 12, 1988.

114. Figures based on the INS, *Statistical Yearbook* and *Annual Reports.* For 2000 data, see INS, *Statistical Yearbook*, 2000, 24.

115. Bozorgmehr, "Misunderstood Minorities," 15.

116. Walbridge, "Middle Easterners and North Africans," 401; Richard H. Curtiss, "Two Arab-American Groups Merge for 'Political Empowerment' in 21st Century," *Washington Report on Middle East Affairs* 19 (Mar. 31, 2000): 33.

117. Hany N. Takla, Maged N. Mikhil, and Mark R. Moussa, "Egyptian Copts," in Levinson and Ember, *American Cultures*, 243–47.

118. Gabriel Abdelsayod, "Copts," in *The New Jersey Ethnic Experience*, ed. Barbara Cunningham (Union City, NJ: Wm. H. Wise and Co., 1977), 120–30.

119. Orfalea, *Before the Flames*, 183; Raff Marcus, "Copts," in *Harvard Encyclopedia of American Ethnic Groups*, ed. Stephan Thernstrom (Cambridge, MA: Harvard University Press, 1980), 242.

120. Nabeel Abraham, "The Yemeni Immigrant Community of Detroit: Background, Emigration and Community Life," in Abraham and Abraham, *Arabs in the New World*, 109–31.

121. Walbridge, "Middle Easterners and North Africans," 400.

122. Shalom Staub, *Yemenis in New York City: The Folklore of Ethnicity* (Philadelphia: Balch Institute Press, 1989), 79.

123. Ibid., 81.

124. Ibid., 81–86.

125. See the essays in Suleiman, *Arabs in America*.

126. *New York Times*, Apr. 27, 2001; Council on American-Islamic Relations, *The Mosque in America: A National Portrait* (Washington, DC: Council on American-Islamic Relations, 2001), 3.

127. *New York Times*, Oct. 25, 2001; Graduate Center of the City University of New York, *American Religious Survey*, 2001, 3; *Christian Science Monitor*, Nov. 29, 2001.

128. Pipes, *Militant Islam*, 138.

129. *Christian Science Monitor*, Nov. 29, 2001.

130. See the report of the Council on American-Islamic Relations, *The Mosque in America,* for details of the study.

131. *New York Times*, Dec. 31, 1985; Lori Anne Salem, "Far-Off and Fascinating Things: Wadeeha Atiyeh and Images of Arabs in the American Popular Theater, 1930–1950," in Suleiman, *Arabs in America*, 272–83.

132. *New York Times*, Aug. 28, 1995. Some of the attacks were directly related to the destruction of the federal building in Oklahoma City.

133. Eric Pooley, "The Arab Connection," *New York*, Mar. 15, 1993.

134. See Council on American-Islamic Relations, *A Rush to Judgment*, 1995; American-Muslim Research Center, *The Price of Ignorance*, 1996; and American-Arab Anti-Discrimination Committee, *1995 Report on Anti-Arab Racism*, 1995; *New York Times*, Aug. 28, 1995.

135. *New York Times*, Dec. 25, 1993; Apr. 2, 2001; Oct. 7, 2001.

136. *USA Today*, May 22, 2002.

137. *USA Today*, May 10, 2002.

138. *New York Times*, Apr. 25, 2002.

139. Reuters, Oct. 11, 2001.

140. *New York Times*, Oct. 15, 2001.

141. *New York Times*, Sept. 19, 2001.

142. U.S. Dept. of State, *Islam in the United States*, 2001.

143. *New York Times*, Sept. 22, 2001.

144. *Atlanta Journal-Constitution*, Jan. 15, 2003.

145. Ibid.

146. *Arab Americans News*, n.d.; WorldNetDaily.com, Aug. 1, 2002; *New York Times*, May 2, 2002.

147. *New York Times*, June 3, 2003.

148. Matthew Brzezinski, "Hady Hassan Omar's Detention," *New York Times Sunday Magazine*, Oct. 27, 2002, 50–52. The ACLU was not alone in pressing for the rights of those detained. *New York Times*, Jan. 23, 2002. For a biting criticism of the INS's detention policies before September 11, 2001, see Michael Welch, *Detained: Immigration Laws and the Expanding I.N.S. Jail Complex* (Philadelphia: Temple University Press, 2002).

149. *New York Times*, Feb. 11, 2003.

150. *USA Today*, Feb. 12, 2003.

151. *New York Times*, June 15, 2002. A "dirty bomb" was a weapon of small size but capable of releasing radiation over a relatively large area.

152. *New York Times*, Oct. 6, 2002.

153. *New York Times*, Dec. 20, 2002.

154. INS, *Special Registration*, Nov. 11, 2002.

155. *Financial Times*, Jan. 29, 2003.

156. *USA Today*, Mar. 25, 2003.

157. *New York Times*, June 4, 2003.

158. *New York Times*, Mar. 9, 2003; Apr. 6, 2003.

159. *New York Times*, Mar. 22, 2003.

160. Maria Jachimowicz and Ramah McKay, "Spotlight on 'Special Registration' Program," Migration Information Source, Apr. 1, 2003; *San Francisco Chronicle*, May 20, 2003.

161. *New York Times*, Apr. 20, 2003.

162. Joseph Suad, "Against the Grain—the Arab," in Suleiman, *Arabs in America*, 265.

163. Ibid., 265–66.

164. *Washington Report on Middle Eastern Affairs*, Mar. 31, 2000.

165. Paula Thomson, "Arab Americans Win Several Races in 2001 Elections," U.S. Dept. of State, *International Information Programs*, Nov. 9, 2001.

166. U.S. Census, Dec. 2000 (American Fact Finder).

NOTES TO CHAPTER 9

1. Immigration and Naturalization Service (INS), *Annual Report*, 2001, 6; Mary Waters, *Black Identities: West Indian Dreams and American Realities* (Cambridge, MA: Harvard University Press, 1999), 36–39, 49–53.

2. Figures are based on INS, *Statistical Year Book*, 2000, 21; INS, *Annual Report*, 2001, 6. The census reported a higher number.

3. Renee C. Romano, *Race Mixing: Black-White Marriage in Postwar America* (Cambridge, MA: Harvard University Press, 2003), 261.

4. *Science*, Jan. 8, 1999.

5. *New York Times*, June 8, 1994.

6. *Journal of Blacks in Higher Education* (Jan. 31, 2000): 60–61.

7. See April Gordon, "The New Diaspora—African Immigration to the United States," *Journal of Third World Studies* 15 (spring 1998): 79–103.

8. Tibbert L. Speer, "A Cracked Door: U.S. Policy Welcomes Only Africa's Brightest and Richest," *Emerge* 6 (Aug. 31, 1995): 36.

9. *Journal of Blacks in Higher Education* (Jan. 31, 2000): 60–61.

10. John Logan, *Black Diversity in Metropolitan America* (Albany, NY: Lewis Mumford Center for Comparative Urban and Regional Research, 2003), 3.

11. *Pittsburgh Post-Gazette*, Mar. 16, 2003.

12. Joseph Takougang, "Recent African Immigrants to the United States: A Historical Perspective," *Western Journal of Black Studies* 19 (spring 1995): 50–51.

13. Roger Cohen, "A Nigerian Discovers America," *New York Times Magazine*, June 6, 1999.

14. Kofi K. Apraku, *African Emigres in the United States: A Missing Link in Africa's Social and Economic Development* (Westport, CT: Praeger, 1991), 4.

15. J. Lorand Matory, "Africans in the United States," *Footnotes: African American History* (Apr. 1, 1993), 1. In 2001–2 the top nations sending students were India, China, Korea, Japan, and Taiwan. *USA Today*, May 6, 2003.

16. *Chicago Tribune*, June 28, 1991.

17. *Washington Times*, Feb. 21, 1993.

18. See Speer, "Cracked Door."

19. *Journal of Blacks in Higher Education* (Sept. 30, 1996).

20. Apraku, *African Emigres*, 2–5.

21. *Emerge*, Aug. 31, 1995, 36; Apraku, *African Emigres*, chap. 1.

22. Speer, "Cracked Door," 36.

23. *San Francisco Chronicle*, Sept. 23, 1993.

24. *Washington Post*, Sept. 21, 1993; *Atlanta Journal-Constitution*, July 2, 1993.

25. See Apraku, *African Emigres*, especially chap. 2. Of course, many of the better-off immigrants sent money home and attempted to keep their traditional cultures alive in the United States as well.

26. *New York Times*, Feb. 21, 1999.

27. INS, *Statistical Yearbook*, 2001, 112–13.

28. *San Francisco Chronicle*, Aug. 27, 2002.

29. INS, *Statistical Yearbook*, 2001, 112–13; see also the excellent summary by Gordon, "New Diaspora," 79–103.

30. *Washington Post*, Feb. 23, 1999.

31. *Washington Report on Middle East Affairs*, June 30, 1998; *Washington Informer*, Dec. 16, 1992.

32. INS, *Statistical Yearbook*, 2001, 113.

33. *New York Times*, Mar. 25, 1998.

34. *Washington Post*, Jan. 16, 1999; *Los Angeles Times*, May 5, 1998.

35. Rogaia Mustafa Abusharaf, *Wanderings: Sudanese Migrants and Exiles in North America* (Ithaca, NY: Cornell University Press, 2002), chap. 3.

36. Ibid., 72–80.

37. Ibid., 8–11.

38. See Gordon, "New Diaspora," 79–103.

39. John Stremlau, "Ending Africa's Wars," *Foreign Affairs* 79 (July–Aug. 2000): n.p. Sources vary. The United Nations, *International Migration Report*, 2002, 28, 68, puts the African total at 3.6 million, which was just under one-third of the world's total of 12 million.

40. *Los Angeles Times*, May 5, 1998.

41. President William J. Clinton, "Refugee Admissions Consultations for FY 2001," *Weekly Compilation of Presidential Documents*, Washington, July 17, 2000.

42. *Washington Post*, Aug. 18, 2001.

43. *Roanoke (VA) Times*, Mar. 29, 2002; INS, *Annual Report*, 2001; INS, *Statistical Yearbook*, 2001, 85. The United States had accepted 75,000 refugees in 2000.

44. *New York Times*, Mar. 10, 2003.

45. *USA Today*, Oct. 13, 2003; Aug. 4, 2003; *Burlington Free Press*, July 24, 2003.

46. U.S. Dept. of Homeland Security, *Yearbook of Immigration Statistics*, 2002, 49–53.

47. *New York Times*, Sept. 15, 2000. An estimated 4,000, the largest number, Liberians lived in Rhode Island.

48. *Providence Journal*, Sept. 27, 1999; *Washington Post*, Sept. 29, 2000.

49. Mark Krikorian, *Here to Stay: There's Nothing as Permanent as a Temporary Refugee* (Washington, DC, Center for Immigration Studies, 1998), 2–4; INS, "News Release," Nov. 7, 2002. For the lobbying behind Salvadoran TPS, see Susan Bibler Coutin, "From Refugees to Immigrants: The Legalization Strategies of Salvadoran Immigrants and Activists," *International Migration Review* 32 (winter 1998): 901–25.

50. Associated Press, Nov. 7, 2000.

51. Sara Corbett, "The Long Road to Fargo," *New York Times Magazine*, Apr. 1, 2001.

52. INS, *Statistical Yearbook*, 2001, 100–101.

53. *San Jose Mercury News*, Nov. 21, 1992.

54. *New York Times*, Aug. 18, 1999.

55. *New York Times*, Apr. 15, 1996; Oct. 12, 1996; Dec. 28, 1996; Aug. 18, 1999.

56. *New York Times*, Mar. 12, 2000.

57. *New York Times*, Apr. 25, 1999.

58. *New York Times*, July 11, 2000.

59. Anna O. Law, "The Diversity Lottery—A Cycle of Unintended Consequences in United States Immigration Policy," *Journal of American Ethnic History* 21 (summer 2002): 3–29.

60. *Wall Street Journal*, Sept. 12, 1997.

61. INS, *Statistical Yearbook*, 2001, 48; P.M. News, "US Postal Workers Frustrate Nigerians," Aug. 26, 1999. Nations were permitted only 3,850 slots of the total of 50,000, but immediate family members were not included in this total. In 2001, the diversity visas were not all used.

62. John A. Arthur, *Invisible Sojourners: African Immigrant Diaspora in the United States* (Westport, CT: Praeger, 2000), 26.

63. INS, *Statistical Yearbook*, 1995, 49.

64. INS, *Statistical Yearbook*, 2001, 43.

65. See Gordon, "New Diaspora."

66. Sylviane Diouf-Kamara, "Senegalese in New York: A Model Minority," *Black Renaissance/Renaissance Noire* 1 (Oct. 31, 1997): 92.

67. *New York Daily News*, April 15, 1999.

68. Ibid.; *New York Times*, June 25, 2002. John Logan (*Black Diversity*, 4) found only 73,851 persons born in Africa in New York City.

69. *San Francisco Chronicle*, Aug. 27, 2002.

70. Sanford J. Ungar, *Fresh Blood: The New American Immigrants* (New York: Simon and Schuster, 1995), 255; *Washington Post*, Feb. 23, 1999; *Cultural Survival Quarterly* 20 (Jan. 31, 1997): 51.

71. Brookings Institution, "The Whole World in a Zip Code: Greater Washington, D.C., as a New Region of Immigration," *Report*, Apr. 2001, 11.

72. *Seattle Scanner* Jan. 6, 1999; *St. Petersburg Times*, Jan. 7, 1998; *St. Louis Post-Dispatch*, Mar. 6, 1995.

73. Associated Press, Aug. 29, 1999; *Minneapolis Star Tribune*, Aug. 15, 1990. For John Logan's different figures, see Logan, *Black Diversity*, 4.

74. Logan, *Black Diversity*, 1–4.

75. David Johnson, "As Somali Civil War Smolders, Bostonians Refugees Adjust to New Life in U.S.," *Washington Report on Middle East Affairs*, June 30, 1998; *San Diego Union-Tribune*, Apr. 18, 1999.

76. *New York Times*, Dec. 29, 1995.

77. See Jon D. Holtzman, *Nuer Journeys, Nuer Lives: Sudanese Refugees in Minnesota* (Boston: Allyn and Bacon, 2000). For other Sudanese, see Abusharaf, *Wanderings*.

78. *Atlanta Journal-Constitution*, Aug. 18, 2002; *Boston Globe*, July 16, 2002; *New York Times*, Oct. 15, 2002.

79. *Boston Globe*, Nov. 20, 2002.

80. Diouf-Kamara, "Senegalese in New York," 92.

81. *Newsday*, Apr. 30, 1995.

82. *New York Times*, Nov. 10, 1985.

83. Paul Stoller, *Money Has No Smell: The Africanization of New York City* (Chicago: University of Chicago Press, 2002), 96–105.

84. Ibid., 96.

85. Quoted in Stoller, "Trading Places: Muslim Merchants from West Africa Expand Their Markets to New York City," *Natural History*, July 2002–Aug. 2002, 50.

86. *New York Times*, July 31, 1986.

87. *Newsday*, Apr. 30, 1995.

88. Stoller, *Money Has No Smell*, 11–14.

89. Ibid., 157–58.

90. Ibid., 21, 153–56.

91. Joel Millman, *The Other Americans: How Immigrants Renew Our Country, Our Economy, and Our Values* (New York: Viking, 1997), chap. 5.

92. *New York Times*, Nov. 18, 1997.

93. *New York Times*, Feb. 14, 1999.

94. Diouf-Kamara, "Senegalese in New York," 92.

95. For the "brain drain," see Peter Lobo and Joseph Salvo, "The African Brain Drain to the United States in the 1990s" (paper presented at the annual meetings of the Population Association of America, Washington, DC, Mar. 2001); Logan, *Black Diversity*, 10.

96. John Logan, *Black Diversity*, 5.

97. Ibid., 6.

98. *New York Times*, Nov. 10, 1999.

99. F. NII-Amoo Dodoo, "Assimilation Differences among Africans in America," *Social Forces* 76 (Dec. 1997): 534.

100. *Chicago Tribune*, June 16, 1993.

101. *San Francisco Chronicle*, Sept. 23, 1993; *Amsterdam News*, July 27, 1996.

102. *Newsday*, July 5, 1994.

103. It will be recalled that persons from North Africa were considered white by the INS.

104. Apraku, *African Emigres*, 4–7.

105. *Minneapolis Star Tribune*, Nov. 19, 2000.

106. *New York Times*, Aug. 21, 2002.

107. For examples of cultural differences and conflicts, see *Detroit Free Press*, Mar. 29, 1998; Leslie Goffe, "Africans in America," *Emerge* 11 (Feb. 2, 2000): 84; *Philadelphia Enquirer*, Sept. 26, 1998.

108. *Los Angles Sentinel*, May 19, 1994.
109. Johnson, "As Somali Civil War Smolders," 67.
110. *Emerge*, Feb. 28, 2000.
111. Millman, *Other Americans*, 202–7.
112. *Seattle Skanner*, Jan. 6, 1999.
113. *Minneapolis Star Tribune*, Aug. 15, 1990.
114. *Morning Call*, Jan. 7, 1997.
115. *Philadelphia Tribune*, Nov. 27, 1998.
116. Abusharaf, *Wanderings*, 81–92.
117. *New York Times*, Jan. 15, 1989; *Washington Post*, May 5, 1998.
118. *St. Petersburg Times*, Jan. 7, 1998.
119. Holtzman, *Nuer Lives*, 123–28.
120. *National Catholic Reporter*, Mar. 27, 1998.
121. *Madison Capital Times*, May 29, 1999; *Boston Globe*, Jan. 11, 1998.
122. Diouf-Kamara, "Senegalese in New York." See also Millman, *Other Americans*, 200–203; Joan D'Alisera, "The Transnational Search for Muslim Identity: Sierra Leoneans in America's Capital" (Ph.D. diss., University of Illinois at Urbana-Champaign, 1997).
123. *New York Times*, Feb. 14, 1999.
124. Holtzman, *Nuer Journeys*, chap. 5.
125. See David M. Reimers, *Still the Golden Door: The Third World Comes to America*, 2nd ed. (New York: Columbia University Press, 1992), chap. 3.
126. INS, *Statistical Yearbook*, 2001, 19.
127. Ibid.
128. Ransford W. Palmer, *Pilgrims from the Sun: West Indian Migration to America* (New York: Twayne, 1995), 52–55.
129. The 2000 census found that less than 10 percent of Dominicans and other Latinos identified themselves as black. *New York Times*, Apr. 28, 2003. About half of Latinos called themselves white, and the rest mostly "other" or some other group.
130. Milton Vickerman, *Crosscurrents: West Indian Immigrants and Race* (New York: Oxford University Press, 1999), 9–12; *Newsday*, Sept. 5, 1993.
131. Nancy Foner, "West Indian Migration to New York: An Overview," in *Islands in the City: West Indian Migration to New York*, ed. Nancy Foner (Berkeley: University of California Press, 2001), 1.
132. Palmer, *Pilgrims*, 18–20; Philip Kasinitz and Milton Vickerman, "West Indian/Caribbeans," in *A Nation of Peoples: A Sourcebook on America's Multicultural Heritage*, ed. Elliott Robert Barkan (Westport, CT: Greenwood Press, 1999), 527–28.
133. Ronald Fernandez, *America's Banquet of Cultures: Harnessing Ethnicity, Race, and Immigration in the Twentieth Century* (Westport, CT: Praeger, 2000), 31.

134. Palmer, *Pilgrims*, 32.

135. Ibid., 32–33; Waters, *Black Identities*, 97–98.

136. Palmer, *Pilgrims*, 33–37.

137. Ibid., 35–41.

138. Waters, *Black Identities*, 102.

139. Ibid., 97–103.

140. Logan, *Black Diversity*, 6.

141. Philip Kasinitz, *Caribbean New York: Black Immigrants and the Politics of Race* (Ithaca, NY: Cornell University Press, 1992), 105–8.

142. Suzanne Model, "Where New York's West Indians Work," in Foner, *Islands in the City*, 57.

143. Roger Waldinger, *Still the Promised City? African-Americans and New Immigrants in Postindustrial New York* (Cambridge, MA: Harvard University Press, 1996), 118–22; Waters, *Black Identities*, 103–16.

144. Kasinitz, *Caribbean New York*, 103; Vickerman, *Crosscurrents*, 63–72.

145. Waters, *Black Identities*, 116.

146. Kasinitz, *Caribbean New York*, 119.

147. Ibid., 119–21.

148. Palmer, *Pilgrims*, 28–30.

149. Waters, *Black Identities*, 153.

150. Ibid., 220–33, 261–67.

151. Vickerman, *Crosscurrents*, chap. 3.

152. *New York Times*, Feb. 1, 2001.

153. Palmer, *Pilgrims*, 26.

154. Kasinitz, *Caribbean New York*, chap. 7.

155. Alex Stepick, *Pride against Prejudice: Haitians in the United States* (Boston: Allyn and Bacon, 1998), 4; Palmer, *Pilgrims*, 11.

156. It was reported in January 1993 that nearly 400 drowned in one incident alone. *New York Times*, Jan. 12, 1993.

157. INS, *Statistical Yearbook*, 2001, 19.

158. *New York Times*, Jan. 16, 1993; Philip G. Scrag, *A Well-Founded Fear: The Congressional Battle to Save Political Asylum in America* (Routledge: New York, 2000), 36.

159. *New York Times*, June 30, 1994.

160. *New York Times*, Sept. 16, 1994.

161. Michael Finkel, "Desperate Passage," *New York Times Magazine*, June 18, 2000.

162. *Miami Herald*, May 3, 2000; May 4; *Fort Lauderdale Sun-Sentinel*, May 4, 2000.

163. A moving account of the journey in 2000 is Finkel, "Desperate Passage."

164. *Naples Daily News*, Aug. 29, 1999.

165. *New York Times*, Mar. 29, 2000.

166. Figures based on INS, *Statistical Yearbook* and *Annual Reports*.

167. This number included 196,000 persons who were born in Haiti and 83,000 who were born in the United States.

168. Steven A. Camarota, *Immigrants in the United States—2002* (Washington, DC: Center for Immigration Studies, 2002), 8.

169. Flore Zephir, *Haitian Immigrants in America: A Sociological and Sociolinguistic Portrait* (Westport, CT: Bergin and Garvey, 1996), 60–62, 102–6, 109–16.

170. Alex Stepick III, "The Refugees Nobody Wants: Haitians in Miami," in *Miami Now! Immigration, Ethnicity and Social Change,* ed. Guillermo J. Grenier and Alex Stepick III (Gainesville: University Press of Florida, 1992), chap. 4.

171. Ibid., 67; Michel S. Laguerre, *American Odyssey: Haitians in New York City* (Ithaca, NY: Cornell University Press, 1984), chap. 5.

172. *New York* Times, June 4, 1994.

173. Laguerre, *American Odyssey,* 93–107.

174. Stepick, "The Refugees," 69–71. For the economic activities of the New York City community, see Laguerre, *American Odyssey,* chap. 5.

175. *Miami Herald,* Sept. 18, 2000.

176. Stepick, "The Refugees," 65.

177. Stepick, *Pride against Prejudice,* 85–92.

178. *New York Times,* Oct. 31, 2002.

179. FAIR, *Immigration Report* (Dec.–Jan. 2002–3), 5. The policy covered only those illegal aliens filing for asylum within the last two years, and it did not include Cubans, who were still covered by the 1966 Cuban Adjustment Act.

NOTES TO CHAPTER 10

1. The standard interpretation of the Displaced Persons Acts is found in Leonard Dinnerstein, *America and the Survivors of the Holocaust* (New York: Columbia University Press, 1982).

2. Gil Loescher and John A. Scanlan, *Calculated Kindness: Refugees and America's Half-Open Door, 1945–Present* (New York: Free Press, 1986), 44–46.

3. Iris Chang, *The Chinese in America: A Narrative History* (New York: Viking, 2003), 242–45.

4. Loescher and Scanlan, *Calculated Kindness,* 172, 195–201. Loescher and Scanlan thought that the pressure to grant parole for Chileans came too late to have much impact. Also, some Chileans did not want to come to the United States because they believed the American government was responsible for the overthrow. See also David M. Reimers, *Still the Golden Door: The Third World Comes to America,* 2nd ed. (New York: Columbia University Press, 1992), 188–89; Diana Kay, *Cubans in Exile: Private Struggles, Public Lives* (Wolfboro, NH: Longwood Academic, 1987), 203.

5. Felix Roberto Masud-Piloto, *With Open Arms: Cuban Migration to the United States* (Totowa, NJ: Rowman and Littlefield, 1988), chap. 2; Miguel Gonzalez-Pando, *Cuban Americans* (Westport, CT: Greenwood Press, 1998), chap. 2.

6. Gonzalez-Pando, *Cuban Americans*, 20–21; Felix Roberto Masud-Piloto, *From Welcomed Exiles to Illegal Immigrants: Cuban Migration to the U.S., 1959–1995* (Lanham, MD: Rowman and Littlefield, 1996), 32–38.

7. Masud-Piloto, *From Welcomed Exiles*, chap. 3.

8. Ibid., 58.

9. Alejandro Portes and Alex Stepick, *City on the Edge: The Transformation of Miami* (Berkeley: University of California Press, 1993), 102–3.

10. See Yvonne M. Code, *Operation Pedro Pan: The Untold Exodus of 14,048 Cuban Children* (New York: Routledge, 1999).

11. Masud-Piloto, *From Welcomed Exiles*, 58–68.

12. Caroline Bettinger-Lopez, *Cuban-Jewish Journeys: Searching for Identity, Home and History in Miami* (Knoxville: University of Tennessee Press, 2000), 10.

13. Masud-Piloto, *From Welcomed Exiles*, 76–82.

14. Maria Christina Garcia, *Havana USA: Cuban Exiles and Cuban Americans in South Florida, 1959–1994* (Berkeley: University of California Press, 1996), chap. 2.

15. Robert S. Kahn, *Other People's Blood: U.S. Immigration Prisons in the Reagan Decade* (Boulder, CO: Westview Press, 1996), 141–45, and chaps. 7–8.

16. Masud-Piloto, *From Welcomed Exiles*, 140.

17. *Washington Post*, Sept. 10, 1994.

18. Masud-Piloto, *From Welcomed Exiles*, 137–44.

19. *New York Times*, Jan. 7, 2000; Jan. 10, 2000.

20. The arrival of the Cubans is treated in Masud-Piloto, *From Welcomed Exiles*.

21. Portes and Stepick, *City on the Edge*, 102–3.

22. Garcia, *Havana USA*, 85.

23. Gonzalez-Pando, *Cuban Americans*, 46; *New York Times*, Apr. 11, 2000.

24. Portes and Stepick, *City on the Edge*, 95–96.

25. Ibid., 99–100.

26. Gonzalez-Pando, *Cuban Americans*, 103.

27. James Crawford, *Hold Your Tongue: Bilingualism and the Politics of English* (New York: Addison-Wesley, 1992), 104–18; David M. Reimers, *Unwelcome Strangers: American Identity and the Turn against Immigration* (New York: Columbia University Press, 1998), 120.

28. *Los Angeles Times*, May 25, 1998.

29. Gonzales-Pando, *Cuban Americans*, 33–34.

30. Manuel Viamonte and Adolfo Leyva de Varona, "The Contribution of Cuban Physicians to the State of Florida," in *Cuban Exiles in Florida: Their Presence and Contributions,* ed. Antonio Jorge, Jaime Suchlicki, and Adolfo Leyva de

Varona (Miami: University of Miami, 1991), 291–308.

31. See Jorge, Suchlicki, and Leyva, *Cuban Exiles*, 309–38.

32. Maria de los Angeles Torres, *In the Land of Mirrors: Cuban Exile Politics in the United States* (Ann Arbor: University of Michigan Press, 1999), 72.

33. Portes and Stepick, *City on the Edge*, chaps. 3, 8.

34. Gonzalez-Pando, *Cuban Americans*, 46.

35. Guillermo J. Grenier and Lisandro Perez, "The Cubans," in *A Nation of Peoples: A Sourcebook on America's Multicultural Heritage*, ed. Elliott Robert Barkan (Westport, CT: Greenwood Press, 1999), 140.

36. Garcia, *Havana USA*, 68–74.

37. Gonzalez-Pando, *Cuban Americans*, 65–70.

38. Roberto Suro, *The Strangers among Us: How Latino Immigration Is Transforming America* (New York: Knopf, 1998), 173.

39. Portes and Stepick, *City on the Edge*, 128.

40. Grenier and Perez, "The Cubans," 146.

41. Grenier and Perez, "The Cubans"; Portes and Stepick, *City on the Edge*, 147–49, 126–37.

42. Leonard Dinnerstein and David M. Reimers, *Ethnic Americans: A History of Immigration* (New York: Columbia University Press, 1999), 146–47.

43. Portes and Stepick, *City on the Edge*, 133.

44. Suro, *Strangers among Us*, 172.

45. Quoted in Portes and Stepick, *City on the Edge*, 128.

46. *New York Times*, June 3, 2000.

47. Suro, *Strangers among Us*, 172.

48. Ibid.

49. U.S. Bureau of the Census, Current Population Reports, *The Hispanic Population in the United States*, Mar. 2000, 6.

50. Ibid., 5.

51. Lawrence E. Harrison, *The Pan-American Dream: Do Latin America's Cultural Values Discourage True Partnership with the United States and Canada?* (New York: Basic Books, 1997), 238.

52. Madeline Zavodny, "Race, Wages and Assimilation among Cuban Immigrants" (paper presented at the meeting of the American Population Association, Atlanta, Georgia, Apr. 2002).

53. Grenier and Perez, "The Cubans," 146–47.

54. *New York Times*, Apr. 11, 2000.

55. Ibid.

56. Garcia, *Havana USA*, 98.

57. Ibid., 88–99.

58. See Bettinger-Lopez, *Cuban-Jewish Journeys*, for a discussion of the Jews settling in Miami.

59. Torres, *In the Land of Mirrors*, 54–61.

60. Quoted in Gonzalez-Pando, *Cuban Americans*, 88.

61. See Torres, *In the Land of Mirrors*, for a discussion of exile politics; and Garcia, *Havana USA*, chap. 4.

62. *New York Times*, Jan. 16, 2000; Apr. 26, 2001.

63. *Miami Herald*, Oct. 23, 1997.

64. Lourdes Cue, "Election 2000: The Latino Factor," *Hispanic,* (Jan./Feb. 2001), 26.

65. *Miami Herald*, Dec. 20, 2000.

66. *New York Times*, Sept. 2, 2001; Mar. 30, 2002.

67. *New York Times*, Mar. 30, 2002.

68. The terms "Indochinese refugees" and "Southeast Asian refugees" will be used here to refer to refugees from Vietnam, Cambodia, and Laos.

69. Ronald Takaki, *Strangers from a Different Shore: A History of Asian Americans* (Boston: Little, Brown, 1989), 448.

70. Reimers, *Still the Golden Door*, 23.

71. Courtland W. Robinson, *Terms of Refuge: The Indochinese Exodus and the International Response* (London: Zed Books, 1998), 18.

72. For the refugee experience, consult Robinson, *Terms of Refuge.*

73. Takaki, *Strangers from a Different Shore*, 452.

74. Robinson, *Terms of Refugee*, 294–96.

75. Canada and France also took in Asian refugees.

76. Robinson, *Terms of Refuge*, 52–62.

77. Ibid., 56–57.

78. Ibid., 171–83.

79. Ibid., 259–67.

80. Thomas A. Bass, *Vietnamerica: The War Comes Home* (New York: Soho Press, 1996), 40; Kieu-Lin Caroline Valverde, "From Dust to Gold: The Vietnamese Amerasian Experience," in *Racially Mixed People in America*, ed. Maria P. Root (New York: Sage, 1992), 144.

81. Min Zhou and Carl Bankston, *Growing Up American: How Vietnamese Children Adapt to Life in the United States* (New York: Russell Sage, 1998), 33; Valverde, "From Dust to Gold," 146–48.

82. For a discussion of their plight, see Bass, *Vietnamerica.*

83. Reimers, *Still the Golden Door*, l77–78.

84. *USA Today*, Mar. 19, 2003.

85. Bass, *Vietnamerica*, 44–46.

86. Valverde, "From Dust to Gold," 156–59; for a particularly biting criticism of the entire program see Bass, *Vietnamerica.*

87. U.S. Department of Justice, Immigration and Naturalization Service, and U.S. Department of Labor, Bureau of International Labor Affairs, *The Triennial Comprehensive Report on Immigration* (Washington, DC: Government Printing Office, 1999), 16; *New York Times*, Nov. 7, 2000.

88. INS, *Statistical Yearbook*, 2001, 63. The figure in 2001 was 730.

89. William Shawcross, *The Quality of Mercy* (New York: Simon and Schuster, 1994), 170.

90. Robinson, *Terms of Refuge*, 74.

91. Ibid., 74–98.

92. Ibid., 103–8; *New York Times*, Dec. 27, 1997.

93. *New York Times*, Nov. 7, 2000. The largest group, as in the past, were Vietnamese.

94. Ibid.

95. Ruben Rumbaut, "Vietnamese, Laotian, and Cambodian Americans," in *Asian Americans: Contemporary Trends and Issues,* ed. Pyong Gap Min (Thousand Oaks, CA: Sage, 1995), 238–39. About 30,000 Vietnamese were arriving in the 1990s, adding to the nearly 800,000 Vietnamese immigrants at the turn of the twenty-first century, but few migrated from the other two nations. Figures based on the INS, *Statistical Yearbook*, 2001, 19. In addition, refugees who had been convicted of crimes in the United States were subject to deportation, and a number were returned to their homelands. *New York Times*, Aug. 9, 2002.

96. Quoted in Rumbaut, "Vietnamese," 242.

97. Hien Duc Do, *The Vietnamese Americans* (Westport, CT: Greenwood Press, 1999), 32–33.

98. *New York Times*, Aug. 23, 2002.

99. Do, *Vietnamese Americans*, 38–45; Nancy J. Smith-Hefner, *Khmer American: Identity and Moral Education in a Diasporic Community* (Berkeley: University of California Press, 1999), chap. 4; Rumbaut, "Vietnamese," 243–45.

100. *Los Angeles Times*, Nov. 2, 1997.

101. *Los Angeles Times*, Mar. 27, 1998.

102. Rumbaut, "Vietnamese," 255.

103. Ibid., 253–56; Do, *Vietnamese Americans*, 79–85.

104. Bruce B. Dunning, "Vietnamese in America: Adaptation," in *Refugees as Immigrants: Cambodians, Laotians, and Vietnamese in America*, ed. David W. Haines (Totowa, NJ: Rowman and Littlefield, 1989), 55–85.

105. Jeremy Hein, *From Vietnam, Laos, and Cambodia: A Refugee Experience in the United States* (New York: Twayne, 1995), 134–40.

106. Nathan Caplan, John K. Whitmore, and Marcella H. Choy, *The Boat People and Achievement in America: A Study of Family Life, Hard Work, and Cultural Values* (Ann Arbor: University of Michigan Press, 1989), 52–57, 145–48.

107. *Washington Post*, Apr. 30, 2000.

108. Quoted in Reimers, *Still the Golden Door*, 186. See also Do, *Vietnamese Americans*, 51–53.

109. Hein, *From Vietnam*, 75–80.

110. *Rocky Mountain News*, Feb. 29, 2000.

111. *New York Times*, Nov. 7, 2000.

112. Hein, *From Vietnam*, 124.

113. Rumbaut, "Vietnamese," 247–48.

114. Hein, *From Vietnam*, 107.

115. Rumbaut, "Vietnamese," 255–60.

116. Hein, *From Vietnam*, 105–10.

117. Ibid., 107.

118. Rumbaut, "Vietnamese," 248–53.

119. Wayne Carroll, "Strangers in a Strange Land: The Status of the Hmong Immigrants in America in the United States in 1990" (unpublished paper, carrolwd@uwec.edu), 10.

120. *Fresno Bee*, May 3, 1993.

121. Smith-Hefner, *Khmer American*, 187.

122. Nancy D. Donnelly, *Changing Lives of Refugee Hmong Women* (Seattle: University of Washington Press, 1994), chap. 3.

123. Jo Ann Koltyk, *New Pioneers in the Heartland: Hmong Life in Wisconsin* (Boston: Allyn and Bacon, 1998), 86. For the general economic positions of the Indochinese refugees, see Rumbaut, "Vietnamese," 246–53.

124. Koltyk, *New Pioneers*, chap. 5.

125. *New York Times*, Sept. 23, 1984.

126. Do, *Vietnamese Americans*, 54–58.

127. *New York Times*, Aug. 31, 1985.

128. Hein, *From Vietnam*, 90.

129. Mary Carol Hopkins, *Braving a New World: Cambodian (Khmer) Refugees in an American City* (Westport, CT: Bergin and Garvey, 1996), 87–93.

130. *New York Times*, Aug. 23, 2002. See also Min Zhou, Carl L. Bankston III, and Rebecca Y. Kim, "Rebuilding Spiritual Lives in the New Land: Religious Practices among Southeast Asian Refugees in the United States," in *Religions in Asian America: Building Faith Communities,* ed. Pyong Gap Min and Jung Ha Kim (Walnut Creek, CA: AltaMira Press, 2002), 58–63.

131. Hein, *From Vietnam*, 118–19.

132. See Hopkins, *Braving a New World*; Koltyk, *New Pioneers*; Smith-Hefner, *Khmer American*; Donnelly, *Changing Lives.*

133. *New York Times*, Oct. 2, 2000. See also Zhou, Bankston, and Kim, "Rebuilding Spiritual Lives in the New Land," 47–52.

134. *New York Times*, Apr. 24, 2000.

135. Ibid.

136. Hein, *From Vietnam*, 105.

137. *Los Angeles Times*, Apr. 28, 2000.

138. Ibid.

139. *New York Times*, Feb. 11, 1999; Feb. 26, 1999. See also Hein, *From Vietnam*, 102–5.

140. Hein, *From Vietnam*, 100–103.

141. See Alejandro Portes and Ruben Rumbaut, *Legacies: The Story of the Immigrant Second Generation* (Berkeley: University of California Press, 2001), for a comparison of the second generation of several groups, including Southeast Asians.

NOTES TO THE EPILOGUE

1. *New York Times*, Mar. 14, 1996; *USA Today*, Sept. 7, 1999.

2. *USA Today*, Apr. 17, 2003.

3. Frank D. Bean and Gillian Stevens, *America's Newcomers and the Dynamics of Diversity* (New York: Russell Sage Foundation, 2003), 260.

4. Renee C. Romano, *Race Mixing: Black-White Marriage in Postwar America* (Cambridge, MA: Harvard University Press, 2003), 249. See also Bean and Stevens, *America's Newcomers and the Dynamics of Diversity,* chap. 8; *USA Today*, Sept. 7, 1999.

5. *USA Today*, Sept. 7, 1999.

6. See Romano's excellent book on this point.

Suggested Reading

GENERAL

Alba, Richard, and Nee, Victor. 2003. *Remaking the American Mainstream: Assimilation and Contemporary American Immigration.* Cambridge, MA: Harvard University Press.

Barkan, Elliott Robert, ed. 1999. *A Nation of Peoples: A Sourcebook on America's Multicultural Heritage.* Westport, CT: Greenwood Press.

Bean, Frank D., and Stevens, Gillian. 2003. *America's Newcomers and the Dynamics of Diversity.* New York: Russell Sage Foundation.

Clark, William A. V. 2003. *Immigrants and the American Dream: Remaking the Middle Class.* New York: Guilford Press.

Daniels, Roger. 2002. *Coming to America.* New York: Perennial Press.

Dinnerstein, Leonard, and Reimers, David. 1999. *Ethnic Americans: A History of Immigration.* New York: Columbia University Press.

Foner, Nancy. 2000. *From Ellis Island to JFK: New York's Two Great Waves of Immigration.* New Haven, CT: Yale University Press.

Fuchs, Lawrence. 1990. *The American Kaleidoscope: Race, Ethnicity and the Civic Culture.* Hanover, NH: Wesleyan University Press.

Portes, Alejandro, and Rumbaut, Rueben. 1996. *Immigrant America: A Portrait.* Berkeley: University of California Press.

Sanjek, Roger. 1998. *The Future of Us All: Race and Neighborhood Politics in New York City.* Ithaca, NY: Cornell University Press.

Takaki, Ronald. 2000. *Double Victory: A Multicultural History of America in World War II.* Boston: Little, Brown.

Waldinger, Roger. 1996. *Still the Promised City? African Americans and the New Immigrants in Postindustrial New York.* Cambridge, MA: Harvard University Press.

Waldinger, Roger, and Lichter, Michael I. 2003. *How the Other Half Works: Immigration and the Social Organization of Labor.* Berkeley: University of California Press.

RACISM AND PREJUDICE

Almaguer, Tomás. 1994. *Racial Fault Lines: The Historical Origins of White Supremacy in California.* Berkeley: University of California Press.

Balderrama, Francisco E., and Rodrigues, Raymond. 1995. *Decade of Betrayal: Mexican Repatriation in the 1930s.* Albuquerque: University of New Mexico Press.

Glenn, Evelyn Nakano. 2002. *Unequal Freedom: How Race and Gender Shaped American Citizenship and Labor.* Cambridge, MA: Harvard University Press.

Gyory, Andrew. 1998. *Closing the Gate: Race, Politics, and the Chinese Exclusion Act.* Chapel Hill: University of North Carolina Press.

King, Desmond. 2000. *Making Americans: Immigration, Race, and the Origins of Diverse Democracy.* Cambridge, MA: Harvard University Press.

Lopez, Ian F. Haney. 1996. *White by Law: The Legal Construction of Race.* New York: New York University Press.

Massey, Douglas S., Durand, Jorge, and Malone, Nolan J. 2002. *Beyond Smoke and Mirrors: Mexican Immigration in an Era of Economic Integration.* New York: Russell Sage Foundation.

Nevins, Joseph. 2002. *Gatekeeper: The Rise of the "Illegal Alien" and the Making of the US-Mexico Boundary.* New York: Routledge.

Reimers, David M. 1998. *Unwelcome Strangers: American Identity and the Turn against Immigration.* New York: Columbia University Press.

Salyer, Lucy E. 1995. *Laws Harsh as Tigers: Chinese Immigration and the Shaping of Modern Immigration Law.* Chapel Hill: University of North Carolina Press.

ASIANS

Abraham, Margaret. 2000. *Speaking the Unspeakable: Marital Violence among South Asian Immigrants in the United States.* New Brunswick, NJ: Rutgers University Press.

Bao, Xiaolan. 2001. *Holding Up More Than Half the Sky: Chinese Women Garment Workers in New York City, 1948–92.* Urbana: University of Illinois Press.

Chan, Sucheng. 1991. *Asian Americans: An Interpretive History.* New York: Twayne.

Chen, Hsiang-shui. 1992. *Chinatown No More: Taiwan Immigrants in Contemporary New York.* Ithaca, NY: Cornell University Press.

Chen, Shehong. 2002. *Being Chinese, Becoming Chinese American.* Urbana: University of Illinois Press.

Do, Hien Duc. 1991. *The Vietnamese Americans.* Westport, CT: Greenwood Press.

Espiritu, Yen Le. 2003. *Home Bound: Filipino American Lives across Cultures, Communities, and Countries.* Berkeley: University of California Press.

Glenn, Evelyn Nakano. 1986. *Issei, Nisei, War Bride: Three Generations of*

Japanese American Women in Domestic Service. Philadelphia: Temple University Press.

Hein, Jeremy. 1995. *From Vietnam, Laos, and Cambodia: A Refugee Experience in the United States*. New York: Twayne.

Hsu, Madeline Yuan-yin. 2000. *Dreaming of Gold, Dreaming of Home: Transnationalism and Migration between the United States and China, 1883–1924*. Stanford, CA: Stanford University Press.

Hurh, Won Moo. 1998. *The Korean Americans*. Westport, CT: Greenwood Press.

Khandelwal, Madhulika S. 2002. *Becoming American, Being Indian: An Immigrant Community in New York City*. Ithaca, NY: Cornell University Press.

Kim, Illsoo. 1981. *New Urban Immigrants: The Korean Community in New York*. Princeton, NJ: Princeton University Press.

Kwong, Peter. 1997. *Forbidden Workers: Illegal Chinese Immigrants and American Labor*. New York: New Press.

Lee, Erika. 2003. *At America's Gates: Chinese Immigration during the Exclusion Era, 1882–1943*. Chapel Hill: University of North Carolina Press.

Leonard, Karen Isaksen. 1997. *The South Asian Americans*. Westport, CT: Greenwood Press.

Min, Pyong Gap, ed. 1995. *Asian Americans: Contemporary Trends and Issues*. Thousand Oaks, CA: Sage.

———. 1998. *Changes and Conflict: Korean Immigrant Families in New York*. Boston: Allyn and Bacon.

Park, Kyeyoung. 1997. *The Korean American Dream: Immigrants and Small Business in New York City*. Ithaca, NY: Cornell University Press.

Posadas, Barbara M. 1999. *Filipino Americans*. Westport, CT: Greenwood Press.

Takaki, Ronald. 1989. *Strangers from a Different Shore: A History of Asian Americans*. Boston: Little, Brown.

Yu, Renqui. 1992. *To Save China, to Save Ourselves: The Chinese Hand Laundry Alliance of New York*. Philadelphia: Temple University Press.

Yuh, Ji-Yeon. 2002. *Beyond the Shadow of Camptown: Korean Military Brides in America*. New York: New York University Press.

Yung, Judy. 1995. *Unbound Feet: A Social History of Chinese Women in San Francisco*. Berkeley: University of California Press.

Zhao, Xiaolian. 2002. *Remaking Chinese America: Immigration, Family and Community, 1940–1965*. New Brunswick, NJ: Rutgers University Press.

Zia, Helen. 2000. *Asian American Dreams: The Emergence of an American People*. New York: Farrar, Straus and Giroux.

BLACKS

Abusharaf, Rogaia Mustafa. 2002. *Wanderings: Sudanese Migrants and Exiles in North America*. Ithaca, NY: Cornell University Press.

Arthur, John A. 2000. *Invisible Sojourners: African Immigrant Diaspora in the United States*. Westport, CT: Praeger.

Berlin, Ira. 1998. *Many Thousands Gone: The First Two Centuries of Slavery in North America*. Cambridge, MA: Harvard University Press.

———. 2003. *Generations of Captivity: A History of African American Slaves*. Cambridge, MA: Harvard University Press.

Breen, T. H., and Innes, Stephen. 1980. *"Myne Owne Ground": Race and Freedom on Virginia's Eastern Shore, 1640–1676*. New York: Oxford University Press.

Foner, Nancy, ed. 2001. *Islands in the City: West Indian Migration to New York*. Berkeley: University of California Press.

Halter, Marilyn. 1993. *Between Race and Ethnicity: Cape Verdean American Immigrants, 1860–1965*. Urbana: University of Illinois Press.

Henke, Holger. 2001. *The West Indians*. Westport, CT: Greenwood Press.

Holtzman, Jon D. 2000. *Nuer Journeys, Nuer Lives: Sudanese Refugees in Minnesota*. Boston: Allyn and Bacon.

James, Winston. 1998. *Holding Aloft the Banner of Ethiopia: Caribbean Radicalism in Early Twentieth-Century America*. New York: Verso.

Kasinitz, Philip. 1992. *Caribbean New York: Black Immigrants and the Politics of Race*. Ithaca, NY: Cornell University Press.

Palmer, Ransford W. 1995. *Pilgrims from the Sun: West Indian Migration to America*. New York: Twayne.

Stepick, Alex. 1998. *Pride against Prejudice: Haitians in the United States*. Boston: Allyn and Bacon.

Stoller, Paul. 2002. *Money Has No Smell: The Africanization of New York City*. Chicago: University of Chicago Press.

Vickerman, Milton. 1999. *Crosscurrents: West Indian Immigrants and Race*. New York: Oxford University Press.

Waters, Mary C. 1999. *Black Identities: West Indian Dreams and American Realities*. Cambridge, MA: Harvard University Press.

Watkins-Owens, Irma. 1996. *Blood Relations: Caribbean Immigrants and the Harlem Community, 1900–1930*. Bloomington: Indiana University Press.

LATINOS

Burns, Allan F. 1993. *Maya in Exile: Guatemalans in Florida*. Philadelphia: Temple University Press.

Camarillo, Albert. 1979. *Chicanos in a Changing Society: From Mexican Pueblos to American Barrios in Santa Barbara and Southern California, 1848–1930*. Cambridge, MA: Harvard University Press.

Cardoso, Lawrence A. 1980. *Mexican Emigration to the United States, 1897–1931*. Tucson: University of Arizona Press.

Coutin, Susan Bibler. 2000. *Legalizing Moves: Salvadoran Immigrants' Struggle for U.S. Residency.* Ann Arbor: University of Michigan Press.

De León, Arnoldo. 1993. *Mexican Americans in Texas: A Brief History.* Arlington Heights, IL: Harlan Davidson.

Fink, Leon. 2003. *The Maya of Morgantown: Work and Community in the Nuevo New South.* Chapel Hill: University of North Carolina Press.

Garcia, Alma M. 2002. *The Mexican Americans.* Westport, CT: Greenwood Press.

Garcia, Juan R. 1996. *Mexicans in the Midwest, 1900–1932.* Tucson: University of Arizona Press.

Garcia, Mario. 1981. *Desert Immigrants: The Mexicans of El Paso, 1880–1920.* New Haven, CT: Yale University Press.

Gonzales, Manuel G. 1999. *Mexicanos: A History of Mexicans in the United States.* Bloomington: Indiana University Press.

Gonzalez, Juan. 2000. *Harvest of Empire: A History of Latinos in the Americas.* New York: Viking.

Grasmuck, Sherri, and Pessar, Patricia P. 1991. *Between Two Islands: Dominican International Migration.* Berkeley: University of California Press.

Mahler, Sarah. 1995. *American Dreaming: Immigrant Life on the Margins.* Princeton, NJ: Princeton University Press.

Margolis, Maxine L. 1994. *Little Brazil: An Ethnography of Brazilian Immigrants in New York City.* Princeton, NJ: Princeton University Press.

Masud-Piloto, Felix Robert. 1988. *With Open Arms: Cuban Migration to the United States.* Totowa, NJ: Rowman and Littlefield.

McWilliams, Carey. Updated by Matt S. Meier. 1990. *North from Mexico: The Spanish-Speaking People of the United States.* Westport, CT: Greenwood Press.

Menchaca, Martha. 2001. *Recovering History, Constructing Race: The Indian, Black, and White Roots of Mexican Americans.* Austin: University of Texas Press.

Menjívar, Cecilia. 2000. *Fragmented Ties: Salvadoran Immigrant Networks in America.* Berkeley: University of California Press.

Monroy, Douglas. 1999. *Rebirth: Mexican Los Angeles from the Great Migration to the Great Depression.* Berkeley: University of California Press.

Pessar, Patricia R. 1995. *A Visa for a Dream: Dominicans in the United States.* Boston: Allyn and Bacon.

Regalado, Samuel O. 1998. *Viva Baseball! Latin Major Leaguers and Their Special Hunger.* Urbana: University of Illinois Press.

Repak, Terry A. 1995. *Waiting on Washington: Central American Workers in the Nation's Capital.* Philadelphia: Temple University Press.

Ruiz, Vicki L. 1998. *From Out of the Shadows: Mexican Women in Twentieth-Century America.* New York: Oxford University Press.

Sanchez, George. 1993. *Becoming Mexican American: Ethnicity, Culture, and Identity in Chicano Los Angeles, 1900–1945.* New York: Oxford University Press.

Stepick, Alex, Grenier, Guillermo, Castro, Max, and Dunn, Marvin. 2003. *This Land Is Our Land: Immigrants and Power in Miami.* Berkeley: University of California Press.

Suro, Roberto. 1998. *The Strangers among Us: How Latino Immigration Is Transforming America.* New York: Knopf.

Valdés, Dionicio Nodín. 2000. *Barrios Norteños: St. Paul and Midwestern Mexican Communities in the Twentieth Century.* Austin: University of Texas Press.

NEAR EASTERNERS

Abraham, Nabeel, and Shryock, Andrew. eds. 2000. *Arab Detroit: From Margins to Mainstream.* Detroit: Wayne State University Press.

Abraham, Sameer Y., and Abraham, Nabeel, eds. 1983. *Arabs in the New World: Studies on Arab-American Communities.* Detroit: Wayne State University Center for Urban Studies.

Bakalian, Anny. 1993. *Armenian Americans: From Being to Feeling Armenian.* New Brunswick, NJ: Transaction.

Bozorgmehr, Mehdi, and Feldman, Alison, eds. 1996. *Middle Eastern Diaspora Communities in America.* New York: Hagap Kevorkian Center for Near Eastern Studies, New York University.

Haddad, Yvonne Yazbeck. ed. 1991. *The Muslims of America.* New York: Oxford University Press.

Hourani, Albert, and Shedhadi, Nadem, eds. 1992. *The Lebanese in the World: A Century of Migration.* London: Center for Lebanese Studies.

Mirkak, Robert. 1983. *Torn between Two Lands: Armenians in America, 1890–World War I.* Cambridge, MA: Harvard University Press.

Naff, Alixa. 1985. *Becoming American: The Early Arab Immigrant Experience.* Carbondale: Southern Illinois University Press.

Orfalea, Gregory. 1988. *Before the Flames: A Quest for a History of Arab Americans.* Austin: University of Texas Press.

Sengstock, Mary E. 1982. *The Chaldean Americans: Changing Conceptions of Ethnic Identity.* New York: Center for Migration Studies.

Shokeid, Moshe. 1988. *Children of Circumstances: Israeli Emigrants in New York.* Ithaca, NY: Cornell University Press.

Staub, Shalom. 1988. *Yemenis in New York City: The Folklore of Ethnicity.* Philadelphia: Balch Institute Press.

Index

Florida International University, 274
Flossmoor (Ill.), 188
Foley, Neil, 87
Foley Enterprises, 110
Foner, Nancy, 184, 251
Ford, (President) Gerald, 276
Ford Motor Company, 229
Foreign Intelligence Surveillance Act,
   230
Foreign miners' tax, 31, 31n. 93, 41
Fort Bliss (Tex.), 177
Fort Wayne (Ind.), 209
Fort Worth (Tex.), 100
Fort Worth Star-Telegram, 184
Fourteenth Amendment, 21, 44
Fox, (President) Vicente, 111
France, 18, 277n. 75
Franciscan missionaries, 23, 27
Franco-Colonial Club, 79
"Free people of color," 17–21; immi-
   grants from Haiti, 22
Fremont (Calif.), 201, 202
French immigrants 11, 17–18, 32, 41
Fresno (Calif.), 208, 217
Fujian (China), 165
Fuzhou (China), 165

Gabriel, Takle, 246–247
Gai, Fakry, 228
Galveston (Tex.), 100
Galveston News, 86
Ganesha Temple (N.Y. City), 194
Garcia, Anastasio Somoza, 127
Garcia, Juan, 96
Garcia, Mario, 88, 91, 93
Garvey, Amy Jacques, 80
Garvey, Marcus, 80–81
Gary (Ind.), 89, 100
Gaye, Elhadji, 246
Gebremarian, Astair, 235
Genital mutilation, as grounds for asy-
   lum, 240–241. *See also women under
   specific groups*
Gentleman's Agreement of 1907 (restric-
   tion on Japanese immigrant labor),
   53, 55, 56–57, 59, 60, 86
Georgetown (Del.), 140
Georgetown (S.C.), 14

Georgetown University, 287
Georgia, 108, 114, 128, 179, 195–196,
   213
Gerefa, Mulegata, 236
German immigrants, 11–12, 15, 86
Germany, 12, 101, 187
Getty Mart, 191
Ghana Homes, 247
Ghanan immigrants, 233, 241, 243
GI Forum, 122
Giuliani, (Mayor) Rudolph, 245
Gold: appeal to Chinese immigrants, 38,
   40–43, 45, 50; appeal to Japanese
   immigrants, 52; placer method,
   31–32, 40, 43; Rush, 30–32, 39,
   40–42; Spanish search for, 22–23;
   value of, 28
Gold, Steven, 215
Golden Venture (cargo steamer), 164
Gonzales, Conchita, 110
Gonzales, Elian, 267, 274–275
Gonzales, Henry, 122
Gonzales, Manuel, 28, 35, 92–93, 102
Gore, (Vice President) Al, 123, 124
Govindarajan, Anita, 201
Graemeen Phone, 199
Graham, Hugh, 190
Grapes of Wrath, 87
Great Britain, 187
Great Depression, 12
Greek immigrants, 12
Green Bay (Wis.), 100
Grenada Mutual Association, 79
Grinberg, David, 228
Guadeloupe, 79, 251
Guam, 276
Guanajuato (Mexico), 107
Guantánamo Bay (Cuba), 255–256,
   266
Guatemala: Caribbean immigration to,
   74; political conflict, 131, 136
Guatemalan immigrants, 125–127,
   131–132, 257, 273; asylum and
   refugee status, 131, 134–135, 145,
   154; illegal, 131–132, 133–134,
   138–140, 143, 149–150; destina-
   tions, 137–140; Mayan Indians,
   143–145; refugees, 135; remittances,

Korean immigrants (*Continued*)
rates, 158, 178–179; religion, 180,
183–184; return to Korea, 183; self-
employment, 180–183; students,
177–178, 235n. 15; women, 60, 176,
179–180, 181, 182–183
Kosovo, 238
Ku Klux Klan, 77, 80, 284
Kuomingtang (Chinese Nationalist
Party), 49
Kurds, 215–216, 220
Kuwait, 219
Kuwaiti refugees, 218n. 79
Kwanghai (China), 40
Kwong, Peter, 165
Kyber Pass (restaurant), 203

La Bahia (Tex.), 24
La Union Filipina, 37
Lackawanna (N.Y.), 230
Lal, Manu, 187
Lam, Tony, 287
Laotian refugees, 262, 263, 276n. 68,
279, 280–281, 282–285, 288;
Hmong refugees, 280–281, 285–286,
287
Laredo (Tex.), 24, 84, 110, 191–192
"Latino," scope and usage of term, 8–9,
26, 142, 145–146
Latin Grammy Awards, 119, 275
Latinos and Latino immigrants. *See spe-
cific groups*
League of United Latin American Citi-
zens (LULAC), 93–94, 94n. 134, 122
Lebanese immigrants, 208–209,
210–211, 217, 222, 226, 229
Lebanon, 222, 224
Lee, Choua, 287
Lee, Daniel, 176
Lee, Erika, 46, 47
Lee, Mary Paik, 60
Lee, Wahn, 48
Legal Immigrant Family Equity Act
(LIFE) (2000), 134–135
Lemon City (Fla.), 75
Leonard, Karen, 61, 188, 192
Lewistown (Maine), 244
Lexington (Ky.), 119

Liberia, 71; TPS status, 136, 136n. 51
Liberian immigrants, 233, 240, 240n.
47, 243; refugees, 135, 237, 239–240
Liberty Evangelical Church, 248
Libyan immigrants, 230
Lisbon (Portugal), 13, 73–74
Little India (magazine), 187
Llucena City (Philippines), 170
Locke, Gary, 167
Loescher, Gil, 262
Logan, John, 108, 125, 147, 233, 243n.
68, 244, 246, 252
L–1 visa program. *See* Visa programs
Long Beach (Calif.), 282. *See also* Los
Angeles (Calif.)
Long Island (N.Y.), 137, 164
Lopez, Albertino, 140
Lopez, Rosa, 138
Los Angeles (Calif.), 20n. 37, 25, 32, 37,
54, 56, 63, 89, 90, 93, 95; African
immigration to, 243, 248, 249; Arab
immigration to, 224; Bangladeshi immigration to, 200; Brazilian immigration to, 155; Central American immigration to, 96, 138, 146; Chinese immigration to, 160–161; Colombian
immigration to, 154; Filipino immigration to, 172; hate violence in, 97;
Hmong immigration to, 287; Iranian
immigration to, 213–214; Iraqi immigration to, 219; Israeli immigration to, 215; Korean immigration to,
179, 180–182, 183, 185; Lebanese
immigration to, 224; Los Angeles–
Long Beach area, 160–161; Mayan
immigration to, 144; Mexican immigration to, 103, 107, 111, 113,
114–115, 118, 120, 122; Nicaraguan
immigration to, 127; popularity
among immigrants, 100; Syrian immigration to, 224; Thai immigration
to, 204; Turkish immigration to,
217–218; women immigrants, 137n.
55
Los Angeles Bangladesh Association,
200
Los Angeles Dodgers, 116
Los Angeles Times, 112

About the Author

DAVID M. REIMERS was educated at Princeton University, Washington University, and the University of Wisconsin, where he received his Ph.D. in American History. He has taught and lectured at a number of American and European universities. In 1999 he retired from New York University, where he specialized in teaching and writing about the history of immigration to the United States. He is the author or coauthor of five books and a number of papers on immigration.